EUROPEAN CITIES

European Societies

Series Editor: Colin Crouch

Very few of the existing sociological texts which compare different European societies on specific topics are accessible to a broad range of scholars and students. The *European Societies* series will help fill this gap in the literature, and attempts to answer questions such as: Is there really such a thing as a 'European model' of society? Do the economic and political integration processes of the European Union also imply convergence in more general aspects of social life, like family or religious behaviour? What do the societies of Western Europe have in common with those further to the east?

The series will cover the main social institutions, although not every author will cover the full range of European countries. As well as surveying existing knowledge in a way that will be useful to students, each book will also seek to contribute to our growing knowledge of what remains in many respects a sociologically unknown continent.

Forthcoming Titles published in the series:

Social Change in Western Europe
Colin Crouch

Religion in Modern Europe
Grace Davie

European Cities

Social Conflicts and Governance

Patrick Le Galès

OXFORD

UNIVERSITY PRESS

OXFORD

UNIVERSITY PRESS

Great Clarendon Street, Oxford OX2 6DP

Oxford University Press is a department of the University of Oxford.
It furthers the University's objective of excellence in research, scholarship,
and education by publishing worldwide in

Oxford New York

Auckland Bangkok Buenos Aires Cape Town Chennai
Dar es Salaam Delhi Hong Kong Istanbul Karachi Kolkata
Kuala Lumpur Madrid Melbourne Mexico City Mumbai Nairobi
São Paulo Shanghai Singapore Taipei Tokyo Toronto
and associated company in Berlin

Oxford is a registered trade mark of Oxford University Press
in the UK and certain other countries

Published in the United States
by Oxford University Press Inc., New York

© Patrick Le Galès 2002

British Library Cataloguing in Publication Data

Data available

Library of Congress Cataloging-in-Publication Data

Le Galès, Patrick.
European cities / Patrick Le Galès.
p. cm.
Includes bibliographical references.
1. Cities and towns—Europe. 2. Urban policy—Europe. 3. Municipal
government—Europe. 4. European cooperation. I. Title.

HT131 .L43 2002   307.76'094—dc21   2002020183

ISBN 0-19-924357-3 (hbk.)
ISBN 0-19-925278-5 (Pbk.)

1 3 5 7 9 10 8 6 4 2

Typeset by Graphicraft Ltd., Hong Kong
Printed in Great Britain by TJ International Ltd, Padstow, Cornwall

PREFACE

WRITING a comparative book takes a long time and requires a good deal of support from generous colleagues. I started the book in the Schuman Centre of the European Institute in Florence. I then moved to CEVIPOF in Science Po, Paris, and did a good deal of writing while teaching at UCLA as a visiting professor. I am very grateful to Erik Neveu, Yves Mény, Michael Storper, and now Pascal Perrineau, who provided excellent working conditions in these places while actively discussing the content of my work.

The book I published jointly with Arnaldo Bagnasco in French in 1997, *Les villes européennes* (*Cities in Contemporary Europe*, 2000), gave me the opportunity to develop working hypotheses and to start to systematize a set of ideas about European cities. My admiration for Arnaldo's subtle mind and incomparably generous spirit grew through our exchanges over ten years or more, in Paris—where he teaches regularly—and in Turin, as well as during our shared work on that book. Arnaldo used to run the Observatoire du Changement Social en Europe Occidentale with Henri Mendras and Vincent Wright in the Poitiers Futuroscope. Their encouragement have been invaluable to me. Vincent's ironic, generous spirit is still sadly missed by us all.

I outlined this book during my stay at the European Institute in Florence in 1997, where I benefited from the extraordinary intellectual environment of the Schuman Centre, directed by Yves Mény, as well as from conversations with Stefano Bartolini, Philippe Schmitter, Adrienne Héritier, Gianfranco Poggi, Martin Rhodes, and Liesbet Hooghe. It was also in Florence that I attended seminars led by Colin Crouch, who had been my professor at Oxford, and he then persuaded me to set to work in earnest. A first draft was written as 'thèse d'habilitation'. During the viva, criticisms and observations from Jean Leca, Bruno Jobert, Jean-Louis Quermonne, Philippe Portier, Yves Mény, and Erik Neveu convinced me to look more deeply at many areas.

As Visiting Professor at UCLA in 1999, at the invitation of Nga Scott and Michael Storper, I was lucky to be able to teach on the book's theme and to pursue some fruitful intellectual exchanges that are reflected here. My thanks are due to the brilliant colony of expatriate Britons in Los Angeles—Perry Anderson, Michael Mann, Allen Scott, John Agnew, and Geoffrey Symcox —for welcoming me, for casting a critical eye over the papers I offered, and for the ability to combine dinner with stimulating conversation.

Since my appointment to CEVIPOF, at Sciences Po Paris, I have benefited from a stimulating intellectual environment in which to pursue this work, in teaching public policy and urban sociology. Jean Leca in particular has more than once encouraged me to pursue research about governance and threw new light on theoretical debates. In CEVIPOF, I enjoyed companionship and discussion with Sophie Duchesne, Florence Haegel, and Nonna Mayer, although I failed to persuade them to focus more on cities. I mainly worked with CEVIPOF's public policy group, where I have been welcomed by Pierre Muller and Guy Groux, and where discussions are always sharp thanks to Richard Balme, Pierre Lascoumes, Nicolas Catzaras, Bruno Palier, and Yves Surel. Nicolas, together with Gina Sandanassamy and Marie-Laure Dagieu, has sorted out many administrative and research management problems, including during coffee breaks around the corner.

Olivier Borraz and Michael Goldsmith have given me the benefit of their critical and attentive reading of all the chapters. Their work on the manuscript, in a spirit of generous criticism, was crucial to editing the book; I am deeply grateful to them. Any errors are, of course, my own, but their help has been invaluable at different times in writing and during our shared teaching.

Some chapters have been discussed and criticized in the context of intellectual companionship and friendships that have endured over many years. Marco Oberti, Paolo Perulli, Edmond Préteceille, Àlan Harding, Peter John, Enzo Mingione, Alan Scott, Pierre Lascoumes, Dominique Lorrain, Christian Lefèvre, Alain Faure, Bernard Jouve, William Gényès, Andy Smith, Emmanuel Négrier, Patrick Hassenteufel, Michael Storper, and Yves Surel are those who have most often read chapters, criticized papers, taken part in open debate, and lent their support.

Others again have given me the benefit of specific criticisms during seminars, teaching, and research projects—notably Michael Keating, John Benington, Mike Geddes, Chris Pickvance, Gerry Stoker, John Mawson, Hussein Kassim, Ash Amin, Mark Thatcher, Michael Parkinson, Carlo Trigilia, Pier Luigi Crosta, Liliana Padovani, Angelo Pichierri, Giovanni Laino, Annick Magnier, Giuseppe Dematteis, Juhani Letho, Matti Heikkila, Anne Haila, Margit Mayer, Hubert Heinelt, Helmut Voelzkow, Jean-Philippe Leresche, Dominique Joye, Yannis Papadopoulos, Stefaan de Rynck, Peter Hall, Roger Keill, John Walton, Neil Fligstein, Wayne Sandholz, Alec Stone and Jeremy Richardson. In France, shared seminars and teaching have enabled me to receive critical comments from Sylvie Biarez, Marc Lazar, Joseph Fontaine, Erik Neveu, Jacques Caillosse, Jacques Lévy, Michel Lallement, Sophie Body-Gendrot, Christian Lequesne, Jean-Louis Laville, Erhard Friedberg, Christine Musselin, Philippe Urfalino, Philippe Estèbe, Jean-Marc Offner, Laurent Davezies, and Pierre Veltz. I must also mention the members of the Editorial Committees of the *International Journal of Urban and Regional Research* and *L'Année de la Régulation*, with whose help I have arrived at a much greater understanding of certain areas and issues. Terry McBride had to increase her workload in order to ensure that the *IJURR* came out on time and that I carried out all my duties. Doctoral students that I followed or supervised have also taught me a lot more than they suspect, and some have already become established researchers my thanks to Patricia

Loncle, Francesca Gelli, Valéria Aniello, Charlotte Halpern, Gilles Pinson, Yann Fournis, and Nicolas Gaubert.

Although I have written some parts in English, writing a book is a different story and the choice of a translator is an absolutely crucial one. Karen George has done a tremendous job in translating and rewriting this book. Our cooperation on the manuscript has proved very effective and a pleasure. The book owes much to her talent.

Finally, I owe much to my family. I hope that Robin and Tiphaine did not suffer too greatly during the time I was researching and writing. Their imagination and vivacity persuaded me not to give up too much time to work. The book is dedicated to Régine, who shares the highs and lows of life with humour and perseverance, and to my father, Georges, who would so much have liked to see the completion of this work.

ACKNOWLEDGEMENTS

I acknowledge with thanks the permission of François Moriconi-Ebrard and the GEOPOLIS database to reproduce Figures 1.1 and 1.2 and Tables 1.1 and 2.3; the permission of Harvard University Press to reproduce Figures 2.1, 2.2, and 2.3, and Table 2.1; and the permission of Oxford University Press to reproduce Figure 5.1.

CONTENTS

LIST OF FIGURES

LIST OF TABLES

I

EUROPEAN CITIES WITHIN
EUROPEAN SOCIETIES

ONE

Introduction

IN 1997, Milan's powerful Chamber of Commerce and Industry, whose leaders later came to power on the city council, published a provocative pamphlet titled 'Milan–City-State: equidistant from Rome and Brussels' (Unnia and Bertaccini 1997). This envisaged the transformation of Milan into a city-state, throwing off the yoke of Italy that was holding it back in European competition. At that time, there was intense debate about transforming the Republic of Italy—in fact, there still is. The Northern League had plans to secede, there were questions about the future of the *Mezzogiorno*, the 'great mayors' of Italy were pressing to organize a political party, and federalism was being discussed. In Milan, tension was strong: the mayor belonged to Umberto Bossi's separatist party, and the city's economic leaders were exasperated by Italy's then centre-left coalition government. In Italy, the memory of city-states remains alive; it is still largely a country of towns, cities, and, increasingly, regions.

This brief example is a contemporary updating of the city-states myth, which now has hardly any meaning in a European political space structured by multiple forms of interdependence, with the state still very present. It illustrates the tensions in play within European societies: the ambiguities and the dynamism of cities, which lie at the heart of this book, and the pressures on the nation-state. Alain Touraine (1997: 414–16), analysing the dissociation of state and nation, has noted:

. . . [its] separation from the globalized economy of cultures, of the global market, and of personal and collective identities. The nation-state created a network of institutions that served to mediate between unity and plurality, past and present, external constraints and internal debates; what we have named 'civil society' itself developed as a system of social relationships. Nowadays, in contrast, there is no longer any mediation between the global market and cultural identities, between the world of objects or techniques and the world of values, between the realm of signs and the realm of meaning . . . At the present time, there can be no mediation between the economy and cultures, between the unity of the global market and the plurality of identities outside the political institutions, of which the main ones are the nation-state, the region, and the city.

This book takes as its subject cities in relation to the transformation of European societies—conventionally organized as national societies—and of the economy, the state, and the sphere of government. The differentiation of social systems and the state's diminishing capacity to structure and dominate flows and groups, to organize institutions, and to impose its culture raise again the classic social science questions about the integration and differentiation of societies, the scales at which different logics are linked together, and the unity and conduct of societies. In this questioning process, Europe, cities, and regions are also seen as possible levels of organization of society—as potential, incomplete societies—providing that they also become intrinsically involved in forms of interdependence between these different levels.

The relationship between society and territories used to be the subject of rural and urban sociology. It is now clearly apparent that, in more mobile societies, the territory—in the sense of a social and political construct—is one of the dimensions constituting the social. But which territories? A now considerable literature has looked first towards the awakening regions.[1] However, European cities have now become likely candidates because of their past role as sites of exchanges, culture, original social relations, and the invention of techniques of government.

Comparative analysis of societies in western Europe highlights enmeshed institutions, social groups, and authorities. Historians and sociologists have raised questions about possibly distinctive features of European societies. Kaelble (1988), Therborn (1985), Mendras (1997) and, especially, Crouch (1999) in his major work on European societies all emphasize the difficulty of the task: church, family, individualism, colonization, the industrial revolution, the state, the welfare state, and culture have all been mobilized to help identify the original structural features of European societies, likely to make them different from other societies. The task is an arduous one, given, on the one hand, the difficulties of defining societies and identifying them empirically and, on the other, the diversity of situations in Europe both between states and within them. Nevertheless, the peculiar territorialization of European societies does emerge as a specific feature. The work of the German historian Gerhard in 1962, reported by Rösener (1994: 30–1) in his history of the European peasantry, underlines the dimension of territorialization of European societies:

According to Gerhard, in relation to a comparatively little hierarchized and extremely mobile American society, the European way of life was distinguished essentially by its social hierarchy and its regional borders. America was characterized by equality, mobility, and modern technology; in Europe, on the other hand, membership of a community based on the land, local rootedness, and cultural tradition played a major role.

This fact, which relates more to the rural environment, has had a bearing on a feature of cities underlined by historians and sociologists: the influence of

---

[1] Jones and Keating (1995); Rhodes (1995); Jeffrey (1997); Loughlin and Keating (1997); Le Galès and Lequesne (1998); Négrier and Jouve (1998).

cities in European societies and, above all, of a particular form of city that brings together public space, social groups, local government, and community. In short, there is an element of permanence about the historically familiar form of the medieval European city. This conclusion contains obvious echoes of Max Weber. In his vast investigation of the emergence of modern European societies, the great German sociologist made a detour through the analysis of urban medieval municipalities in order to show at what point they became a crucible for emerging Western European societies. Although the initial shaping and the subsequent trajectory of each national society produced a particular relationship between society and territory, especially in cities, this relationship is now altering. Consequently, the first objective of the book is to examine changes in this relationship between nation-state and cities, stressing the implications for groups and actors within cities.

European integration processes are today shaping a dynamic that questions the social sciences and to some extent challenges conventional categories of thinking, which are most often nationally based. The processes institutionalizing Europe, the shaping of a political unit that would be a strange form of state, and the dynamics of Europeanization are the subjects of increasingly detailed, in-depth research. Interest in European integration and top-down perspectives are now combining with bottom-up perspectives centred on the actors, territories, groups, and institutions that are involved in Europeanization processes whether they like it or not. The city-based approach therefore seems to be continuing along a line of analysis that has proved fertile in the past for the study of European societies. This book aims to take up this thread again and use it to contribute to the analysis of contemporary European societies. Leaving aside radical hypotheses on postmodernity, the book takes as its starting-point European societies in the form in which they have developed, at least since the nineteenth century: that is, national societies framed by a state.

Cities, States, and the European Union

The making of the European Union (EU) gives a different meaning to the term 'European cities', going beyond sociological and geographical analysis. They are now part of a polity in the making. This questions the forms of interdependence between cities and states, a research avenue whose importance for understanding the making of the state has been fully demonstrated in the works of Charles Tilly and of historians.

Although there is no lack of excellent literature on medieval, Renaissance, or industrial European cities, recent works on the genesis of the modern state[2]

[2] Genet (1990); Tilly and Blockmans (1994), Lévy (1997).

have systematically examined the influence of cities on the making of European states. In other words, while the classic literature on the making of states tended to contrast the selfish interests of the narrow-minded city burghers with the noble elites who presided over the making of nation-states, the works of Charles Tilly and Wim Blockmans (1994) or of Genet (1990) have now thrown a great deal of light on the links between urbanization and the making of the state. Thus, they tie in with Weber and the roots of the original trajectory of Western Europe. In following this through, the essential role of cities in these processes has been strongly re-evaluated in terms of political and cultural invention and of accumulation of wealth, which have contributed to the way other types of states have been fashioned, as has the fact that cities and the social groups within them have played an enduring role in European states. This role has, moreover, sometimes been hidden by the anti-urban ideologies of the English gentry and middle classes, the Spanish aristocracy, the French Jacobins, or those who developed universalist welfare states in northern Europe.

The following hypotheses and propositions have been inspired by this literature.

1. In Western Europe, the relationship between cities and nation-states is central to understanding changes to states and European societies. Although cities were finally absorbed by what appears a posteriori as the triumph of the nation-states, their social, economic, and political influences have survived well beyond that point, notably in the countries where they were powerful.
2. In the light of the long history of European cities and of this relationship with states, when the constraint of the state loosened, for whatever reasons, a new context for sub-national entities—European cities and regions—emerged, expressed particularly through opportunities to develop forms of autonomy and integration, and strategic capacities, as well as pressures towards fragmentation.
3. This is probably the case today. Globalization and European integration processes are at work in reshaping states and national societies, as well as having implications for cities and for actors within cities. During the twentieth century, European societies were characterized by embedded forms of a capitalism that was more institutionalized and more territorialized than in the United States, for instance. In the difficult search for a European road, cities are not simply going to be dismantled under the influence of macro trends. Opposing those who forecast the decline of European cities and the fading of their charms, I will try to show how these cities, and the actors within them, are adapting to the new conditions in order to contribute actively to the building of this European road and to developing new forms of territorialization and institutionalization, and of compromise between social integration, culture, and economic development combined with the requirement to improve the environment.

4. The actors of these changes in cities come from associations, firms, and special interests, but also from local government and politics, which make differentiated modes of governance in European cities.

European integration processes are manifested especially by a vast movement of redistribution of authority that is contesting the state's monopoly of violence and enabling a loosening of constraint. In these conditions, as Bagnasco and Le Galès (2000) have shown elsewhere, we are really in an 'historical interlude' in which there are multiple competing centres and interdependent forms of authority that favour the autonomy of cities. One example of this is the regional urban leagues in northern Germany in the fourteenth century, which were born of the impotence of the higher level of government. Faced with the risk of anarchy, the cities cooperated in an alliance in order to defend their trading privileges and avoid conflicts (Pichierri 1997). In today's Europe, redistribution of authority should not be confused with anarchy and impotence at the centre. European states are being reshaped and remain powerful, but the institutionalization of the European Union is gradually imposing a certain level of organization on the rules of the game.

All this sketches out a research perspective that ties in with Max Weber's analyses. Its originality lies in the fact that the city is conceived as an integrated local society—most of the time incomplete—and as a complex social formation. As Bagnasco and Negri (1994: 16) have stressed, Weber analysed cities as a group—therefore, equipped with an administrative apparatus and with a leader—regulating the economy. The creation of the city as collective actor came about through the formation of confederacies of burghers: a bourgeoisie as collective actor, which can take different forms. Consequently, looking at the development of cities does not, in terms of methods, involve abandoning the idea of local societies or of the collective actor city, even though the context differs strongly and even though local society is not viewed as established. This analysis suggests we should look at the interplay and conflicts of social groups, interests, and institutions, and the way in which, to some extent, regulations have been put in place through conflicts and the logics of integration. In most European cities, the nation-state has played an essential role in the development of hierarchical, bureaucratic forms of regulation. The structuring of local authorities, and frequently of local governments, was largely determined by the national context.

Now, however, the 'deconstruction' of the category 'national society or nation' is on the agenda.[3] The language of networks, interconnectedness, interactions, actors, and organizations seems to be more relevant than that of social structures or class relations. 'With the decline of the idea of society, the social world is presented as a jigsaw, a set of enmeshed organizations, practices, aspirations, cultural models, and collective behaviours, from which it seems

[3] Dubet and Martucelli (1998) talk about the 'decline of the idea of society' in the sense of the society produced by the democratic and industrial revolutions. See also Bell (1976); Beck, Giddens, and Lash (1994).

dangerous to extract some kind of principles of unity and organization' (Dubet and Martucelli 1998: 52). Social scientists are going back to their classic questions. What is it that holds society together? What are the models of domination? How are collective issues constructed? How do social groups build up? At what scale? In short, what is it that produces society, contingent and random though it may be? This book makes a small contribution to that agenda, examining the role of European cities in these changes.

Collective Actor, Local Society, and Governance

The research perspective adopted here requires clarification of three key ideas that run through this book: collective actor, local society, and governance.

The dimension of integration and of the social order constructed in the city raises, in updated terms, one of the central issues of the social sciences, of sociology in particular. The founding fathers of sociology asked questions about the effects of social disorganization in the cities of modern industrial society—first European and, later, American society—on concentrations of working-class people and then on the diversity of immigrant populations. From Weber to the Chicago School, mechanisms for integrating socially and culturally different populations have been at the heart of urban sociological research. With the exception of industrial cities, ports, and capital cities, European cities appeared for a long time to be sheltered from the issues of different communities 'living together'. This is no longer the case. Open borders, immigration, and people's mobility are helping to transform European urban societies. What is more, increasingly large poor populations have appeared, especially during the 1980s, in cities hit by unemployment and the various processes that are together described as 'disaffiliation' or 'social exclusion'. Integration and social cohesion discourses have become increasingly widespread, yet the—incredibly vague—issue of cohesion has arisen just as mechanisms for integration through the labour market, the family, institutions, and nation-state-level public policies have seemed, at best, to be stalled and, at worst, impotent (Castel 1995; Mingione 1996; Paugam 1996; Harloe 2001). Fear of seeing concentrations of the new 'dangerous classes' develop in the centre or on the periphery of cities has gradually come to occupy some minds.

Social and cultural conflicts structure groups and organize the development of cities. The issue of the making of urban society necessarily calls for thinking on political regulation, which, again, is updating the old questions. Historians have shown the importance of local government issues for industrial cities in the UK; and in his fine book *The Chicago Sociological Tradition* (2001) Chapoulie recalls that in American cities in the early twentieth century, beyond models of interaction and competition in urban ecology, the issue of the government of cities was an acute one. Consequently, thinking on government and modes of governance of cities provides the second main theme for my book.

When thinking in terms of cities as collective actor, it is essential to avoid the stumbling block of reifying the city as a single actor, examined mainly from the point of view of elected political actors. This means taking into account the diversity of the actors, groups, and institutions that make up the city. The myth of the European city feeds the imaginary picture, and frequently the strategies, of European actors, but these cities are also diverse and riddled with conflicts. Anthropologists highlight multiple identities, the urban mosaic, the diversity of experiences. The city does not have a single will to act, and conflicts lie at the heart of the social and political dynamic. Some groups have no territorial base and are of little or no consequence to the city. The term 'actor city' may lead to privileging instrumental rationality and a desocialized, depoliticized view of the world in terms of consensus and decision-making. Just like the common good of the state, the common good of a city is a fiction created and sustained by the actors at a given moment (Lascoumes and Le Bourhis 1998). Although the development of a common good for a city may enable collective strategies to be put into effect, it is also intended to reduce conflicts between the different social groups and organizations, even to impose a hegemonic plan—in the Gramscian sense—the aim of legitimizing the domination of certain social groups which develop an instrumental vision of unity in order play the game of competition between cities (Préteceille 2000).

The collective-actor issue is an old one for sociology, whether of classes, groups, or organizations, opposing those mainly concerned with individual actors and those interested in institutions and collective bodies such as classes. Following Weber, sociologists—of organizations, for example—very often agree on a view of the individual actor. For Friedberg (1993: 193), for example, a strategic actor—an individual one, that is—is 'an empirical actor, whose behaviours are the expression of intentions, of thinking, of anticipations, and of calculations, and cannot, in any case, be entirely explained by prior elements'. Individual actors are seen as the only ones capable of having goals and objectives: Friedberg, citing Cyert and Olsen, adds: 'only individuals—not organizations—can have objectives, and the goals of an organization must from now on be understood as the product of a compromise within a dominant coalition that is capable of imposing its preferences on other participants and of obtaining their co-operation . . .' (Friedberg 1992: 361). He agrees to consider a collective actor on certain conditions, which correspond to the presuppositions of methodological individualism:

. . . at the end of the day, it may be perfectly acceptable to treat some groups as collective actors, but this is on condition that not only the common interests, on which these collective actors are built and which maintain them, have been demonstrated, but also the empirical integration mechanisms that provide them with a capacity to act as a group and that help, in their turn, to define and maintain common interests. (Friedberg 1993: 201)

This position has its own logic and rigour, and serves as a reference point and a useful basis for the questions of those who venture beyond the individual actor, as in the questions and criticisms that this writer addresses to neo-institutional sociologists.[4] It puts us on our guard by stressing the individual actors within cities and the importance of integration mechanisms. From the same perspective, Boudon does not talk about 'collective actor' but about 'organized group'. 'By organized group, I understand a group equipped with a collective decision-making mechanism. One could then go on to talk about a semi-organized group, in relation to latent groups (i.e. a set of individuals sharing a common interest) "represented" by professional organizations defending their interests' (Boudon 1992: 8). Thus, Boudon has put his finger on a central element of the collective actor: the collective decision-making mechanism.

Should we think of a city as a collective actor that can have objectives and goals? From my perspective, collective actors within cities, and possibly cities as collective actors, do not emerge solely from the interplay of individual actors. Cities are also to some extent social structures and institutions that guide actors' anticipations, structure their interests, and influence their view of the world. Following the Italian sociologist of organizations, Pichierri (1997), my definition of collective actor city does not correspond to the paradigm of methodological individualism. Five elements seem to be important in identifying a collective actor: a collective decision-making system, common interests—or those perceived as such—integration mechanisms, internal and external representation of the collective actor, and a capacity for innovation. Moreover, Pichierri stresses that this type of collective actor is all the more relevant when applied to particular types of organization with '*legame debole*' or 'weak ties': situations where there are weak hierarchies, strong interdependence, or strong autonomy. Some of the problems of defining a collective actor are problems of a political order, of defining common interests and collective choices, of integration of local society, and of the selection and exclusion of actors and groups.

This issue of the collective actor may be analysed in a sociological perspective on condition that we do not confine ourselves to the common instrumental view that privileges the optimum solution to problems of coordination—the 'problem-solving view'—while rejecting the political dimension and social relations.[5] It remains the case that thinking of the city as a collective actor still carries the risk of drifting off the point, but this can be largely avoided

---

[4] For example, Powell and Di Maggio (1991); March and Olsen (1989).
[5] Bourdin (2000: 317) does not say anything different: 'It is really a matter of defining common interests, a strategy, an identity, friends and enemies, or, at least, allies and competitors. If all that exists, and a spokesperson or an authority is clearly competent to express it, then one can, in fact, talk about an actor.'

by taking into account actors, groups, organizations, even individuals and their relationships within the city. The issue of the collective actor is not peculiar to cities. On the contrary, at all levels individuals, groups, and organizations are increasingly and systematically claiming the status of actor: in public policies, for example. Our societies are frequently characterized as societies of actors or societies of organizations. It is, for instance, difficult to read a European Union, state, regional, or city-generated public document without seeing mention of the necessity to consult the actors and involve them in decision-making and implementation of public policy. Representations of society have been saturated by all those claiming the status of actor, a key argument in justifying the novelty of a more complex society, rightly or wrongly. The absence of any monopoly of domination in Europe or at the world scale and the absence of universal belief in one religion—or in any other structuring principle—favour and encourage the search for common rules and values on the part of all sections of society and at different levels. Since the major principles for structuring hierarchies are less effective—calling into question the nation-state—the door is open for all sorts of individuals, groups, and organizations to claim the status of actor. Linking these phenomena to the processes of globalization of cultural models, Meyer (2000: 237–8) underlines the ambiguities of this triumph of the actor:

Tremendous premiums in the modern system go with actorhood, so that social life tends to be reorganised around its claims . . . and all sorts of social structures reform themselves as formal organizations and thus as legitimated actors. The claims of actorhood are rewarding, exorbitant and utterly unrealistic. Under elaborate, standardized and very general rules, actors are thought to have clear purposes, means-ends technologies and analysed resources. They are to have unified decision sovereignty, effective control over their internal activities and clearly defined boundaries. They are to have complete and accurate analyses of their environments. They are, in short, to be little gods . . . Faced with now-rationalized uncertainties and the legitimated requirements of actorhood to deal with these uncertainties, modern actors stabilize themselves by creating, and using rules of various kinds . . . The point is that the 'first interest' or problem of the modern actor is—not to accomplish prior goals of some sort—but to be an actor. This requires discovering goals, technologies, resources, sovereignty, control and boundaries.

In other words, all organizations want to become actors, but most of them are clearly aware that the classic definition of the collective actor in the international game relates to the figure of the nation-state, which is out of their range. This profound uncertainty both constrains and facilitates mobilization within groups and organizations to attain the status of actor and to gain recognition as such by others, thus marking a strong dependence on outside models of legitimization. As applied to European cities, this analysis clearly highlights the role that the European Commission has played in legitimizing actors over about 20 years. More generally, the actors within cities mobilize to gain recognition of their territory as an actor. Internal mobilization towards this status meets outside injunctions and produces a dynamic, notably but not solely in the fashion of a discourse. Most regions and cities aspire to be recognized as actors of European governance, but most of the actors within them have only a vague notion what this represents, and that determines the fortunes of some of the models driven by the Commission and of the public and private bodies that drive all sorts of models and norms.

Local Society

Cities do not develop solely according to interactions and contingencies: groups, actors, and organizations oppose one another, enter into conflict, cooperate, produce representations to institutionalize collective forms of action, implement policies, structure inequalities, and defend their interests. Consequently, they can, in part, be studied as incomplete local societies.

Local societies are the result of interaction between multiple actors working at different levels, some of whose actions are guided by local society and take on a particular pattern over time. They are stabilized by a set of organizations linked to the state in varying degrees: hospitals, schools, universities, harbours, and social and cultural centres. Social movements, associations, sometimes even families, are deployed in different organizations and help to shape—although always partially and with only occasional stability— a degree of coherence and a certain local social and political order. In the tradition of Weber, the city as local society is analysed in terms of aggregation, integration, and representation of groups and interests.

European cities are incomplete societies: they constitute only one of the levels at which social actors interact, represent themselves, are mutually interdependent. In the face of fragmentation, the issue that always used to be key for sociologists—that of social differentiation and integration—is coming to a head again in cities. The metropolis is a clear representation of the prospect of mosaic, fragmentation, and differentiation. It is hard to see, for example, how the concept of local society could have any meaning for Paris or London. In medium-sized European cities, on the other hand, the concept is often meaningful, providing that we disaggregate this collective actor and analyse the interplay of social groups and organizations in such cities. Lovering (1995; 1999) has vigorously criticized the drift towards this kind of analysis of actor cities, which he refers to as the risk of 'new localism': privileging local strategies, the capacity of local actors, and local forms of regulation. According to him, the strategies of groups and actors cannot come to fruition independently of broader changes: that is, in the terms used in this book, changes to the structure of constraints and opportunities, the reshaping of the state, and economic restructuring. The construction of this book represents an attempt to consider cities—in the sense of localities or incomplete urban societies—in relation to these changes; but this does not exclude consideration of cities as local societies.

More specifically, the issue of the regulation of local societies has been a fundamental question in Italian sociology, which enjoys both a rich anthropological tradition and the presence of differentiated local societies, enabling it to highlight the informal economy, the dynamism of localized family relations, the interplay of associations, reciprocity, culture, and ways of life, the density of localized horizontal relations, and local social formations (Paci 1996; Bagnasco 1999). Examination of local societies has been fruitful for understanding the dynamics of local economies and the reshaping of cities, and has helped to highlight local forms of regulation. According to Saraceno *et al.* (1998), a local society requires specific constellations of economic conditions, actors and processes, social and political cultures, including patterns of family and kinship arrangements, of organization and participating in civil society. It should be relatively stable over some time.

Cities may be more or less structured in their economic and cultural exchanges and the different actors may be related to each other in the same local context with long-term strategies, investing their resources in a coordinated way and adding to the social capital riches. In this case the society appears as well structured and visible, and one can detect forms of—relative—integration. If not, the city reveals itself as less structured and as such no longer a significant subject for study: somewhere where decisions are made externally by separate actors. (Bagnasco and Le Galès 2000: 21–2).

Governance

The object of this book is precisely to make the link between changes in the state, the economy, and society which are causing upheaval in the model of the nation-state and altering the constraints and opportunities for sub-national territories. The second part will identify the pressures that are pushing these territories either towards social and political fragmentation or towards attempts to create internal coherence and develop strategies to help them evolve towards being actors of European governance. However, this argument is meaningful only if the groups and special interest actors who may come together within cities, aside from the city council, are clearly identified. They mobilize in order to strengthen the city as an urban society and as a site of governance, but they meet various forms of resistance and face conflicts and failures.

The sociology of governance is intrinsically part of a thinking that attempts to integrate economic, political, and social changes at different scales, while privileging access through the territorial level. Such a bias seeks to tie in with the approaches taken by Max Weber and later Karl Polanyi, which fall into the frame of what is called economic sociology and/or political economy (Swedberg 1987). This is not an easy business, given the confusion and the interest aroused by the notion of governance and the dozens of definitions that are current, as well as the multitude of normative or instrumentalized usages. Governance is used by the elites of the state and cities as a strategy of adaptation to the external constraints that are helping to reshape the role and work of politics (Pierre 2000). The popularity of the idea at all levels of government in Europe, and especially in Brussels, clearly shows its potential in terms of instrumentalization. The worst thing is the ideological use that is made of it, within a neo-liberal perspective, to discredit the state, government, the political, and even democracy.

Consequently, my choice has its perils. 'Governance' can have different kinds of usage in the social sciences (Kooiman 2000a). In brief, for American new institutional economists (Williamson 1995), governance means coordination in order to increase the efficiency of the firm. They propose a concept of governance that brings together law, economics, and the sociology of organizations to account for the development of coordination mechanisms in firms which enable the reduction of transaction costs at the micro-level and the improvement of the firm's efficiency. The coordination of these different transactions leads to the development of institutions of governance: market relations, hierarchies, or hybrid forms of contracts. Thus, the firm can be analysed as a structure or mode of governance within which different types of transactions are settled.[6]

In economic sociology, the perspective of governance of the economy has been conceptualized by drawing on Karl Polanyi and Max Weber, on historians, and on sociologists of organizations to account for the proliferation of different forms of rootedness and of regulation of the economy in capitalist countries. Contrary to what the economists suggest, the issue is not only one of improving the efficiency of firms but also of taking into account conflicts of authority, the interplay of social groups, and control mechanisms: in other words, the particular division of labour between the market, social structures, and political structures. These writers have proposed a typology of mechanisms of governance, often viewed as regulations linked together within modes of governance: market, networks, hierarchies—state and large private sector organizations—communities, associations. In this perspective, the concept of regulation is defined in the following terms (Lange and Regini 1989)[7] on the basis of three dimensions: (1) the mode of coordinating diverse activities or relationships among actors; (2) the allocation of resources in relation to these activities or these actors; and (3) the structuring of conflicts—prevented or resolved. Consequently, the word 'regulation' can be used, for example, when highlighting relatively stabilized relationships between actors or social

---

[6] This perspective has been taken up in the economic geography and regional economics literature, as well as in economic approaches to public policy.

[7] 'We define as regulation the mode or form (or better, the different modes) by which a determinate set of activities and/or relationships among actors is coordinated, the related resources allocated, and the related conflicts, whether real or potential, structured (that is prevented or reconciled).' Introduction, in Lange and Regini (1989: 12 ff.).

groups, relationships which allow the distribution of resources according to explicit or implicit norms and rules.

Many authors have proposed typologies to identify, on the one hand, types of regulation and, on the other, the outcome of different combinations. For example, classically, three ideal-typical forms of regulation may be identified (Hollingsworth and Boyer 1997; Crouch *et al.* 2001).

1. State regulation—frequently identified with hierarchical or political regulation —where the state structures conflicts, distributes resources, and coordinates activities and groups. This type of regulation implies domination and control as well as the capacity to sanction. This description can also fit certain large, hierarchized organizations, where authority is the principal moving force, even if only informally.
2. Market regulation: since the emergence of capitalism, this type of regulation has played a growing role in organizing exchanges between supply and demand, adjusted through prices or sometimes through volumes . . .
3. Cooperative/reciprocal regulation—sometimes called regulation through social or political exchange—based on values and norms, on a single identity, and on the trust that expresses forms of exchange and/or solidarity between the members of a community, a clan, a family, or a district.

Sociologists of governance, who have worked more on the economy, have generally retained a simplistic view of the state and of political forms of regulation. The latter is the area of interest to political science, and deservedly so, since this political dimension is a deep-seated, historical component of European cities.[8] Governance there is defined as a process of coordinating actors, social groups, and institutions to attain particular goals, discussed and defined collectively in fragmented, uncertain environments. Thus, governance relates to all the institutions, networks, directives, regulations, norms, political and social usages, public and private actors that contribute to the stability of a society and of a political regime, to its orientation, to its capacity to direct, and to its capacity to provide services and guarantee its own legitimacy.

In the linkages between these different senses, we can discern the existence of a specialized sphere of regulation of society: the political. Political specialization

may be understood as the affirmation of roles—the roles of what we call 'government' and those who govern. The characteristic of someone who governs is his or her recognized ability to impose decisions that concern the whole of society, to arbitrate in confrontations between groups or sections relating to the whole of society, and to make rules based on the totality of decisions that have

---

[8] This point is also stressed by Sebastiani (1998). British writers such as Gerry Stoker or Peter John do not fall into such extremes. Nevertheless, on the basis of the UK situation, they emphasize the passage—in their eyes now inescapable—from local government to local governance, with an improvement in terms of efficiency in view.

reference value in identical situations. Government's particular authority is established by the fact that it can 'legitimately' have recourse to sanctions against the recalcitrant: every order of sanction, through to disapproval provoked to the point of unusual punishments—but, above all, the sanction of violence, through recourse to coercion. (Lagroye 1997: 128)

In Western Europe, the state has constituted the form of government by coercion: thus, the form of political organization. Consequently, for political sociology, the notion of governance must be related to that of government. Leca (1995: 3 ff.) has conceptualized government on the basis of four elements:

(1) The general principles for building and organizing a collectivity . . . its representative 'regime' with four characteristics (election of those who govern, the latter's relative independence, freedom of public opinion, and 'trial by discussion . . . democratized by the extension of the electorate and of opinion) (Manin 1995) . . .
(2) The body, like the constellation of bodies that teach, make decisions, allocate resources, levy taxes, and administer . . . is a differentiated body made up of professionals—politicians and civil servants . . .
(3) The way in which the body functions internally and in its relationships with its multiple environments, the process . . . Government is a process that is both genuinely multi-directional and theoretically transitively ordered on the basis of a dominant goal . . . However, the workings of democracy make us prisoners of the necessary illusion that government makes not just choices, but ordered and coherent choices, so as to accomplish two different and perhaps contradictory tasks: efficient, effective 'problem-solving' and 'responding to demands' . . . Government is in fact a process of stewardship and of leadership: autonomy and independent innovation.[9]
(4) Finally, government is what 'comes out of' government in sense 3, all its 'products': allocative, normative, incentive, dissuasive, and coercive measures, 'programmes' and 'policies', whose immediate effects and outcomes can be assessed in terms of performance . . . Government performance has been conventionally evaluated in terms of equality and of efficiency, the first being assumed to be fulfilled by welfare state redistribution policies, the second by policies that develop economic activities in order to produce more wealth—socially aggregated, whatever its distribution between particular groups . . .

To make things simple, we should perhaps view the characteristics of governance on the basis of points (3) and (4).

The issue of governance has emerged in part from studying the European Union—since it takes decisions and conducts public policies in the absence of government—and from the literature on the failures of government, which are, according to Mayntz (1993; 1999), its inability to enforce regulations, the refusal of some groups to recognize its legitimacy, its poor appreciation of the relationships between means and ends, and the absence of competence

---

[9] Decision-making and management: in a forward-moving view, March and Olsen (1995) in 'democratic governance' stress the distinction between processes of aggregation of interests and demands and the role of guidance and direction

or instrument of government. In a perspective marked by the German context, she stresses society's capacity for self-regulation as well as the capacity of some sectors to resist the state's authority. Dutch academics working with Kooiman at the Erasmus University of Rotterdam, accustomed to thinking of the nation-state on the basis of cities and the interplay of 'pillars'—Christian, Liberal, and Socialist—have been fairly quick to perceive how difficult it is for the state to guide or orient society. Kooiman (2000b) has defined governance as 'all these interactive arrangements in which public as well as private actors participate aimed at solving societal problems or creating societal opportunities, attending to the institutions within which these governance activities take place and the stimulation of normative debates on the principles underlying all governance activities'. More oriented towards political science, Schmitter (forthcoming, 2002), puts more emphasis on outcomes, or the decisions made: 'Governance is a method/mechanism for dealing with a broad range of problems/conflicts in which actors regularly arrive at mutually satisfactory and binding decisions by negotiating with each other and cooperation in the implementation of these decisions.' All those inspired by the sociology of organizations and public policy networks, including British writers like Rhodes (2000), stress horizontal forms of interaction between actors, forms of interdependence, the regularity and rules of interaction and exchange, the autonomy of sectors and networks in relation to the state, the temporal dimension, the processes of coordination of political and social actors, and, frequently, the constraints associated with decision-making.

Even though public policy networks may have the importance that these writers ascribe to them—a matter that merits close examination from an empirical standpoint—it remains the case that the steering or linking together of networks cannot be reduced to simple resolution of coordination problems. Some political actors—governments, for example—have particular resources —although perhaps not a monopoly of them—for directing the behaviour of actors and networks, for arbitrating between the different networks, and for legitimizing their choices (Papadopoulos 1998; Duran 1999; Le Galès 2001a). Governance has not replaced government. Linkages between networks are not just a question of coordinating things at the lowest possible cost. This raises issues of collective choices, values, open debate, confrontation between diverse interests, the common good—however situated—and legitimacy: in short, political issues.

The significance of this sociology of governance lies in its thinking on the linkages between different modes of regulation of society as it tries to better discern the respective places of political and social regulation and the changes to them within this economic sociology/political economy perspective. Since the late nineteenth century—more precisely, since the Second World War —the categories we have used to analyse the political have been basically national and linked to the state. Present-day interest in issues of governance clearly stems from a transformation in the role of the state and in the modes of political regulation that attach to it. Consequently, this idea of governance clearly falls within a conceptual frame that is situated on—almost dated by— a trajectory of formation. Although the logics of reshaping the state, and the power and monopoly implications of this, can be demonstrated (Poggi 1996; Jessop 1995; Mann 1997), the notion of governance clearly constitutes an opportunity to construct a conceptual frame legitimized by a set of logical propositions on the one hand and by empirical observations on the other.

Therefore, governance has appeared over a well-defined period, and this allows us to formulate research questions, to identify the elements of an explanatory system, and to elaborate a system of hypotheses whose productiveness and relevance in empirical terms will be seen later (Borraz and Le Galès 2001). Developed precisely to allow comparative research, this idea may enable, for example, the development of ideal types of modes of governance. It is not a matter of developing a theory on the basis of this single idea, but for the moment, it seems to me, a question of exploring an interesting avenue to help explain changes, as well as permanent features, and, in particular, contemporary forms of the state and of public policy. As Jessop (1995) has suggested, governance is in the process of conceptualization, with empirical and theoretical literature converging in this direction. In the current state of affairs, governance does not actually constitute a concept rooted in a theory, or, a fortiori, a theory. It is more of an idea; at best, a second-rank concept which does not so much draw immediate responses as enable the formulation of questions. These questions, which are part of an analysis of changes to the state and to public policy and also, more generally, to economic, social, and political regulation, present a threefold advantage: they reveal the limits of existing analytical frames faced with phenomena that they cannot account for; they suggest modified relationships between variables; and they sketch out the lines along which empirical research should respond. A sociological approach to governance enables us to formulate questions and to draw the axes of research, whose answers and results will be able to contribute to the construction of a renewed theoretical frame. In doing so, this sociology of governance aims to distance itself as much as possible from any vision of 'good governance', which most often relates to a classical economist's view of the search for institutions that would guarantee the optimum functioning of the market, or to a neo-liberal plan to justify the imposition of market discipline on European societies. Governance is not a matter of efficiency or a miracle problem-solver: after the way that the failures of state and market have been highlighted, no one can doubt that the failures of governance will prove at least as noteworthy.

Elements of Method

Writing on European cities is an impossible task for at least two reasons: the diversity of cases and the lack of data. In the preface to his overview of social change in Europe, Crouch (1999) makes it clear that one of the limitations of his work results from the absence of comparable data at a sub-national scale, which has obliged him to draw comparisons between countries. Beyond population figures and figures comparing cities within a given nation-state, there is not much on offer: clearly a primary limitation of this book. However, apart from the analytical perspective, the originality of this work probably lies in the materials I have mobilized; this method also throws light on the limits of this book and of this type of exercise.

If you aspire to do any work on European cities, your first approach must be to immerse yourself in the works of historians who have analysed the development of European cities, the transformations of capitalism, and the development of the nation-state in Europe. Given the initial hypothesis of the loosening constraint of the state, it seemed vital to go back to the link between cities and nation-states. I cannot claim any originality in this area: this book has been fuelled by the works of Pirenne, Rokkan, Blockmans, Tilly, Mann, Genet, Barel, Bairoch, Briggs, Thomson, Mumford, Berengo, Hohenberg and Lees, Badie and Birnbaum, Anderson, the *Annales* historians and, of course, Weber, as well as numerous historical monographs. This approach then leads to questions about changes to nation-states in Europe and about links with globalization processes and the European integration project. Consideration of the longevity of European cities and analysis of the link between nation-states and cities are, therefore, central. I have tried to respect all these sources as far as possible, and to use the points that are salient to the structure of my book's arguments. The use of direct quotation acknowledges the origin of ideas and developments.

The second element of the method draws on comparative and empirical studies; although these lie at the origin of this book, I do not give a precise account of them here. The book is the outcome of different types of research carried out over several years: monographs on French, British, and—fewer— Italian cities, work on the formation of social groups, surveys of organizations representing private interests in cities, comparison of public policies and of Europeanization processes. These comparative research projects and regular, frequent visits, first to the UK and then to Italy, lend special weight to the arguments I will develop, although the ambition is for the book to propose an analysis that relates to European cities more broadly. As far as Scandinavia, south-western Europe, and, especially, Germany are concerned, the analyses presented in this book mobilize work carried out by others and take into account the available quantitative data. Although the arguments presented have, in the past, seemed relevant for countries other than the first three mentioned, Germany remains problematic, betraying my lack of knowledge of the country and its culture. This difficulty reflects a fundamental one for all work that deals with the sociological and political science literature on Europe: how to show a pattern in the political and social phenomena that relate to Europe without misrepresenting the extraordinary diversity of European societies and states. In much of the literature, the writers' perspectives are profoundly influenced by their origins and the countries they know best: for me, France, the UK, and Italy. For example, it is well-known how far Esping-Andersen's (1990) fundamental work on welfare state models has remained relevant to the Scandinavian countries and the UK, while his typology has been criticized in relation to the countries of southern Europe and to France.

Analysis here is limited to western Europe, for two reasons: (1) I am drawing on socio-historical arguments that stress the particular features of Western Europe, especially since the Second World War; (2) there is a substantial accumulation of comparative knowledge of the major countries of the European Union. However, there is no doubt that reconsideration of the issues that differentiate western from eastern Europe should now be a research priority.

The third element of the method is central to the origins of the book: the question of scales. Although, following in the footsteps of geographers, writers in the social sciences have increasingly systematically incorporated the issue of levels of analysis, those who have carried out empirical research at these various levels are less numerous. Since I have been involved in research into cities, then into regions, into the public policies of states—France, the UK, and Italy, both urban and regional policy—and more recently into European Union regional and urban policies, I have tried to use this research in the book to give a detailed account of interrelationships between these different levels, whether in the public sphere or in the sphere of private or associative actors. This effort to combine scales probably represents one of the original features of this book, as it attempts to demonstrate the importance of forms of interdependence and the limits of reasoning in terms of levels. However, everything is not to be found everywhere. The difficulty lies precisely in reconstructing the combination and the particular linkages, sometimes between cities and state, sometimes between cities and the European Union, sometimes in more localized phenomena, sometimes primarily falling within the logics of globalization. The effort to demonstrate linkages between scales does not exclude analysis at the 'intermediate' level of the city. Use of this intermediate level does not solve the problems, since it is often hard to know whether it is an original level of structuring and regulation of the political or the social, or a level that is shot through with macro- or micro-logics, made more visible at this scale. The analysis will aim to show the relevance of this angle of approach, which, in the case of European cities, clarifies subdivisions and highlights the interplay of political and social actors.

Can We Define 'European Cities' as a Category, despite Metropolization Processes?

In the medieval period, the city was a social structure and a collective actor:

In all of them, in fact, the burghers formed a corps, a *universitas*, a *communitas*, a *communio*, all the members of which, conjointly answerable to one another, constituted the inseparable parts. Whatever might be the origin of its enfranchisement, the city of the Middle Ages did not consist in a simple collection of individuals; it was itself an individual, but a collective individual, a legal person. (Pirenne 1971: 129–30)

These conditions obviously no longer apply nowadays, and this might lead us to question the relevance of the project. The perspective outlined above could appear, at first sight, fundamentally conservative. This would be the case if we were celebrating local identity, endogenous development, or the social capital of pacified, protected communities in the European city, so that we could more easily shut out the horrid smell of Europe, of foreigners, or of immigrants. It would also be the case if we were simply updating the myth of the urbanity of the European city: balanced, welcoming, innovative, and dynamic, isolated from any restructuring of the labour market, from globalization processes, social conflicts, reorganized power relations, new forms of domination, deregulation of transport, telecommunications, and energy services, as well as from pollution and from persistent and developing forms of poverty. Finally, it would be the case if we were simply legitimizing a European model sheltered within the borders of the illusory 'fortress Europe', so that we could more easily ignore what happens around the Mediterranean and in Africa, distance ourselves from the United States, and remain almost unmoved by changes in the faraway lands of Asia or South America. Europe is only a part of the world and is in the making. The European dynamic represents an opportunity and a focus for major research, on condition that we do not use it as a pretext to seal ourselves inside a Eurocentric view. Often, Europeanization processes play a role in accelerating trends that are actually more linked to globalization processes. Crouch (1999) has shown, moreover, that some basic structures of European societies were similar to those of North America and sometimes of Japan. European societies are capitalist societies, and the peculiarly European dimension of capitalism cannot be a difference of nature. Consequently, the analysis requires a great deal of subtlety if it is to account for changes that are combining at different scales.

Urban sociology has long privileged analytical models of the convergence of cities, whether based on models of urban ecology inspired by writers from the University of Chicago, or in the context of the Marxist and neo-Marxist tradition that privileges the decisive influence of newly-globalized capitalism on social structures, modes of government, and urban policies. This tradition is alive, and comprises an important body of research on global cities (Sassen 1991) and on metropolises and flows (Castells 1996). In theoretical terms, if the urban is growing everywhere, then either it reflects a vague general pattern or there are different types of urban models of cities, which may become differentiated since they are different types of social, political, cultural, and economic structures. This does not exclude the possibility that all those models will to a certain extent follow the same path. The book argues that, given the longevity of European cities, it is possible to take the view that the general trends of social change are being expressed in an original way, combining with existing structures and with the strategies of actors in European cities.

Yet focusing on European cities nowadays goes hand in hand with analysing forms of interdependence between scales and between levels of government, multilevel strategies of social actors, and linkages between forms of mobility and local societies. It would be a vain exercise to work on European cities without applying oneself at all to the global strategies of major firms like Olympia, Dexia, Deutsche Post, Innogy, Suez, RWE, Vivendi or Italcenti, ABB, to the retailing strategies of the Spanish and Italian clothing groups, to the transnational communities that weave links on both sides of the Mediterranean, to the competition rules drawn up and then imposed in the European Union context, or to the restructuring of welfare states. We must first move through national perspectives on cities, and then compare European cities with cities on other continents, including in terms of the dissemination of models.

Is the European city an outmoded or obsolete subject for research? If that were the case, this book would be merely an exercise in nostalgia. Therefore, it is necessary to consider some of the writers committed to a radically opposed research direction, in order to see, in compressed form, the arguments they bring to bear. Several arguments may be opposed a priori to the approach I have taken.

1. The fragmentation of cities is said to render illusory any perspective that was in the slightest bit integrated: urban research has highlighted the instability of the city; its disorder; the diversity of experiences, of contradictory representations; the city as mosaic, as space of varied interactions, of otherness, of opposed and enmeshed cultures, of ephemera, of spectacle; the city as unceasing movement, as a space riddled with networks and actors whose interests and allegiances are either unknown or multiple;[10] the city of multiple competing interests, of fragmentation of organizations and actors; the 'ungovernable' city with its extreme pluralism (Yates 1977). In terms of method, the revival of work by ethnologists, interactionist sociologists, and ethnomethodologists has considerably enriched this sphere.[11] 'Metropolitan catastrophe' has made the city a 'centrifugal territorial aggregation' (Dematteis 2000), which is said to mark both the triumph and the end of cities. Increasing urban concentration has been accompanied by apparently inescapable, unlimited dispersal into conurbations and into urban regions with fluctuating outlines. The development of modern societies since the nineteenth century has radically changed the context for cities. The term 'metropolis', contrasted with

---

[10] See, for example, Ruggiero (2000); Agier (1999); and especially Henri Lefèvre's work.
[11] Nas (1998); Duneier (1999); Bourgois (1995).

the medieval city, has been used to describe and analyse first the biggest modern European cities and then American cities. 'Metropolization is not only the growth and proliferation of large conurbations, but also the increasing concentration within them of populations, activities, and wealth' (Ascher 1995: 16). The notion of city may be supposed to refer to a relatively enclosed space, but the notion of metropolis marks both a change of scale and a multiplication of relationships and functions, which would render obsolete both analysis of cities in the Weberian sense and analysis of local societies viewed in a narrow sense.

2. Cities have expanded, fragmented, and organized into networks like those in northern Italy or the Netherlands, and this is said to be rendering traditional spatial representations obsolete. Many writers stress the unending extension of the suburbs, the development of 'non-places' (Augé 1992), anonymously similar urban spaces—motorway slip roads, shopping centres, residential developments, areas of commodified leisure facilities, car parks, railway stations and airports, office blocks, and leisure parks—and megalopolises—'post-cities'—in different parts of the world.[12] In short, this is the time of 'citizens without cities' (Agier 1999), where new forms and experiences are being invented. Architects and urban planners are rushing passionately forward to an urban world, apparently liberated from the classic constraints— of the state, of rules, of slowness, of the social substrate, of fixedness—and dazzled by the speed, fluidity, and scales of urbanization of Asian or African megalopolises, by a globalization of innovative urban thought at the cutting edge of the cyberworld, and by the invention of forms that are feasible thanks to technologies. Measured against all this, the spatial images of the classic European cities singularly lack attraction—unless it is as museums.

3. The power of globalized capitalism and of global cities is said to be making European cities—except the largest ones—insignificant. In the Marxist perspective formulated by David Harvey (1989), for example, mobile capitalism is increasingly laying down the law to cities organized and disciplined according to the imperatives of competition and of economic development, and this is making differences between cities a secondary issue. Attempts have been made to characterize cities in rich countries in this perspective, or at least to put American and European cities in the same category. In a different register, Saskia Sassen (1991; 2000) and other writers who focus on 'global cities' have highlighted a link between a type of economic development and an urban form that seems to be limited to the biggest metropolises: in Europe, London, Paris, and to a lesser extent the Randstad, Milan, Rome, Frankfurt, and perhaps Berlin.

4. Cities are also concentrations of capital in the material form of infrastructures and concentrations of technologies. In this regard, they are chiefly places of technological change affecting transport, building and public

---

[12] See Koolhaas *et al.* (2001), a fine book, teeming with ideas.

works, information and communication technologies, and the management of infrastructures. Patsy Healey (1995: 146) emphasizes four dimensions that link technological innovations and cities: (1) the role of information and communication technologies in all aspects of urban life, in surveillance-style communications, and in the management of infrastructures; (2) changing perceptions of priorities, costs, and benefits: for example, the environmental effects of increasing speeds of travel; (3) pressures for very heavy investments in the new infrastructures that favour travel; and (4) the mode of management of infrastructures and changing scales linked to globalization processes that relate to the strategies of firms and the strengthening of competition logics.

5. The importance of mobility is said to disqualify the idea of society and to be strengthened by information and communication technologies; the 'space of flows' is said to be outclassing 'places'. John Urry's (2000) manifesto analyses the different dimensions of mobilities, which, according to him, are turning our societies—and cities in particular—upside down and challenging the traditional categories of sociology: 'Social processes have to be rethought as involving multiple mobilities with novel spaces and temporalities. Notions of such mobile persons can be transferred, metaphorically and literally, to the mobility of other entities, of ideas, images, technologies, monies, wastes and so on' (Urry 2000: 188). Other writers stress networks, the labyrinthine city, the nomads and rootless people who populate the cities, and Martinotti's (1992; 1999*a*) 'city users': tourists, business people, those who come only to work, consumers of services. Cities are nodes on networks that go beyond them, where flows and transactions are managed (Perulli 1999 [*a* OR *b*?]; Tarrius 2000). Consequently, mobilities and networks are said to be destroying the old reality and representation of the city. In the postmodern view of 'suburbia' beyond cities, these are cities without urbanity, said to be becoming the twenty-first -century norm, and Los Angeles is the emblematic case where the extremes of different worlds coexist (Dear 2000). In Europe, urban flagship projects are emblematic of this desire of cities to reaffirm their importance and to take their place in European and globalized networks, as witnessed by the rebuilding of the Potzdamer Platz in Berlin or the regeneration of the London Docklands.

This is serious. Placed end to end like this, the weight of these arguments implies that the main determinants and characteristics of the urban turn of this new century have very little to do with Weberian urban sociology or the 'new political economy of cities' presented earlier. These arguments will be discussed throughout the book and taken up again in the Conclusion. I will not be dismissing them out of hand, but discussing them, since these writers draw attention to many innovative, frequently profound changes: changes whose implications for cities raise many different types of questions.

We should note from now on that the prophecy of a post-city era is simply the updated version of another of the classic myths of Western societies: the end of cities, a myth whose limitations have often been exposed before. The breakup of the city is far from being the end of the story, for it does not admit of other processes: integration, network linkages, or governance. Although the city is an unceasing movement, it is also the locus of collective action, of innovation, of interest-aggregation mechanisms, of negotiation, and of conflict. All this demands more precise description and qualification. Mobility, rightly put forward as being a major phenomenon, does not concern the whole of society, and it does not inevitably contradict aggregation processes, rootedness, the invention of urban identities, or the making of urban society. Finally, we should note the possibility that the urbanization now becoming general throughout Europe and beyond will lead to processes of convergence and to the domination of an urban form. However, we can hypothesize that one effect of this trend will be that sociologists will have to think more precisely about different types of cities.

The objective of the first part of the book is to characterize one category of European cities more precisely: that of medium-sized cities and regional capitals. According to Eurostat statisticians, European societies have become urban societies, with from 75 per cent to 85 per cent of individuals, depending on country, living in urban areas. This justifies differentiating certain types of urban area: for example, medium-sized European cities. If we set aside London, Paris, the Randstad, and the Rhine/Ruhr region, western Europe is made up mainly of medium-sized cities with populations of between 200,000 and 2 million. Notions of metropolises or medium-sized cities are all relative: a great metropolis in France would be seen as a small city in Asia. My intention is not to dwell on different categories of cities according to size or to economic or political specialization, since there is excellent literature from geographers who have worked on this. All of it is useful, but I am interested in picking out what represents the core of the European urban structure nowadays, and differentiating it from the biggest metropolises: essentially, from Paris and London. Some people have already made up their minds to view medium-sized cities as urban regions with certain similarities to large metropolises. However, despite real pressures towards dislocation and sprawl, these cities remain places of aggregation of interests and places of representation.

Through work on the Geopolis database, Moriconi-Ebrard (2000) has come up with an authoritative account of the populations of the world's cities. Table 1.1 brings together figures from his work.

A few points are worth mentioning. The first is that, of course, European cities, apart from Paris and London, are not among the giant megalopolises now growing all over the world. Second, in many cases the growth of large conurbations means that cities within them have lost ground and even social meaning. The Ruhr is an interesting exception, because most of the cities within it have retained a strong sense of identity and their own political organizations and social groups. The idea of the city is invariably now strictly contrasted with that of the metropolis: this is particularly important when

TABLE 1.1. *The largest conurbations in the world (2000)*

Conurbation	Ranking of conurbations	Population of city in 2000 ('000s)	Population of conurbation in 2000 ('000s)	Population of city in 1900 ('000s)
Tokyo	1	7,769	29,896	1,496
New York	2	7,459	24,719	3,437
Seoul	3	9,831	20,674	150
Mexico	4	8,591	19,081	419
São Paulo	5	10,286	17,396	240
Manila	6	1,711	16,740	209
Los Angeles	7	3,642	15,807	123
Bombay	9	11,536	15,769	822
Djakarta	10	9,966	15,086	170
Osaka	11	2,851	15,039	852
Delhi	12	9,426	13,592	238
Calcutta	13	4,630	12,619	1,481
Buenos Aires	14	2,957	12,297	833
Shanghai	15	9,755	11,960	840
Cairo	16	7,078	11,633	570
Rio	17	5,625	10,628	692
Moscow	18	8,272	10,046	1,096
Istanbul	19	8,793	9,981	900
Paris	21	2,122	9,850	2,678
Dhaka	22	9,801	9,801	127
Karachi	23	9,661	9,661	132
London	24	7,263	9,166	4,505
Chicago	25	2,833	9,076	1,699
Madrid	48	2,903	4,669	540
Brussels	51	960	4,424	219
Barcelona	61	1,501	3,994	533
Manchester	64	429	3,976	540
Milan	69	1,241	3,822	524
Berlin	70	3,417	3,755	1,889
Athens	79	662	3,227	181
Rotterdam	88	581	3,122	372
Naples	92	1,032	3,047	610
Rome	99	2,625	2,826	414
Birmingham	117	925	2,456	518
Lisbon	124	567	2,356	359
Hamburg	133	1,701	2,196	706
Vienna	149	1,625	1,928	1,750

Note: The boundaries of the conurbations in 2000 differ considerably from those in 1900.

Source: Moriconi-Ebrard (2000: 315–20). The figures are taken from the GEOPOLIS database.

Moriconi-Ebrard analyses the dynamics of cities, conurbations, and now city-regions, and the complex relationship between them. For example, the importance of Manchester as a city-region is not in contradiction with the fact that social and political actors within the city—or within the conurbation—have been active in promoting and regenerating the city, trying to make it an actor within European governance. The same applies to Lisbon, Brussels, or Naples. A third point is that, after much thought, this geographer sets a level of 2 million people as distinguishing the megalopolis from the city. In the European case, this makes a lot of sense, as only Paris, London, Madrid, Berlin, and Rome reach that limit, with a few more if one takes into account conurbations. Fourth, he stresses that the boundaries of the city, and often of the conurbation, have changed a lot over time. The final important point—a view supported by the 1999 Urban Audit—is that there is no single, clear-cut pattern by which a city loses population in favour of the conurbation first and the city-region second. This is an important part of the story. However, many cities in Europe have continued to grow, particularly in France and in Scandinavia, and over the past 20 years some that lost ground are on the rise again, for instance in the UK. Some are also in decline, in Spain and Italy for example. It follows from this that to look at European cities through American eyes—obsessed by the decline of cities and the rise

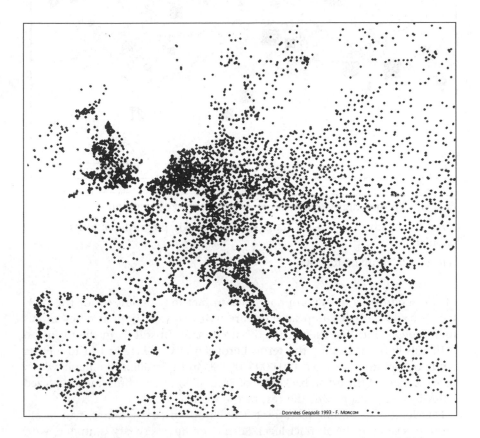

Données Geopolis 1993 - F. Moriconi

FIG. 1.1. The urban structure of Europe; towns with more than 10,000 inhabitants in 1990

Source: Moriconi-Ebrard (2000).

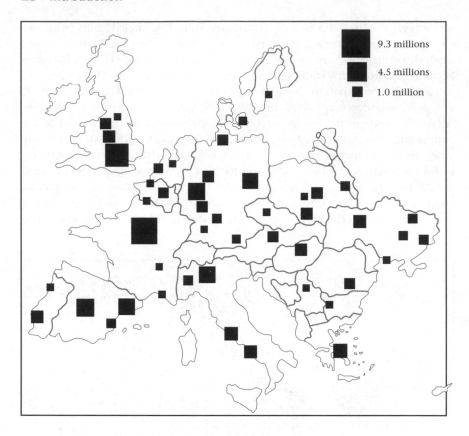

Fig. 1.2. European cities with more than 1 million inhabitants

Note: The relative size of each state is approximately proportional to its population

Source: Moriconi-Ebrard (2000).

of the suburbs—is not appropriate, and in fact may be less so for the USA, too. It could be that European cities are trying to exist both as cities and as metropolises, but that their strength and dynamism still lie in their centres.

In this book, therefore, the term 'European city' will refer to those cities with populations of between 150,000–200,000 and 1.5 million–2 million, which provide most of the urban backbone of Europe: in other words, medium-sized cities by comparison with the rest of the world.

Developing an outline picture of 'the European city' requires, first of all, more precision at the abstract level. Seen close up, every city is unique, with its own characteristics and history. Some features common to most cities in the same country become apparent only when we look at the whole national picture: for example, the historic centres of Italian cities, or the way that, in

French cities, churches are physically confronted by buildings that represent the state. At a more general level of abstraction, and in relation to other, theoretical questions, we may choose to employ the categories of 'city', 'urban', or even 'Western city'. This is not a normative choice in praise of the old European city, but derives from the aim of asking questions about change in European societies, their form of territorialization, the reshaping of the state, and the hypothesis presented earlier about the different forms of the urban.[13]

The nature of the contemporary city is as a local or regional 'socio-economy' whose very usefulness to the forces of global capitalism is precisely as an ensemble of specific, differentiated and localised relations. These relations consist of concrete relations between persons and organisations that are central to the economic functioning of those entities. Cities are sites where such relations are conventional, and they are different from one city to another. What is distinctive about cities is the ways in which groups of actors—tied together by their relations and conventions—engage in specific processes of economic and social reflexivity . . . These 'worlds' of urban action must become the focus of urban theory, analysis, and policy. (Storper 1997: 222–3)

In the first part of the book, I will try to show that European cities are a relatively robust category of 'urban world' and that they are not only subject to the diktat of the markets. Within them, groups and institutions are mobilizing to seek new models of integration, governance, principles of organization, and norms of behaviour. Finally, this book has no pretensions to an all-encompassing view of European cities. Many questions have been omitted, particularly those about the shape taken by European cities, as have issues of aesthetics and culture. I have also left out some of the more sensitive and less well-known issues, such as urban violence, forms of mobility, and environmental issues, even though they are crucial to the future of cities.

Presentation of the Book

This preliminary introduction to the issues involved is complemented by a second, historical introduction that reveals the long history of European cities, from the Middle Ages to the mid-twentieth century. In trying to understand the transformations of actors within cities and then come to understand cities as collective actors, careful consideration must first be given to the social, economic, and political changes to the nation-state that are profoundly transforming the environment of urban actors and of cities and are creating lasting alterations in the structure of constraint and opportunity. Therefore, the second part of this book is devoted to changes in the state, to the erosion

---

[13] Lévy (1997) also raises many important points following that line of analysis in his book on the geography of Europe.

of national societies, and to processes of globalization and re-territorialization of the economy, all of which, in Europe, have direct implications for actors, social groups, and organizations within cities. These chapters will gradually build up a particular image of European cities. The third part of the book takes as its subject the actors of European cities and the modes of governance that are allowing some cities to become collective actors. The way changes combine in this context is creating the conditions for cities to constitute collective actors. They also help us to understand the reshaping of urban actors and local governments, as well as attempts to structure modes of governance. The chapter on actors, groups, and organizations in European cities is complemented by a chapter on changes to urban governments. Urban governments are not being dragged to oblivion in the wake of the disappearing state: they are adapting, reshaping, and engaging in a modified dynamics. Finally, the conclusion discusses the place of European cities in European societies, on the basis of a typology of modes of governance.

TWO

The Long History
of the European City

THE golden age of late medieval cities is a European myth, associating the
city with civility and urbanity. Lepetit (1988: 60) identifies two clear dimensions to this myth: 'In its origins, the city is immovable. Two founding myths
command its existence and form the basis of its supremacy. Cities are fixed
within space and time by their walls and by their foundation in time
immemorial and their past splendour.' Benevolo (1993) also emphasizes
that this bond still forms part of the European identity. The city represents
a kind of ideal of urbanity, in which the mutual cooperation of citizens inside
the city goes hand in hand with openness to the outside and with the
circulation of goods and ideas (Zidjderveld 1998). In retrospect, this heritage
of the monumental and the urbane seems rather magical by comparison with
the common view of the hell of mining towns and industrial areas or the
anonymity of the metropolis. Political autonomy, social structure—that is,
associations—economy, culture, and town planning all seem to have come
together to create an urban ideal which is now lost. But it is clear that reconstructing the city in this guise must mask very diverse situations and uncertain trajectories, especially from the standpoint of the actors of the time (Barel
1975).

Highlighting the longevity of European cities is not merely a conservative
project, aimed at reaffirming their resistance to change and the original nature
of their structures. Nowadays, the nation-state is facing strong pressures, and
the recurrence of this imagined picture of European cities is no accident. It
offers a cognitive frame of reference for thinking through and putting into
practice interactions, interdependencies, and networks of relationships that
cut across national boundaries. There has been no shortage of instances of
updating the myth, especially since the late 1980s. The Mayor of Barcelona,
Pasqual Maragal, and his planners have made liberal use of it in their reorganization of that city. In Venice, the philosopher-mayor, Massimo Cacciari,
used his own writings about the European archipelago of cities to mobilize
his coalition and to make proposals for the institutional framework of Italy.
Georges Frèche, the mayor of Montpellier, and the author of a thesis on the

history of Toulouse, has compared himself—perhaps more often than can be justified—to a Renaissance Medici in order to legitimize his ambitious urban development plans and his cultural investments. More recently, the political, economic, and cultural elites of Copenhagen, Hamburg, Stockholm, and Helsinki have launched an increasing number of political initiatives relating to infrastructures and to representations, which aim to revive a large trading space from the North Sea to the Baltic.

The myth of the European city has been rehabilitated and reinvented by urban elites seeking a role and an identity for their cities. Yet this heritage is not solely mythical: its accumulated legacy is a visible one. The Galileo Chair at the University of Padua, the bankers' houses and palaces of Amsterdam, Bourges, and Frankfurt, the palaces of the Medici, the Strozzi, and the Antinori in Florence, the cathedrals of Salisbury and Mainz and the lanes of St James of Compostella, the port districts of Barcelona, Copenhagen, and Stockholm, the Jewish ghetto in Venice and the Dutch houses in Norwich, the canals of Bruges and Leiden and the belfries of Lille and Brussels are all familiar features of those cities.

From the time when an enlarged European market and a European form of politics began to take shape, more and more questions have been raised about the foundations of European societies. In their uncertain quest, sociologists and historians have highlighted the legacy of peasant societies or of religion, the role of the state, the influence of the Industrial Revolution on the formation of national societies and all that came with it—a working class, trade unions, left-wing parties, the welfare state—and cities. In his inquiry into the specific features of twentieth-century European societies, the historian Hartmut Kaelble (1988: 62) has stressed Europe's original urban route:

The scale of the European city is another facet of urban development in Europe that was equally important . . . The medium-sized town of between 20,000 and 100,000 inhabitants played a more significant and more enduring role in twentieth century Europe than elsewhere. About a third of the urban population of Europe lived in towns like Cambridge, Aarhus, Lund, Delft, Liège, Tübingen, Aix-en-Provence, and Ravenna. Especially in the post-war age, the figure for American and Australian towns of comparable size was lower, as it was in Japan and Canada.

Colin Crouch (1999) also argues convincingly that European societies are distinctive in their levels of institutionalization and territorialization. The deep roots of European societies in territories—above all in states, but also in cities, regions, and rural micro-regions—are directly tied to the strongly territorial nature of the economic and the political. The 'Europe of Cities' is a good example of this distinctive feature.

European cities are one of the structuring elements of modern European societies. Since the end of the Middle Ages, Western cities have been the crucible for the social, political, and economic organization of European nation-states. This chapter takes the work of various historians as its starting point in order to demonstrate the longevity of European cities and the relative stability of the European urban framework. Cities also offer an adaptable key to understanding the way nation-states have been shaped, since they form a part of national trajectories. The importance of this relationship between cities and states in Europe is that transformations of states alter the political conditions in which cities exist.

Cities in Medieval Europe: The Crucible of European Societies

In his classic chapter 'The City' in *Economy and Society* (1978), Max Weber portrays the medieval Western city as having the following characteristic features: a fortification; a market and a specifically urban economy of consumption, exchange, and production; a court of law and the ability to ordain a set of rules and laws; a structure based on associations—of guilds—and at least partial political autonomy, expressed in particular through the existence of an administrative body and the participation of the burghers in local government, and sometimes even through the existence of an army and an actual policy of foreign expansion. He saw two additional features as essential in law: rules relating to landed property—since cities were not subject to the taxes and constraints of feudalism—and to the legal status of individuals in the cities, and citizenship associated with affiliation to a guild and with relative freedom. These features, which are combined in the unique model of the Western city, differ by their very nature, their institutions and their social structures. This combination of political autonomy, religious culture, specifically urban economy, and differentiated social structure, all surrounded by a wall, made the Western city an original sociological category and a structuring element in the Europe of the Middle Ages. The period from the tenth to the fifteenth centuries is considered to have seen the rise of European cities, with the emergence of large urban trading centres and, as the golden age of the medieval city came to an end, with architectural renewal and cultural expansion. This urban Europe reached its high point at the end of the Middle Ages, when feudal structures were gradually fading, but before the states had established their domination everywhere.

The medieval city played a key role in the invention of Europe, which had previously been a part of the Roman Empire and at the periphery of a world centred on the Mediterranean. The remarkable adventure of the European city seems to have begun around the tenth century. Its starting point was when 'Europe rose as Rome fell': in other words, as these two processes occurred over time. The break with the East and the Byzantine Empire established the dominant influence of the Church in the invention of Europe. Conflict with Islam cut Africa off from Europe and, for a time, drove Europeans out of the

Mediterranean. As a direct consequence, the centre of gravity of the new formation moved north, towards the Franks and the Germans. The end of the barbarian invasions left Europe with uncertain eastern boundaries. The revolution in agriculture enabled cities to take off economically. This geo-political reality, which gradually took shape after the tenth century, was coupled with the gradual cultural and social 'invention' of Europe, within which the Church and the cities were to play an essential role (Delanty 1995; Crouzet and Furet 1998).

The playing field was now marked out. Cities would rise in a Europe made up of peasant societies, the Church, knights, and landed gentry. At first insinuating themselves into the gaps in the feudal system, they would go on to become the crucible for the gradual emergence or the reappearance of the main features of modern European societies: social classes, capitalism, culture and education, political autonomy in religious matters, rationality, political institutions, democracy.

The true Europe was the Europe of cities in the middle of the countryside, the Europe that finally came into being from the twelfth century, a Europe that was not just covered with a sprinkling of little white churches, but a Europe covered with a tapestry of cities, real cities, cities that were not just fortresses, not just granaries and centres of rural administration. These were real cities, with their municipal statutes and their burghers; burghers who were first and foremost merchants, and merchants who were warriors, men of moral fibre and remarkable depth, always on the move, always with some plan on the go, always ready to set off on an adventure or a trading expedition, weapon in hand; men with an irrepressible energy that neither natural nor mental barriers, nor scruples of any kind, could halt; men of remarkable vigour who enriched humanity with a new species, the merchant-conqueror, and who already had their own spirit, an attitude to gain that we call the capitalist approach, but also a spirit of criticism and of rationalism, somewhat terse, opposed to any mysticism; realistic and calculating, they wore away their original prejudices by rubbing them up against other prejudices . . . (Fevre 1999: 155)[1]

For Pirenne ([1969 OR 1971?]), the development of trade and commerce, and then of production, lies at the origin of the development of medieval European cities. In fact, their creation may be linked to other factors (Bairoch 1985; Hohenberg and Hollen Lees 1985). Some of the cities that became prosperous again during this era had survived the breakup of the Roman Empire, particularly in Italy and on the Mediterranean, though much more rarely in the north, except in the Rhine Valley and in France. The Church also played an essential role since its territorial organization ensured the permanence of smaller cities: for a time, the religious authorities were to fulfil the task of

---

[1] The enthusiasm of various authors for the dynamics of European cities often leads to exaggeration of the contrast with peasant societies, which, despite their apparent resistance to change, also underwent transformation and were gradually drawn into economic and social changes, interdependently with cities. See, in particular, Rösener (1994) and Mendras (1976; 1997).

framing and organizing urban society. Other cities were created at a stroke by monarchies in the course of formation—Aix-la-Chapelle, for example— or for strategic and military reasons, like Newcastle or some Spanish cities during the conflicts of the *Reconquista*. In northern Europe in the twelfth century, the sovereigns or religious authorities of small, newly forming states created Copenhagen in 1180 and then Stockholm. Another major factor contributing to a city's development could be its establishment as an important political power, as was the case with Paris from the Capetians onwards, with London and Naples under the Angevin Kings and with the papacy at Rome. However, it is true that strong urban growth was rooted in trade, which augmented the wealth of merchants, and in artisan production. Cities prospered from the influx of new inhabitants, rural artisans and traders— craftsmen producing food, tailors, smiths, taverners, and so on—and others who were passing through or were trying to escape the peasant's hard lot. This growth of cities can be seen in the numbers of inhabitants and in the creation of new districts and new buildings. With development, other functions appeared or were strengthened: lawyers, jurists and notaries trained in places like Bologna or Padua, bankers, small shopkeepers, and various artisans. The major banking families of Florence, Augsburg, Bruges, and Cologne, and later of Frankfurt, London, and Amsterdam, had financial relationships throughout Europe and investments even farther afield.

The cities most involved in this dynamic were those that linked west and east: in the south, Mediterranean cities, especially Italian ones—Venice, Genoa, Pisa, Naples; in the north, the new Baltic cities of Lübeck, Hamburg, Danzig, and Rostock, as well as Bruges and Cologne. These cities, which could be described as typical of the maritime model of European cities, were at the heart of economic flows, and organized the major trade routes. Pirenne (1969) explains that, in the south, the cities of the fertile Lombardy plain were carried forward in the wake of Venetian commerce, while the commercial activities of Scandinavian sailors stimulated the economies of the northern coast from Flanders to Russia.

In his book on the Hanseatic League, Philippe Dollinger (1970: 13) describes the dynamics of northern cities:

In north-west Germany the future Hansa cities of any importance were almost all old-established towns, whose urban character had developed slowly from the tenth to the thirteenth century, in the way so often described, but with a number of local variations. This entailed an increase in population in certain favourably situated settlements as artisans moved in from the country and merchants set up permanent establishments; the amalgamation, within a single fortified area, of a merchant quarter—called *wiek* in north Germany—and an older administrative centre, either ecclesiastical or lay; the development of a uniform code of law, peculiar to the town and its inhabitants and dealing especially with matters of real estate and trade; the creation of a community of burgesses, often bound together by oath; the preponderant influence in this community (at least in the more important centres) of the merchants, sometimes grouped together in

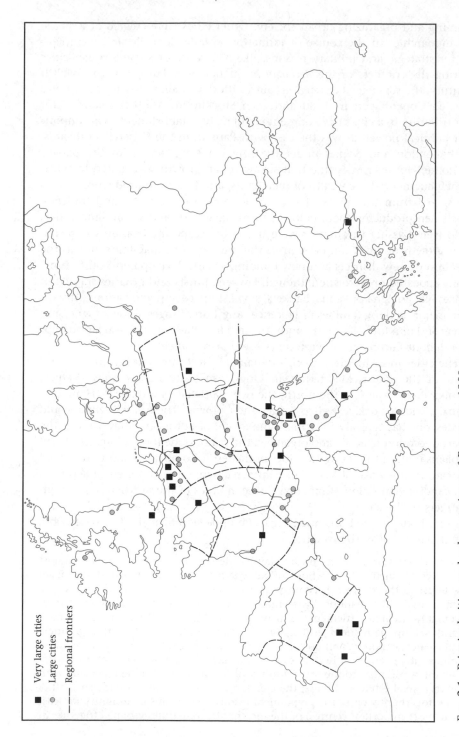

FIG. 2.1. Principal cities and urban regions of Europe, c. 1350

Source: Hohenberg and Hollen Lees (1985).

Very large cities
Large cities
Regional frontiers

a guild; the annexation of the government by the richest families, or patriciate; the growing independence of the town in relation to the local feudal lord; and, finally, the development of administrative institutions controlled by the burgesses, among which the council (*Rat*) . . . became everywhere the controlling organ in the now fully developed town.

By the end of the fifteenth century, Europe had just over 150 cities with more than 10,000 inhabitants and, by 1650, nearly 200 of this size. A European urban system had been formed with a 'backbone' that had grown out of early capitalism, the religious inheritance, and the exercise of active political will. The shape of this Europe of merchants was organized around trade through Italy, the Hanseatic League, Bruges and Antwerp, with the Rhine-Rhône corridor as its main highway. As Pirenne ([1969 OR 1971?]: 66) has noted, 'Italian merchants . . . are made mention of at Paris; and at the beginning of the twelfth century the fairs of Flanders were already drawing a considerable number of their compatriots. Nothing could be more natural than . . . the attraction which trade spontaneously exerts upon trade'. The west of Europe, on the other hand, seems to have been rather isolated. Of the 150 cities identified in 1500, only three were in England: London, Norwich, and Bristol. The absence of major regional centres seems to have been a characteristic of the British Isles, although England had a tight network of small market towns and fairs. Spain—apart from Barcelona, Valencia, and some cities in Aragon—Portugal, and western France—with the exception of Bordeaux—were also isolated. It would take the opening up of America to give new impetus to Europe's Atlantic shore. Scandinavia had several major cities, but the heart of Europe beat first in Italy and in the southern Netherlands—Antwerp, Bruges, and so forth—which were the two most urbanized regions because they were the most dynamic in their pursuit of early capitalism.

Physically, the medieval European city was characterized by a citadel, an enclosing wall and a marketplace, a built-up area around a focal point, administrative and public buildings, churches, monuments, squares, areas for commerce and trade, and development radiating out from the centre. The creation of belfries, campaniles, public buildings, cathedrals, and numerous palaces often reveals competition between different powers—bishop, lord, burghers, sometimes the state—between the great families or between cities themselves. The end of the Middle Ages was an intense period of construction of palaces and churches (Heers 1990; Benevolo 1993). The creation of streets and public squares has rightly been highlighted as a key element in the organization of communes and local democracy, but hospices, prisons, and parvises should not be forgotten in this regard. The medieval city was a building site. The town-planning revival that began in Italian cities spread to a large number of other European cities, particularly after the fourteenth century.

Contrary to the feudal order and despite the bishops' reservations, burghers—merchants, bankers, artisans, shopkeepers, and lawyers—were the new actors of this European urban expansion and of the cities' autonomy from the old feudal order. This bourgeoisie of early mercantile capitalism gradually invented itself as a social class with its own interests but also with its own ways of life, consumption behaviours, values, ideas, organizations, distinctive law, strategic marriages, formation of clans, rivalries between great families trying to monopolize power, prestige, and wealth, and with emerging social class relations (Angiolini and Roche 1995; Lane 1973). Social hierarchies were established through reversals of fortune, alliances with overlords, or the acquisition of positions of power within the guild or the commune. District or parish, guild, and family were the three elements that shaped the social structure of cities in the Middle Ages. Citizenship resulted from the aggregation of groups and networks.

Citizens originally established themselves as a social group in opposition to the aristocracy and the landed gentry. But sometimes they merged with them: in Italian cities, for example. The word 'citizen' can have different meanings:

. . . the concept of citizenship (*Bürgertum*) . . . First . . . may include certain social categories or classes which have some specific communal or economic interest . . . Second, in the political sense, citizenship signifies membership in the state, with its connotation as the holder of certain political rights. Finally, by citizens in the class sense, we understand those strata which are drawn together, in contrast with the bureaucracy or the proletariat and others outside their circle, as 'persons of property and culture,' entrepreneurs, recipients of funded incomes, and in general all persons of academic culture, a certain class standard of living, and a certain social prestige. (Weber 1951: 315)

The medieval city was the crucible of European societies, in which new cultural and political models developed, along with new social relations and cultural and organizational innovations, furthered by interactions between the various populations. The city as 'exchange multiplier', according to Fernand Braudel (1979), promoted mechanisms for learning a collective way of life, for innovation and spreading innovation, rapid accumulation, transformation of behaviours, interplay of competition and cooperation, and processes of social differentiation engendered by proximity. European cities also became seats of learning, arts, and science. City burghers went on to create schools and institutes that were autonomous of the religious authorities. Starting in Italy in the twelfth century—Bologna in 1088, Padua, then Salerno, Naples, Rome, Sienna, Florence, and so forth—the movement for the creation of universities spread to Spain—Salamanca, Seville, Lisbon; to England—Oxford and Cambridge; to Ireland—Dublin; and to France—Montpellier, Toulouse, Paris, and Orleans. Although launched later, the movement to create universities in central and northern Europe was no less vigorous, from Cologne to Prague, from Strasbourg to Vienna, from Heidelberg to Cracow or Louvain (Jehel and Racinet 1996). The Europe of cities in the fourteenth century had about a hundred universities, which organized a dense traffic in ideas, students,

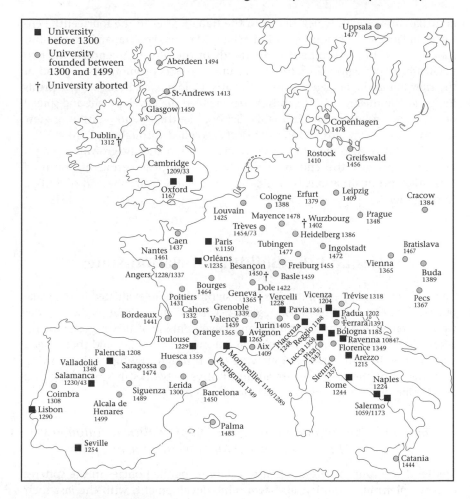

FIG. 2.2. European universities in the Middle Ages

Source: Jehel and Racinet (1996)

and intellectual elites. Some universities provided a full programme of education from a very early stage. Galileo, for example, came from the University of Padua, where astronomy, medicine, mathematics, and law were all studied. The Europe of cities in the Middle Ages was not just the Europe of early capitalism and of merchants, but also the Europe of cities of intellectuals, universities, and culture.[2]

This was a dynamic that continued during the Renaissance, despite the reactions of the nobility and the increasing strength of states. It was originally

[2] For an overview of European cities at the end of the Middle Ages, see Berengo (1999).

an urban movement, which began in the Italian cities in the fourteenth century—in Florence, obviously, and in Milan, Mantua, Ferrara, and Rome—but also operated in the southern Netherlands in the fifteenth century: the two most urbanized regions in Europe. Cultural contacts promoted the spread of the new Italian Renaissance culture to Paris, Cologne, and Prague. The printing press, the theatre, and the universities enabled the development and spread of ideas and of books. The Humanist School like the one in Strasbourg grew up; and humanists, artists, and architects travelled throughout Europe.[3]

As the Middle Ages drew to a close, feudal reaction and the growing strength of states presaged the end of a distinctive historical period of confused authority and of situations that differed remarkably from one end of Europe to the other.

Cities and the Building of Nation-States

The making of European states has been significantly re-evaluated in the wake of a new generation of historical research. This has shown that medieval cities were characterized by the creation and development of urban government, a key element in their relative political autonomy, which would then play a decisive role in state-making. Following this through highlights the growing importance of the state and its administrative networks in structuring and developing cities: the 'continental' model of cities.

The Municipal Revolution and the Fragile Political Autonomy of Cities: The Origins of Urban Government in Europe

Medieval communes were the first to establish public policies in the spheres of town planning, security, and economic development, with the last their main concern. Fiscal, legal, and military tools and statistical techniques developed in the cities were later to prove invaluable in consolidating states.

The municipal revolution, which contributed to the making of nation-states, took the form of a movement, from the tenth century onwards, to create communes by obtaining titles and charters from their overlords. This movement continued by various means throughout the Middle Ages and in England, in a limited form, into the fifteenth century. The emergence of urban government was part of a logic of defence against other cities, against the nobility, and against any rival power, as well as a determination to acquire rights and privileges. It allowed merchants, shopkeepers, and artisans to

---

[3] Erasmus' elegant turn of phrase, cited in Burke (2000: 129), 'I would like to be a citizen of the world', meaning '. . . of the European community of knowledge', illustrates this dynamic.

exercise and develop their trades in the face of various more or less institutionalized groups in the city.

Numerous claims to authority stand side by side, overlapping and often conflicting with each other. Episcopal powers of seigneurial and political nature; appropriated vicontiel and other political office powers resting partly on chartered privileges and partly on usurpation; powers of great urban feudatories or freed *ministeriales* of the king or the bishops (*capitanei*); those of rural or urban subfeudatories (*valvassores*) of the *capitanei*; . . . occupational unions of the urban economic classes; judicial powers based on manorial law, on feudal law, on territorial law and on ecclesiastic law—all these are found in the same city. (Weber 1978: 1251)

The burghers formed sworn confederacies—*coniurationes*—guilds, and corporations to defend their economic interests, their status and their autonomy, and later to organize the communes internally and to defend themselves against other cities. Weber stresses this point: 'all *coniurationes* and city unions of the Occident, beginning with those of early Antiquity, were coalitions of the *armed* strata of the cities' (1978: 1262).

The power of the burghers would lead gradually to the creation of more or less democratic institutions and the creation of a distinctive urban form of law. This process came about through alliances between these *coniurationes* and some of the other existing authorities and interests, and through a complex interplay of relationships with overlords. Municipal institutions were also subject to conflicts of interest between the petty bourgeoisie, the great patrician families, the overlords, and the king's representatives. A commune was characterized by its own political rights, by autonomous courts and economic policy, and less frequently—except in the case of Italian cities and urban leagues—by international policy and a military force. The acquisition of this municipal autonomy was gradual and the time it took varied enormously, although it happened earlier in Italy. It came about when a charter was granted by the higher authorities—prince, bishop, king, or emperor—defining the rights, duties, and privileges of the corporation, according to circumstances, the wealth of the burghers, the needs of one overlord or another, or as a result of compromise. This movement tended to create a political authority that made the city a collective actor and strengthened the coherence of urban society in the face of other powers. The municipal movement changed the way the hand of politics was dealt in Europe, and foreshadowed the development of the modern state. In these urban communes democracy was shaped and reinvented, as was, in particular, the concept of citizen as member of a municipal corporation, taxpayer, and inheritor of property. Within feudalism, this concept of citizenship represented a radical innovation. One of the consequences of this dynamic would be the development of an 'urban patriotism', of a form of collective mobilization located in cities.

Urban governments were the result of compromises between the different interests—associations, families, or districts—that gave structure to political life. Despite the infinite variety of situations, forms of municipal power were generally organized around a grouping of all citizens, with a council, various committees, and an executive authority. The combination of mechanisms for appointing councils and officials of the executive took many forms, such as co-option, elections, or drawing lots, and was, moreover, likely to vary over time, reflecting the interests of the dominant families, the balance of power with the nobility, or royal interventions, as well as revolts, social conflicts, coups, and various sophisticated ways of seizing power by one family or small group. The histories of cities are replete with such rivalries between families or guilds, with changes of alliance and reversals of fortune. Often, a small number of families managed to remain on the councils and control the government of the communes, and were all the more likely to do so if they accumulated wealth and inheritance, succeeded in arranging alliances through marriage, and avoided sudden bankruptcies. The development of urban oligarchies was, therefore, a fairly common feature of the medieval cities of Europe, from north to south and, to a lesser degree, from east to west. Confrontations between groups, families, and interests saw the elaboration of mechanisms for representation, delegation, and compromise. Cities were a laboratory for experiments in democracy, which sometimes resulted— though rarely and belatedly—in emancipation from all higher authorities. More often, cities would gradually attempt to be recognized as speaking directly to the emperor or king in order to assert their interests themselves, without the nobility as intermediary.

The gradual strengthening of the communes in a context of urban growth would foster a dynamic of institutionalization and the creation of norms, rules, and procedures. Church prelates played a decisive role in the administration of a number of cities, but gradually associations of burghers took up the reins of municipal government and found themselves having to manage urban growth. They began to experiment with and develop various techniques of government. The invention of urban government involved the differentiation of roles, special responsibilities, and administrative functions—magistrates, aldermen, lawyers, and so on. Moreover, it was often this increase in the power of urban administrations that provided the reason for a section of the urban nobility to merge with the burghers. These medieval city administrators were faced with some formidable tasks: constructing public facilities and building whole districts, managing social disorder, reviving town planning, and managing settlement or urban leagues. These same city administrators would be mobilized by the central state when it needed local and regional bases or administrators at the centre. Techniques and instruments of government were also developed within the context of these urban governments. Special attention was paid to financial techniques and the management of borrowing. The accumulation of wealth in the cities very soon made certain families, such as the Medici of Florence and the Fuggers of Augsburg, bankers to the sovereigns of Europe. At an equally early stage, the emergent political authorities tried to capture part of this wealth, by negotiation or by force. The 'calculating burghers' of the Italian city-states—the chief of which were Venice and Florence—as well as of the Hanseatic League developed investment calculations, statistical models, and management techniques, and experimented with all kinds of fiscal instruments (Isaacs and Prak 1996).

Similarly, urban law and constitutions were an important dimension of the institutionalization of urban governments, both in scope and in scale. In the case of France, Rigaudière (1988: 70) also shows that cities

. . . had already been contributing, since the thirteenth century, to developing a body of legislation that royalty wanted to impose more generally. The very diverse regulations that they enacted often served as the model for royal decisions. Thus, there was a genuine transfer of administrative techniques and political know-how from the city to the state. Urban law, although diverse at the outset, became, as it were, the crucible for a new legal experiment, on which the monarchy was able to draw with some success. The direction of this process was unquestionably from the city to the state, while state law was further enriched by the large-scale presence of former urban magistrates within the royal administration at local level.

This line of argument is even more pertinent in the case of England and Wales, where common law was made as royal courts resolved disputes and rulings made in local and seignorial courts.

States Against Cities?
'Conquering Princes and Calculating Burghers'

Although urban communes contributed to the formation of states, the modern state in Western Europe developed in opposition to cities: 'voracious states' got the better of 'obstructing cities'.[4] Historical research has sometimes put forward a somewhat Manichaean history of state formation, taking two opposed views. On the one hand, medieval European cities have been seen as conservative forces hindering the formation of nation-states. Cities are suspected of being the strongholds of a merchant society that ran counter to any idea of political community, by implication counter to the political order of the nation-state, superior and noble as this was. By contrast, others have pointed to the heroic resistance of proud cities, the seats of culture, innovation, diversity, and progress, ravaged by kings greedy for conquest and by brutal states with their force and their blind bureaucratic rationality. The work of European historians and political sociologists such as Rokkan and Tilly has thrown light on the complex relations between cities and states, where confrontation was just one approach among several.

There is no doubt that, in the long term, the state became the dominant, even the monopoly, form of organization of power. Weber's opinion on this

---

[4] Blockmans (1988), from the title of which the second part of the present subsection's heading is taken.

is incontrovertible: 'On the Continent, the modern patrimonial bureaucratic state eventually deprived most of them [the cities] of their political autonomy as well as of their military powers, except for police purposes' (1978: 1324). The modern state took shape at the end of the Middle Ages. Genet has defined it as follows:

... the 'modern state' was a new form of state: it came fully into being between 1270 and 1360 in the west (in France and, especially, in England, but also in Castile, Scotland and Aragon) through a combination of means. A non-feudal relationship was established between king and subject, representative assemblies were developed, a state taxation system was set up, and state activity (and service) in the areas of justice and warfare intensified. Corollaries to the rapid crystallization of all these elements (some of which already had a long history behind them) were the appearance of a specific ideology of the state and the increased autonomy of the field of politics. (Bulst and Genet 1988: 339)

Charles Tilly notes that the 500 political entities that existed in the West at the end of the Middle Ages had, by the end of the nineteenth century, become just 30 nation-states, and that these had been arrived at by long processes and various routes. The works of Tilly, Blockmans, and Genet tie in with Weber and the origins of the original trajectory of Western Europe. In following this through, the role of cities in these processes has been re-evaluated in terms of political and cultural inventions and accumulation of wealth, as has the fact that cities, and the social groups within them, have played an enduring, though often hidden, role in European states. These authors have thus brought to light the importance of cities in the emergence of modern states and the forms these have taken. In his comparative work on the formation of the state in Europe, particularly the sections undertaken in collaboration with Rokkan, Tilly (1975) has highlighted the way in which the nation-state was formed, notably how it gradually brought a clearly delimited territory under control through a monopoly of violence and coercion. Looking at these issues again, over 20 years later, we come to a sort of impasse, since the authors did not discuss the European regions that did not transform into states at the same time as others and where diverse political forms persisted for a long while. Tilly argues that the formation of nation-states in Europe arose out of constraints caused by war. The success of the national state model can be explained by its ability to mobilize the human, technical, and financial resources needed to wage war on other states—and not necessarily just national ones. This was not, however, a uniform process, since several types of state organization coexisted in Europe before the fifteenth century: empires, kingdoms, principalities, and city-states were all in conflict with one another. Tilly (1990) is interested, therefore, in those state transformations that enable him to highlight the importance of the relationship between city and state. In his view, the existence of cities—places, first and foremost, where wealth is accumulated—represents a key constraint on the formation of nation-states. He thus elaborates an analytical framework that endeavours to identify several types of state formation processes on the basis of the influence of coercion and of capital, according to the interplay of landed gentry, urban bourgeoisies, and the power of the monarch.[5]

From the thirteenth to the fifteenth centuries, the feudal system remained dominant wherever urbanization was weak, for example in Spain, France, Scotland, Wales, Ireland, eastern Europe, and Scandinavia. But in southern England, the United Provinces, western Germany and northern Italy, cities were dominant or else resisted the landed gentry either by associating themselves with the sovereign—in England—by creating leagues—in Germany—or by becoming powerful city-states—Genoa, Venice—occasionally vaguely attached to an empire. In some cases, national governments' strategies can be seen in the way they associated themselves with city burghers, giving them charters or exempting them from taxation, in order to fund foreign wars—the Republic of the United Provinces, for example, hardly existed outside the assembly of cities and provinces—or domestic adventures to get rid of burdensome barons, as in Aragon and Castile. At the same time, in Poland the rural nobility that elected the kings managed to prevent cities from playing too significant a role. States used various means to control cities: legitimacy disputes, the creation of national ideologies, force, heavy taxation, granting peerages and privileges to urban elites, and political integration. In most cases, cities were unable to resist the processes of national state formation, except where the feudal system was particularly weak—the Netherlands, Switzerland —or where it was a question of city-states or dense city networks—Italy, parts of Germany. Even the latter proved incapable of containing the rise in military power of France, Spain, and England.

The powerful cities of northern and southern Europe seem to have constituted barriers to the formation of certain kinds of state. The cities of Flanders, Germany, and Italy are, therefore, the favoured observation ground on which to study the 'coercion versus capital' confrontation (Tilly 1990). The Italian city-states present the best known counter-example to the argument put forward above. Venice retained a formal attachment to the Byzantine empire for a long time, and this guaranteed its complete autonomy even before it set itself up as a quasi-state on dry land. Economic power fostered political independence. Conflicts between cities and higher authorities—the Germanic and Byzantine empires, the Pope, the Hapsburgs, the kingdom of France or

---

[5] Tilly (1994: 8, 9) writes: 'For Europe it [his book] explores the possibility that the variable distribution of cities and systems of cities by region and era significantly and independently constrained the multiple paths of state transformation. It argues that states, as repositories of armed forces, grow differently in different environments and that the character of the urban networks within such environments systematically affects the path of state transformation . . . The varying intersections between the processes by which capital and coercion concentrated and came under state control help explain the geographic pattern of European state formation, the differentiated incorporation of urban oligarchies and institutions into consolidated state structure, and the shift in state power from the Mediterranean to the Atlantic.'

the kingdom of Spain—would be endemic throughout the Middle Ages and beyond, until the final triumph of the nation-state only late in the nineteenth century, with the unification of Germany and of Italy. From the twelfth century onwards, a lengthy conflict set the Lombard cities in opposition to Emperor Frederick Barbarossa and ended with the crushing of Milan. From the thirteenth century, the cities of Flanders were in revolt against annexation by the King of France, ending with the battle of Courtrai and ignominious retreat by the French. In the same period, tensions also increased between German cities, princes, and the imperial power. Organized urban government and economic development were formidable assets to invest in the subsequent acquisition of military force or the purchase of the good graces of more powerful protectors.

Cities formed alliances—in Italy and Germany, these were the urban leagues—which differed in form and longevity, in order to defend themselves against the extension of the power of states. Such regional leagues—the Saxon League, the Rhineland League—went on to prosper in the end, relying on the dynamism of the city burghers and their accumulation of wealth. Most of these cities did not desire inevitable transformation into city-states. A remote attachment to the emperor, to whom they submitted in exchange for a certain tribute when it seemed sensible, was most often seen as the most beneficial solution. Recognizing the emperor as sovereign in no way prevented them from joining dynamic urban leagues in order to protect themselves from immediate dangers. The Hanseatic League provides the consummate example of a city alliance, as well as the longest-lasting: from roughly the tenth century to the mid-seventeenth. Its model offers the most perfect counter-example to linear, functionalist views, which see the growth of the state in terms of coercion, since the Hanseatic League was based on a very low level of institutionalization. As Dollinger (1964: xvii–xviii) has written:

... in spite of these structural weaknesses and the conflicting interests inevitable in an association of towns so different and so distant from one another, the Hansa was able to hold its own for nearly five hundred years. The secret of its long life is to be found not in coercion, which played no appreciable role, but in the realisation of common interests which bound the members of the community together. This sense of solidarity was founded on the determination to control the commerce of northern Europe. . . . As long as this economic interdependence continued, the Hansa survived.

Originally a grouping of northern German merchants, the Hanseatic League became a powerful association of between 100 and 200 cities, depending on the period in question, stretching from the Netherlands to the Baltic Sea. Dollinger points out the political and economic motivations of the Hanseatic League: to defend merchants' autonomy and legal status, but above all to protect them abroad so as to guarantee commercial expansion. Permanent tensions with the Scandinavian states—war with Denmark—with

Russia, occasionally with France, and with England over the protection of trading posts sometimes degenerated into open conflicts, in which the Hanseatic League brought its power of economic blockade fully into play while also ensuring the support of other political powers, empires, principalities, or rival states through the use of diplomacy or money. With no cumbersome administration, no specific forms of organization, and a low level of institutionalization, and without the characteristic features of a state, the Hanseatic League went on to become the chief military power in northern Europe.

In the fifteenth century, this Europe of cities succumbed to the onslaught of nation-states. In the north, states consolidated their position and promoted their own markets. The Hanseatic cities were in competition with the cities of the Netherlands unified by Burgundy, with Scandinavian cities encouraged by the powerful Danish state, and with English cities. In the late Middle Ages, the German cities sustained major defeats against the princes and against Frederick II. Military and economic pressures would finally get the better of the Hanseatic League. The south saw the Italian cities, which had been concerned for a very long time with fighting each other, succumb: some asserted themselves over others—Sienna, Fiesole, and Lucca came under the control of Florence—and some fell to foreign invasions, as in the case of Naples. France came to govern Genoa and Milan. Coercion triumphed over capital.

In France and in England, the capital city became established in the late Middle Ages as the dominant city. Although merchant cities existed, they were neither numerous nor powerful: Toulouse and Lyons in France, Norwich and Bristol in England. There was no conflict between the development of a modern state and the existence of a belt of cities with only vague impulses towards independence from the Crown. On the contrary, and particularly given the fears associated with war—the English invasion of the southwest, or the Hundred Years War—cities attempted to loosen the feudal overlords' grip and to ensure some political stability by rallying to the Crown. In both these countries, the Crown established its ascendancy by passing judgement in disputes between cities and between burghers and overlords. This mechanism, where the state became institutionalized through resolving disputes, led to recognition of the king's sovereignty, and so played a fundamental role in England. In France, the model of the 'good city' (Chevalier 1982) symbolizes the integration of cities into the modern state. At first, the relationship between cities and crown was fairly well-balanced. The king, still in a fragile position, was eager for political and military support against the English and against the Burgundians, for capital, and for local and regional bases. In order to win the cooperation of the cities, he showed great respect for their autonomy, intervening very little in urban affairs. Some historians talk in terms of the kings of France using an 'urban policy' in their political attempts to draw the cities in as partners in public planning: a policy that matured into respect for autonomy, including military autonomy, and granting privileges to the cities. Chevalier (1988) suggests that this was, therefore, an alliance rather than a form of subordination. Thus, Rigaudière (1993: 19) notes, in relation to the 'good cities':

Outposts of the monarch's policy and strong points for transmitting his orders, they were also closely associated with all decisions of influence . . . In their refusal to remain passively submissive to the new legal order that royalty intended to create, they succeeded in making their voices heard and in demanding recognition of their wide autonomy to make regulations. Strengthened by this power, they were able to establish that their aptitude for government equalled their ability to take part in developing the legal order under construction. Powers to regulate, judge, and tax were also attributes of power that, each time a city was partly or totally recognized as possessing them, went further towards erasing traditional categories, so that, from the mid-thirteenth century, two distinct groups of urban communities had formed. The city that had not been recognized as a body capable of autonomous action can be contrasted with the 'good city', which, within the context of the privileged relationship that it maintained with royalty, enjoyed autonomy and—probably even more so—a substantial degree of trust. As a centre of decision-making and an outpost of royal policy, the 'good city' was at once a model for and an agent of state-building, underpinning the activities of the state and stimulating its birth.

A gradual shift took place: the consolidation of the kingdom tipped the balance towards the king. He was able to bring into play the threat of force, enlist the urban administrative elites, re-examine privileges granted in order to sell them, increase his hold over wealth created—which thus no longer benefited the urban economy—and gradually replace the burghers with representatives of the state. On France, Lepetit (1988: 121) concludes:

Between the end of the thirteenth century and the beginning of the eighteenth, the 'good cities' came to constitute an original model of urbanization, within which social and political characteristics occupied a central position. By that time, the city was a fourth power, alongside the king, the Church and the aristocracy, allied to the developing state yet threatened by it. In *Ancien Régime* France, therefore, the history of municipal institutions and the history of the ways in which people rose up the social ladder both provide a record of the continuous weakening of the autonomous social formations that cities had once represented. In a certain sense, social and political histories of the seventeenth and eighteenth centuries have rightly developed without regard to any spatial limits, viewing the city as a convenient observatory: the demise of the 'good cities' justifies this approach. By the end of the *Ancien Régime*, the specific nature of the urban object lay elsewhere, in its relationship to the economy and to the territory. The genesis of the modern city is economic, functioning within the context of economic development and the state's growing hold over territory.

The English situation was similar, apart from the fact that interdependence between cities and the Crown was probably less strong, despite significant internal conflicts. Centralization made itself much less felt, and the corporations retained greater autonomy for longer—which was the envy of the French up to de Tocqueville's day and beyond. England established itself as the country of 'self-government', where the urban oligarchies had acquired great autonomy, even though it had to wait until the fifteenth century for any significant development of charters (Ruggiu 1997). The central authority did not replace urban oligarchies with its appointed representatives. What is more, England remained a fairly non-urbanized country. While French cities became involved in the centralization process, allowing regional capitals, particularly the cities where the *Parlement* sat, to benefit from any important development, England had no major regional centres apart from Norwich and Bristol. The burghers of small fair towns and market towns were therefore the natural allies of the Crown, bearing no relation to city-states. The absence of powerful urban networks allowed the state to develop without coercion, and towns acted as a useful counterweight to the nobility. Poussou *et al.* (1983) has compared England to the Paris Basin: London's rapid growth hindered the emergence of regional capitals, while the influence of towns was limited.

Finally, in Spain the phase of growth and increasing autonomy for cities was soon interrupted by the 'seigneuralization' movement and the attachment of cities to the domains of the nobility (Rucquoi 1990). Outside Barcelona, Valencia, and a few other cities, Spain was characterized by the powerful role of the nobility in the genesis of the modern state, despite the strong resistance of the Barcelona burghers. In small, centralized, essentially agrarian states, such as Denmark or Portugal, cities were never to be an autonomous force, even in the background. To the east, in Poland and Bohemia, on the fringes of empire, only capital cities managed to develop, with the exception of Danzig for a time. Jehel and Racinet (1996: 336) have concluded:

By the end of the Middle Ages, English and French cities understood that they could have no political ambitions of their own. From then on, regardless of the various forms their history took, they were no longer able to conceive of themselves outside the higher authority of the kingdom; they subordinated their interests to those of the whole kingdom. They threw in their lot with the future of the newly-forming nation, which, by the end of the fifteenth century, had merged with the monarchy. The evolution of politics, therefore, was a major reorganizing factor, which exerted a great deal of influence on urban development. It explained the flourishing administrative, religious, judicial and university functions of a certain type of city—the regional capital. All forms of higher authority promoted the latter's rapid development. Thus, the late Middle Ages saw cities confirmed as capitals, varying in their degree of splendour, at the same time as the number of sovereign states increased. This development had socio-political consequences: the more the city was integrated into the state, the further those who made it their business to serve the city rose.

By the sixteenth century, the picture was clear. First, modern states had expanded to well outside the European urban belt, although urban networks still represent a key factor for understanding the development of states and the forms they took. The merchant cities of the Mediterranean, Germany, Switzerland, Flanders, and the Netherlands resisted conquest by large states for quite a long time—sometimes for a very long time. Second, from the end of the Middle Ages in France, England, and Spain, and a little later in the

Netherlands and Scandinavian countries, cities and citizens contributed to the development of the state, sometimes through very sophisticated forms of cooperation. Third, as Tilly and others have shown, wars played a fundamental role in the triumph of states. Ruinous, incessant wars were central to establishing the domination of states, even more so since they involved an increase in the use of human and technical resources. The cities resisted the states for a time, but in the end the states imposed themselves by force, except on the Hanseatic League and Venice. Fourth, in both models the city burghers took part in state formation, since they were involved in the birth of central administration as advisers to the king, as war financiers, as investors in the national debt, and, in urban government, perfecting supervisory tools and techniques. Finally, this dynamic of confrontation between state and city took place over time. Blockmans (1988) has clearly shown that, when state formation took place before the phase of urban growth, this growth did not reach its full potential—in England and Scandinavia, for example. In contrast, if the creation of the state took place when the urban network was already solidly established, the cities retained an influential degree of importance and could block the state's development.

But the weaknesses of cities, too, became apparent over time: rivalries between families, religious conflicts—in England, for example—that would become crucial during the Reformation, particularly in Germany, and social conflicts. 'The urban élites' natural desire to preserve their domination, which was threatened by equally natural efforts on the part of other social strata of citizens to gain power and get into government, not infrequently drove these élites to renounce part of their autonomy in favour of another territorial authority, which would guarantee to maintain the existing social equilibrium' (Isaacs and Prak 1996: 304). In the face of pressure from citizens, the urban oligarchies of the Italian and German cities did not hesitate to form alliances or to submit to a prince or overlord. This was partly because the late medieval crisis ruined some cities, which got into long-term debt, and intensified the problems they had to manage, notably the problem of the poor, victims of the crisis.

Apart from city-states, which were an exception, many European cities did not need complete independence in order to effect dynamic organization of their economic and urban development. Most of them enjoyed a fairly high degree of political autonomy, maintaining vertical ties to an overlord, a prince, a bishop, a king, or an emperor, which varied in strength but in no way hindered the smooth running of commerce. In addition, these vertical ties did not stifle major transverse political and economic networks or even prevent a city from belonging to many different ones. As Weber has shown, this period of economic growth and redistribution of authority in cities especially favoured those cities that were able to deploy all their energies.

Although the golden age of European cities came to an end in the fifteenth century, cities continued to play a major political role within empires and sometimes within states, as the creation of the Republic of the Netherlands, German and Italian cities or, to a lesser extent, French regional capitals shows. Thus, the state became the main organizational force in the European urban system.

Both European city models—maritime and continental—organized an urban system that remained relatively stable until the Industrial Revolution. State domination, first in the west, north, and east, then at the centre of western Europe, gradually came to be established as the second, but strongest, organizing principle of the urban system. Even during the period of early urban growth, this strength was apparent to a minor, but certainly not insignificant, degree. With the domination of the state, it became an established fact. In terms of ideal type, the administrative city, the continental city involved in a hierarchical relationship with the state, and a string of cities with weak transverse networks can be contrasted with the model of interdependent merchant-burgher cities, predominantly maritime, which prospered through various forms of flow and exchange. The producing, trading, risk-taking burghers were joined by the administrative burghers who managed and formed ties with the centre. As the domination of the centre became more established, local and regional administrative and political bases became more important. In most cases, the term 'bourgeoisie' tends to include both these types. Even after the victory of the princes in Germany, corporations of merchants continued to play a decisive role in urban government, at least until the nineteenth century (François 1995), and this was equally true of Dutch cities.

In most European countries, these two structuring principles combined to create a very varied landscape of cities. Such combinations did not exclude some very clear remaining differences between those cities that continued to control their resources and engage in production and finance.

In France and England, administrative logic was predominant but did not have a monopoly. Gradually, in the complex interplay of relations between Crown and cities, various distinctions confirmed the political role of the most important cities, and hierarchies were formed. 'Good cities' were able to increase the extent of their influence. We can now see what is fundamentally different about this model: to some degree it was the state that defined, sustained, and strengthened the city. This power faced concurrent pressures from cities for recognition of their jurisdiction in one sphere or another, or for the grant of a parliament. With some exceptions, states had a tendency to respect existing forces and to sustain hierarchies. Conversely, even in lands dominated by market logic, ties with the state—or with whatever carried out its functions—were also a significant asset to development: these ties could mean cities being granted rights and privileges or obtaining the financial resources to build a fortress or palace, or to rebuild a whole district. Italian, German, and Dutch cities provide the perfect illustration of this. In most cases, the two principles combined to give depth and considerable stability to the urban system established in the late Middle Ages.

The main features of the urban Europe that emerged were the spread of cities and the dynamism of regional capitals: cathedral cities that had become more or less successful merchant cities and, subsequently, centres of legal, political, cultural, or military functions (Hohenberg and Hollen Lees 1985), or else producer or small market towns that had become administrative centres and later found that this helped to further their economic development. The influence of these regional capitals and the stability of the urban system that emerged were fundamentally characteristic of Europe—of continental Europe, that is: England was somewhat exceptional, given its low level of urbanization and the domination of London, which undoubtedly prevented the opening up of regional capitals.

Industrial Cities, Metropolises, and Cities Bound to the Nation-State

This urban framework, although it was robust, obviously could not remain unchanged. The two revolutions—the democratic and the Industrial—that swept across Europe in the nineteenth century sustained the nation-state and transformed the cities.

The reader is probably very familiar with the history of industrialization, since it is fairly recent. The combination of industrialization and the advent of the nation-state in its contemporary form promoted the growth of the great European capitals. Finally, in the twentieth century, capitalism and the state together intensified and completed the urbanization of the continent. Even though the major capitals already existed, the twentieth century saw the advent of the big city: the metropolis. This section simply attempts to emphasize some salient points that are particularly useful to my argument.

Industrial Cities and Industry in the City

The end of the seventeenth century saw the gradual beginnings of a second capitalist movement—industrial capitalism this time—which would lead to the formation of industrial societies and a new wave of urbanization. The industrial cities of Britain were emblematic of this movement. In the nineteenth century, the city became the site of capitalist development, and was no longer improved for its own sake.

With this new wave of urbanization, the urban phenomenon spread massively across northern Europe, but had considerably less impact in the south. Cities underwent a change of scale. Concentration in great metropolises and large industrial areas lent a different dynamic to cities, changing them both socially and physically.

As De Vries (1984) has shown, it is easier to see the impact of the Industrial Revolution with the benefit of hindsight, since the spectacularly large scale of industrial urbanization actually did little to challenge existing urban hierarchies. Outside Great Britain, its greatest impact was in creating the industrial cities of the German Ruhr, Wallonia, and Upper Silesia in Prussia, with a lesser effect on the ports and industrial areas of Scandinavia, Holland, and France. The impact of the Industrial Revolution was much more limited in southern Europe, with the exception of Bilbao and the Asturias, and it was not until the end of the nineteenth century that the impact of industrialization was seen in the north-west triangle of Italy, in Barcelona, in the Basque country, in Oporto, and in Lisbon. This was because, as industrialization developed, it tended to be of equal benefit to the major cities that already existed, the regional capitals, and, above all, the great metropolises. Today, when the cycle of what are now viewed as 'old industries'—the coal industry, traditional iron and steel production, mining, and, to a lesser extent, shipbuilding—has come to an end in most European countries, it has become apparent that, in the final analysis, this industrial interlude did not destroy the existing European urban system. It added a new layer of cities but its impact was massive only in Britain. Beyond, its influence is decreasing over time.

The Industrial Revolution, which began about 1750 in England, gave rise to a vast movement of industrialization and urbanization, and of economic and technical development. The accompanying urban transformation is well-known: on the one hand, a new type of industrial city emerged, most often around coal mining, textiles, or iron and steel, then later chemicals, electricity, and mechanical engineering. At the same time, since the city and industrialization went hand in hand, the great metropolises became industrial cities, with major ports and some regional capitals following the trend.

However, in the western Europe of 1800, industrialization and urbanization did not yet go hand in hand. Europe had many rural localities with their own localized industries, or rather 'proto-industries'—a term that is debated. The Industrial Revolution did not begin in the most urbanized areas of the Netherlands or of Italy, but in England, which was relatively non-urbanized. At first, the localization of industrial areas either resulted from the development of existing textile industries or was totally dependent on deposits of coal or minerals or on rivers. Therefore, an industrial area would often grow up outside the existing urban structure or else would incorporate boroughs, villages, and small towns, as in the Ruhr.

Although activities remained proto-industrial in scope and scale, the seventeenth century saw them beginning to concentrate in one place—Liège, for example: '. . . coal mining attracted a multitude of fuel-hungry activities to the valley of the Meuse: alum pits, breweries, distilleries, nail makers and farriers, sulphur and vitriol works, and powder mills' (Leboutte 1997: 76). Although it took off again later, the decline of this Liège industrial area can be explained by customs disputes, the dispersal of textile

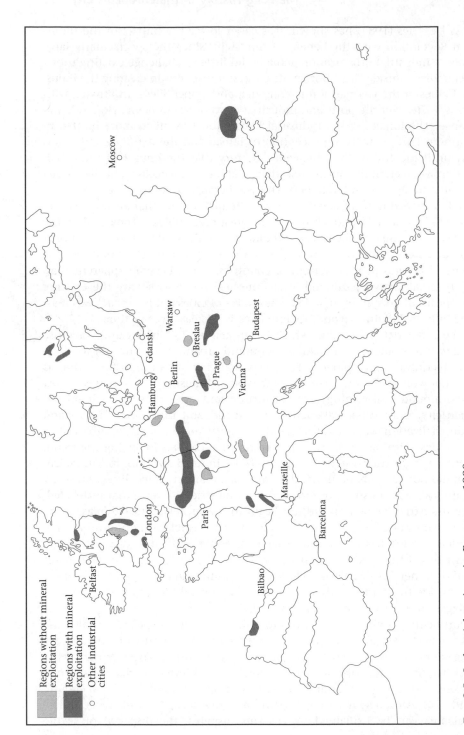

FIG. 2.3. Industrial regions in Europe, c. 1880

Source: Hohenberg and Hollen Lees (1985).

production into the countryside, and competition from the English. Standardization and mechanization were the dynamic driving forces of the Industrial Revolution, which next spread across Wallonia by virtue of John Cockerill setting up there. In Great Britain, some villages near mines began to develop, becoming towns of up to 10,000 people like Bradford. Regional capitals situated not far from such dynamic proto-industry, such as Leeds or, to a lesser extent, Lille, then began to develop from their commercial and trading functions.

The industry-city equation, so typical of the British situation, came about only gradually, whether through the aggregation and development of originally rural areas into cities or through the growth of industry in small and large towns, which then became metropolises. Concealed behind the traditional picture of the industrial city, Europe has, and always has had, very diverse forms of city, each with its own history, including its history within the nation-state.[6]

But, in all these cases, industry-driven urban growth was very rapid. All historians stress the dramatic impact on workers of this uncontrolled urbanization around factories, in city centres and in suburbs.

Hohenberg and Hollen Lees (1985) distinguish three processes at work during the early Industrial Revolution: (1) the profound transformation of mining towns, with the extraordinarily rapid growth of population— movement from the land and immigration—that was to lead to the creation of very dense industrial regions with a lot of small towns, such as Wallonia, the Ruhr—Düsseldorf, Bochum, Essen, and so forth—the Black Country in the English Midlands, Yorkshire, Lancashire, north-east England, parts of Wales and Scotland, the mining area of north-east France, and industrial centres such as Birmingham, Saint-Etienne, and Bilbao; (2) the gradual adaptation of new technologies and scientific progress to existing activities, including textiles in Lancashire and northern France, cutlery in Sheffield, and silk in Lyons; and (3) the de-industrialization and decline of rural regions, small towns, and regional capitals in western France, south-west England, north Wales, Flanders, and Italy.

In his analysis of *The Life and Death of European Industrial Areas, 1750–2000*, Leboutte (1997) highlights the supremacy of coal in terms of localization and 'the tyranny of fixed costs': in other words, costs and means of transport. The effect was twofold: on the one hand, industrial development strengthened and diversified around early industrial concentrations, for example in British industrial cities or in the Ruhr—coal, iron and steel, followed by the development of other activities, mechanical engineering and then chemical and metallurgical industries; while, on the other hand, industrial ports developed. Liverpool, Hull, Rotterdam, and—later—Genoa,

---

[6] Despite Briggs' clear rejection of any models, his work on *Victorian Cities* (1962) is a fascinating account of the range of dynamics in various British industrial cities.

and Le Havre were places where trade was concentrated, and these became centres of industrial activity.

Leboutte (1997: 148) has also clearly demonstrated the impact of techno-logical innovations, such as the Bessemer converter, in various areas:

In a short space of time, all iron and steel firms were condemned to this inno-vation, a change made all the more difficult because the Bessemer converter uses non-phosphorous ores, which most industrial areas did not have. Stocks had to be brought in at great expense from Sweden, Algeria, the Isle of Elba, the French Pyrenees, and the Basque country. This new market in ores prefigured the change to a worldwide iron and steel industry, which became imperative after 1945. The enormous quantities of ores that had to be imported stimulated shipbuild-ing and guaranteed a key role for large ports, such as Rotterdam and Emden. The supremacy of supplies heralded a coastal iron and steel industry: Jimuiden in the Netherlands, Dunkirk in France, Piombino (in Tuscany), Cornigliano (Genoa), Bagnoli (Naples), Trieste, Gijón and Bilbao.

The second phase of the Industrial Revolution, during the last half of the nineteenth century, was linked to transport—railways and canals—which increased the pace of movement and of concentration. The development of chemicals, metallurgy, mechanical engineering, plant manufacture, and, not least, the finance sector strengthened the role of industrializing regional capitals, which were gradually adapting to new sectors and new techno-logies, such as Stuttgart, Lyons, Turin, Liège, Barcelona, Munich, Lausanne, Copenhagen, Lille, Nancy, and Milan, combining the structures of an older European urban world with the dynamic energies of new economic develop-ment (Hohenberg and Hollen Lees 1985). Industrialization and transport increased the pace of concentration in large cities that had no mining deposits, in particular London, Paris, Berlin, Vienna, Moscow, Turin, Milan, and Madrid. Cities became places where capital was tied up in major fixed assets, with labour forces that varied in composition and size, and with a high level of internal diversity.

In European countries where industrial areas did not extend to the size of those in the Ruhr or Great Britain, the existing major cities profited most from such developments. In the case of France, if we set aside Saint-Étienne and Lille-Roubaix-Tourcoing, the fact that the strongest growth was recorded by the biggest cities—Paris, Lyons, Marseilles—demonstrates the stability of the urban hierarchy. Most European countries saw both a growth in towns and industrial areas, including a port town, and a strengthening of the major cities.

The classic view is that industrial cities are characterized by their social struc-ture and by their form and organization. There is no need to recall the ter-rible conditions in these cities, with workers packed in to meet the needs of factories (Engels 1969). The growth of cities was fostered by substantial flows of migration. In the majority of cases, these were most often over a short distance within the same country; however, transnational flows of migration to the most dynamic cities and industrial areas were soon established. In the

Ruhr, flows of migration came at first from Prussia and the north, and later—about 1890—from Poland. In the Nord-Pas de Calais region of France, the first to settle were Germans and Belgians, followed mostly by Italians and Poles. Although these cities had large firms and major entrepreneurs, they were above all workers' cities, a crucible for working-class organization, which got under way gradually and often with difficulty (Thompson 1963; Hobsbawn 1987). Bit by bit, within these cities of 'the labouring classes, the dangerous classes' (Chevallier 1958), from these concentrations of poverty, of various immigrant groups, of all sorts of workers with different religions, there would emerge forms of trade union and political organization and mutual aid societies. The model of the big industrial firm would produce a type of working-class urban society that would then be reproduced wherever economic conditions permitted. This process took decades. Some of these cities became 'social formations' in the Gramscian sense, where social structure and social relations took the form of a class society, diametrically opposed to that of the medieval city: what Mumford (1961) called 'Coketown'. Working-class culture was organized around work, clubs, cafés, dances, and sport, although with considerable variations from one city to another and one country to another.

Even beyond the structuring opposition between the bourgeoisie and the newly forming working class, these industrial cities were socially diverse places: artisans continued to exist and to develop, and the number of shops increased, if only to feed the abundant populations of vagrants, prostitutes, and white-collar office workers. The larger the city, the greater this diversity; all the same, these groups were marginalized in the industrial cities, although obviously there were large variations from one place to another. In the most striking instances, the working population commonly represented 70 per cent to 80 per cent of the city's population, although this remained exceptional in southern Europe.

The industrial city took the form of this combination of industries, workers' housing—slums, social housing, suburban houses—minimal communal amenities, and transport routes. In industrial cities, overpopulated working-class districts mixed with factories in city centres, driving out the bourgeoisie, in a configuration that reversed that of the old European cities, where industrial activities and working populations had most often been pushed out to the periphery, into what became the suburbs. The rise of trams and railways was instrumental in allowing the development of suburbs either as a form of protection for the middle classes fleeing the city or to accommodate the working classes being pushed out by the gentrification of the centre. The rise of social democratic urban governments (see Chapter 6) permitted solid public policies for the creation of collective amenities, such as social housing or health centres. This social formation remained the established one throughout the twentieth century, until the 1960s, when the decline of traditional industrial activities became more pronounced.

TABLE 2.1. *The principal cities in the European urban hierarchy, 1750–1950 (population in thousands)*

	1750		1850		1950	
Rank	City	Population	City	Population	City	Population
1	London	676	London	2,320	London	8,860
2	Paris	560	Paris	1,314	Paris	5,900
3	Naples	324	St Petersberg	502	Moscow	5,100
4	Amsterdam	219	Berlin	446	Ruhr	4,900
5	Lisbon	213	Vienna	426	Berlin	3,707
6	Vienna	169	Liverpool	422	Leningrad	2,700
7	Moscow	161	Naples	416	Manchester	2,382
8	Venice	158	Manchester	412	Birmingham	2,196
9	Rome	157	Moscow	373	Vienna	1,755
10	St Petersburg	138	Glasgow	346	Rome	1,665
11	Dublin	125	Birmingham	294	Hamburg	1,580
12	Palermo	124	Dublin	263	Madrid	1,527
13	Madrid	123	Madrid	263	Budapest	1,500
14	Milan	123	Lisbon	257	Barcelona	1,425
15	Lyon	115	Lyon	254	Milan	1,400
16	Berlin	113	Amsterdam	225	Glasgow	1,320
17	Hamburg	90	Brussels	208	Liverpool	1,260
18	Marseilles	88	Edinburgh	194	Naples	1,210
19	Rouen	88	Hamburg	193	Leeds	1,164
20	Copenhagen	79	Marseilles	193	Copenhagen	1,150
21	Florence	74	Milan	193	Athens	1,140
22	Genoa	72	Leeds	184	Bucharest	1,100
23	Grenada	70	Palermo	182	Katowice	977
24	Barcelona	70	Rome	170	Brussels	964
25	Seville	68	Barcelona	167	Amsterdam	940
26	Bologna	66	Warsaw	163	Prague	938
27	Bordeaux	64	Budapest	156	Stockholm	889
28	Turin	60	Bristol	150	Lisbon	885
29	Valencia	60	Sheffield	143	Munich	870
30	Cadiz	60	Bordeaux	142	Newcastle	830
31	Stockholm	60	Venice	141	Rotterdam	803
32	Dresden	60	Turin	138	Warsaw	803
33	Prague	58	Copenhagen	135	Kiev	800
34	Brussels	55	Munich	125	Kharkov	730
35	Edinburgh	55	Prague	117	Sheffield	730
36	Lille	54	Breslau	114	Turin	725
37	Cork	53	Wolverhampton	112	Cologne	692
38	Breslau	52	Newcastle	111	Frankfurt	680
39	Königsberg	52	Valencia	110	Genoa	676
40	Leyden	50	Ghent	108	Lodz	675

Source: Hohenberg and Hollen Lees (1985).

Capital Cities

For observers of the nineteenth century, the development of very big cities—the capitals of states and, in some cases, of empires—is the second main phenomenon, and a disturbing one. Capital cities of states benefited from the consolidation of states, the shift of political life onto the national level, and the strengthening of the states'—and therefore the bureaucracies'—capacity for control, as well as from industrial development. They absorbed a large part of the flow of migration, thus providing sizeable reserves of labour. With

TABLE 2.2. *Population of selected capital cities in the nineteenth century*

City	1800	1910
Vienna	231,000	2 million
Berlin	172,000	2.071 million
Prague	70,000	0.6 million
Paris	835,000*	2.888 million
London	959,000	4.522 million

*1831 estimate.

Sources: Moriconi-Ebrard (2000); Hohenberg and Hollen Lees (1985).

the leadership of the states, they were the first beneficiaries of the transport revolution, from tramways to road and rail networks. These were ministerial and military cities. Open to the world in an era that saw increasing numbers of different kinds of exchanges, discoveries, and technical innovations, they established their role by organizing universal exhibitions and great fairs. Concerned with public health and safety, governments organized major improvement works, created wide avenues, and constructed new public buildings: stations, squares, and monuments that symbolized their dynamism and technical progress. These cities were also places of speculation, of public and private investment in housing, and of financial capital (Harvey 1985*a*).

As university cities and cultural centres, they were the focus of unrest and the sites of the political and social revolts that punctuated the nineteenth century. Finally, the great metropolis became the site of consumption, a place of department stores and wide avenues. Simmel (1965) as a sociologist, and Müsil (1965) as a writer have both given accounts of the transformation of the urban experience in these big cities at the turn of the twentieth century.

Contemporary European Cities: Early Beginnings

Certain features of contemporary European cities will be explored in detail in the remaining chapters of the book, particularly in relation to changing forms of the state and the economy. However, a few guidelines are useful at this stage.

Despite categorization difficulties, there are data that provide an account of the urban hierarchy. If we again use the indicator of population size to characterize cities—a point we shall have to come back to—a classic map of urban Europe emerges. These data and the picture they provide can be read as emphasizing certain points. The length of time over which the urban population and economy have developed has enabled a large number of cities, regardless of their differing fortunes, to draw increasing advantage from cycles of economic change. The stability of the urban system in Europe can be seen in the relatively stable classification of cities in order of size, both within nations and throughout Europe as a whole. The history of the making of urban Europe

TABLE 2.3. *Urban growth, 1950–2000*

Rank	Metropolitan area	Country	1950 City	1950 Metro. area	1960 City	1960 Metro. area	1970 City	1970 Metro. area	1980 City	1980 Metro. area	1990 City	1990 Metro. area	2000 City	2000 Metro. area	Number of communes in the metro. area
1	Essen	Germany	508,841	7,808,452	696,971	9,688,354	680,447	10,226,814	591,393	9,956,803	574,907	9,904,859	570,893	9,962,743	89
2	Paris	France	2,790,938	6,459,414	2,803,672	7,602,414	2,493,449	8,721,288	2,206,503	9,152,603	2,151,663	9,647,289	2,121,499	9,849,666	458
3	London	Britain	8,197,000	9,343,900	7,992,300	9,476,127	7,452,400	9,143,134	6,784,329	8,550,681	6,628,276	8,420,947	7,262,467	9,160,487	107
4	Madrid	Spain	1,645,215	1,726,726	2,259,931	2,393,282	3,146,071	3,565,035	3,184,435	4,308,222	3,094,882	4,638,838	2,899,826	4,658,427	23
5	Brussels	Belgium	1,821,90	3,656,671	171,972	3,922,078	161,589	4,211,301	141,051	4,283,532	136,649	4,317,368	133,812	4,423,523	171
6	Barcelona	Spain	1,280,179	1,840,509	1,557,863	2,424,623	1,745,142	3,396,969	1,754,011	3,945,656	1,688,367	4,040,254	1,501,561	3,988,393	86
7	Manchester	Britain	703,100	4,281,700	661,791	4,382,531	549,650	4,396,167	456,345	4,181,836	417,691	4,002,445	429,200	3,976,124	99
8	Milan	Italy	1,238,765	2,318,707	1,540,138	2,985,811	1,712,556	3,749,630	1,620,151	3,973,675	1,396,670	3,886,601	1,301,264	3,890,644	171
9	Berlin	Germany	3,336,026	3,665,000	3,252,691	3,605,000	3,208,719	3,565,000	3,053,825	3,396,000	3,421,722	3,698,953	3,417,348	3,755,223	47
10	Athens	Greece	559,189	1,369,918	621,017	1,820,084	839,447	2,512,339	883,848	3,056,534	782,749	3,186,922	695,751	3,349,716	71
11	Rotterdam	N'lands	678,556	2,363,351	736,057	2,682,355	695,338	2,889,288	593,226	2,872,665	580,721	2,970,635	592,677	3,116,490	63
12	Naples	Italy	990,082	1,925,729	1,159,770	2,265,163	1,221,034	2,557,823	1,214,154	2,820,514	1,084,499	2,887,922	1,001,544	2,973,487	74
13	Rome	Italy	1,592,458	1,664,717	2,112,576	2,208,356	2,699,737	2,830,724	2,832,910	2,992,531	2,783,294	2,961,823	2,701,373	2,897,788	9
14	Birmingham	Britain	1,116,200	2,320,500	1,110,683	2,476,902	1,014,670	2,540,609	932,300	2,476,157	883,071	2,423,397	925,038	2,456,183	32
15	Lisbon	Portugal	773,104	1,137,671	800,128	1,346,906	782,266	1,693,717	822,052	2,206,129	678,109	2,281,331	566,636	2,344,824	58
16	Hamburg	Germany	1,603,718	1,860,354	1,813,388	2,095,897	1,792,359	2,173,501	1,646,144	2,105,707	1,639,239	2,115,556	1,700,769	2,195,830	38
17	Vienna	Austria	1,614,956	1,828,907	1,626,683	1,841,354	1,620,599	1,857,776	1,533,068	1,792,829	1,539,677	1,822,456	1,625,265	1,928,221	47
18	Lille/ Kortrijk	France/ Belgium	208,146	1,352,873	212,411	1,456,134	202,827	1,581,074	173,563	1,632,443	172,490	1,661,359	186,395	1,696,813	102
19	Leeds	Britain	505,300	1,664,000	510,676	1,650,167	496,009	1,671,580	438,272	1,612,428	425,404	1,612,218	436,200	1,659,893	29
20	Munich	Germany	828,772	969,045	1,062,402	1,245,630	1,293,649	1,555,822	1,304,066	1,673,268	1,217,803	1,608,020	1,167,864	1,576,104	34
21	Frankfurt am Main	Germany	545,532	963,319	688,102	1,237,637	698,610	1,416,566	629,054	1,408,761	639,990	1,425,907	635,237	1,439,695	31
22	Lyon	France	470,099	845,275	521,370	998,302	503,821	1,209,062	423,593	1,292,499	416,319	1,352,904	449,614	1,416,093	113
23	Turin	Italy	686,861	820,274	981,300	1,177,437	1,149,175	1,524,921	1,123,383	1,571,788	980,601	1,460,616	902,345	1,400,320	22
24	Copenhagen	Denmark	768,200	1,212,200	721,400	1,360,000	622,800	1,402,900	491,251	1,379,023	467,179	1,338,717	498,008	1,396,666	28
25	Marseilles	France	649,490	820,528	749,798	971,740	895,273	1,221,284	882,855	1,319,616	800,491	1,316,328	798,136	1,354,571	38
26	Stockholm	Sweden	742,049	919,105	806,031	1,056,925	710,627	1,135,146	648,991	1,157,077	673,320	1,229,069	737,006	1,346,291	16
27	Valencia	Spain	509,075	707,916	505,066	766,080	653,690	1,056,257	742,244	1,262,591	774,819	1,341,260	730,423	1,332,319	44
28	Glasgow	Britain	1,089,767	1,526,879	1,055,017	1,504,359	897,483	1,581,299	710,636	1,439,092	635,610	1,342,916	622,930	1,317,411	36
29	Oporto	Portugal	280,129	735,593	302,450	837,089	310,437	943,687	333,516	1,112,862	305,661	1,172,663	266,638	1,258,077	107
30	Stuttgart	Germany	496,532	824,026	625,176	1,074,198	632,641	1,204,350	581,201	1,178,684	575,325	1,184,989	584,862	1,210,544	23
31	Douai/ Péruwelz	France/ Belgium	40,392	1,109,206	46,633	1,237,210	47,882	1,280,417	43,227	1,238,935	42,192	1,215,211	42,882	1,202,742	211
32	Newcastle	Britain	291,800	1,203,500	269,678	1,269,348	222,209	1,263,275	192,048	1,211,388	187,348	1,190,625	190,457	1,178,500	30
33	Amsterdam	N'lands	841,230	1,031,444	872,556	1,106,538	825,906	1,139,339	714,154	1,073,445	698,679	1,086,093	733,406	1,158,310	11
34	Bielefeld	Germany	252,292	872,583	297,971	960,633	314,276	1,027,219	312,575	1,051,070	317,060	1,074,724	322,169	1,118,606	23
35	Seville	Spain	376,627	481,126	442,300	574,428	548,072	719,502	643,429	869,471	699,580	986,318	707,477	1,050,941	17
36	Helsinki	Finland	369,380	369,400	452,777	542,700	514,652	683,800	483,036	755,200	490,249	888,900	553,542	1,037,958	7

No.	City	Country	1	2	3	4	5	6	7	8	9	10	11	12	Rank
37	Zürich	Sw'land	381,931	630,362	437,955	793,716	423,357	926,932	371,597	943,447	365,229	981,483	334,649	985,624	87
38	Dublin	Ireland	535,385	651,122	541,176	686,591	581,516	808,098	574,891	935,149	505,324	938,825	506,993	978,282	8
39	Bilbao	Spain	212,844	429,524	276,113	603,713	369,329	859,193	387,720	975,365	373,773	968,361	357,958	944,527	40
40	Florence	Italy	367,252	657,157	428,252	774,532	455,086	914,862	449,504	971,405	408,666	948,462	375,580	924,858	16
41	South Hants	Britain	233,600	618,300	215,077	686,762	197,431	789,321	178,342	815,192	182,748	851,940	192,133	904,278	22
42	Nice	France	228,183	410,025	281,097	510,635	329,368	654,855	338,919	764,161	342,447	856,877	342,780	893,366	50
43	Mannheim	Germany	245,074	638,661	307,863	782,207	331,889	863,775	304,210	846,948	308,185	868,649	309,454	891,244	21
44	Bremen	Germany	443,562	641,786	553,953	754,587	582,015	812,302	555,718	824,971	547,762	827,815	543,982	838,710	12
45	Genoa	Italy	676,891	818,267	771,533	928,831	812,714	998,373	769,442	968,630	688,757	881,440	634,232	826,163	22
46	Salonica	Greece	213,924	296,380	247,308	371,243	334,884	535,591	399,902	689,113	386,155	743,409	372,659	805,645	15
47	Oslo	Norway	432,598	502,969	471,235	580,608	485,687	644,264	453,348	642,996	459,743	684,783	506,416	778,998	11
48	Toulouse	France	266,765	315,860	310,313	375,908	371,758	501,890	354,273	579,706	359,568	670,574	394,748	775,512	73
49	Palermo	Italy	479,288	530,584	574,839	630,849	635,690	694,113	694,125	760,069	698,958	775,934	681,538	773,425	5
50	Bordeaux	France	281,964	484,346	279,779	520,758	251,815	601,230	211,805	658,273	210,476	722,090	216,061	768,655	53
51	Hanover	Germany	472,947	573,013	600,206	720,156	581,745	773,957	536,039	757,467	509,428	739,127	517,574	753,631	8
52	Nuremberg	Germany	378,358	570,460	466,326	673,530	503,944	732,575	484,330	723,553	489,688	735,784	486,424	749,155	12
53	Dresden	Germany	498,200	776,000	508,000	778,000	506,500	790,000	525,500	807,000	501,914	763,410	447,029	715,862	28
54	Nottingham	Britain	308,000	598,800	311,899	626,922	300,630	657,444	274,680	660,789	271,558	679,365	285,867	705,943	23
55	Aachen/Heerlen	Germany/N'lands	171,020	520,002	212,429	633,181	230,573	672,858	244,334	693,860	239,412	695,769	243,527	703,393	15
56	Sheffield	Britain	512,900	700,300	540,385	746,016	520,327	723,389	484,094	699,788	461,339	681,172	463,053	685,500	11
57	Malaga	Spain	269,726	305,495	293,968	333,313	365,645	430,694	459,558	558,281	528,066	672,072	502,891	683,923	6
58	Oviedo	Spain	106,002	305,860	127,058	381,247	154,117	510,630	186,528	624,159	202,815	656,179	198,926	662,110	10
59	Liège	Belgium	242,884	668,842	249,394	693,994	240,617	702,018	215,869	685,691	195,907	665,413	184,907	658,961	25
60	Catania	Italy	292,151	395,623	355,191	472,593	395,344	538,599	382,739	588,418	338,645	603,968	337,041	652,378	18
61	Bari	Italy	262,956	476,007	306,173	530,206	351,277	596,926	369,275	647,876	345,773	653,028	331,995	652,196	11
62	Saragossa	Spain	264,360	267,423	326,316	330,078	479,845	484,682	579,688	586,304	619,134	628,006	605,483	617,266	3
63	Palmas, Las	Spain	153,262	296,819	193,862	352,237	287,038	460,705	358,406	559,335	356,018	577,815	349,022	605,657	14
64	Belfast	Britain	443,671	545,292	415,856	551,695	362,082	563,771	317,851	555,787	281,890	546,383	286,200	584,621	8
65	Bristol	Britain	443,000	521,000	438,038	536,670	426,657	555,264	394,830	541,316	385,541	543,709	402,267	573,000	19
66	Charleroi	Belgium	234,932	608,201	240,791	629,530	237,046	631,093	223,305	615,131	207,304	596,234	200,071	565,026	19
67	Leipzig	Germany	620,000	759,000	588,000	723,000	586,500	718,000	562,500	684,000	525,962	634,982	423,827	560,812	18
68	Nantes	France	211,934	299,711	236,007	350,606	259,097	420,176	244,480	463,905	245,697	576,067	273,759	551,718	20
69	Bologna	Italy	328,897	401,282	430,254	510,803	484,574	605,510	462,898	613,608	410,842	497,435	380,562	550,415	11
70	Salerno	Italy	88,007	333,250	113,685	391,642	150,122	455,507	157,148	497,867	149,963	524,453	141,889	540,100	19
71	Toulon	France	133,688	260,096	156,836	310,023	176,983	395,159	180,015	457,393	167,421	502,442	159,693	532,121	27
72	Utrecht	N'lands	218,468	341,482	255,424	398,988	278,808	455,094	236,656	472,729	230,828	498,966	234,142	523,333	10
73	Gothenburg	Sweden	368,226	402,989	421,303	464,715	464,674	525,865	432,592	497,195	432,441	502,373	465,845	518,069	4
74	Geneva/Annemasse	Sw'land/France	142,288	228,372	174,781	294,074	173,724	383,028	157,184	426,145	170,410	473,598	172,989	506,660	64
75	Wiesbaden	Germany	227,202	362,165	258,130	441,868	261,991	477,025	275,441	507,416	258,587	480,526	268,481	503,036	6
76	Metz	France	81,761	316,833	99,676	423,753	108,911	496,277	113,637	491,052	119,710	479,390	124,357	487,398	78
77	Basel/Lörrach/Saint-Louis	S'land/Germany/France	180,341	329,124	205,722	418,984	212,599	494,697	183,330	481,333	178,581	486,132	168,542	483,575	35
78	Brighton	Britain	158,000	377,100	163,159	416,173	161,351	442,043	148,567	439,352	148,309	450,567	158,367	481,776	15
79	Leicester	Britain	285,200	355,200	288,065	404,342	284,208	424,932	282,685	438,023	281,595	451,257	302,133	481,284	21

TABLE 2.3. (Cont'd)

Rank	Metropolitan area	Country	1950 City	1950 Metro. area	1960 City	1960 Metro. area	1970 City	1970 Metro. area	1980 City	1980 Metro. area	1990 City	1990 Metro. area	2000 City	2000 Metro. area	Number of communes in the metro. area
80	Saarbrücken/Forbach	Germany/France	189,865	445,162	212,981	511,037	212,637	524,175	193,726	489,907	191,079	481,644	185,615	469,991	28
81	Murcia	Spain	212,986	287,363	243,575	322,177	237,744	320,654	283,586	378,298	332,926	436,540	353,141	466,193	7
82	Strasbourg/Kehl	France/Germany	188,573	276,564	222,253	329,751	250,671	387,093	249,872	412,440	252,665	433,877	265,751	462,357	21
83	Southend on Sea	Britain	151,900	238,500	165,093	329,558	162,770	398,253	158,247	426,978	159,294	438,838	178,700	458,822	10
84	Edinburgh	Britain	466,761	483,771	468,361	485,633	453,584	485,482	404,087	443,386	403,277	444,028	414,208	457,576	4
85	Venice	Italy	313,133	401,587	343,385	441,285	361,059	481,132	348,217	487,344	313,790	462,147	288,267	441,260	9
86	Chemnitz	Germany	260,000	504,300	295,700	529,600	302,200	529,499	326,600	533,500	305,848	497,795	245,521	434,357	32
87	Grenoble	France	109,508	174,141	146,453	243,191	163,024	348,105	158,936	392,200	150,829	403,150	153,672	418,120	33
88	Bournemouth	Britain	144,900	270,700	54,296	301,101	153,869	342,331	149,716	369,748	162,764	406,750	161,767	418,057	13
89	Hasselt	Belgium	43,193	242,536	51,671	289,754	58,868	341,171	64,228	377,406	66,469	395,227	68,130	415,007	17
90	Palma de Mallorca	Spain	136,814	144,100	159,084	167,536	234,098	245,861	297,239	324,143	308,194	354,604	337,845	395,695	3
91	Santa Cruz de Tenerife	Spain	103,446	162,197	133,100	208,620	151,361	253,456	186,811	322,660	201,452	349,904	222,109	394,752	5
92	Middlesbrough	Britain	147,300	333,200	164,762	379,086	157,313	405,682	152,189	401,354	146,980	396,332	148,133	393,655	5
93	Rouen	France	112,313	272,042	119,834	318,198	118,630	377,916	105,025	385,286	102,830	385,878	107,129	392,044	32
94	Padua	Italy	164,121	245,714	193,653	284,318	227,060	342,838	234,291	372,492	217,488	374,522	210,514	384,964	15
95	Karlsruhe	Germany	215,952	272,341	260,855	328,450	287,301	374,262	271,961	371,698	272,851	374,867	277,672	382,209	6
96	Reading	Britain	114,200	156,200	126,797	205,522	139,799	268,427	134,829	307,193	132,869	339,375	149,833	376,209	18
97	Cardiff	Britain	243,700	265,300	289,853	315,549	287,598	318,979	274,707	306,768	285,542	317,718	336,733	371,009	3
98	Stoke-on-Trent	Britain	275,200	369,500	277,251	387,225	265,258	376,057	254,761	367,366	252,900	367,141	256,400	369,136	6
99	Bergamo	Italy	101,804	227,129	113,414	260,833	125,342	307,043	122,727	336,141	115,813	347,772	117,626	367,791	35
100	Coruña, A	Spain	133,844	201,626	177,502	245,539	189,654	256,835	228,106	309,357	250,583	344,410	242,323	360,550	9
101	Eindhoven	N'lands	141,874	200,545	170,815	245,868	194,700	300,458	195,172	330,126	192,311	337,892	202,654	359,777	8
102	Augsburg	Germany	208,243	250,921	241,177	297,378	254,177	330,301	248,243	338,717	253,515	352,793	252,783	359,409	7
103	Alicante	Spain	104,222	122,416	121,527	144,027	184,716	219,617	244,442	293,248	272,641	336,828	269,774	355,625	5
104	Grenada	Spain	154,378	195,106	157,178	201,762	190,429	244,711	254,670	318,310	285,186	368,506	236,359	352,663	16
105	Vigo	Spain	137,873	181,051	144,914	189,347	197,144	249,547	252,409	317,170	276,054	345,890	278,596	352,444	5
106	Coventry	Britain	263,000	288,000	318,354	349,468	336,746	377,291	317,528	360,111	306,250	347,885	309,700	348,373	2
107	Valladolid	Spain	125,010	129,217	151,807	157,265	236,341	242,188	320,349	328,990	344,293	359,257	320,122	344,765	5
108	Berne	S'land	144,091	242,406	162,440	285,019	162,437	329,087	145,932	340,264	136,699	351,125	122,161	334,330	48
109	Nancy	France	119,372	226,573	127,792	263,220	118,208	305,777	99,091	325,309	99,469	330,631	104,196	332,830	38
110	Brugge	Belgium	94,937	247,353	103,677	269,378	116,175	298,128	117,940	309,479	117,130	321,027	116,414	331,100	12

111	Osnabrück	Germany	126,375	230,527	157,189	272,836	165,014	302,710	157,148	306,474	162,240	318,069	164,197	330,072	10
112	Hull	Britain	299,200	334,900	303,961	346,347	285,970	341,607	272,713	333,537	262,570	324,526	265,333	328,568	3
113	Lausanne	S'land	104,659	177,599	125,447	224,220	136,903	283,183	127,752	297,601	128,080	329,884	113,294	327,628	83
114	Brescia	Italy	138,493	206,616	168,572	240,725	204,976	288,393	207,081	310,786	195,982	313,863	193,000	323,676	17
115	Montpellier	France	95,412	106,335	113,618	128,183	170,843	197,512	195,745	244,962	208,479	280,311	227,808	321,647	15
116	Swansea	Britain	161,000	297,600	167,322	307,592	173,413	331,483	171,423	319,334	172,000	320,711	172,400	320,940	11
117	Cordoba	Spain	165,403	165,403	198,148	198,148	235,632	235,632	279,879	279,879	307,811	307,811	314,602	314,602	1
118	Donostia-San Sebastian	Spain	113,776	159,897	135,149	197,219	165,829	271,231	174,667	300,443	175,975	298,706	179,880	301,758	10
119	Cagliari	Italy	133,542	157,231	177,405	208,086	217,994	259,223	232,513	291,824	222,729	304,350	203,448	299,814	3
120	Tours	France	92,780	146,804	104,773	173,375	132,032	231,330	134,279	268,216	129,601	283,585	133,280	299,659	23
121	Kiel	Germany	246,306	275,544	277,466	314,291	271,506	319,800	250,422	310,287	244,571	305,164	237,370	299,363	10
122	Saint-Étienne	France	187,158	284,079	205,242	314,715	222,241	339,625	208,660	329,019	198,836	321,663	177,696	295,043	19
123	Coblenz	Germany	80,569	220,635	112,819	275,517	119,378	293,399	113,995	288,346	108,335	285,071	109,635	293,081	18
124	Verona	Italy	173,519	190,433	215,166	236,094	260,084	286,951	265,966	296,597	257,066	290,156	256,370	290,697	3
125	Linz	Austria	183,564	230,085	195,085	252,601	204,042	276,948	200,008	285,557	202,981	297,893	185,533	286,253	11
126	Preston	Britain	119,300	221,000	113,341	230,949	98,088	246,798	88,429	264,021	89,455	279,142	92,508	286,082	12
127	Kassel	Germany	161,760	201,233	203,498	249,830	213,976	277,315	196,152	277,443	192,928	278,855	196,803	285,886	7
128	Caserta	Italy	41,798	168,207	47,378	185,562	58,334	208,407	65,488	239,205	68,682	261,073	74,630	280,945	15
129	Blackpool	Britain	147,200	228,400	153,185	252,791	151,860	268,005	149,649	267,474	150,118	272,829	151,033	276,858	6
130	Rennes	France	119,159	133,994	145,104	163,717	186,351	213,689	195,562	235,952	197,777	250,110	207,436	275,425	10
131	Arnhem	N'lands	104,291	184,847	126,421	221,367	132,645	249,817	128,281	255,919	130,960	264,920	138,620	273,898	8
132	Aldershot	Britain	37,700	139,800	31,225	157,115	33,390	218,934	36,316	257,205	34,566	265,366	33,225	273,300	10
133	Enschede/Gronau	N'lands/Germany	107,689	191,044	124,814	221,965	140,222	248,402	143,693	260,574	146,260	262,674	149,851	272,468	3
134	Halle	Germany	289,100	302,600	276,200	289,200	292,500	305,000	324,400	336,400	316,913	328,337	255,123	272,356	12
135	Plymouth	Britain	226,800	234,300	230,406	242,099	239,452	254,165	244,501	263,363	249,415	269,087	251,533	270,751	3
136	Malmö	Sweden	197,335	202,792	232,401	238,878	264,484	276,043	234,764	249,066	233,398	247,958	254,633	269,495	2
137	Orléans	France	73,492	112,219	82,445	136,701	99,060	181,239	103,583	217,326	105,334	243,712	114,239	266,088	19
138	Blackburn	Britain	111,300	276,500	106,242	270,671	101,816	262,222	100,601	269,555	96,401	265,433	95,943	265,399	12
139	Münster	Germany	150,999	150,999	214,238	214,238	251,758	251,758	270,617	270,617	256,261	256,261	265,234	265,234	1
140	Graz	Austria	225,390	234,079	236,245	248,400	247,945	263,354	243,283	260,612	237,916	258,202	240,769	263,541	8
141	Massa	Italy	49,647	209,457	56,125	226,263	62,148	245,876	65,335	259,268	66,605	261,965	68,025	263,173	11
142	Amersfoort	N'lands	63,014	123,208	74,770	149,157	84,541	178,873	88,231	205,407	100,681	228,509	127,531	261,821	5
143	Taranto	Italy	165,863	185,690	191,198	211,955	222,967	244,895	241,940	271,199	233,773	270,273	222,644	261,022	5
144	Pamplona/Iruña	Spain	72,394	81,560	97,880	107,817	147,168	183,797	179,523	229,692	190,374	252,534	187,711	260,732	7
145	Clermont-Ferrand	France	110,801	150,555	124,139	76,638	76,638	230,611	149,553	255,005	136,208	254,532	137,273	259,117	17
146	Messina	Italy	216,699	216,699	250,201	250,201	251,160	251,160	259,016	259,016	235,082	235,082	258,227	258,227	1
147	Rimini	Italy	67,332	129,384	89,661	172,790	114,882	220,695	126,599	243,122	127,942	248,304	131,383	258,176	8
148	Cadiz	Spain	100,249	154,506	117,871	188,398	135,743	215,499	155,624	256,054	157,396	276,972	140,105	255,689	3
149	Avignon	France	61,479	132,214	70,320	154,039	87,576	197,085	89,543	224,470	86,911	239,884	85,796	255,538	22
150	Lübeck	Germany	239,304	267,117	236,313	263,014	239,155	268,504	221,013	255,751	213,843	252,565	213,364	252,839	4
151	Le Havre	France	145,386	178,204	181,358	220,946	210,541	254,266	203,859	257,205	195,715	254,506	190,228	247,713	14
152	Tampere	Finland	107,041	101,200	132,673	128,000	159,327	153,860	166,228	161,600	171,294	218,800	194,141	247,340	5
153	Brunswick	Germany	247,906	247,906	274,853	274,853	271,424	271,424	261,409	261,409	257,575	257,575	244,444	244,444	1
154	Derby	Britain	196,800	196,800	212,720	212,720	219,582	219,582	218,215	219,661	222,820	224,189	240,500	241,710	2

TABLE 2.3. (Cont'd)

Rank	Metropolitan area	Country	1950 City	1950 Metro. area	1960 City	1960 Metro. area	1970 City	1970 Metro. area	1980 City	1980 Metro. area	1990 City	1990 Metro. area	2000 City	2000 Metro. area	Number of communes in the metro. area
155	Dijon	France	107,024	123,932	130,146	153,604	147,368	198,738	143,559	219,633	146,791	233,178	150,306	240,414	17
156	Magdeburg	Germany	261,000	267,000	263,100	269,000	273,000	278,000	288,000	292,500	285,842	290,244	233,808	240,386	3
157	Breda	N'lands	98,719	132,689	122,821	162,431	142,105	192,379	143,220	209,040	151,238	223,149	161,402	238,889	3
158	Luton	Britain	110,400	127,600	140,044	165,047	161,405	193,233	165,439	214,895	172,071	222,581	185,367	236,613	5
159	Barnsley	Britain	75,700	228,100	74,704	233,276	75,395	235,786	70,587	237,443	69,096	235,491	69,001	235,916	14
160	Mulhouse	France	95,478	152,777	106,652	178,187	116,553	207,839	113,352	223,761	108,413	228,291	110,637	235,326	19
161	Salzburg/Freilassing	Germany/Austria	102,409	147,450	107,706	159,562	127,715	189,501	139,229	209,622	143,886	224,632	144,947	235,261	13
162	Tarragona	Spain	40,084	81,005	45,273	92,658	78,238	149,510	108,133	207,814	112,689	225,742	113,569	230,778	5
163	Algeciras/Gibraltar	Spain/Gibraltar	52,732	15,928	66,317	173,299	81,662	184,958	85,634	198,637	99,886	221,340	102,053	230,720	5
164	Angers	France	98,448	123,886	112,145	144,228	131,394	175,675	136,425	198,040	141,678	212,190	152,651	228,938	12
165	Turku	Finland	105,499	101,900	129,569	119,000	154,888	153,400	163,680	156,700	159,680	206,000	172,698	227,253	3
166	Santander	Spain	102,462	121,539	118,435	141,500	149,704	177,784	177,303	210,656	194,568	232,283	182,620	226,292	4
167	The Medway	Britain	70,700	162,200	72,910	177,237	86,862	207,983	96,747	224,255	99,716	231,542	93,667	223,517	6
168	Valetta	Malta	18,566	194,336	17,323	200,934	14,130	200,405	10,752	206,363	9,202	217,944	7,060	219,548	31
169	Vitoria-Gasteiz	Spain	53,571	53,571	74,936	74,936	137,990	137,990	187,002	187,002	207,946	207,946	219,393	219,393	1
170	Mons	Belgium	84,994	225,274	87,963	227,185	93,363	230,144	94,142	227,538	91,895	222,836	90,804	219,156	8
171	Freiburg im Breisgau	Germany	116,338	120,504	150,791	156,897	174,316	183,725	174,403	189,495	189,391	205,613	202,077	218,709	4
172	Århus	Denmark	116,724	150,900	131,752	177,300	232,637	199,000	245,929	182,623	262,783	201,014	285,433	217,608	1
173	Reims	France	129,716	123,376	146,915	140,816	161,829	178,041	177,520	201,341	180,803	209,833	188,121	217,487	8
174	Tilburg	N'lands		136,947		156,143	166,348	177,893	170,672	187,358	177,060	196,061	194,395	216,696	2
175	Elx	Spain	55,877	68,513	73,320	87,367	122,663	139,564	158,729	179,177	184,964	207,435	191,779	215,929	2
176	Trieste	Italy	272,496	272,496	272,698	272,698	271,984	271,984	254,729	254,729	233,657	233,657	215,776	215,776	1
177	Nijmegen	N'lands	111,537	133,285	130,418	155,509	149,404	182,997	147,398	190,258	145,265	197,971	152,368	211,625	5
178	Brest	France	92,220	116,832	129,849	155,591	158,027	189,207	158,685	202,759	148,003	204,578	149,867	210,838	8
179	Gandia	Spain	23,936	102,314	25,982	107,152	36,342	129,193	47,239	157,754	51,638	178,015	58,722	207,543	29
180	Darmstadt	Germany	97,785	128,873	136,065	174,857	143,245	197,522	138,238	200,854	138,227	204,477	136,496	205,975	4
181	Bergen	Norway	112,725	143,266	115,826	152,059	208,064	181,706	207,768	180,981	212,590	187,271	230,084	205,144	1
182	Rostock	Germany	133,100	134,000	161,700	162,700	198,800	199,800	236,000	237,000	250,803	251,767	200,740	204,108	3
183	Northampton	Britain	104,500	104,500	124,100	124,100	133,673	136,785	156,096	160,401	181,903	186,315	199,333	203,725	3
184	Aberdeen	Britain	182,783	184,483	185,390	187,288	182,071	201,547	178,802	205,160	181,179	208,495	176,273	203,497	5
185	Caen	France	60,467	80,523	85,727	115,029	113,193	161,944	115,436	184,924	112,878	191,710	114,145	200,602	18
186	Erfurt	Germany	205,000	205,000	203,000	203,000	213,000	213,000	228,000	228,000	229,623	229,623	199,431	199,431	1

Table 2.3. (Cont'd)

International agglomerations by country

Agglomeration	Country													
Aachen/Heerlen	Germany	171,020	303,728	212,429	375,053	30,573	400,622	244,334	414,579	239,412	411,904	243,527	420,055	6
Aachen/Heerlen	N'lands	77,827	216,274	90,255	258,128	94,728	272,236	91,047	279,281	94,195	283,865	95,037	283,338	9
Algeciras/Gibraltar	Spain	52,732	131,160	66,317	151,743	81,662	160,286	85,634	172,328	99,886	194,659	102,053	201,420	4
Algeciras/Gibraltar	Gibraltar	20,768	20,768	21,556	21,556	24,672	24,672	26,309	26,309	26,681	26,681	29,300	29,300	1
Basel/Lörrach/Saint-Louis	S'land	180,341	258,339	205,722	323,914	212,599	380,098	183,330	366,473	178,581	368,040	168,542	361,238	25
Basel/Lörrach/Saint-Louis	Germany	29,792	52,187	39,218	71,901	45,135	85,719	41,324	82,226	42,274	84,554	44,056	87,646	4
Basel/Lörrach/Saint-Louis	France	9,005	18,598	11,828	23,169	15,796	28,880	18,511	32,634	19,559	33,538	20,019	34,691	6
Douai/Péruwelz	France	40,392	1,064,987	46,633	1,192,731	47,882	1,236,616	43,227	1,196,766	42,192	1,173,369	42,882	1,160,912	207
Douai/Péruwelz A	Belgium	7,124	14,447	7,276	14,800	7,106	14,477	6,825	13,798	6,897	13,826	6,808	13,491	2
Douai/Péruwelz B	Belgium	17,592	29,772	17,336	29,679	17,262	29,324	16,704	28,371	16,547	28,016	16,890	28,339	2
Enschede/Gronau	N'lands	107,689	156,780	124,814	186,271	140,222	209,874	143,693	219,295	146,260	222,442	149,851	230,024	2
Enschede/Gronau	Germany	34,264	34,264	35,694	35,694	38,528	38,528	41,279	41,279	40,232	40,232	42,444	42,444	1
Geneva/Annemasse	S'land	142,288	196,149	174,781	253,525	173,724	322,858	157,184	343,907	170,410	374,621	172,989	398,886	43
Geneva/Annemasse	France	9,538	32,223	12,894	40,549	18,959	60,170	25,469	82,238	27,657	98,977	27,196	107,774	21
Lille/Kortrijk	France	208,146	767,761	212,411	842,759	202,827	933,961	173,563	969,359	172,490	988,611	186,395	1,014,102	65
Lille/Kortrijk A	Belgium	67,430	548,680	71,969	576,678	77,008	610,216	76,009	626,864	76,125	636,890	74,636	647,386	35
Lille/Kortrijk B	Belgium	18,090	36,432	18,000	36,697	18,330	36,897	18,102	36,220	17,865	35,858	17,531	35,325	2
Saarbrücken/Forbach	Germany	189,865	370,368	212,981	408,469	212,637	412,470	193,726	377,747	191,079	370,591	185,615	365,412	10
Saarbrücken/Forbach	France	14,761	74,794	21,678	102,568	23,782	111,705	26,688	112,160	26,947	111,053	22,270	104,579	18
Salzburg/Freilassing	Austria	102,409	134,282	107,706	144,586	127,715	171,611	139,229	188,944	143,886	201,880	144,947	211,107	11
Salzburg/Freilassing	Germany	7,197	13,168	9,135	14,976	11,395	17,890	12,791	20,678	13,989	22,752	14,655	24,154	2
Strasbourg/Kehl	France	188,573	262,521	222,253	306,628	250,671	358,254	249,872	382,496	252,665	403,996	265,751	430,564	20
Strasbourg/Kehl	Germany	14,043	14,043	23,123	23,123	28,839	28,839	29,944	29,944	29,881	29,881	31,793	31,793	1

Source: Moriconi-Ebrard (2000).

(Hohenberg and Hollen Lees 1985) is perfectly clear on this point. The largest medieval cities were frequently best placed to be the first to benefit from technological innovation, economic development, and new forms of political organization. Despite some reverses, they were able to diversify and to achieve growth that was relatively well sustained. Later historical developments, including marked urban growth in Europe since the 1950s, have also tended to strengthen the cities at the top of the urban hierarchy within nations. The great age of European cities and the relative stability of the urban system—what Cattan *et al.* (1999) call 'meta-stability'—therefore constitute a primary distinguishing feature of European cities. These tables show the longevity of European cities, their process of formation and becoming established, the old urban framework, the industrial cities, and the capital cities. As far as France is concerned, Lepetit (1988: 51) reminds us that this is hardly astonishing.

The old balances had been established over a long period, but they were not part of an unchanging history. The permanence of city sites should not mislead us. It is not surprising to find the same names on the lists of cities over a long period. In a world marked very early on by high population densities, there is not an infinite number of potential node points. And the town, even the small town, offers advantages—some of them natural in origin—that act to prevent it withering away completely.

This in no way implies resistance to change. Wars, revolutions, and economic or other crises certainly shaped the fate of many a city; but the system as a whole, especially the hierarchies that formed, remained remarkably stable over the centuries. The relative homogeneity of European cities is heightened by the fact that, overall, the major waves of urbanization were broadly similar, despite time lags and variations from one country to another. This can also be seen in the preservation in a large number of cities—except nineteenth-century industrial cities or those bombed during the Second World War—of historical centres and medieval or Renaissance quarters, or those dating from the eighteenth or nineteenth centuries. This longevity manifests itself in town halls, churches, palaces, and other buildings belonging to one period or another and reflecting the wealth of the city and its bourgeoisie and the influence of the state at different times.

These structural effects are reinforced by a distributive effect. Europe has few very large cities of several million inhabitants. Although London and Paris can probably be classed as global cities, which are also the ones most subject to international competition in economic development, other European cities of this size are rare. Thanks to their work in building databases on European and world cities (Moriconi-Ebrard 2000), Cattan *et al.* are able to highlight the factors that distinguish Europe. With a degree of urbanization comparable to that of Japan and the United States, Europe is characterized, first, by its very large number of cities and their marked proximity to one another: 'for an urban population that is 30 per cent higher than that of the

United States, the European urban community alone has three times as many urban areas of over 10,000 inhabitants—3,500 as against 1,000' (Cattan *et al.* 1999: 23); second, by the fact that the major cities of Europe are not huge: large metropolises with a population of over 2 or 3 million are rare, and 'if one compares the total number of urban areas of over 200,000, the average size is of the order of 800,000 in Europe, as against 1.3 million in the United States and Japan . . . the top 30 American cities are markedly larger than the top 30 European cities' (Cattan *et al.* 1999: 26); and third, by the relative importance of small- and medium-sized cities: Europe distinguishes itself by its relatively large number of urban areas of between 200,000 and 1–2 million inhabitants. In 1990, the European Union contained 225 urban areas of 200,000 or more, 40 or so of these exceeding 1 million, and a very small number 2 million.

Given that to some extent size goes with social, political, and economic diversity and complexity, these facts provide a very important contextual element for the analysis of European cities, one that is accounted for partly by the age of cities that came into being before the development of different forms of transport. The relatively stable core of Europe's urban system is made up of medium-sized and reasonably large cities which are fairly close to one another, and a few metropolises This importance of regional capital cities has already been noted by historians in relation to medieval and Renaissance European cities.

This structural effect combines with the morphology of the regional capital city—or, to be precise, of its commonest version—and has been well described by generations of geographers and historians. Unlike American cities, which are organized around a geometric plan, or 'grid', European cities are characterized by a built-up area around a focal point: administrative and public buildings, churches, monuments, squares, areas for commerce and trade, and development that radiates out from this centre. The city is, in origin, a trading centre and a site for fairs. The medieval city evolved little by little, partly as a result of the development of such towns and partly because walls and identifiable town boundaries gradually disappeared to make way for faubourgs—that is, districts beyond the walls—and peripheral urban spaces.

This built-up town model, characteristic of the medieval city, has not remained unchanged. The logic of the metropolis exerted a strong influence on the way in which the urban space broke up and became increasingly complex. Revolutions in technology, starting with roads and railways, had an impact on the development of cities and the forms they took. Finally, every state made its mark, in the shape of public buildings, networks, forms of urban planning, and the development of forms of housing. It was a mark that varied considerably according to country: the ascendancy of the Jacobin French state, with its prefectures and stations, had little in common with that of the Italian or Swedish states. Despite these significant differences, the centre, whether historic or not, continues to hold meaning in most European cities and has preserved its historic influence, for example, as a place for citizens to gather at protest meetings. The way authority is organized also still has meaning in relation to the centre. European cities have remained relatively built-up in nature, even though important developments have taken place, and the imagined picture of the city is still a reality.

These features are less evident in cities that developed as a result of the Industrial Revolution. These nineteenth century industrial cities, which saw extraordinary growth, were organized around factories, transport junctions, and workers' housing, with the bourgeoisie going to live in residential sub-urbs. However, even in these instances the logic of a focal point surrounded by a built-up area made itself felt. Thus, as Briggs (1962) has shown, the development of Victorian cities in the second half of the nineteenth century was accompanied, on the one hand, by the building of imposing town halls and the organization of a city centre, as in Leeds, Manchester, and Birmingham and, on the other hand, by strong civic pride, which encouraged the planning and creation of all sorts of monuments and symbolic sites, to confirm the city's power and wealth. Consequently, most European industrial cities had a centre, come what may. In addition, in many European cities industrial development was added on to existing structures. Sometimes for objective reasons, but most often because it suited the dominant social groups, industries and the associated workers' housing were established on the periphery of existing cities, with the centre retained in its historic form, as in Barcelona, Stockholm, Munich, Lyons, Milan, Turin, and Copenhagen.

As urbanization accelerated in the late nineteenth and the twentieth centuries, the initial urban system was broadly respected, partly at the expense of the periphery. Despite certain differences, some central city districts still had very much the same social status, with wealthy districts tending to stay wealthy and vice versa.

Conclusion: The Longevity of the Urban System and the Myth of the European City

Acknowledging the longevity of European cities does more than just rehabilitate a myth: it underlines the dynamics and the strategy of actors within cities. Although the urban revolution first took place outside traditional cities, the old European cities, or at least some of them, benefited from it. But this did not happen spontaneously. Entrepreneurs, economic and political elites, and social groups mobilized to organize economic development, for instance. Groups and individuals within cities were actors in these transformations, with varying fortunes. Lepetit provides an example of the mobilization of cities, in this case within the state. In his study of modern French cities (Lepetit 1988), he examines the capacity of state administrations to secure the growth of cities and to structure the urban network, looking in particular at the formation of a road network and the redrawing of the administrative map during the French Revolution. The central administration played a determining role in the growth of cities: the continental logic of city development. Networks were formed at the instigation of royalty and imposed on cities. On the other hand, Lepetit also stresses the cities' capacity for resistance. Road networks essentially respected existing urban hierarchies, which can be explained both on technical grounds and by the intense pressures mounted by the elites of these cities within the state. The redrawing of the political and administrative map during the revolutionary period certainly involved some setbacks for regional capitals, but Lepetit has shown that it was exceptional for large cities to be marginalized by the new geography of power. Social and political actors within the cities proved extremely active in defending their interests and in reorienting certain sections of networks. Similar instances could easily be found elsewhere, in the Netherlands for example.

In the face of economic and political change within centralized states, and even during a phase of capitalism when cities were merely sites for the concentration of phenomena whose source and dynamic lay elsewhere, European cities were not just passive spaces obeying logics that transcended them. Although politically and economically outclassed, various urban interests, groups, and elites had strategies that allowed them to play a greater or lesser role in structuring new trends, and so they were able to turn changes to their advantage with varying degrees of success. The social and political logics of such cities do not have much in common with medieval cities. However, cities continued to play a role within states: somewhat less in small centralized states, somewhat more in the Netherlands and in Italy. The relative stability of urban hierarchies in Europe can also be explained by these social dynamics.

Even though Europe at one time dominated the world hierarchy of cities in terms of population size, this is clearly no longer the case: there are now only a dozen European cities in the top 100 cities in the world, and none in the top 20. This may indicate either the decline of European cities or a different mode of organization of societies, which have become strongly territorial in nature as they adapt to new conditions. The essential point of our analysis to be noted at this juncture is the importance of old cities in the European network: regional capitals or the capital cities of small states, cities where trade, production, culture, universities, and administrative functions mingle. Figures need to be updated to take account of the new upsurge in urbanization and the continued growth of urban populations in Europe since the 1950s. This structural basis of European societies is still essential to any understanding of the contemporary dynamics of European cities.

Great Britain seems to be a partial exception to this history. Until the Industrial Revolution, the country was not very highly urbanized. In this context, London's extraordinary development must be viewed alongside the weakness of the regional capitals compared with those in the rest of Europe

(Poussou *et al.* 1983). British elites were not anti-urban as such: they lived between London, the economic and political capital, and their country estates. However, they made no contribution to the development of other cities in the kingdom and took no interest in any of them, apart from Edinburgh, Dublin, and Cardiff. The industrial towns that became de facto Britain's major provincial cities were rejected by the British elites of the time. Opposition to the cities was to become a central feature of the identities of both the aristocracy and the middle classes (Bédarida 1990; Lowe, Murdoch, and Cox 1995).

Once collective actors and social structures, cities have now been integrated into national societies and states. This relationship between states and cities is central to understanding the formation of states and, to some extent, the development of cities. So any nation-state transformation could have consequences for European cities.

What is more, the adventure of the powerful city-states and the political autonomy that medieval cities enjoyed seem all the more spectacular because we are now used to thinking in terms of the state. But, despite their power, very few cities could claim total sovereignty. Most Italian cities had attachments to the emperor, with limited exceptions such as Florence, Milan, or Genoa at certain times. Even Venice preferred to recognize the authority of the Emperor of Constantinople for several centuries rather than acquire full sovereignty. The same held good for German cities, including the Hanseatic League, where those who wanted to gain independence at any price were rare indeed. By contrast, urban elites were very concerned with their political autonomy: securing their own defence, enforcing rules that favoured their commercial enterprises, developing their own courts, and avoiding de facto control or domination by higher authorities. However, except in certain cases, seeking independence was not the norm, and historically, even at the end of the Middle Ages, independent city-states have been a rare phenomenon, however spectacular. Most often, the cities with greatest autonomy were those attached to an overlord. When they needed to defend their interests, they organized themselves into urban leagues and alliances, as in the Netherlands and Germany.

Consequently, for most of the time the relationship between cities and states has not been one of competition between city-states and states but one of complex interactions, shifts in the balance of power, and cooperation, and a search for autonomy and interdependence. The golden age of European cities was clearly round about the end of the Middle Ages:

The fifteenth and sixteenth centuries witnessed a great transformation of European societies. Preconditions of this transformation date back to the growth of towns in the tenth to twelfth centuries, when urban communities developed their economies rapidly and achieved political autonomy. But the turn from the authority of kings to government by popular mandate had its more immediate social and intellectual antecedents in the decades around 1500 . . . [they] witnessed not only economic growth, European expansion overseas, and the

Reformation; they also witnessed the rise of Humanism, the invention of printing, and the early development of modern sciences. (Bendix 1978: 9)

As we have seen, cities were still enjoying strong growth and the urban bourgeoisies were accumulating wealth. The structures of feudalism were weaker
over almost all Europe, and there were varying outcomes. The landed gentry was less able to apply different types of constraint to hinder the development of cities. Finally, although the military power of states was imposed
gradually, numerous conflicts demanded that states mobilize their resources,
and so they needed the cities. Even Spanish sovereigns enriched by South
American gold had a hard time with the Netherlands. The existence of varied political forms—empires, states, principalities, duchies, even city-states—
sometimes creates an image of relative anarchy, particularly within the
Germanic and Byzantine empires, and the reality was one of highly confused
authority, to say the least. But it was precisely within this context of confused authority that the thriving medieval cities found the greatest room for
manoeuvre. By financing sovereigns and maintaining their own defences, they
gained considerable capacities for negotiation with their overlord. This gave
them the scope to acquire rights and privileges, to pursue the accumulation of wealth without paying too much tax to the overlord, to assert their
rights in military or commercial conflicts, and to organize their own institutions so as to conduct their affairs efficiently, following their own wishes.
Although the logic was the same across almost all Europe, there were considerable variations from one city to another. Enmeshed authorities and rules
on the one hand and incessant conflicts on the other make it unrealistic to
attempt the construction of a precise model, capable of integrating all the
different cases. In the opposite scenario, when nation-states established their
domination and were able to concentrate resources, authority, legitimacy, and
force, cities lost a large part of their political autonomy and their room for
manoeuvre. Putting down roots in the nation-state, urban elites still played
along with the political centre, but they no longer controlled the rules of the
game, and their capacity to take part was greatly diminished—although, again,
there were considerable differences between the situations in the Netherlands and Italy on the one hand and Sweden and France on the other.

This book's argument will attempt to reflect all the above. In other words:

. . . with the problems facing national States, the crisis in international relations
and the construction of Europe, there could emerge a new climate of doubt and
uncertainty for the higher authorities: a new historical interlude—whose stability and length we can only surmise—that may once more bring some political
space to cities. This space may be limited, yet the room for manoeuvre is growing for cities. The social and political actors are aware of this and are developing
their strategies accordingly. (Bagnasco and Le Galès 2000: 7)

This hypothesis is seductive, and it justifies the attention now being paid to
cities again. However, it becomes meaningful only if we can demonstrate that

'confused authority' is not just a formulaic expression: a task I undertake in the next chapter.

The attention devoted to the longevity and size of European cities does not signal a return to the cosy ideas through which some people have attempted to isolate the 'good' European city, the old city, or the working-class city from the winds of social change. Rather, this historical detour has enabled me to identify some key variables: relations with the state, involvement in a certain type of capitalism, and involvement in national societies. The next chapter takes as its aim the analysis of how these variables have changed, in an attempt to understand the rules laid down for cities on the new playing field.

II

A 'HISTORICAL INTERLUDE FOR EUROPEAN CITIES'?

THREE

The Loosening Grip of the State and the Redistribution of Authority Within the European Union: A New Set of Parameters to Structure Modes of Urban Governance

B Y the end of the Middle Ages, European cities had become collective actors. We have seen that there were two central variables favouring cities: a particular type of trade capitalism and a political situation in which powers were unevenly distributed. Emergent states were still fragile, and power and rules were enmeshed at different levels. Then, with varying degrees of difficulty, the nation-states established their authority. Society and capitalism were organized within the limits of the state and under its supervision. A key hypothesis of this book is that, if the state is changing, a new set of constraints and opportunities is emerging for cities, a context in which some of them may become actors of European governance and more structured as local societies. It makes sense only if we are able to demonstrate that something has changed for the nation-state: that is, to identify the argument and to provide evidence of state restructuring, of the institutionalization of Europe, and of the implications for cities and regions. European cities are not organized solely by the state but, increasingly, in relation to cities and regions in other countries—the horizontal dimension of European institutionalization—and in relation to Brussels—the vertical, multi-level dimension.

Given that European countries are overwhelmingly urban, the state cannot ignore the fates of cities, the places where wealth is produced and where the major public services operate (Gurr and King 1987). From the mid- or late nineteenth century in Europe, the state has taken charge of the large institutions and the production of collective goods that contribute to the

well-being of city dwellers (Wolman and Goldsmith 1992). Seen from a political angle, cities—meaning here urban governments—became agents of the
state, as local and regional bases for putting national policies into practice
and for legitimizing a form of territorial management by the state (see
Chapter 7). It follows that a different set of political institutions, especially
when modified in relation to the European integration process, will structure
a different pattern of constraints and opportunities for cities and actors within
cities. This chapter concentrates first on the restructuring of the state and
second on the impact of the institutionalization of the European Union.

A first definition of European cities is that they are now included within
the European polity. In the mid-1980s, cities were not party to the European
polity, or were so only to a very small extent. Fifteen years later the European polity has developed, specific programmes and funds exist, networks
have proliferated, and consultation procedures on urban issues have been
established with the Parliament, the Committee of the Regions, and associations of cities. There are numerous access points for cities in Brussels and
Strasbourg (Marks and Hooghe 1996; McCarthy 1997). The European Union
has produced indicators, urban programmes, and working papers, and has
developed public policy categories and territories. Like any political centre
on a trajectory of formation, the European Commission is preoccupied with
the legitimacy of these forms of intervention. In line with the movement
initiated by Jacques Delors, cities—although less so than regions—seem to be
potential local bases for the implementation of European programmes, for
the mobilization of citizens on behalf of the European integration project,
and for the participation of coalitions that aim to advance this project. This
to some extent recalls what Lepetit (1988), Blockmans and Tilly (1994), and
Genet (1990) had to say about state formation (see Chapter 2).

This chapter argues that the nation-state today plays less of a determining
role in structuring and steering society, and that therefore sub-national territories, viewed as political and social constructs, are likely to be one of the
intermediate levels at which actors, groups, and institutions can be structured.
Since the moment when 'state coercion' lessened, cities and regions have
emerged as one possible level of political regulation, even though such
territories do not have the characteristics of nation-states. My argument
demands evidence of both the relaxation of state control and the dynamics
of European integration. Examination of the dynamics of European integration and Europeanization is therefore required to provide evidence of the
current fluid situation: of what Hooghe and Marks (2001) call 'European multi-
level governance'.

The loosening of the state's grip and the processes of Europeanization
in sub-national territories are the main threads of this chapter, since any
political analysis of the redistribution of authority and its implications for
cities must involve both taking stock of states and a consideration of the
Europeanization process. The argument about the changing role of the state

and the reshaping of territorial politics therefore concerns both cities and regions alike. Although regions will be sidelined in this book, for reasons explained in the Introduction, it remains the case that, in some countries, they are at the forefront of the restructuring process.

Two last points of information. In this chapter, given its political focus, the term 'city' is used in the sense of 'urban local authority'; and the implications for urban governments of the changes outlined will be examined, in Chapter 7. The emphasis of the first part of the book is on providing a picture of constraints and opportunities.

The Reshaping of the State in Europe

For cities, the triumph of the nation-state in Europe represented a loss of political autonomy and the imposition of rules and national categories. The influence of the state in European societies increased throughout the twentieth century, especially following the two world wars. This expansion of the state, and of the welfare state in particular, played a part in structuring relations between the state and sub-national territories, among them cities: relations classically examined in terms of centre-periphery relations (Unwin and Rokkan 1983). This general process varied from state to state and took different forms.

The reshaping of the state and the blurring of its representations produce effects which might be likened to a sort of 'unlocking': opening the field to sub-national territories and to cities in particular. With European governance in the making, any transformation of the state's role promotes significant transformations in modes of government and/or governance of sub-national territories. In addition, a detour through the issue of state transformation is justified by the fact that any lessening of state coercion also transforms the interplay of constraints and opportunities for cities and regions. Despite 'the inevitable incoherence of the state' (Jobert 1995), its meaning and power in Western Europe remain massive. Its role and strategies in this context are giving way to contradictory interpretations of state transformation, which make the classic definition of the state obsolete. The exceptional congruence organized in the nation-state seems to have had its day. But the state has not disappeared: it is undergoing reshaping (Wright and Cassese, 1996).

The Classic View of the State in Western Europe

Although a transformation of the Western state is well under way, it is still necessary both to define precise terms, so as not to confuse the reshaping of the state with its demise, and to clarify the main lines along which reshaping is taking place.[1] The point of departure is provided by classic sociological definitions such as Max Weber's: he highlights the political and institutional dimension of the state, which claims a 'monopoly of legitimate violence'. Badie and Birnbaum (1994) underline the aspect of internal sociology: the state is a public space that has formed in the face of a civil society, aiming to ensure the monopoly of public functions for those allegiances that have priority in constructing civil obedience, and to differentiate between the political and the social by recruiting its own staff and producing its own institutions. Finally, authors such as Hintze (1991), Tilly (1975), Mann (1986), Giddens (1987), and Gellner (1983) have stressed the importance of war, coercion, and the enforcement of law and order in the dynamics of the making of European states.

The modern Western state, an original political form resulting from historically located social processes, has become the legitimate mode of political organization for European societies. It has taken various forms since the end of the nineteenth century, but these have always been characterized by: control of a bounded territory, enclosed within borders; a centralized bureaucracy, differentiated from other social forces; a minimal degree of secularism separating the political space from the religious space; a body of law protecting the state's borders; a strong concept of citizenship, which attaches citizens directly to the state and limits the ascendancy of intermediate groups and communities; a taxation system; a currency; forces ensuring a monopoly of violence in order to protect its citizens—the police and the armed forces.[2] Concretely, states established their authority through taxation, through enforcing borders—both by guaranteeing the safety of their citizens and by making war—through the development of legal rules, and through a currency. The sovereignty of the state, imperfect and relative as it may have been, acquired full meaning within a system where states were viewed as independent of one another, where there was no legal power superior to the state. But this Westphalian concept of the state is now being called into question (Badie 1999).

Apart from any question of concepts, the way the state is perceived is inevitably blurred by the concrete view of its multiplicity of functions and organizations. In fact, the state is also a set of institutions and narratives:

---

[1] This book does not aim to deal with the consolidation of states after the fifteenth century, for which see Badie and Birnbaum (1994), Bendix (1978), Tilly (1990), Elias (1962), Poggi (1990). The literature on state-building considers a set of variables, including cities: see, in particular, Eisendstadt and Rokkan (1973) and Rokkan (1975). The making of the state has been the subject of a sizeable theoretical and empirical body of work, giving an account of a long process unfolding from the twelfth century to the present day. See, for example, the classic works of Poggi, Anderson, Strayer, Badie and Birnbaum, Bendix and Elias, and, for an excellent presentation in French: 'La formation de l'État européen', Chapter 2 of Lagroye (1997). Badie and Birnbaum (1994) have clearly highlighted differing analyses of state-building and political sociology approaches.   [2] Hermet *et al.* (1998).

'Any general definition of the state would need to refer to state discourse as well as state institutions ... The core of the state apparatus comprises a distinct ensemble of institutions and organizations whose socially accepted function is to define and enforce collectively binding decisions on the members of a society in the name of their common interest or general will' (Jessop 1990: 341). To avoid erring on the opposite side, and giving too abstract a definition of the state, we must agree with Jessop when he makes it clear that: (1) the boundaries between the state and society are always in doubt, especially at the micro-level of organizations; (2) the nature of state functions and organizations will depend on the nature of the social formation and its history, and will differ from one country to another—and the capitalist state is different from others; (3) the forms in which legitimacy is institutionalized will also vary; (4) apart from violence, the state can employ a whole range of means of intervention, which are frequently contradictory; (5) societies are no more a natural phenomenon than are states: like states, they are built, transformed and reproduced; and (6) the common interest is always an illusory construction, which inevitably involves differentiated selection processes and the differential articulation of interests, values, and opinions.

Since the late nineteenth century, the influence of European states in society has grown considerably, especially with the development of the welfare state. In most European countries, state expenditure has increased, particularly during and after the two world wars, as has the proportion of GDP that it represents. In retrospect, the decades following the Second World War seem like a kind of golden age of the 'modernizing state', when, in a context of economic growth, state intervention grew and became more differentiated into increasingly diverse and complex sectors. For a long time, public policy in European countries enabled institutional arrangements to be structured as a successful public policy/market mix so as to allow economic development, the growth of state public policies, and a fairly high degree of social cohesion: that is, the 'Keynesian compromise'. European countries experienced both a higher rate of growth than that of the United States and a fairly low level of social inequalities.[3]

Table 3.1 gives a rough picture of the extent of state influence. These figures translate into investments, staffing, and public policies of all kinds. Of course, European countries have not all evolved in the same way or at the same rate. However, such growth has represented a long-term trend accentuated by wars.

Going beyond figures alone, comparative analysis of the different institutional arrangements of economy and state in Europe has suggested that there are different combinations of public policy and economic regulation. The UK

[3] All this has been thoroughly analysed in the political economy literature on different forms of institutionalization of various types of capitalism (Crouch and Streeck 1996; Boyer 1986; Hollingsworth and Boyer 1997).

TABLE 3.1. *State expenditure as a percentage of GDP, 1870–1994*

Country	c. 1870	c. 1913	c. 1937	1960	1994
Britain	9.4	12.7	30.0	32.2	42.9
France	12.6	17.0	29.0	34.6	54.9
Germany	10.0	14.8	42.4	32.4	49.0
Italy	11.9	11.1	24.5	30.1	53.9
Japan	8.8	8.3	25.4	17.5	35.8
USA	3.9	1.8	8.6	27.0	33.5
Singapore	n/a	n/a	n/a	n/a	19.0

Source: World Bank (1996).

was distinguished by a powerful centralized state, which gave a large role to market regulation and involved a low level of direct state intervention in society. By contrast, institutionalization of the economy seems to be a particular feature of mainland European societies, with the market viewed as a social and political phenomenon and the state as an indispensable regulatory instrument generating long-term advantages (Schonfeld 1965). During the postwar decades, European states extended their activities and their supervisory role in relation to an increasing number of issues across a wide range of areas of social and political life and economic activity, by controlling a growing proportion of resources (Poggi 1996). This institutionalization took different forms—in France, it was more state-led than in Germany, where the social partners were central—but, at the end of the day, most countries achieved economic growth, along with declining social and spatial inequalities.

In retrospect, and with due regard to the bias by which retrospective views tend to erase conflicts and disputes, the state in the 1960s seems to have been legitimate, innovative, and growing. It organized arrangements with social groups and institutions, regulated conflicts, and controlled the market in a context of optimism and faith in progress. Except by free-market and Marxist critics, this extension of the role of the state was broadly accepted, if only because it coincided with a substantial improvement in the living conditions of populations. Consequently, the state became the legitimate form to guide and direct society, with society itself seen within the frame of the nation. Cities were included within this frame.

From Municipality to State: Models of Local Government Institutionalization in Europe

For over 100 years, local government was closely integrated within nation-states, which organized the politics, the policies, the roles, the resources, and the functions of local governments.

The cycle of urbanization linked to the Industrial Revolution continued in most European countries from the last third of the nineteenth century into the early twentieth century, in parallel with the consolidation of nation-states. One effect of this consolidation was the recognition of legal status for local authorities in the second half of the nineteenth century. Thus, they became an integral part of the state, organized according to rules and principles defined in the national context. Local governments, particularly in northern Europe, devised urban social policies in response to the pressures created by industrialization. Indeed, welfare states were partly invented in cities.

In the course of the nineteenth century, the recognition of local government within European nation-states came about rapidly in the north and later in the south. These local governments were gradually institutionalized by means that varied according to the particular forms taken by the state, social compromises, the dynamism of industrial bourgeoisies, the formation of the labour movement, the longevity of municipal autonomy and its institutions, and the advances of democracy. The fact that Scandinavian states were fairly long-established and relatively socially homogeneous facilitated the rapid shaping of municipal governments, which obtained legal status and a fairly high degree of autonomy from 1837 onwards in Norway, 1857 in Denmark, and 1862 in Sweden. Once legally recognized, municipalities went on to become privileged sites of democratization, political participation, and bureaucratic modernization. In Germany, cities retained a form of autonomy into the nineteenth century. Modern local government was able to develop rapidly there, strengthening the tradition of municipal democracy within the imperial German state, so that it became a fundamental element of German democracy after 1945: 'From 1807, Prussian municipal legislation granted them autonomous status . . . The development of participatory institutions accompanied the creation of a particularly efficient local bureaucracy' (Gabriel 1999: 17). In Britain, local authorities have never gained institutional recognition, since there is no written constitution; but this did not prevent their rapid development in the nineteenth century (Stoker 1995). However, in the model of rigid separation between 'high politics' and local 'low politics' (Bulpitt 1983), local authorities are merely the creations of Parliament.

In the Netherlands, more than anywhere else, two distinctive features— powerful trading cities and the original sixteenth- and seventeenth-century venture to create a Dutch Republic, which hinged on its cities—suggest a remarkable continuity of institutions in the 'Dutch model' (Daalder and Irwin 1989; Thoonen 1991) and of solid municipal democracy. During the making of the unitary system of government, 'local autonomy continued to be viewed as a key element of the system of government . . . the organization of the territorial state of the Netherlands provided for a single level of local government (*gemeenten*) and a uniform regime of municipal urban government, whatever the nature of the local authority concerned: urban, suburban or rural' (Denters 1999: 227). At its formation, Belgium inherited a Napoleonic administrative system, which, as in the Netherlands, took account of the strong tradition of local autonomy. When Belgium gained its independence in 1830, it was quick to write into the constitution the organizing principles of municipal government, and the latter's status was recognized from 1836. As highlighted in Chapter 2, Italy has always and above all been characterized by a rich past of autonomy and independence for cities; and its current population still feels this. This autonomy and independence were recognized at the time of Italian unity and at the time of the First Republic, before the country underwent the vicissitudes of fascism. In France, the Revolution suppressed municipal corporations, and it was left to the state at the time of the Third Republic to take the initiative on major laws granting municipal freedoms—notably, in 1884. In the face of social and political initiatives taken by large *communes*, the state used its *préfets* on the ground and the *Conseil d'État* in Paris to limit cities' autonomy and to ensure the political pre-eminence of the state in terms of resources and expertise. In contrast, the *commune* was preserved by the Revolution, and has remained a—frequently mythologized—foundation of French democracy. The city, however, appeared as a threat to the Jacobin Republic. In Spain, the *Code Napoléon* defined 9,000 *municipios*, closely controlled by the central political authority. It was not until the Second Republic in the 1930s that there was increased regional autonomy and growth in local government, though local government was then reduced to its simplest expression during Franco's regime.

During this period—somewhat earlier in Great Britain, a little later in southern Europe—problems accumulated in those European cities that were affected, to a greater or lesser extent, by urbanization. 'Urban life would bring its own dangers: crime, crowd violence, riots, unpredictable labour market cycles, and mass epidemics. None of these problems could be resolved with certainty' (de Swaan 1995: 166). Public health issues combined with political and social concerns to prompt urban elites and social actors to embark on public policies (Topalov 1990). Local governments, as they have always done, tried to maintain order and prevent riots, acting either independently or jointly with the state. In northern Europe and in France, urban elites first organized the city, then built and rebuilt, destroying a range of unhealthy working-class neighbourhoods. Enclaves and suburbs were developed, either as refuges for the bourgeoisie or—more or less anarchically—for and by the working classes.

In the name of free movement and of modernism, urban governments and the state built roads and streets, constructed sewerage, gas, and transport networks, provided street lighting, organized refuse collection, modernized firefighting through the use of fire stations, and created abattoirs. 'Thus, there are two key concepts in the urban arrangements of the nineteenth century: the idea of policing and the idea of network' (de Swaan 1995: 171). The vast literature on social reformers, the labour movement, and the late nineteenth-century bourgeoisie has attempted to demonstrate the motivations of the urban elites who embarked on social policies and laid the groundwork for the welfare state (Topalov 1990). Cities played a key role in what de Swaan

(1995: 22) has called the 'process of collectivizing medical care, education, and income maintenance'. The movement frequently called the 'Haussmanization' of Europe's major cities helped to spread the ideas, know-how, and doctrines of town planning, as well as promoting the existence of professional town planners.

The innovative urban policies of local governments in this era were not established without difficulty. The aristocracy and the urban bourgeoisie, who owned the land and paid the taxes, demonstrated reservations and hostility towards these developments. In many cities, the petty bourgeoisie of independent artisans, shopkeepers and professionals was vigorously opposed to local government interventionism and to the institutionalization of municipal government. At the same time, in the major cities of northern Europe, the labour movement was pushing for the development of social policies, frequently against the state. This gave birth to the movement for municipal socialism, whose effects would be felt particularly in Germany, but also, to a lesser extent, in England and Denmark, and later in France. It was not until the 1930s that the government of most of Britain's major industrial cities was won by the Labour Party, which invented an original model of municipal management directed towards providing services to the working class. For their part, the powerful German and Scandinavian municipalities organized the direct provision of numerous public services. France experimented with water concessions, and the state very quickly intervened to limit the municipalities' room for manoeuvre.

Housing, as a very particular kind of good, was at the heart of initiatives that tied social issues closely to the urban question. Private and public local—and, later, central—initiatives combined to launch the social housing movement, first in Scandinavia, the Netherlands, and the UK, then in France (Harloe 1995). Urban governments were at the forefront of all these initiatives. This example clearly highlights the division of labour between the market, civil society, the state, and local authorities. This was not a given at the outset but became institutionalized after conflicts between the state and local authorities, between the private and the public sectors, and between social groups. In every state, these conflicts shaped representations, groups, and institutions. The production of housing was to take a particular form in each country: centralized to varying degrees, allowing differing amounts of room for public sector mechanisms or for cooperatives, investing heavily in social housing—or not—and acting as an expression of how far voluntarist policies formed an integral part of different views of society.

In cities—above all in the largest and the most industrialized—public service administration became professionalized. Town planners, for example, played an increasing role in organizing cities, met each other within professional organizations, observed what was happening in the United States, and laid the foundations of a form of town planning that relied on growing public interventionism.

City councils running cities made sense within the nation-state. Globalization and European integration processes are now altering this parameter. Since the state is the key variable for assessing the political autonomy of cities, we need to make a detour through the impact of these processes on the dynamics of states.

Redistribution of Authority: European Integration and Beyond

Globalization and European integration are two processes that are disturbing the workings of the state, even though the state is itself an actor and a driving force of these processes. Cities are also part of the processes and have to respond to them. The processes are leading to the dislocation of traditional political communities and to a reordering of scales and actors, who are escaping the control of the nation-state. 'A new world scene is taking shape, one which is sometimes aterritorial, sometimes subject to the competition of several contradictory territorial logics and sometimes—though increasingly rarely—commonplace nation-state' (Badie 1995: 14). For the moment, we propose to look at these two processes solely in terms of their political logic; other dimensions will be considered in Chapters 4 and 5.

Today's European Union is an original political entity: if not a state, then a form of state (Caporaso 1996). Nevertheless, it is characterized by a developed system of governance that has, among other things, a fairly small civil service with limited capacities and low tax receipts which cannot rise above a certain ceiling, but also a substantial rule-making and conflict-resolution capacity through the European Court of Justice (Stone Sweet 2000). In some sectors, it can now be appropriately described as a regulatory state. Majone defines the regulatory state as no longer—or, at least, less frequently— dealing with redistribution or major social policies but with regulation as such; public interventions are 'supposed to eliminate or reduce the inefficiencies engendered by particular types of market failure' . . . such as 'monopoly power', 'negative externalities', 'information failures' or 'inadequate provision of public goods' (1996a: 28–9).[4] European supra-national modes of governance have now come into being, structured by systems of rules that apply to the whole territory of the Union and by trans-national networks of actors (Sandholz and Stone Sweet 1998).

The European space born of the European Communities project was originally viewed as a relatively traditional international space for interactions between sovereign states (Moravscik 1999). This European integration project resulted from negotiations between nation-states as well as from pressures

---

[4] He gives public health, the environment, and safety as examples of collective goods. European agencies, such as the Environmental Agency, created in 1994, or the Agency for the Evaluation of Medicinal Products, promote integration by non-regulatory means, relying instead on national administrative bodies. Majone (1996b) stresses their role in terms of governance by networks and by information.

generated by firms involved in ever-increasing volumes of trade within the area of Europe. Fifty years later, the European Union, although it still does not have the attributes of a state, produces public policies, rules, procedures, and norms in an original form (Mény, Muller, and Quermonne 1995; Kohler-Koch and Eising 1999; Scharpf 1999; Stone Sweet, Sandholz, and Fligstein 2001). These rules and policies are gradually being imposed across the whole territory of the EU, while increasingly dense networks of trans-national actors are mobilizing and organizing in order to exert pressure on policies. Consequently, any analysis of European integration from the point of view of institutionalization requires the European space to be viewed as a set of public policy spheres, structured by organizations, committees, agencies, groups, networks, and rules. This space is gradually being reshaped, but not very coherently, and with very significant differences between realms and times.

Modes of action, frequently original, are becoming more concrete, inspired by consultants and associative interests or, more often, resulting from hybridization of existing national or regional models (Héritier, Hill, and Mingers 1996; Wallace and Wallace 2000; Lequesne 2001). In turn, the institutionalization of European governance is generating tensions with long-institutionalized national spaces for regulating public policy. Interactions entail processes of transfer, adaptation, and hybridization, as well as dynamic conflicts that produce new rules and help to structure an original public policy space.[5] Any representation of European governance that stressed only odd links and interconnected public policy hierarchies would fail to address the logics of state reshaping and the temporal dynamics of institutionalization, which lend stability to actors' behaviour. Structures are starting to appear. The term 'institution' is used in the sense that North (1990) suggests: a set of rules, norms, and procedures that governs the behaviour of actors and organizations. Thus, European institutions provide a stable frame within which anticipation reduces uncertainties. Regularity in the behaviour of European actors is achieved through cognitive and normative matrices, coordinated sets of values, beliefs, and principles of action, assimilated by the actors to varying degrees and guiding their practices (Pierson 1998; Sandholz and Stone Sweet 1998).

However, institutionalization also produces uncertainties in terms of outcomes. Although institutions constitute a constraining framework for the actors within a given sub-system, experience shows that they can be used in unexpected, creative ways. In other words, the fluid situation created by the

---

[5] Hassenteufel and Surel (2000) have usefully proposed to distinguish three types of approach to the study of public policies in Europe: one which gives greatest prominence to the way Community policies are implemented, one which sees the EU as the place where Community policies are produced, and one which stresses the co-production of activities by myriad actors at different levels. See also A. Smith (1995); Wallace and Wallace (2000).

institutionalization of Europe gives different actors with less power than the nation-states—regions and cities, for example—a chance to develop initiatives, set up projects, or obtain resources. From this point of view, the example of the European integration project offers a large number of striking instances relating particularly to the special role played by the European Court of Justice as a conflict-regulating, institutionalizing body (Weiler 1994; Dehousse 1995; Stone Sweet 2000). The Commission and the Parliament take decisions and play the role of political entrepreneur, creating coalitions with states and with non-state actors at various levels. In doing so, the Commission is structuring a trans-national policy-making system and contributing to the formation of a public space. The term 'European governance' has been widely used to describe this strange 'polity'. The use of this term originates from three features of the EU: (1) the interpenetration of different levels of government; (2) the proliferation of actors and organized non-state interests, and the existence of public policy networks that display varying degrees of organization, alongside political and social sub-systems with many forms of interdependence; and (3) the fact that, even though responsibility for decision-making and policy has not been delegated to an elected government, decisions are made and rules are imposed on all citizens. 'European governance' takes into account multiple interactions and the production of rules and public policies. In other words, the term 'governance' is used to describe the process of government at the European level 'because authoritative allocation takes place without or outside government' (Kohler Koch and Eising 1999). It poses crucial problems of legitimacy. Before he goes on to highlight the possibilities offered by output-oriented legitimization and the efficiency of public policy in solving problems, Scharpf (1999: 187) emphasizes the three areas of deficit for classic input-oriented legitimization, namely, 'the lack of a pre-existing sense of collective identity, the lack of Europe-wide policy discourses, and the lack of a Europe-wide institutional infrastructure that could assure the political accountability of office-holders to a European constituency'. Within this polity in the making, everybody—groups and local governments, in particular—can claim to be an actor; dynamic European cities are no exception.

In terms of the redistribution of authority, the effects of globalization processes are in many ways mixed with Europeanization processes: in the area of law and rules, for example. The proliferation and differentiation of state actors and, especially, non-state actors—individuals, groups, cities, regions, organizations, associations, and firms—form a second key element in political globalization processes (Cziempel and Rosenau 1991; Smouts 1998). This political world scene has no government, no real legitimate political centre, no government responsible for world affairs, except economic affairs to some extent; yet norms, representations, and rules have developed, conflicts are increasing, ways of resolving conflicts are being organized, and regulations are appearing—all of which bring us back to the term 'governance'. The state itself acts within networks and organizations and retains a great deal of room for manoeuvre in multiple transactions and interactions. However, whether on a European or on a world scale, it has become just one actor among many.

The logics of trans-national flows and interactions represent points of disjunction for the classic concept of the state (Held *et al.* 1999). This development of flows has the effect of trans-nationalizing political power and strengthening interdependence between different types of actor, as well as economic, military, and political forms of interdependence (Meyer 2000). European integration and globalization processes are accelerating the development of trans-national forms of interdependence. They are leading to a reordering of scales that accentuates the fragmentation of governmental organizations. The assumed coherence of national public policies, organized around stable interactions between the state, ministers, and collective interests—the latter organized solely or mainly at the national level—is no longer relevant (Balme 1996; Marks and Hooghe 2001; Keating and Loughlin 1997).

Consequently, the state is losing its centrality in, and its—relative—monopoly of, public policy processes, and this is opening the field for political entrepreneurs, for instance actors within cities benefiting from a long tradition and legitimacy to mobilize around the territorial identity.

The Loosening Grip of the State

Discourses announcing the demise of the state are not new—Marx and the thesis of the decaying state spring to mind—and they are now taking on a new vigour in the light not only of the state's internal fragmentation and differentiation but also of the effects of globalization and European integration.[6] However, the long history of the nation-state in Europe urges caution in making assumptions about the possibility of radical changes. Of course, in most European countries, although to an unequal extent, market regulation and the private sector play an increasing role, and the changing scale of capitalism has created a precarious balance for the state (Sklair 2000; Jessop 2000; Leca 1996). Given its deep historical roots and the resources at its disposal, any announcement of the demise of the state is certainly premature. Mann (1997) and Wright and Cassese (1996) find unlimited opportunities to mock all those who prophesy the state's decay. A brief examination of some points of disjunction for the state is of value here, in order to understand what has changed for cities and for actors within

---

[6] The titles of relevant books and articles speak volumes in this regard: 'the dismantling state', 'the virtual state', 'the retreating state' (Strange 1996), 'the hollowing out of the state' Castells (1996–98), 'the destatisation process' (Jessop 1997*a*),'the splintered state' '[l'État en miettes]' (Dupuy and Thoenig 1996), some even have a question mark . . . 'the state, obsolete or obstinate?' (Hoffman 1995). On the other hand, other expressions, including 'the organisational state', 'the strategic state', 'the enabling state', and 'the regulatory state', tend to suggest new forms of action on the part of the state.

cities.[7] The approach used is to present and analyse the various phenomena separately, while acknowledging that this underestimates their dynamics and the effects of the way they interact.

For Europeans, the first point of disjunction is symbolized by currency and the European Central Bank, as the Euro replaces national currencies which symbolized national identities.

Second, the monopoly of legitimate violence: the thesis put forward by Mann (1997) and Anderson (1992) is strong: after the Second World War, the end of armed conflicts between European nation-states enabled states to relax domestic coercion. No longer mobilized to the same extent by the imperatives of war or preparation for war, states have tended to let territorial differentiation processes simply unfold. They have allowed social and political actors greater autonomy. The development of post-militarist tendencies in relative terms—by comparison with the period 1850–1945, for example—has lessened coercion, leaving the field open for an end to the legitimate monopoly of violence and for the decline of what Mann calls 'hard politics': politics defined in terms of control and domination in a context of possible war. This, according to Anderson, was the prime logic giving rise to various dynamics of decentralization all over Europe. So what remains of states' independent capacity to protect their citizens? Even though states retain an essential security, order maintenance, and protection role, they have lost their autonomy. Interdependence in the areas of technology, information, and industrial systems renders the idea of conflict between European states obsolete. The 'third pillar' of European integration includes a security dimension. There are increasing signs that a power higher than the nation-state is in the making and is amassing elements of coercion, at various levels: the Schengen agreements, a hesitant start on the Europeanization of police forces (Bigo 1996), the appointment of Javier Solana in charge of the Common Security policy, integrated NATO operations, and the creation of a 'Eurocorps'. Armies have had to face radical reorganization. Boesne and Dandekker (1997) stress the impact of the professionalization of armies, changing objectives, uncertainties as to what constitutes a threat and who the enemy is, the growing number of joint actions—as well as their limitations—and the introduction of market mechanisms. The outcome of all this is that no single state can any longer ensure the protection of its citizens and that, in addition, the classic idea of the link between state and violence (Giddens 1987) may be less central. In terms of the classic concept of sovereignty, even if the reality was very

---

[7] It is also worth emphasizing two clear limits to this exercise. First, to make presentation easier, this approach largely follows the list of state characteristics given in the first section; but this analytical division blocks any attempt to take into account the interactions and dynamics between the developments being described, despite the fact that these are crucial. Second, this presentation aims to link together the changes at work, at least in the major European countries; yet this masks their essential differences on some points. Work on these linkages, which will need to be fairly systematic, has not been carried out as yet.

different (Badie 1999), the existence and increasing strength of focal areas of constraint, in competition with the state, render both the idea of the state's monopoly of violence and that of the state's sovereignty in Europe obsolete (Caporaso 1996).

Borders constitute a third, widely acknowledged point of disjunction (Ruggie 1993; Badie 1995). Borders have not disappeared from European states, but their importance has diminished or been transformed. Sociologists of globalization have pointed to the increased number of different flows: capital, telecommunications, tourism, pollution, ideas, knowledge, norms, immigrants, business, social movements (Held and McGrew 1993). This proliferation of flows jeopardizes the state's vision of control over its borders. Ethnic minority networks have their own logic, and many studies have shown that there continue to be exchanges with countries of origin, thus creating trans-national social spaces (Sassen 1998; Faist 1999; Cesari 1994). Cities are, of course, the places that function as initial entry points for these flows, so they face the destabilizing impact of any increases in immigration, for instance.

The European Union is playing a major role in the gradual erosion of national borders within the EU. From the start, the creation of the enlarged market was expressed in steady moves towards reduction of customs barriers and all types of impediment to the free movement of goods. The European Union also actively promotes the free movement of persons: for citizens of states that are signatories to the Schengen agreements, passport controls at borders are a thing of the past. The European Union also finances numerous exchange programmes to encourage mobility and to develop cooperation between trans-border regions: for instance the INTERREG programmes. Consequently, the state's control over a national territory enclosed within borders, incomplete as it may have been, is now less relevant.

Fourth, the state is also defined by a legal system. Even though the most positivist version of the legal state has always been, in part, a fiction (Chevallier 1994), it remains the case that the law constitutes one of the pillars of the state and represents a fundamental factor differentiating states. Here again, the challenge is fairly radical. First, for states inside the EU, a significant proportion of new legislation originates at the European level. The numerous conflicts between Commission and member states and the judgments of the European Court of Justice provide an account of this very strong dynamics of integrating Europe through law, norms, rules, and institutions (Weiler 1994; Stone Sweet 2000). Second, international agreements on human rights, nuclear disarmament, environmental issues, and trade represent an increasing source of norms and rules that are gradually being imposed on states, and constitute another point of disjunction for the legal state. Third, large firms, banks, and accountancy and auditing firms are a major source of norms, financial and accounting rules (Dezalay and Garth 1998), various different types of contract, and legal practices, including arbitration in disputes (Cutler 1997; Arnaud 1998). This dynamic, in which the area of civil law is party to globalization processes, creates a new *lex mercatoria*, recalling that of the medieval merchants, which redefines the boundaries between public and private—even within states—promotes exchanges through standardization of rules, and constitutes a kind of private, global system of governance. Countries with strong traditions of national public laws are finding this dynamic particularly destabilizing (Caillosse 1999).

Fifth, the differentiation of the state: for many years, literature in the sociology of organizations, public policies, governance, public policy networks, and state and administrative reform has stressed the fragmentation and differentiation of state scenarios, which have become splintered and incoherent (Rhodes 1997; Dupuy and Thoenig 1986; Dente 1990; Rouban 1998; Commaille and Jobert 1999). The state seems to be a series of interconnected agencies, organizations, flexible rules, and negotiations, where an increasing number of actors plays a part in public policy, in one way or another. The view of public policies as forward-moving and rational has been widely questioned. Public policy is often characterized by ad hoc or contingency arrangements, enmeshed networks, the blurring of boundaries between sectors, a proliferation of actors, various constraints, multiple aims, heterogeneity, cross-linking of issues, the coming together of heterogeneous actors, changing scales of reference territories, adjustments between contradictory social interests, and the increasing complexity of instruments for intervention. All this blurs the boundaries and suggests a crumbling state. The state's capacity to steer is called into question (Poncela and Lascoumes 1998). Public policies no longer inevitably obey political logics. Public policies—or, to be more precise, the social interests represented, the groups, networks, and organizations—have their own autonomy and now they, in their turn, are structuring politics. European integration processes are emphasizing centrifugal trends within states. The making of a European political space has created a movement towards the redistribution of authority: in relation to the European Court of Justice, for example. The process of European integration has considerably increased interdependence among states—or between segments of the state—and this has reinforced coordination problems, even though the existing fragmentation of states might have favoured the extension of EU powers (Dehousse 1996). The state has lost some of its centrality. This redistribution of authority—a mosaic or some kind of anarchy—does not necessarily simply lead to fragmentation. Power relations and hierarchies have not disappeared (Jobert 1999): they are realigning and redeploying. The proliferation of rules intensifies the state's difficulties in lending coherence to the whole.

Sixth, taxation and public investment: the power to levy taxes is also one of the bases of modern states and the motive force of the state's capacity for effective action. Appreciable changes are in motion. The state must take into account both top-down and bottom-up pressures. European integration processes have brought pressures towards fiscal harmonization. At the same time, research institutes, international organizations—which never hesitate to offer normative opinions criticizing 'the burden of the state' (OECD 2001)—and the press—the financial press especially—have produced numbers of studies that tend to act as a pressure on states. This has not placed formal constraints on states, but in practice exerts pressure that makes it difficult for them to maintain differences in taxation. The legitimacy of the state in this sphere is being undermined. Obviously, what is at stake in this taxation debate is the place of the state in society and the economy. The neo-liberal version of globalization and Europeanization actively contests the issues of redistribution, defining the common interest and delimiting the public sphere. In areas that are conventionally viewed as part of the state-financed, state-run public infrastructure—transport, roads and bridges, hospitals, schools and universities—constraints imposed on state resources—or, in some places, on the allocation of existing resources—have been used to justify the development of private forms of investment, such as the UK's Private Finance Initiatives for hospitals and schools or major infrastructures, with the support of the EU. In tandem with this anti-tax pressure, there is a new round of commodification of state intervention, with the same type of reasoning being applied to social insurance, health expenditure, and pensions (Palier and Bonnoli 2000).

Equally, there are bottom-up pressures. The restructuring of the state can also be explained by pressures from civil society and social actors, who no longer have the same trust in the state (Jobert 1999). Increased power of local and regional levels of government in Europe and decentralization of the management of scarcity, with the latter encouraged by the state, have most often been accompanied by transfers of resources, though not without conflicts and contrasting developments. Although the burden of the state, measured in terms of the share of GDP represented by mandatory deductions, shows only a marginal withdrawal of the state in Europe, except in the UK and the Netherlands, this does not mean that there is no significant challenge to the state's capacity to control and direct public investment. Regional and local authorities, especially cities, are now responsible for the greater part of public employment in Europe.

These figures naturally call for more detailed explanation. Centralized states have frequently retained tight control over local public investment by defining financial and legal parameters, such as *post hoc* capping sanctions in the UK. Broadly, however, local and regional authorities are responsible for between 50 per cent and 70 per cent of public investment in Europe. These indicators must be linked to figures on local taxation (see Chapter 7), but, in part, they illustrate a lower capacity for state intervention.

Seventh, the state and economy: the issue of the state's economic sovereignty has formed the subject of a huge literature, which has come to some contrasting conclusions (Cohen 1996). European states have retained a strong capacity for intervention in and regulation of the economy, but they

TABLE 3.2. *Local share of gross fixed capital formation in total GFCF for 1996 in Europe*

Country		Local GFCF as % of national GFCF	Local GFCF as % of GFCF in public services
Germany	*Länder*	2.2	20.5
	Municipalities	6.6	62.1
Austria	*Bundesländer*	1.6	13.8
	Municipalities	7.4	63.5
Belgium		4.0	58.9
Denmark		6.2	63.6
Spain		10.3*	59.3
Finland		8.6	50.9
France		12.6	71.8
Greece		n/a	n/a
Ireland		10.9*	80.1
Italy		8.8	66.9
Netherlands		10.1	74.2
Portugal		7.4**	47.9
United Kingdom		5.3	59.3
Sweden		10.2	54.2

*1995   **1992

Source: Ministère de l'Intérieur (1998).

have lost a significant part of their power. Economic globalization—notably, of financial markets and of firms—and dematerialization processes are leading to the 'disembeddedness' of the economy (Strange 1993; Castells 1996). However, this argument involves a number of clearly evident paradoxes and limitations (Hirst and Thomson 1999; Boyer and Drache 1996; Scott 1998) in relation, for instance, to how far the state is playing an active role in these processes, how far leading national firms have adapted to globalization, how important national innovation systems and organizations remain to firms (Whitley 1993), and the extent of non-internationalized exchanges and sectors (Storper 1997). Consequently, even if we avoid bowing to simplistic globalization ideology, we have to agree that, by comparison with the 1960s, states have lost a part of their capacity to direct and constrain economic actors, notably major firms, through rules and taxes. Large-scale movements towards economic deregulation, privatization, and transfers to the European level, as with central banks, have challenged the state's influence as an actively interventionist participant in the economy. Large firms now tend to obey other logics. Because of these changes of scale and because the largest firms have acquired greater influence, the economy is now somewhat less institutionalized. Although they seem to remain rooted in their national environment, large national firms are now being managed according to norms and constraints other than national planning, industrial peace, industrial policy, urban and regional policy, and the state's funding needs. European forms of capitalism have taken a certain neo-liberal turn, and shareholders and pension funds now play a much greater role than, for instance, employers and unions negotiating at the national level or local and regional political elites. Lastly, the European Union plays an increasingly central role in defining the rules of the economic game through trade agreements, environmental standards, competition policy, regional policy, and labour market regulation. In the final analysis, national regulation of the economy has been broadly undermined over the past 30 years (Crouch and Streeck 1996) because of the dynamics associated with large firms and with changes in the world economy.

This brief survey is oversimplified and, therefore, somewhat inadequate. Welfare state reforms, the issue of citizenship, and the way that the state chooses to structure domestic matters have not been addressed. However, drawing together the various different points made above, we can come to one fairly clear conclusion: the classic definition of the state in terms of 'hard politics'—that is, in terms of a monopoly of violence within the national territory—no longer corresponds to the reality of contemporary European states. The state has seen a major change: it has developed a strategic role that is a question not just of legitimacy but of the relationship of the state to the territory.[8]

The most systematic interpretation of the developments presented above is that of Marxist writers who stress the transformation of capitalism as the explanatory factor. They interpret state retreat, especially in the economic sphere, as the sign of a failure of the political and of social actors in the face of firms and of the dominant economic actors. The emergence of a European governance is a concrete expression of the replacement of governments by forms of governance that aim to adapt the state to capitalism. In the most interesting neo-Gramscian version of this argument, Bob Jessop has theorized this transformation of the state as being from the Keynesian national welfare state to the post-national Schumpeterian workfare state (Jessop 1994; 2000). This new state form is characteristic of Western countries and, he suggests, has the following objectives: (1) through supply-side policies, to promote innovation in terms of products, processes, organization, and markets in the globalized economies in order to reinforce a country's competitiveness; and (2) to subordinate social policies to requirements for labour market flexibility and to the constraints of international economic competition, especially 'welfare to work' policies intended to discipline the workforce (Peck 1996). Taking the effects of globalization processes on the state as the starting point of their

---

[8] '. . . everything is taking place as if territorial integration were no longer capable of its previous achievements and as if other forms of control, mobilization and association were being substituted for integration' (Badie 1995: 132). Postmodernist writers, such as Ruggie (1993), have suggested that we radically change our concept of the state to take account of this reality, in which states are partly detached from a national territory; they also point to the fragmentation of the state, its withdrawal from certain spheres, and the challenge to a whole set of stabilized, centralized social and political forces. This view of the postmodern state is also very evident in the works of legal scholars who no longer adhere to a positivist view of the law.

TABLE 3.3. *Fiscal revenue of EU member states and selected other states as percentage of GDP, 1965–1999*

Member state	1965	1975	1985	1995	1999
Sweden	35.0	43.4	48.3	47.6	52.1
Denmark	29.9	41.4	47.4	49.4	50.6
Finland	30.3	37.07	40.0	45.0	46.5
France	34.5	36.9	43.8	44.0	46.0
Belgium	31.3	41.6	46.3	44.8	45.4
Austria	33.9	37.7	41.6	41.5	44.3
Italy	25.5	26.2	34.4	41.2	43.0
Luxembourg	27.7	39.6	45.3	41.9	42.1
Netherlands	32.8	43.0	42.4	42.0	40.3
United Kingdom	30.4	35.4	37.7	35.2	36.6
Germany	31.6	36.0	32.9	38.2	37.7
Greece	18.2	21.0	28.6	31.7	37.1
Spain	14.7	19.5	27.6	32.8	35.1
Portugal	15.8	21.3	27.1	32.7	34.5
Ireland	24.9	30.2	35.1	33.1	31.9
EU average	29.1	33.4	36.8	39.4	40.7
USA	24.7	26.9	26.1	27.6	28.9*
Japan	18.3	20.9	27.6	28.4	27.7
Australia	22.4	26.6	29.1	29.4	29.9*

*1998

Source: OECD (2001: 188).

analyses, Strange (1993) and Cerny (1989) come to fairly similar conclusions. European states are becoming 'competitive states'. In a post-militarist European space, 'hard politics' is being replaced by the logic of economic competition, and the state, under the auspices of Europe, is reorganizing in this direction, taking economic competitiveness as its main priority. Cities used to be mobilized for war, sometimes even created for the purposes of war (Chapter 2). They are now mobilized in the name of economic competitiveness.

But this interpretation does not really meet the case, at least for the time being. Although European welfare states have reorganized, they have not gone very far in cutting tax revenues, except, to some extent, in the UK, Ireland, and the Netherlands.[9]

Most nation-states are also very actively revitalizing national education systems. In most European states, the population has certainly not espoused neo-liberal ideas. The logic of public policy is to intervene in the market through political decisions and bureaucratic logics rather than to correct market failures. Although existing redistributive mechanisms have generally remained in place and continue to have large-scale effects, they are no longer growing and, in most European countries, the political objective of

---

[9] Although comparative analyses such as Esping-Andersen's (1990) tend more to stress 'frozen welfare states in Europe', Palier and Bonoli (2000) have shown that the conditions for 'defrosting' are gradually being established.

reducing inequalities has now become secondary. In addition, there is an increasing number of regulatory agencies or authorities. The great waves of privatization in the 1980s and 1990s made it necessary to create new rules (Wright 1993) and regulatory authorities for, among other areas, telecommunications, energy, transport, water, and the media. Frequently with the encouragement of Brussels—a marker of the Europeanization of public policy—states have created national agencies that take over Brussels' areas of responsibility: for example, the environment, health, or food and drug standards. Here we come to the heart of what the transformation of states means. Are these new agencies a sign of the state's retreat in favour of experts, private interests, and associations, which could be interpreted in terms of 'governance versus government'? Or do these authorities reveal a transformation in modes of public policy, with greater efficiency on the part of state intervention and with modes of public policy leaving more room for procedures, for open public debate, for coalition-building, and for mobilization—a transformation that gives an equally central role to the political in creating new norms and directions?

The fluid power situation created by the European integration process should not be interpreted solely in terms of state retreat. The making of the European Union is still in part under the control of the member states (Moravscik 1999), and Prodi's Commission is facing hostile member states reluctant to deepen the integration process. In some areas, including regional policy, there is growing pressure towards returning control to the national level. Any idea of increasing the resources of the EU is abruptly set aside. European states have knowingly used the EU to reform their economies in the coal and steel sectors, their welfare states, or the state apparatus itself. States use a definition of Europe that acts as a system of constraint, justifying domestic reforms. Equally, however, the European integration process has its own institutional and political dynamics, which goes well beyond the states' control.

The state in Western Europe has to face the fact that intergovernmental networks have outstripped or bypassed it (Balme 1996). The state no longer has a monopoly in representing its citizens abroad, with both the EU and local authorities taking on part of this role. This is an essential point in any defence of the thesis that the state's grip is loosening. Local authorities and pressure groups that are marginal in the national political system have found that the European political space in the making offers them the possibility of organizing trans-nationally and at the European level. The field is open, therefore, and actors have more autonomy and more opportunities. Yet this is equally true of the state and its elites, notably its administrative elites. This open field, along with the loosening of constraints, also gives the state apparatus—and especially the upper echelons of its civil service—the opportunity to regain certain areas of autonomy in regard to organized interests, cities, or the most disadvantaged groups and territories. Distance has become a resource for higher levels of authority. The EU enables state elites to distance themselves from a given subject, to opt for a non-decision, or to avoid responsibilities. To a certain extent, in the economic, energy, banking, and urban and regional policy fields political and administrative elites have swapped a system of national—political—constraints for a European one. Their whole game lies in stressing this distancing from national social and political constraints and in minimizing or controlling the effects of constraints created by Brussels. In the area of urban or regional policies, the EU has given a new role to the apparatus of the central state; but, because of the way cities and regions are organized by Brussels, the game is a complicated one and unstable over time.

The Europeanization of Cities Illustrates the Dynamics of Overlapping Powers and the Making of Europe as a Polity

As a result of the institutionalization of Europe, the category 'European city' makes greater political sense. European public policies, rules, procedures, conflict-solving mechanisms, debates, and norms are now relevant to all cities within the EU. Europeanization processes provide a new structure of opportunities for cities and incentives to engage with other actors to promote their spatial or sectoral interests through both vertical and horizontal networks. But they also represent a new structure of constraints, of rules which limit their autonomy and overlap with national or regional institutions. The EU therefore sets new parameters within which urban governance modes may be organized and are encouraged.

Keating (1998: 185) has shown in detail the importance of the EU in structuring the 'new territorial politics' in Western Europe, within and beyond the state: 'The new territorial politics is focused less on territorial management and national integration, and more on territorial competition, within national arenas but also within Europe and the wider market.' Many arguments in this section apply to both regions and cities, but the main focus here is on cities.

From a political and institutional standpoint, the institutionalization of Europe is the main factor creating a different sort of polity in Europe, a different frame of opportunities and constraints for political entrepreneurs in cities and regions, which have the chance—if they want to take it—to operate beyond the limits of national centre-periphery relations. At that level, the argument makes sense for all sub-national entities; but because EU programmes have been organized in terms of regional policy and because of the dynamics of regional movements and identities since the 1960s, most of the arguments up to now have been based on regions.

Europeanization

Europeanization processes have potentially very destabilizing effects on cities. At first, Europe represented an international stage for cities and their elected representatives; it gave a form of recognition, a new political legitimacy for representing citizens beyond the state's borders, with possibilities for integrating horizontal and vertical networks and bypassing the state, and with access to new resources: in other words, new room for manoeuvre and new opportunities for political entrepreneurs. Europe seemed to represent modernization, the culture of a new generation of elected representatives. The second stage saw the constraining, destabilizing effects of this European governance come fully to light. The criteria that have to be observed in order to obtain funding seem even more rigid and strict than those pertaining to national programmes. Behind flexible networks and forms of interdependence lie complex rules, the difficulty of exerting pressure on choices, and the constraints of coalitions and networks. Elected representatives have finally discovered the limits of their activities: norms that seem to have come upon them like a bolt from the blue. Thus, the European integration dynamic has a destabilizing effect because of the uncertainties associated with it.

New opportunities, constraints, and uncertainties form a background which alter the traditional conditions of urban societies and local governments. This does not determine the way cities are changing, but it does contribute to shaping the environment under which modes of governance are likely to emerge.

Europeanization and globalization processes are intimately connected with the local, and are fed at local levels. Cities, regions, and states all take part in these processes. Assessing the speed and impact of these changes is very important, yet it is also difficult, and so attempts up now have been rather limited (Bartolini 1998). Until recently, the term 'Europeanization' described any change that was in any way related to European integration. Useful descriptions of European organizations, with the indispensable addition of detailed empirical studies of structures—parties, central civil services, and parliaments—and public policies, form a sizeable literature on Europeanization, brought into perspective by the debate about explanations of the development of the EU. Since the Treaty of Amsterdam and the introduction of the single currency, the research agenda has developed in such a way as to highlight Europeanization mechanisms and processes: in other words, the theoretical framework has been consolidated to explain change and resistance at different levels and in different sectors.[10] Radaelli (2000: 2) defines Europeanization as 'a set of processes through which the EU political, social and economic dynamics become part of the logic of domestic

[10] Hassenteufel and Surel (2000), Radaelli (2000), as well as the following collaborative projects: Héritier (1999); Stone Sweet, Sandholz, and Fligstein (2001); Green-Cowles, Caporaso, and Risse (2001); and Hix and Goetz (2000).

discourse, identities, political structures and public policies'. Europeanization does not mean convergence or harmonization. Not all local authorities in Europe have fallen into line overnight with injunctions from Brussels to follow the norms, policies, and modes of organization that Brussels wants. In fact, putting the emphasis on processes stresses that changes are the outcome of varied mechanisms, and that resistance makes as much sense as adaptation. Europeanization processes affect individuals, organizations, and institutions within cities, which may adapt, resist, or change (Goldsmith and Klausen 1997).

Powell and Di Maggio's (1991) analysis of mechanisms of institutional change in terms of coercive, mimetic, and normative isomorphism is useful here. In their analysis of the homogenization process of large American organizations, they define the concept of isomorphism as

a constraining process that forces one unit of the population [of organisations] to resemble other units that face the same set of environmental conditions . . . Organisations compete not just for resources and customers, but for political power and institutional legitimacy, for social as well as economic fitness . . . Coercive iso-morphism stems from political influence and the problem of legitimacy. It results from both formal and informal pressures exerted on organisations by other organisations upon which they are dependent and by cultural expectations in the society within which organisations function. Mimetic isomorphism results from standard response to uncertainties, a powerful force that encourages imitation . . . A third source of isomorphic organisational change is normative and stems primarily from professionalisation. (1991: 66 ff.)

Cities are changing, within the frame of Europeanization processes, in response to the constraints and policies of the European Union—coercive isomorphism—of mimetism, and, to a lesser extent, of normative isomorphism, with the latter involving the role of professional networks, consultants, and consultant-driven models.

For cities—and for regions—the making of the European Union represents a significant political opening. All of a sudden, the old opposition between state and cities, between centres and peripheries, has become one dimension among others, although still a major one. The political playing field has seen changes of scale and a proliferation of new players; above all, no player any longer possesses a monopoly of rule-production or of coercion. This factor is almost automatically transforming hierarchical relations between levels.

This opening of the field offers new potential for local and regional authorities: lodging appeals against state decisions through the European Court of Justice, organizing lobbying in Brussels to influence decisions and policies, acquiring resources and expertise independently of the state, developing horizontal trans-national relationships with other local authorities, getting deeply involved in various networks for certain policies, claiming to repres-ent and defend the interests of their citizens, and questioning the state's formulation of the common interest. In the pattern of institutionalization presented above, the more the EU—and, in particular, certain of its policies —becomes institutionalized, the more the actors tend to react by organizing to contest and defend their interests; and, in doing so, they contribute to the production of new rules that foster the institutionalization dynamic (Stone Sweet, Sandholz, and Fligstein 2001). This fundamental trend within the European context grows stronger with globalization.

Thus, cities and regions are becoming sites of sustained geographical reshaping, even though they used to be fixed points for subjections to sovereignty. This ebb and flow is allowing the local to sketch out multiple, overlapping communities of responsibility. In these conditions, any local authority will tend towards a twofold challenge to the principle of sovereignty: it will loosen the constraints of hierarchy in order to promote responsible behaviour on the part of its citizens, and it will become active in a set of regions and trans-national spaces that is itself constantly becoming more complex.

A Growing Role Within Regional Policy

The example of Structural Funds policy perfectly illustrates this dynamic. Although it was introduced to support the transition of regions integrating into the enlarged market from a relatively backward economic position, in southern Europe, or at risk of suffering from competition, this policy was implemented in such a way that it protected dominant economic interests in the disadvantaged regions and, in particular, in the cities.[11]

In the late 1980s, Jacques Delors, then President of the European Commission, set in motion a dynamic towards recognizing local and regional authorities as actors in the European polity. With the entry of Spain, Greece, and Portugal to the European Community, the Commission, under Delors, developed an ambitious regional policy. This began as one of the social compensations for the implementation of the enlarged market, laid down in the context of the Maastricht Treaty, and it went on to generate the mixed outcomes that we are familiar with. As usual, the Commission organized numerous consultation exercises, aiming to make local and regional authorities into partners in European governance, to bypass the nation-states, to mobilize coalitions for the Commission's projects, and to increase the legitimacy of the European integration project in the eyes of its citizens. This 'Delors dynamic' for integrating local and regional authorities has taken different forms, but we can pick out from the generally confused picture: the Mediterranean integrated programmes (1985), the creation of the Committee of the Regions as a consultative body to the Commission—something which at that

[11] McAleavey and de Rynck (1997); Davezies (1998*b*).

time appeared to supporters of the Europe of the Regions to be a major innovation—the two-pronged reform of the Structural Funds, the introduction of
the principle of subsidiarity into treaties (Faure 1997), the funding of trans-
national networks (Article 10 of the Structural Funds; the Community
Initiatives programmes), the development of indicators, and the commissioning
of studies.[12] This sphere of European public policy has become institutionalized: budgets have increased and norms, categories, and rules have developed,
producing, in their turn, conflicts of interpretation with member states, with
DG Competition—that is, the body in charge of competition policy—and with
cities and regions, which have led to the production of more precise rules
and norms and to the formal involvement of an increasing number of different actors.

The development of Structural Funds policy and related principles contributed to establishing a discourse on the making of the Europe of the Regions
and, a little later, on the Europe of Cities. Consequently, the Delors Commission recognized regions and cities as political actors, fully integrated
within European governance. The Commission thus legitimized regions and
cities attempting to establish their role within national political systems
(Hooghe 1996). It also provided significant funding for regions in the south
of Europe and in Ireland, and cities within them benefited from it. Taking this line was a smart move on the Commission's part, since the more it
legitimizes these cities and regions, the more they recognize the Commission's legitimacy. Almost independently of existing—strongly contrasting—
political realities, therefore, the Commission has created a pressure on—or,
at least, has encouraged—cities and regions to become political actors in Europe.
The institutionalization of local and regional government representation
within the Committee of the Regions has strengthened this movement.

Regional policy offered the first opportunity to put these discourses into
practice. Well-understood interests and questions of legitimacy are two powerful forces driving regional and local authorities to organize their own direct
access to Brussels. Despite the sometimes appalled reactions of certain
nation-states, various regions and local authorities have now opened offices
in Brussels on a grand scale. British cities and counties, marginalized in their
own country, who have been major beneficiaries of Structural Funds for industrial conversion were among the swiftest to organize (John 1994), as were
the large regions. Birmingham—from 1984—Catalonia, and the German
Länder were quickest off the mark. A decade later, everyone—or almost
everyone—is on the bandwagon (Goldsmith and Klausen 1997). Italian local
authorities and those in small centralized countries have been among the last
to join the movement (Ercole 1997), while the Scandinavians were mobilizing on a large scale as part of their preparations for integration into the

---

[12] There is an extensive literature on this dynamic. See, in particular, A. Smith (1995),
Hooghe and Keating (1995), Hooghe (1996; 1999), and Heinelt and Smith (1996).

European Union.[13] At the same time, Commission officials systematically visit European cities and regions to prepare Structural Fund programmes or White Papers on transport, the environment, and the cities.

Thus, since the late 1980s, the urban question has found a place within a formerly reticent DG XVI, now DG Regio, in charge of regional policy. Without going into detail about the confusion surrounding all this, we should note the following factors: consultations by Jacques Delors' forecasting unit; the influence of Commissioner Bruce Millan, from the Glasgow Labour Party, who was particularly sensitive to issues of the decline of European industrial cities; the Committee of the Regions; the interest of the Environment DG;[14] the pressure from those large northern member states that are fairly favourable to urban programmes, which enable them to maximize the funding they can get from Structural Funds; the dynamics of British, Dutch, and French urban policies—City Challenge programmes and *Contrats de villes* went on to form the basis of the URBAN Programme; pressures from the European Parliament after 1992; the impact of studies commissioned by DG XVI, notably 'Urbanization and functioning of cities in the European Community' (1992), taken up again in the document 'Europe 2000 Plus'; the dissemination of the results of pilot or experimental programmes—Urban Pilot Projects, *'Quartiers en crise'*; the UN Conference on Sustainable Human Settlement Development in an Urbanizing World—Habitat II; the opportunity offered by the end of Poverty 3, which was not renewed; as well as effective lobbying by transnational networks of cities, notably Eurocities (Salone 1997), which relies on political and academic entrepreneurs.

An urban coalition has gradually organized, finding intermediaries among Commissioners, member state representatives to the Commission, and in the Parliament. Despite DG XVI's reservations, German hostility, and early expressions of reservations by southern member states, the URBAN Programme for the renewal of urban neighbourhoods has been launched. The Commission also produced in 1997 a document titled 'Europe's cities, community measures in urban areas', which has strengthened this dynamic. URBAN is a Community Initiatives programme. The first phase included a budget of 880 million ecus for 110 cities, including depressed neighbourhoods. The URBAN programme has as its objectives: promoting local employment, revitalizing depressed neighbourhoods both socially and economically, providing social

---

[13] These lobbying offices often consist of two people, but large regions such as Wales, Catalonia, or Bavaria can easily employ 20. The offices play a role in relaying information on European policies for their sponsor, lobbying within the Commission, taking part in various networks, and sometimes negotiating with the Commission. These local authority lobbies form only a small proportion of some 15,000 people working in the Brussels lobbies (Mazey and Richardson 2001). See Mazey and Richardson (1993), John (1994), and Greenwood (1997) on the workings of the lobbies and their integration into the workings of the European Union.

[14] CEC (1990).

and other services, improving living conditions and the urban environment and public spaces, and improving local strategies and decision-making processes so as to involve local communities. A second phase is now on the way:

In the context of the Structural Funds reform envisaged for the new funding round, this urban coalition, through a small group within DG XVI, launched an increasing number of initiatives. The 1997–9 phase was characterized by competition between different cognitive frames of reference, aiming to define not only the issues at stake for cities but also the public policy priorities and, therefore, ultimately, the funding priorities. One example was the way in which the Germans and Scandinavians put forward environmental issues, while DG XI (Environment) was also stressing sustainable development and Agenda 21. The British promoted issues of economic competitiveness, efficiency, democracy, citizen choice, and service management, in line with the policies of Conservative governments.[15] The French preferred to promote social themes, more in line with their urban policy. The Commission then put out a paper titled 'Towards a European Urban Agenda' (1997) and later issued the 'Agenda 2000' document, which proposed the reorganization of the Structural Funds. In this, the Commission reaffirmed the importance of cities, including in terms of legitimacy—cities as close to citizens, and as actors in the success of European policies—as well as the principles for action enshrined in the treaties or promoted through policies: subsidiarity, partnership, social cohesion and economic efficiency, sustainable development, and strengthening the local capacity to act. The most important point to be established was the promotion of the transverse urban dimension within all European policies, including economic and social cohesion policy.

All this was the subject of debate, notably in the setting of the Vienna European Urban Forum (May *et al.* 1998). This forum provided the chance for urban policy actors, including many city mayors, and Commission representatives to engage in direct dialogue about the European urban agenda. All the themes of urban policy were discussed: the environment, quality of life and sustainable development, social exclusion, economic competitiveness, transport and European networks,[16] housing, partnership approaches, the application of new technologies to renewing the built environment, and issues of health, culture, governance, and trans-national cooperation.

Next in line were the 'Agenda 2000' discussion and the agreement made at the Berlin summit. Although the document stimulated broad discussion, the chief decisions were, finally, to freeze the Structural Funds, except for some money made available to countries negotiating entry to the EU, and an organizational change that slightly reduced the population covered. The urban lobby proved to be very active throughout the debate, with, for instance, strong

---

[15] See Clarke (1997) and other papers presented to the EU conference hosted by the Dutch presidency in Rotterdam, 28–30 May 1997.
[16] See debates at the European Urban Forum in Vienna, 27–28 November 1998.

support expressed within the European Parliament. The Commission was to start URBAN II, and the 'urban priority' element of the Structural Funds was strengthened.

However, great uncertainty surrounds this policy area, and it would be misleading to tell a story of straightforward institutionalization. Within the context of enlargement and frozen resources for regional policy, it has become quite obvious that the delayed reform of Structural Funds will become a major issue in the next two years, and should lead to a transfer of funds towards new member states. With Santer, and then Prodi, at the head of the Commission, the Delors dynamics of associating cities and regions with the making of Europe has been in decline. Over the past few years, member states have monitored the Commission closely, and prevented most clear moves towards European integration. In different policy areas, including agriculture and regional policy, some member states—most notably Germany—are advocating a return to control at the national level. These debates, like the document on the governance of the European Union commissioned by Prodi, reveal the extent of the mobilization of the German *Länder* and of autonomous communities in Belgium and Spain to prevent further moves that might undermine their autonomy. German *Länder* in particular have powerfully opposed the development of an urban anti-poverty policy, alongside member states who are less keen to finance regional policy if they will no longer benefit. As a minor part of regional policy, therefore, urban policy is not secure, despite the institutionalization and professionalization of urban interests in Brussels. These mobilize and support minor EU initiatives, such as the Urban Audit, which aims to collect and standardize statistics on European cities. They are also active in voicing the interests of cities within other policy areas.

Coping with New Rules and Norms

These urban policy initiatives are only one of the elements of European public policy to have had a direct impact on cities. Although at first seduced by the new political horizons of the European Union, local authorities have gradually learned that EU institutionalization is accompanied by a new set of constraints.

Partnership provides one instance of these norms. In the European context, 'partnership' conventionally refers either to the relationship between the Commission and the different levels of representative government—the French variant—or to the relationship between 'the social partners', including employers' and trade union organizations, within the Economic and Social Committee—the German variant, later relating to other north European member states as well, and drawing on their corporatist heritage. With the 1998 reform of the Structural Funds on the one hand (DG XVI) and anti-poverty programmes on the other (DG V), partnership became a key concept in European politics, a normative framework which was to become progressively more of a constraint (Hooghe 1996; Benington and Geddes 2001). The notion of partnership has become the organizing principle of the Structural Fund programmes. The European Parliament took it up in 1997 in relation to the creation of territorial employment pacts. This EU variant of 'partnership' refers to a broad local alliance between public authorities, private organizations, 'the social partners', and the population. It has been expressed in many different ways in different European countries (A. Smith 1995); but participation is always organized around two dimensions: different levels of government, and organizations outside the public authorities, including 'the social partners' and representatives of minority groups. This second dimension of partnership did not make much sense in countries such as France, given the role of politics and the leadership of public policy by mayors and state representatives, or in the small centralized northern countries. More than one writer has seen the mark of state retreat on this partnership and has suspected the Commission of taking up British neo-liberal social policies: not an unfounded suspicion. As the years have gone by, the Commission has increasingly required this principle to be taken into account in getting joint funding from Europe and in assessment procedures. Member states who have not taken the rules seriously or who have not been able to implement them, such as Italy, have found that failure to comply with this principle has cost them dear. Whether they like it or not, all the public authorities involved in European programmes such as LEADER, URBAN, Poverty 3, NOW, INTERREG, and now the Employment Strategy (Jouen 2000) have had to learn the rhetoric of partnership and the management and assessment rules that go with it. This has not been achieved without tensions and disputes—often well-founded—about a European norm which, over time, has become a precise, rigid rule, bureaucratically cumbersome to set up and with clarification often arriving only at the end of the implementation process. For its part, the Commission is absolutely delighted to have compelled member states to provide evidence of innovation in these areas (Benington and Geddes 2001; Laino and Padovani 2000). The Commission-sponsored push to define indicators for generalized benchmarking has increased the effort involved in rationalization and the related constraints.

Other strong constraints have also developed, for example in relation to the environment. Gradually, the Commission and the environmental protection associations, major pollution treatment firms in the urban services sector, some local authorities, consumer defence groups, and representatives of member states have developed new air quality and waste treatment standards in Brussels (Lenschow 1999). Following these through, observation tools, observatories, and benchmarking tools to categorize countries or cities have been developed, specifying precise time limits for implementing some of these operations. Many elected representatives must now commit themselves to sizeable investments in order to meet these new standards.

The institutionalization of the European Union also implies that rules will place limits on potential urban governments action. For example, the forms of aid that local authorities can give firms are now very severely limited (Wishdale 1998). Until the mid-1980s, regulation of aid to firms seemed to be the poor relation of competition policy under DG IV (Cini and McGowan 1998), but since then successive Commissioners have accelerated the neo-liberal trend in this sphere. After many conflicts with member states, firms, local authorities, and even DG XVI, DG Competition was successful in imposing very strict limits, including for small and medium enterprises (SME's), through the impetus given by Commissioners Leon Brittan and Karel van Miert, well supported by the European Court of Justice. Mayors suddenly discovered that European rules could limit their activities just as effectively as the state, if not more so . . . and that room for political negotiation within the system was more limited for local authorities. In a similar vein, the rules concerning public markets and conditions for invitations to tender have destabilized local authorities, especially cities, because they challenge both existing rules and the close ties of certain service providers to the financing of political life in Italy, Belgium, and France. Other policies have indirect effects, such as the deregulation of telecommunications and—tough this is more limited at the moment—of road and rail transport, as well as of gas and electricity. In various policy areas, the development of rules inevitably impacts on cities in one way or another: the new White Paper on transport, the procurement rules, energy policy, and the debate about the definition of public services, to mention just a few current issues, have a direct impact on cities whether they like it or not.

Horizontal Interactions through Transnational Networks of Local Authorities

Beyond top-down programmes and rules—that is, largely coercive and normative institutionalization—the increased density of trans-national relations and networks among social and political actors is a key indicator of the institutionalization of Europe at levels beyond and below nation-states. Indeed, as far as cities and regions are concerned, hundreds of horizontal networks have now spread all over the EU, nearly always related in one way or another to EU programmes and incentives. For some time now, interactions between individuals and groups have been routinely organized within networks of cities from different member states (Bache, Georges, and Rhodes 1996; Benington and Harvey 1999).

These trans-national networks of local authorities are not new in Europe. Vion (2001) has traced the history of networks since at least the beginning of the twentieth century. Municipal reform movements were very dynamic before and after the First World War (Saunier 2000), involving European cities in close dialogue with US cities. Twinning agreements went through a golden period in the aftermath of the Second World War, linking German cities and towns with the rest of Europe, and before the cold war, linking western to eastern European towns and cities. The focus was very much on cultural exchanges, day-to-day life, associations, and peace-related issues. Scandinavian towns also have a long tradition of mutual cooperation. The Council of European Communes and Regions was created in the 1950s, reflecting all this dynamism.

The institutionalization of the EU has provided a new impetus and focus for trans-national networks of local and regional authorities: cities in particular, because they have more resources. In most countries, despite resistance from nation-states, especially the most centralized ones, local authorities—especially regions—have developed political and economic relations with other regions in the EU, a dynamic that is demonstrated by the INTERREG programme. Treaties are now being signed between autonomous communities. To the great surprise of both the UK and France, the *Conseil Général* of the *département* of Seine Maritime, similar to a County Council, has bought Newhaven Harbour in order to develop the maritime connection between Dieppe and Newhaven, with the blessing and under the formal auspices of the EU. Plans for cooperation are spreading across border areas everywhere, even though their impact is limited so far.

Originally, trans-national networks of local authorities were often based on sectoral issues (Benington and Harvey 1999): mining towns—the Coalfields Communities Campaigns—ports, or cities with aerospace, fashion, defence, ceramics, textiles, or shipbuilding industries. The diverse range of interests represented has now extended to cities with historical walls or towers. Specific networks of cities and regions have also organized to represent their own collective interests, such as the Conference of Peripheral Maritime Regions (CRPM), the Atlantic Arc, the *Club des Eurométropoles*, the network of medium-sized towns, the association of cities with an industrial tradition (RETI), or Eurocities.

Eurocities has gone from six founder members in 1986—Birmingham, Barcelona, Lyons, Milan, Frankfurt, and Rotterdam—to a hundred or so members—all cities with populations over 250,000—with an office staff of about 15 people in Brussels, closely linked to experts such as EURICUR in Rotterdam, the Dortmund Town Planning Institute, the Turin Polytechnic, or the European Institute for Urban Affairs in Liverpool. Eurocities' objectives are defined in terms of active lobbying within the European Union—in other words, ensuring that the problems of large cities are taken into account transversely in European public policies—and of developing ways to exchange experiences and expertise within the network. Among other things, Eurocities has played an important role in defining the URBAN programme as well as in developing the Commission's 'Urban Audit' pilot scheme and in developing statistical indicators that may contribute to forms of benchmarking. Some of these networks have been funded under the various Community Initiatives programmes at the Commission's instigation, or under the RECITE Programme for regions and cities in Europe (1991). The latter has expressly encouraged the formation and development of multiple networks in order to share the advantages of information and representatives who can be mobilized within coalitions, and thus to promote the European integration process through trans-national interactions.

Benington and Harvey (1999) suggest differentiating a third type, that of thematic networks organized around particular European Union programmes: LEDA, LEADER, ELAINE (ethnic relations), 'Urban neighbourhoods in crisis', the European Anti-Poverty Network, and URBAN. These trans-national networks often involve different types of actors, and cities are members alongside others.

Even though it is not a complete list, this catalogue highlights the proliferation of organized networks within European governance, as well as the increasing number of points of access to the EU for cities who want it. Without taking a purely functionalist view, it is true that these trans-national networks are an indicator that cities are involved in a web of very varied, horizontal forms of interdependence. These trans-national networks are privileged sites for obtaining information, exchanging experiences, ideas, and knowledge of various kinds, and challenging European programmes or states: therefore, they are also places for learning policy norms and styles. Individuals within organizations in cities very often mention the importance of these networks in 'learning Europe', that is, not only understanding the dynamics of policy-making at the EU level, or how to obtain funds, but also making sense of new repertoires and norms, understanding the logic and uncertainty associated with some programmes, understanding the dynamics of coalition-building and the diversity of interests represented within the EU, and, not least, understanding profoundly different institutional settings.

One difficulty is to interpret the impact of these networks. Mimetic institutionalization is evidently taking place: social and political actors within cities learn from each other, and both behavioural norms and norms for implementing EU programmes emerge. There are also fairly clear impacts on the organizational structure of urban governments: no 'European city' could now join a European network without some access to Brussels for lobbying and some kind of 'European Unit' operating within the council itself. All over Europe, local authority managers are learning and building a kind of new urban management culture. Magnier (2001) argues that a diffuse version of public management is gaining ground in most urban local authorities, a construction which takes place mainly within trans-national networks of professionals and cities: an example of normative isomorphism.

These trans-national networks of cities are only one piece within the jigsaw of European governance. They have serious limitations in terms of steering, of reaching constraining decisions, and of accountability. Most of them are de facto related to some kind of EU funding, in particular when associations and voluntary sector organizations are involved (Benington and Harvey 1999). The participation of social actors beyond the urban political elites and their bureaucracies is not often sustained over time (Fisher 2001). The institutionalization of these trans-national network tends to favour cities because they have the bureaucracy to sustain the exchanges over time, to provide goals, and to commit resources. Vion (2001) argues that trans-national networks of local authorities—including twinning links, which are becoming less popular—have undergone a profound transformation. Once enshrined within the post-war ideals of peace and cultural exchange, they are now oriented toward the construction of the EU and economic development. Once easygoing social occasions, they have become subject to the rationale of auditing and evaluation. Once supported by local associations, they now mainly concern economic and political interests: hence the marginalization of social actors. In other words, Vion argues that these networks used to reflect a Europe of communities embedded within their nation-states, where political and economic concerns were marginal. They now reflect a Europe within which political and economic entrepreneurs try to promote cities in Europe in order to gain in terms of both power and economic development.

Last but not least, their structuring impact is often limited, since trans-national networks reflect existing power structures and hierarchies. Although they bring some fluidity to these, they do not replace them.

Conclusion

The European integration process has taken the form of a vast movement of redistribution of authority. We can agree with Poggi (1996) that the reshaping of the state along the lines I have sketched out above seems to mark the beginning of 'a new phase of the state story' and perhaps, as an indirect outcome, the end of a cycle for the state. This cycle began in the second half of the nineteenth century and was marked by the structuring of the state and its growth, which seemed to be unlimited. In this context, cities, whatever the room for manoeuvre in their particular contexts, found themselves operating within the centre-periphery paradigm, within hierarchies and national policies, in a political space dominated by the nation-state. This is no longer the case. Closely interconnected processes of reshaping the state and Europeanization are rendering this view of things obsolete. Cities and regions, even with Brussels' support, are not on the way to replacing the state. However, the central state's grip has been loosened, and Europe is witnessing increasingly unstable intergovernmental relations, with the cooperation-competition model accompanied by the creation of networks. This reshaping of the state should not be confused with a weakening of the state. Retreat may actually allow state elites—finance ministries naturally spring to mind

—to pursue their main objectives, and to impose changes by acting on the various levels of government. Most central governments have been able to make use of 'the constraints of Europe', which they have been active in developing, in order to impose reforms on national social actors. Conversely, many decentralization reforms have allowed central governments to 'decentralize penury' (Mény and Wright 1985), giving sub-national governments the responsibility of managing scarcity and painful restructuring.

The emphasis placed on forms of interdependence, the flexibility of interdependence, and the minimal impact of hierarchies in multi-level European governance contrasts with the logic of a state mobilized for war, coercion, and hierarchies. This period of redistribution of authority, favouring the autonomy of cities, has been matched by a period of peace and relative economic prosperity in Europe. One can easily imagine that a war involving either European nation-states or the European Union would soon challenge the political and economic dynamics that favour cities. Another hypothesis is that the consolidation of the European Union into a form closer to the classic centralized state would have a similar effect, putting an end to the relative autonomy of cities. In other words, the current situation is an historical interlude whose duration is uncertain.

This situation, in which the redistribution of authority is linked to apparent Europeanization processes, involves dynamics that have implications for cities. Public policy changes in the direction of contractual relations, negotiation, assessment, and monitoring provide good illustrations of these concerns. Public policy that alters the parameters of the institutions within which the actors must act autonomously leads not to retreat on the part of higher authorities but to a transformation in forms of coercion. The introduction of a logic with varying quasi-market or contract rules, whether by the state or by the European Union, weakens the actors, making them dependent and reactive within broad principles. What is more, the public policy norms and models driven either by the Commission or from within trans-national networks do not easily combine with either existing modes or the vertical logics within states. Cities, and actors within them, have to face this complexity: they must play the European game when it is required—for instance, for funding from a European programme—or operate within a network; but they will also comply with the rules of the more classic national game, in which the financial stakes are usually higher and there is, obviously, more deep-rooted institutionalization.

Cities have become more or less involved in this European institutionalization dynamic. Their representatives have learned new roles, repertoires, and modes of action, and have found legitimacy on this larger playing field, which has increased their room for manoeuvre in relation to the state. They also learn how to obtain funds, from small sums for innovative programmes to very large sums for industrial cities in crisis in poor regions. Following Weber and Hirschman, Bartolini (1998: 9) insists that the form of the modern state, 'the case in which a strongly differentiated internal hierarchical order manages to control the external territorial and functional boundaries—and to correspondingly reduce exit options—so closely as to insulate domestic structuring processes from external influence . . . is simply the contingent historical result of a specific configuration'. Apart from the most clear-cut cases of exit—that is, secession—Europeanization offers cities a relative capacity to escape the constraints and hierarchies of the national political system—that is, partial exit. There is an almost automatic risk that engagement in challenging this national order will decrease. The state's capacity to structure its territory is being questioned. However, no local authority can really completely escape the national territory, although there are some exceptional cases. As Bartolini reminds us, looking at the areas that interest us, capacities for exit are shared very unequally between cities and regions. Cities and regions that have the most interest in and capacities for escaping the constraints of the system represent the greatest potential threat to the state's authority; they may therefore gain additional capacities to influence changes in the balance of power and the system in favour of the simple fact of having potential possibilities for exit, however limited. Emphasizing internal political structuring processes, linked with the formation of boundaries political, economic, and cultural, may create a fertile setting for us to better understand the dynamics of Europeanization and their consequences for cities.

For urban governments, the European Union represents a powerful agent for opening up access and for internationalization (Goldsmith 1992). European cities have Europeanized to a greater or lesser extent. This chapter stresses the various dimensions of this that need to be taken into account: organizations, representations, and forms of interdependence, for example. Although they have not been treated exhaustively, processes of change were highlighted that are, in a general sense, moving in this direction: the role of coercion—coercive isomorphism—linked to European rules, to funding, and to public policies, and the role of mimetism and competition, in membership of multiple networks, for example, which enable cities to learn norms and rules and to position themselves strategically. European governance is presented as a playing field on which the actors are permanently involved in the logics of cooperation and interdependence, as well as of political cooperation. This does not in any way signal a homogeneous movement or an orderly progress of cities along the primrose path of Europeanization. In their comparison of the level of Europeanization in local authorities in several European countries in the mid-1990s, Goldsmith and Klausen (1997) have in fact concluded that the pathways followed are not only an important factor but also extraordinarily heterogeneous. These findings echo the institutional dynamics within member states. As I have argued before (Le Galès 1998), there is no such thing as a Europe of regions or cities in the making; instead, we have a 'variable-geometry' Europe within which cities and regions sometimes becomes actors or systems of action. The EU is also being built from below, by social and political actors in regions and cities: constructing, resisting, fighting, and adapting to new rules, opportunities, and constraints.

The reshaping of the state and European integration are creating strong pressures on cities, combining financial and political incentives. Faced with changes of scale, cities are at times unable to change anything and can mount only marginal resistance in the face of legal changes. In the context of the constraints and opportunities, actors within cities have a strong incentive to develop their own strategies with different actors: indeed, these are conditions that have become necessary for most European funding. The European Union seems to be saying to cities 'opportunities exist—seize them' and, at the same time, 'heaven [that is, the EU] helps those who help themselves'. As much through the discourses and representations that they drive forward as through public policies, the EU and, to a lesser extent, states are pushing cities to become actors of European governance at the risk of losing out in terms of economic and social cohesion and of privileged access to national resources, not to speak of the risk of marginalization in the European space.

States have retained influence and considerable resources as well as capacities for control, but their effective room for manoeuvre has been reduced under the burden of pressures from Europe, from local and regional authorities, from financial markets, and from the interests of the most privileged social groups.

FOUR

European Cities: A More Diverse but Robust Social Structure Within Eroding National Societies

O VER centuries, European societies have come to be structured as national societies, within which cities were mostly organized in relation to the national social structure. Classes and social relations were less specifically urban, and the European city lost its social originality (Saunders 1979). The category of 'European city' did not make sense any more, as, despite some similarities, each nation-state followed its own path. This process, although never fully completed, reached its peak during the decades following the Second World War.

Classically, the concept of society is taken to refer to three ideas: of intensity of relations between individuals and groups, of capacity and autonomy, and, finally, of territory. A society may be defined as a human grouping characterized by culture, institutions, values, and ideas. In Western Europe, 'the abstract idea of society cannot be separated from the concrete reality of national society, since it is defined as a network of institutions, controls, and education, which relates to a territory and a government' (Touraine 1990); 'The end of the 19th century saw an industrial economy, a social grouping, a political system, and a modern culture become interlocked, within a territory controlled by the state, so that a national society is a structured community, into which all these elements have been integrated' (Lapeyronnie 1993: 32). Gellner (1983) points out that society appears to be a complete whole, in which, at a historically located time, a culture, social structures, an industrial economy, and a political system are congruent. The nation-state represents a horizon beyond which society cannot travel. 'During the period of intense European national territorial rivalry from the late nineteenth century onwards . . . national self-images became entrenched in the consciousness of most people living in European countries. Hence, the macro sociological concepts such as social system, social structure, and total society

... were effectively synonyms with nations ... Thinking about humankind as a whole or even new transnational regional identities, has little or no emotional significance' (Kilminster 1997: 268). In this model, the nation-state has the monopoly over structuring identities, and what is left—local and regional identities—seem to be remnants of tradition, gradually being eroded by the modernizing force of the nation-state. This national society results both from the political project of elites and from the pressures of groups sharing a language and a culture in the sense characterized by Gellner (1983: 7) as 'a system of ideas and signs and associations and ways of behaving and communicating'.

Closely linked to the political project of the making of the nation-state, national society has been constructed, both socially and historically and with varying degrees of proactive politics, in such a way as to erase internal differences. This homogeneity is particularly marked for the Scandinavian nation-states, except the Lapps. However, even in the case of France, where the Jacobin elites toiled unceasingly, Mendras (1997) has emphasized that, despite the long history of the state, despite religious unity and the influence of the Church, despite the *Code civil* and the coinage, not to speak of roads, railways, municipalities, and schools, local and regional diversity in France really became blurred only in the 1960s, with the advent of mass consumption and television. These surviving local and regional societies and their tradition of dynamism have also provided a touchstone for Italian sociology (Pace 1998). After a period in which Marxist and American influences led sociologists to study modernization and backwardness in Italian society, a new generation rediscovered living local urban societies (Paci 1996), as well as territorial forms of regulation (Bagnasco and Trigilia 1993). Similarly, in their different ways, the religious contrasts between northern and southern Germany, the oppositions between Catalonia and Spain, the cultural differences between Scotland and England or between the Walloons and the Flemish have not disappeared.

National society also meant industrial society, capitalist society, and class society. Therborn (1985) has identified 'the European industrial trajectory' as an essential element differentiating European societies, with industry as the main provider of employment. Industrial capitalism organized society into classes in Europe more than elsewhere, but especially so in Britain, which is often regarded as the model of class-based society. But the same process occurred in Germany, Belgium, Scandinavia, France, and—later and to a lesser extent —in southern Europe, the Netherlands, and Ireland. The industrial cities mentioned in Chapter 2 represent the urban expression of this transformation. Working-class organizations, trade unions, and communist and social democratic parties exerted pressure within the state to obtain forms of compensation through the welfare state. Redistributive policies limited or reduced social inequalities. The economy was attached to, even embedded within, a set of rules and social compromises (Regini 1995). This European political economy was strengthened after 1945 by the Keynesian compromise—that original form of regulation, the great trade-off between capital and national society—which fostered the dynamic of growth and the reduction of inequalities (Crouch 1999). Despite the image of industrial society, the peasantry as a social group had not disappeared in France, even by the 1960s; and the traditional petty bourgeoisie—shopkeepers, artisans, small business people—is even today one of the pillars of Italian society.

Large organizations were a powerful means of mobilizing this national society: parties, trade unions, the Church, employers' organizations, and large associations structured society and defended their interests at the centre. In the late nineteenth century, and frequently a little later, parties were organized around social—or class—religious, and territorial cleavages. The state itself has played a direct part in structuring national societies. From the time of Bismarck onwards, state employees formed a social group apart (Kocka 1989). Later, 'the democratic class struggle' (Korpi 1983) contributed to the 'decommodification' of a part of the labour market: in other words, the development of an important section of the labour market that is not regulated by market logics. The development of the welfare state was accompanied by a substantial increase in white-collar and other middle-class jobs in the public sector, especially after 1945, and this was a key factor in the consolidation of national societies (Esping-Andersen 1990; Hassenteufel 1998). In most European countries, these public-sector lower-middle classes came to play an essential role in the social—new social movements—and political dynamic of European societies, including in cities (Kriesi *et al.* 1995).

Within western Europe, each national society has followed its own trajectory and undergone its own form of development, contrasting with others. Differences of language, social structure, and culture were simply reinforced by the strengthening of the nation-state throughout the twentieth century. Here again, we see the Weberian process: that is, the dual movement in which borders are strengthened and inside is differentiated from outside, while an internal order is organized and a national society gradually homogenizes (Bartolini 1998), despite international relations and international commerce. These different elements of national societies have been more or less in place since the late nineteenth century in most European countries and, frequently, much longer. Crouch (1999) stresses that the social compromise forged after the Second World War gave a new vigour to this model. European industrial capitalist societies were organized around the state, its citizens' rights, and its institutions.

Even today, most social structures are to be found within the national context, and European societies function there. However, the cycle of a century of reinforced national structuring of European societies is perhaps now coming to an end. Trans-national networks, Europeanization and globalization processes, and pressures from cities and regions are damaging the model of national society, even though this has never been completely realized.

Since European societies have become essentially urban societies, the transformation of national societies can be revealed largely through analyses of the transformation of cities. However, in line with my initial proposition, the emphasis here is on the category of medium-sized European cities, with roughly 200,000 to 2 million inhabitants, the cities which make up the framework of urban Europe. Some of the factors involved are not different in larger metropolises, such as Paris and London, but simply more concentrated. The differentiation of national societies may give cities, or some of them, the opportunity to play a more important role in structuring and organizing society, if they themselves are not restructured or disorganized by flows that pass through them and fragmentation processes that affect them just as much.

I want to emphasize the embeddedness of European cities within national societies, European cities are stabilized by the welfare state and public services. The bulk of the population of most European cities consists of a large body of public-sector employees, along with middle-class white-collar workers and the petty bourgeoisie, although this is less true where welfare states are smaller, such as in southern Europe or the UK. The second point to note is that robustness does not imply homogeneity or stable social order: social conflicts and spatial polarization have increased as new forms of poverty have emerged, associated with the economic crisis and the de-industrialization process. Third, European cities are becoming more diverse, in response to individualization, Europeanization, and globalization processes. These translate into flows of migrants, tourists, business people or students, and possibly a new international urban elite in the making. It follows that the erosion of national societies is deregulating traditional process of identify formation and providing an opportunity for political entrepreneurs, including at the urban level, to encourage alternative identities.

Robust European Cities Stabilized by the State and the Welfare State

European cities are not unchanging. However, the relative stability of their situation in the *longue durée* combines with their internal diversity and social consumption groups, protected by the welfare state, to give them a relative robustness. The Oxford English Dictionary defines 'robust' as 'tending to strength . . . vigorous . . . strongly built'. In relative terms, these cities have a capacity for resistance, a solid constitution that is not necessarily given to smaller, industrial, or isolated cities.

The classic distinction between the logic of production and the logic of collective consumption as elements of the social structure of European cities

TABLE 4.1. *Public administration: total expenditure as percentage of GDP, 1985–2000*

	1985	1990	1995	2000
Austria	50.2	48.6	52.5	47.6
Belgium	57.3	50.8	50.3	47.0
Germany	45.6	43.8	46.3	42.9
Denmark	n/a	53.6	56.6	50.2
Finland	42.3	44.4	54.3	43.6
France	51.9	49.5	53.5	51.4
Greece	43.9	47.5	54.6	50.9
Ireland	n/a	39.0	39.2	38.9
Italy	49.8	52.4	51.1	44.4
Luxembourg	n/a	41.0	42.9	39.5
Netherlands	51.9	49.4	47.7	41.5
Portugal	39.5	39.5	41.1	41.5
Spain	39.7	41.6	44.0	38.7
Sweden	60.4	55.9	62.1	52.7
United Kingdom	n/a	41.9	44.4	39.2
European Union	48.3	46.7	48.7	44.2
USA	33.8	33.6	32.9	29.4

Source: OECD (2001: 278).

was identified by Saunders, following Weber.[1] A characteristic of cities is their concentration of collective consumer services, traditionally linked to the development of the welfare state and collectively organized and managed; broadly known as public services, they are provided in a non-market context and at least partly financed from taxation (Dunleavy 1981): health services—especially hospitals—social services, schools, higher education establishments, and the provision of various services such as leisure, housing, socio-cultural activities, possibly water, energy, and transport. These spheres are the main ones affected by the growth in public expenditure and public sector employment, especially during the period of more rapid development.

With the exception of the UK, where industrialization and urbanization took place much earlier, it was only after the Second World War that European nation-states saw, simultaneously, higher levels of industrial development, urbanization, and welfare state development. As the drift from the countryside gathered pace and then came to an end, social, education, and health services naturally tended to be set up in cities. In most European cities, including in the UK, social housing, new hospitals, infrastructures, public transport, schools, social services, and universities were built and operated within the whole urban system. The large university-educated cohort of

---

[1] This consideration of cities as a collective consumption category was one of the major innovations of urban sociology in the 1970s and 1980s, from Castells (1983) to Dunleavy (1981) and Saunders (1979; 1986). This literature ties in with research in France on the public-sector middle classes and the production of public amenities. Taking a somewhat functionalist neo-Marxist stance, Castells presents a preliminary analysis of the city and consumption in *The Urban Question* (1977).

the baby-boom generation was integrated into the public or quasi-public sector on a massive scale, especially women. This process was more accentuated in continental Europe, less so in the south. Indeed, public expenditure excluding military expenditure, measured as a percentage of GDP, increased from just over 20 per cent in 1960 to 33–35 per cent in 1995 in the UK, a little less in Greece, Portugal, and Ireland, nearly 40 per cent in France, about 45 per cent in Denmark and Finland, and even more in Sweden. By way of comparison, it is useful to note that the figures for the USA and Japan in 1995 were 23.1 per cent and 9 per cent respectively!

From the point of view of social structure, Europe, despite great internal diversity, remains a completely different world from the United States or Japan.

These developments were reflected in employment figures. In his analysis of changes in post-industrial social structures, Esping-Andersen (1993) very clearly demonstrates the role of the welfare state and of education in structuring Western societies, in combination with the structure of production and the industrial relations system. The figures for Scandinavian states are obviously more spectacular than those for the UK or, to a lesser extent, Germany.

Welfare states are undergoing major internal reorganization, but, as far as the mass of their populations is concerned, cuts and job losses have not been substantial as yet, except in the UK and, to a lesser extent, the Netherlands. This means that, up to now, public employment, as a relatively stable form of employment, has been maintained, providing a solid pillar of stability for national and local societies, and benefiting women especially.

These observations take on their full meaning when applied to cities. In the European context, cities are most often the capitals of small nation-states, regional capitals, or centres of economic regions. In all these cases, the cities have played a particularly important role as local or regional bases for a welfare state organized at the national level. In other words, not only is the welfare state more developed in Europe than elsewhere, as is demonstrated by public facilities and infrastructures on the one hand and by the significant percentage of public or quasi-public sector jobs on the other, but the territorialization of this welfare state has reflected and strengthened existing hierarchies of cities, especially the category of regional capitals. This represents another example of path dependent processes, in line with Lepetit's observations about the period of state-building (see Chapter 2).

This general trend and structural component masks great diversity among European cities, and particularly between cities in northern as against southern Europe. Statistics on employment in cities, although difficult to compare as between one country and another, express this reality. In French cities, in most municipalities that are in the centre of conurbations over 50 per cent of jobs are in the public sector; sometimes, in the case of the less industrialized regional capitals such as Montpellier, Rennes, or Toulon, this can reach 70 per cent. Re-calculated to the scale of the whole conurbation, this represents a good third of all jobs.

TABLE 4.2. *Private, state, and municipal jobs in Nordic cities as percentage of total*

City	Private	State	Municipal
Alborg	56	11	33
Århus	57	11	32
Odense	59	8	33
Helsinki	62	21	17
Oulu	59	28	13
Tampere	70	7	22
Turku	62	16	22
Stockholm	75	10	15
Gothenburg	71	7	22
Malmö	71	7	22

Source: Nordstat (1999).

In the Scandinavian countries the figures can be easily compared. The higher proportion of welfare state employees, especially in the social services, is counterbalanced by the universalist ideology, which helps to create very high equality in the spatial distribution of these services, with a lower concentration in the cities.

There have not been many studies of the links between the welfare state and cities, since urban research has almost all concentrated on the effects of production and of capitalism, especially industrial capitalism, in shaping cities (Letho 2000). The factors presented here suggest that, thanks to public services and the welfare state, European cities have a stable employment base. Broadly, a third of city employment is rooted in the public or quasi-public sector, sometimes beyond 40 per cent, which means that, in the short and medium terms, a large section of the workforce is escaping the logics of the market, globalized as these now are. In addition, these jobs offer social services to the population, provide a substantial proportion of female employment, make life easier for households, and partly protect populations from the effects of economic risks—even though this last has proved less effective since the 1980s. The situation in the UK is somewhat different. State public expenditure there is traditionally lower than in continental Europe—but not in comparison with Ireland or the south of Europe. This trend became more pronounced after Mrs Thatcher came to power in 1979, with the introduction of market mechanisms, privatization of housing, transport, and energy, and tax reductions.

Up to the present day, European cities have been able to count on an element of stability: local government, state agencies and services, hospitals, schools, universities, social and cultural centres, research centres, and the forces of law and order have together contributed a great deal to the organization and stability of cities. In more sociological terms, based on the Italian case, Bagnasco and Negri (1994) have attributed a dual role to the middle classes and lower-middle classes—*classi medie e ceti medi*—in stabilizing local urban societies and in social innovation. This means that, in some cities, from the point of view of the production of goods and services, public or quasi-public sector employees—or some of them—may organize as a social group (Le Galès 1993). This is not very often the case, yet the relevance of a social class paradigm can be blurred by these vaguely defined intermediate social groups. From the point of view of consumption of collective welfare state services, the 'thirty glorious years' from 1947 to 1976 allowed the middle strata to gain in strength; the stratum that includes both blue-collar and white-collar workers, who have become more similar by virtue of their increased purchasing power, is relatively more uniform and stable, with lifestyles and consumption patterns that are now more uniform, centred on leisure and working hours. The middle strata have always been the main beneficiaries of public services. By contrast, those who did not get in at the right time, that is, by the 1970s—those who came too late have been identified by Chauvel (1998*a*) as 'a sacrificed generation'—or who have remained outside this system, as have some women, young people, those who have left the labour market early, immigrants, lone-parent families, and unskilled people, may find themselves on exclusion trajectories from which they run the risk of forming social groups of 'the excluded' in various European cities (Mingione 1996; Oberti 1996). It would not stretch things too far to describe this second line of social demarcation as 'status stratification', a term that traditionally relates to particular ways of life and to consumption possibilities recognized socially or through political guarantees. Apart from the most industrial cities, medium-sized European cities have been and largely remain cities where these status groups have played a central role. From the 1970s onwards, evidence of this has appeared through urban social movements linked to public amenities, schools, and housing, complemented by research on issues of urban poverty and the process of exclusion.

These public-sector middle classes and lower-middle classes have gradually gained influence in many European cities. A whole literature in political science has studied the decline of the working class as the main supporter of social democratic parties in the 1970s (Seyd 1990). The rise of the middle strata has translated into social movements, associations, and new political elites in social democratic and Green parties, particularly in cities (Sellers 2001), as well as into public policies (see Chapter 6).

This important first step in sustaining the claim of European cities to be robust is complemented by a second element. Geographers are fully aware that the simple effect of concentration of population leads almost automatically to the development of market services and to building development: big or small business, artisans, retailing, shopkeepers, the professions, consulting, banking, insurance, property development, leisure, public buildings, and other works. This development also encompasses social services in the private sector, with jobs ranging from the worst kind of temporary work to the most prestigious, best-paid jobs. These forms of employment mainly involve the existing population and are not likely just to vanish from one day to the next. In a large number of European cities, most especially in southern Europe, they make up another third of the employment structure. Finally, large firms generally set up their regional offices, depots, and warehouses in the kind of regional capitals under consideration here. Individual or collective market services develop according to the potential market and therefore, in most cases, according to the size of the surrounding population, or depending on other criteria such as wealth or existing transport networks. The meta-stability of the urban system tends to reinforce transport networks between existing cities, reflecting existing hierarchies; and the territorial distribution of new services tends to reflect existing patterns of cities.

Of course, the situation varies a lot from one city to another, and frequently from one country to another. The remarkable staying power of the traditional petty bourgeoisie in Italy, protected for a long time by the Christian Democrats, means that these strata still provide between 15 per cent and 20 per cent of jobs in Italy, a much higher proportion than in other European countries. Although dispersed, these strata are most naturally found in cities; so, all in all, these groups represent a second stable pillar of employment in cities, helping to produce wealth and not too sensitive to the hazards of international finance.

European cities, therefore, are not just crossroads for flows of travellers, not merely aggregations of individuals buffeted by the strong wind of globalization, or cosy local societies that are gradually becoming dislocated. The middle strata of the public, or quasi-public, sector and the traditional petty bourgeoisie form two pillars of urban societies in European cities: two relatively robust, relatively stable pillars, with educational, occupational, and inheritance strategies. In most cases these categories and their integration into the city mitigate the most extreme effects of polarization. The 'dual city' (Mollenkopf and Castells 1989) scenario that can be evoked for New York does not seem to be the most appropriate one to use in considering European cities. However, this does not mean that pressures towards polarization, identified at the level of national societies, are not also present at city level.

Poverty and Social Segregation

The jobs of the two groups identified above confirm the social hierarchy as a whole. In the public or quasi-public sector, senior managers of various bodies have both high educational qualifications and comfortable levels of income. In the private sector, professionals, shopkeepers, artisans, and small business people form a conventionally bourgeois base. Depending on the situation, a privileged section of these groups may organize into a true local bourgeoisie, with educational and inheritance strategies and ways of life that are clearly identified in spatial terms. But insecure, low-skilled, low-paid jobs are also to be found on both sides of the public-private divide, and can be closely linked to the most disadvantaged populations.

Poverty: In or Out of the City?

The theme of the fragmented society appears in the literature throughout Europe. The crumbling of society's 'pillars' has been recorded in the Netherlands and Belgium; social classes no longer play the structuring role that they had in industrial society. Inequalities are changing and often strengthening, but lines of social cleavage are becoming blurred. Post-industrial capitalism is, at the moment, producing a much less legible class structure than in the preceding period, given especially the absence of a large working class—although this does not mean that class relations have disappeared.

The social changes of the last 20 years have also got a lot to do with economic restructuring: they reflect the decline of industry, the high rate of unemployment in European societies since the mid-1970s, and the erosion of the wage-earner society. Labour market changes, with movements towards increasing insecurity in relation to work for some categories, or even their exclusion from the labour market, present a strong contrast to new opportunities for the most highly skilled people, new sectors of employment, and rewards for those who belong to the globalized networks of excellence. It is, therefore, surprising that some sociologists have abandoned the language of social class at a time when capitalism is undergoing a new phase of expansion, and the political counterweight that used to keep capitalism in check is somewhat less effective. As Marx, Weber, and Polanyi clearly showed, when capitalism structures social relations, the society is more likely to be organized around social classes. In other words, if capitalism is playing a larger part in the current phase—whose length we do not yet know—then structuring in terms of social classes is likely to become more important for our societies. However, these classes will not be the same as those we knew before, and the principle of social structuring may combine with others, such as status group or membership of ethnic, religious, territorial, or sexual groups.

Neither the increased wealth of European societies nor the implementation of social policies has led to the abolition of poverty. On the contrary, forms of poverty re-emerged in the late 1970s in Europe generally and in the early 1990s in northern Europe. Social trends that we hoped were in the process of disappearing—poverty, deprivation, riots, homelessness, and marginality—have been returning. And other, equally painful, terms have come into vogue: social exclusion, social disqualification, disaffiliation, outsider or disadvantaged districts, ghettos, *la galère*, the underclass.

Three processes are at work in combination: (1) change in the job market, de-industrialization, the increasing insecurity of part of the workforce, and the effects of unemployment; (2) the increasing fragility of social bonds, notably family ties, which especially disadvantages lone mothers; and (3) the restriction or withdrawal of social policies and the effects this has on citizenship, for example in the sphere of housing. First and foremost, exclusion and disqualification processes are running at full throttle; work is no longer the great integrator of society, the family is becoming increasingly vulnerable, and the welfare state is not able to stand up to the resurgence of poverty recorded in all European countries over the last 20 years. Types of family structures, labour markets, and welfare states have combined in such a way that different types and different experiences of poverty have emerged in Europe (Morris 1995; Mingione 1996; 1997; Gallie and Paugam 2000). Castel, in his account of wage-earning, has analysed how the wage-earning condition is crumbling away. He proposes:

a general hypothesis to account for the complementary nature of what happens along an axis of integration through work—from attachment to a steady job, to complete absence of work, through participation in insecure, casual, seasonal, or similar forms of occupation—and along another axis, that of involvement in relationships via family and sociability networks—from integration by means of strong relationships, through fragile relationships, to social isolation. These connections describe different zones of density of social relations: a zone of integration, a zone of vulnerability, a zone of assistance, and a zone of exclusion—or rather, of disaffiliation. (Castel 1995: 414)

In all European countries, the description of new forms of poverty is the object of a major effort of classification. The contrast between those who are at the core of the job market and those who are on its periphery or outside it does seem to represent a strong dynamic tension within Western societies (Esping-Andersen 1993; 1999a).

It is not always easy to gain a clear picture of poverty, and there is now a proliferation of statistical surveys and qualitative studies in Europe, all attempting to account for the processes and populations involved. These surveys show several things in particular: the quantitative size of the problem, with 60 million statistically poor people in 1996 in Europe—in other words, with an income lower than 60 per cent of the median income (Atkinson, Glaude, and Olier 2001); the diversity of situations, processes, contexts, and experiences of poverty; diversity as between countries, resulting from effects linked to the welfare state, the labour market, and the family: about 20 per cent of children are living in poverty in the UK and in Italy, as against fewer than 5 per cent in Scandinavia and Finland, which shows that the welfare state does have some impact; and the diversity of the processes and populations involved, with immigrants, educationally failed young people, lone mothers, old people, and couples particularly affected. As things stand, this diversity makes the use of the term 'sub-proletarian class' inappropriate, and blind to the particular reality in some local areas. However, diverse poor populations in more affluent societies are now a common trend all over Europe.

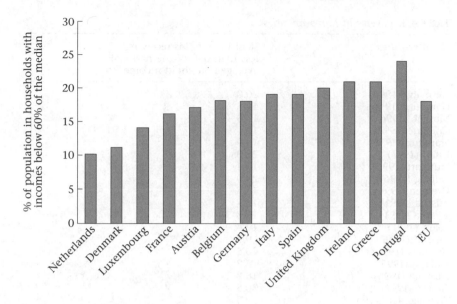

FIG. 4.1. Financial poverty in the European Union, 1994

Source: Atkinson (2000).

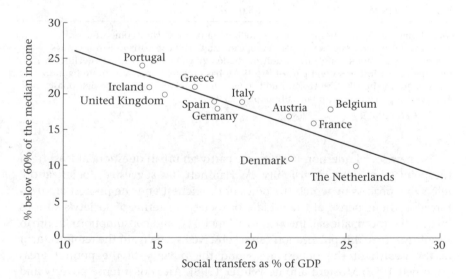

FIG. 4.2. Financial poverty and social transfers, 1992

Note: the data relate solely to social security transfers, and exclude other state transfers.

Source: Atkinson (2000).

TABLE 4.3. *Poverty in European cities*

Country/Cities	% of households receiving less than half of the national average household income
Germany (1993)	20.0
Hamburg (1996)	19.8
Munich (1996)	16.0
Cologne (1997)	18.9
Frankfurt (1996)	18.9
Essen (1997)	20.0
Stuttgart (1996)	16.4
Leipzig (1996)	23.0
Dresden (1996)	16.8
Austria (1991)	16.7
Vienna (1991)	15.8
Spain (1991)	19.4
Madrid (1996)	9.7
Valencia (1996)	20.5
Finland (1995)	2.2
Helsinki (1995)	18.2
Greece (1994)	30.5
Thessaloniki (1994)	32.3
Netherlands (1996)	18.6
Amsterdam (1996)	34.1
Rotterdam (1996)	28.7
UK (1991)	48.9
Leeds (1996)	30.2
Edinburgh (1996)	55.0

Note: Figures apply to cities only, not to their conurbations. They come from an experimental programme to compare European cities. The comparison is not always obvious; see caveats in the Urban Audit methodology guidelines. Also, the decline of unemployment in the second part of the 1990s has probably improved those figures, for instance in the UK. The Urban Audit scheme included 58 cities in the first phase. The average percentage of financially poor is 23.2%.

Source: CEC (2001).

This new social question has become partly an urban question, at least from the point of view of its visibility. As Hamnett has suggested, 'polarization' refers to a process by which the poles of the richest and the poorest are reinforced at the expense of the middle of society, in terms of society's various inequalities (occupational, income, social mobility, and consumption). In urban sociology terms, this polarization can be observed spatially, in the reinforcement of the wealth of the richest areas and the poverty of the poorest areas (Hamnett 1997; Musterd and de Winter 1998). Areas of intense poverty and areas of intense wealth exist and are increasing within cities, thus recreating a mosaic of spatial inequalities and conflicts.

In cities, national models of integration—economic, political, and social— can be seen as having reached a series of impasses. The concentration of poverty in certain districts has caught the imagination (Bourdieu 1993). The spiral of decline in city-centre districts, former working-class districts, and, in ports, seamen's districts is known as 'inner city crisis'. It first affected those historic industrial cities marked by de-industrialization—Birmingham, Glasgow, Bradford, Sheffield, Coventry, Manchester—then other industrial cities— Saint-Étienne and Le Creusot, Lille, certain cities in the Ruhr, Liège—ports— Naples, Genoa, Marseilles, Bilbao, Barcelona, Oporto, Le Havre, Liverpool —and also cities such as Brussels or Frankfurt and small industrial cities. This decline of crisis-ridden central urban districts was all the more visible because immigrants from outside these communities had settled in them during the 1960s and later. Apart from central districts, many working-class districts had been organized, anarchically or in a planned fashion, on the periphery of cities, notably in France, the UK, and the Netherlands, but also in some German, Spanish, and Italian cities. This concentration of vulnerable, deprived populations produces self-reinforcing effects as the immobility of such populations intensifies their districts' separate cultures: the logic of 'urban relegation'. Adverse comment, public policies, and the media can all contribute to the stigmatizing of certain districts within cities.

The 'dual city' model stresses this social polarization and has been developed with reference to the American situation; a priori it seems able to account for social and spatial divisions in Berlin, London, or Paris—but Hamnett (1995) and Préteceille (1995; 2000) show it does not work for London or Paris—and more broadly in European cities. However, the situation is more complicated in the latter: some distinct structural polarizations exist, but they are not the norm. Everywhere, districts are experiencing spirals of decline. In some central or peripheral districts, poverty is becoming structural, and economic and social indicators reveal dreadful situations of exclusion. In addition, poverty can often be hidden or distributed across a large part of the city, not remaining enclosed in a single area: this is more often the case in Italian or Scandinavian cities, for example. Moreover, all this does not determine the 'lived experience' of poverty in different contexts.

Associating crisis-ridden districts with poverty produces a doubly mistaken perspective. In some European cities—for instance, Helsinki, and also Amsterdam, Stuttgart, and Naples (Musterd and Ostendorf 1998; Mingione 1996)—poverty is less concentrated in crisis-ridden districts. It is more diffuse, sometimes less visible, and spread across the whole—or almost the whole—city. In addition, the populations of the districts targeted are not homogeneous. Very strong differences can exist, even from one building to another or from one staircase to another (Oberti 1995). In their surveys of districts on the periphery of Bordeaux, Avenel (1999) and Villechaise-Dupont (2000) stress that there are two factors unifying the populations of these districts: the view of others outside the district, and their economic exclusion from the way of life of the middle classes. Unlike the literature on excluded social classes and isolation, they and others emphasize the cultural proximity of the populations in deprived districts to the middle classes. By contrast to the concept of ghettoes, relatively powerful logics of social integration are found in such districts. Italian and Dutch researchers (Engbersen *et al.* 1993) have come to similar conclusions, although, as usual, there is great diversity from one city to the next. All, however, stress that there are dangers in terms of how things may develop and the potential emergence of socially excluded groups in the most disadvantaged districts. Finally, independently of well-defined districts, disadvantaged social groups have been pushed out to the periphery of cities, into suburban areas and into buildings put up in formerly rural municipalities. Polluting industrial activities and waste management are also flung out onto the periphery in this way. Frankfurt, Keil, and Ronnenberg have highlighted the political dynamic of how undesirable activities and social groups have been rejected, first by the city centre, then by independent municipalities in the suburbs, and then by those even further out.

Thus, although it is not necessary to mobilize the myth of the American ghetto as contrast and foil, poverty, crisis-ridden districts, and the increasing vulnerability of whole chunks of society have also become the common lot of European cities. Recent surveys, such as that conducted by the ESOPO team (Saraceno *et al.* 1998), have opened the way to challenging nationally based views of poverty and to emphasizing the originality of urban situations. Family structures, type of welfare state, and labour market combine with variables more specifically linked to particular cities—social groups, local authorities and public policies, associations and their coordination—to account for very diverse situations.

Although economic and social inequalities are more pronounced in the United States than in Europe, European cities have a certain reputation for manifesting the phenomena of social segregation. To the European imagination, ghettoes and 'gated communities'—districts or small towns protected by walls and fences, kept under surveillance, and entered only through checkpoints—or the nightmarish Los Angeles described by Davis in *The City of Quartz* (1990) seem to run counter to the idea of citizenship, public space, political community, and central square: the city in the classic sense. The contrast is exaggerated, since many American cities do not correspond to these visions. Moreover, European cities have also changed (Burtenshaw, Bateman, and Ashworand 1991; Musterd and de Winter 1998) and are not distinguished by significantly lower levels of social segregation. Of course, spatial segregation processes are more marked in the largest metropolises because of the concentration of higher-status groups (Tabard 1993), but Préteceille (2000) has rightly noted that social segregation may sometimes be more marked in medium-sized cities. Given that Europe has more medium-sized and moderately large cities, segregation processes are frequently less marked or less visible. Studies of segregation have emphasized first and foremost the processes of segregation of disadvantaged populations: immigrants, poor people, and workers. On this level, social segregation processes are more pronounced in the United States, since such populations live in central districts or near to city centres and have black skins: relative levels of poverty measured by the indicators show a higher proportion of poor populations. As Body-Gendrot (1992) has emphasized, comparison of the main central districts of New York, Los Angeles, London, Paris, and Rome inevitably leads to the conclusion that there is a much greater concentration of poverty in the United States. Poverty in suburban districts of Rome or Paris is obviously more discreet.

The Bourgeoisie

Another new characteristic of Europe is the dynamics in the upper strata, who seem to be benefiting to the full from the opportunities created by globalization processes. In some European countries, the incomes of the richest 10 per cent are tending to increase strongly, which indicates a trend towards the Americanization of European societies, such as the spectacular increase of inequalities in the UK during the Thatcher years; but in some other countries—France and Nordic countries, for instance—those inequalities seem to have remain pretty stable (Atkinson *et al.* 2001). Income hierarchies do not correspond to social positions or educational hierarchies (Chauvel 1998); social classifications work less well as predictors of individual or household behaviour. Social groups are more difficult to apprehend, and different types of conflict, such as generational ones, are superimposed on the picture (Chauvel 1998).

However, social segregation also involves the middle and upper classes. In his study of inequalities in French cities, Davezies notes that inequalities are growing in a similar way in all of them; he sees no particular urban features but rather the accentuation of trends in French society: 'the rise in sociospatial inequality in France seems to be an overall social phenomenon in an urbanized society, not a truly urban phenomenon' (Davezies 1998c: 63). He highlights two overall mechanisms, which apply to France and can be presumed to apply in other European countries: the clear increase in the household incomes of the rich in relation to others, and the social specialization of rich local authorities, sometimes within larger urban areas. State expenditure remains the most massive mechanism of redistribution to reduce inequalities. Most analyses of social segregation in European cities show evidence of the importance of the state and social groups linked to the state, countering the assumption of a simple movement of polarization in European cities (Maertens and Vervaeke 1997).

The upper classes in particular have a strong capacity to choose where they live, and they use it. Pinçon and Pinçon-Charlot (1989; 2000) have identified the 'spatial stamp' of the bourgeoisie: a way of building and organizing 'good districts' in cities, especially the largest ones. This geographical mutual reinforcement enables them to deploy inheritance and reproduction strategies: 'this spatial segregation, pushed to the extreme, is in fact an aggregation, the choice of a social group, of a class, through which it is expressing its awareness of the group's deep community of interests' (Pinçon and Pinçon-Charlot: 2000: 54). The same thing was shown by Butler and Savage's (1995) research on the UK middle classes, particularly in relation to educational strategies. European cities differ significantly from US ones on this point. Historically—and this is linked to the role of the city centre in European cities —the most privileged social strata—the cultural, political, and economic elites— have remained in the cities and in their centres, except in the UK. They have maintained and reproduced their presence, and they have accumulated economic, social, cultural, and political capital. New groups of managers and professionals have followed the same logic by settling either in residential suburbs on the periphery or in city centres. European cities are rarely distinguished by urban crisis in the city centre, except in nineteenth-century industrial cities, ports, and some special cases such as Brussels or Frankfurt. On the contrary, their bourgeoisies have often been sufficiently active to push the building of factories and social housing out towards the periphery: more so in France and southern Europe, and less so in Scandinavia.

Again, the UK constitutes an exception to this. Anti-urban feeling among elites in England had developed before the nineteenth century. The British middle classes had a unique experience of large-scale industrialization. The rural environment, small towns, and the 'English countryside' became symbols of eternal England, the refuge of the middle classes. The initial shock of the founding of industry and the profoundly anti-urban culture of British elites caused an early middle-class and aristocratic (Carradine 1990) departure into the suburbs, which, among other things, led on to town planning and the creation of parks and protected spaces in cities. This distinction has been reinforced over the years: 'Not only is the countryside regarded as an "anchor" for "new traditionalist" class and gender identities, it is also a "white" space. It is now increasingly apparent that ethnic minority groups are confined to the city' (Lowe, Murdoch, and Cox 1995: 79; Gilroy 1987).

By contrast, European bourgeoisies and aristocracies have not systematically deserted the centres of old European cities, and their presence has become more pronounced again since the 1980s. Comparative studies of social mobility show higher rates of upper-class segregation in European cities, and not merely in the larger metropolises (Burtenshaw, Bateman, and Ashworth 1991). However, some sections of the middle and upper strata have gradually settled on the peripheries of cities. In most European cities, it is easy to distinguish those suburban local authorities where there are concentrations of well-off households, including the richest: historically, they tend to lie to the west. In Scandinavian and Italian cities, the phenomenon was initially limited but is now gaining momentum. It is more common in Germany and France. Areas of suburban houses or peri-urban developments and small, ethnically and socially homogeneous residential towns, largely of owner-occupiers, have developed on the periphery of cities, and these benefit from the two movements of urban growth and dispersal. Horizontal dispersal has gradually affected European cities but has not led to the decline of city centres, except in the cases mentioned above. Good districts and residential suburbs are especially visible in the biggest cities because there are more important households there, particularly in capital cities, close to government; but most European cities are experiencing this phenomenon on a lesser scale.

In Chapter 2, which dealt with the long history of European cities, I noted how the fact that cities found a place in a state-organized national space helped to strengthen the power and legitimacy of those who served the state, for example the bourgeoisie of lawyers. The public-sector middle classes are now massively represented in the policy elites of European cities. The reasons for this are to be found in the links between the state and capitalism. European societies are evolving alongside European integration and globalization processes, which have an important economic dimension. The hypothesis here is that the current upsurge of capitalism, which is expressed in the extension of market logics into more and more varied sections of social life, has consequences for social stratification. As cities are at the heart of exchange flows and logics of accumulation, the individuals and groups most involved in the private sector and/or in Europe and in globalization processes should see their social and economic influence in cities increase, despite some conflicts.

The logics of social differentiation in the biggest cities seem more pronounced than in the medium-sized ones, but, up to now, these have resembled differences of degree more than differences in the nature of the phenomena. One way of exploring this further would be to start with Robert Merton's research on a small American town, Rovere, in the 1950s. Merton (1965: 300) proposed the following distinction between 'localites' and 'cosmopolitans':

Rovere has few residents who command a following outside that community. The chief criterion for distinguishing the two is found in their orientation toward Rovere. The localite largely confines his interests to this community. Rovere is essentially his world. Devoting little thought or energy to the Great Society, he is preoccupied with local problems, to the virtual exclusion of the national and international scene. He is, strictly speaking, parochial. Contrariwise with the cosmopolitan type. He has some interest in Rovere and must of course maintain a minimum of relations within the community since he, too, exerts influence there. But he is also oriented significantly to the world outside Rovere, and regards himself as an integral part of that world. He resides in Rovere but lives in the Great Society.

The idea of society is linked to interactions and to the representation of territory. This division between localites and cosmopolitans could probably be refined to meet the case of European cities. Mobility, interactions, and representations of the world are generally accompanied, as Merton showed, by different social practices and types of integration into the locality. If only at an exploratory level, it would be interesting to distinguish, in European cities, between localites in Merton's sense, nationals—a classic distinction within the context of centre-periphery national models—Europeans, and cosmopolitans. In all cities, people in senior positions, whether in the public sector or the private sector, are induced to move elsewhere on a regular basis, for professional reasons. Managers in public bodies—town halls, chambers of commerce, universities, or the apparatus of the state itself—go to the capital city, since that is the location of the higher echelons of the state apparatus, or, increasingly often, to Brussels. Private-sector managers tend to move to their firm's head office, which may be in or near the capital or else in London, Brussels, Amsterdam, or even the United States. Professionals are doing the same. Both have increasingly regular horizontal contacts with other firms, cities, establishments, suppliers, and customers. Beyond the traditional bourgeoisie, social groups with rather better educational qualifications and cultural resources have regular trans-national interactions on differing scales.

Involvement at different scales and mobility now seems to be an important principle of social differentiation. The labour market is one expression of these pressures. The phenomenon of metropolization has concrete consequences for the labour market. Thus, cities play an important role in terms of social mobility, since the most prestigious, best-paid jobs are over-represented in them. In France, the Paris region plays a filtering role: the size of the flows of those entering and leaving is not accidental. Those who stay are more often the most highly skilled in their field, with much greater career prospects in the Paris region. In the UK, the major urban region of south-east England plays an 'escalator' role in upward social movement and reproduction: 'The South East is hence a kind of machine for upward social mobility, in which people at the bottom are promoted relatively quickly, and those at the top disperse elsewhere, so allowing more promotions to take place within' (Savage *et al.* 1992: 182). More generally, social mobility and spatial mobility are closely linked, notably for private sector managers (Butler and Savage 1995). This phenomenon is being accentuated by the presence of working women and their level of qualifications. It is hard to envisage anyone having two careers in management outside the cities, even the largest of them, as is the case in Denmark, Portugal, or Italy. The influence of the state in society is no longer growing; a section of the hierarchies is rather to be found in Brussels, and there is a rising wave of 'commodification' and globalization: therefore, the private-sector workforce is coming to play a larger role in European societies, and especially in cities. On the one hand, individuals are concentrated in the cities where labour markets are most favourable; on the other hand, the most prestigious services, in employment terms, have also chosen to set up in the cities where these social groups live. These phenomena affect the biggest cities more, but also have an effect on regional capitals.

Societies are now organized through overlapping scales, and, since cities form an integral part of these societies, they tend to be increasingly involved in various kinds of networks.

More Social and Cultural Diversity
Within European Cities

Globalization

The changes of scale in society are partly linked to transformations of capitalism and to the pressure of market logics (see Chapter 5). In these two dynamics, cities are in the front line, and are gradually losing the structure imposed on them by national society. Urban societies are, if only to a limited extent, becoming disembedded from national societies. European cities are rooted in national societies, but they also form nodes where flows and interactions are greater; they have growing populations and take an active part in the production of wealth and in commercial and cultural exchanges. Seen from below—that is, from the cities' point of view—the political processes of European integration and globalization are interwoven and reinforce each other. In the search for the different dimensions of globalization, as soon as one attempts to formalize, analyse, break down, or decipher the phenomenon, its plural forms assert themselves, exposing the diversity of the processes in train, which often have little connection with one another. Globalization processes actually represent more than one form of globalization (Wallerstein 2000).

The globalization literature takes as its starting point the proliferation of interactions and flows on increasingly distant scales, facilitated by technological changes, which has contributed to the emerging consideration of a world perceived as a whole.[2] Although there are many difficulties in accounting for these processes, we must at least distinguish the neo-liberal political project to extend the rule of the market from the impact of social processes: the rhetoric of uniform domination by markets versus diversity of cultures (A. Scott 1997). Globalization processes are contested, varied, and very unequally advanced as between one sector and another or one place and another. There is no need for this book to give an account of all the debates on these issues: the conflicts between the critics and the hyperglobalists,[3] between Marxists and postmodernists, the debates about the extent of the phenomena, about the diversity of the processes unfolding and their tenuous links to one another, and about the periodization of globalization into waves in the history of humanity. The authoritative work by Held *et al.* on

---

[2] In order to avoid a vast number of notes on this subject, the reader is referred to Held *et al.* (1999), Robertson (1992), A. Scott (1998), Sklair (2001), Appaduraï (1996), to the special issue of *International Sociology*, 15/2 (2000), and to the symposium in *International Journal of Urban and Regional Research*, 24/2 (2000).

[3] 'Hyperglobalization as the ultra-modernist narratives of capitalism . . . it masquerades as a defence of economic freedom or laissez-faire . . . with its teleology of utopian simplicity, is at best a naive fairy tale, far less plausible than the dark (if partial) Gibsonian vision of the future (or the present already?) of sinister data corporations and their symbiotic mafia' (Lloyd 2000: 262, 272).

globalization gives the following definition, stressing the diversity of processes unfolding and their historicity, and suggesting different types of empirical checks:

a process (or a set of processes) which embodies a transformation in the spatial organization of social relations and transactions—assessed in terms of their extensivity, intensity, velocity and impact—generating transcontinental or inter-regional flows and networks of activity, interaction and the exercise of power . . . In this context, flows refer to the movements of physical artefacts, people, symbolic tokens and information across space and time, while networks refer to regularized or patterned interactions between independent agents, nodes of activity, or sites of power. (Held *et al* 1999: 16)

Taking a more operational approach, J. Meyer (2000: 233) suggests a distinction between different dimensions of globalization:

First it means the increased political and military interdependence of a set of sovereign nation-states and the expanded and strengthened set of organizations involved: here states are the main actors conceptualized. Second, it means the increased economic interdependencies of a set of national or subnational economies and the relevant multilateral and international public and private organizations: here states and firms are the main originating actors. Third, it means an expanded flow of individual persons among societies through socio-economic migration, travel and political expulsion: states and individuals are the main actors discussed. Fourth, globalization means the expanded interdependence of expressive culture through intensified global communication . . . All types of actors from individuals to organisations to national states are involved. Fifth, globalization means the expanded flow of instrumental culture around the world. Put simply, common models of social order become authoritative in different social settings.

Starting from a theoretical analysis that interprets these processes as a fundamental transformation of societies, Giddens, Lash and Urry, Robertson, Appaduraï, and Sklair all propose that the hypothesis of a global society in the making should be taken seriously. In other words, the dynamic of flows, interactions, and the strategies of collective actors and individuals is such that society today is on the road to being reshaped on the global scale, starting from globalization processes. Social systems with absolutely no linkages to the nation-state context are on a trajectory of formation. Culture, representations, social movements—including environmental and human rights movements—and capitalism—or, at least, the vanguard forces of these processes—are exiting the nation-states. The global scale is thus a new level for structuring major cultural and social conflicts of interest, and regulation of these. For example, social movements are developing new repertoires and new rules that have a meaning on this scale and this scale alone, and these are gradually imposing themselves (D. Meyer and Tarrow 1998). Anti-globalization mobilizations in Seattle, Gothenburg, and Genoa are spectacular illustrations of this. These dynamics are eroding national societies. In these processes, nation-states are not disappearing: they are simply becoming less

relevant in structuring social groups, conflicts, representations, policy repertoires, and interests. Thus, Appaduraï (1996), from a cultural point of view,
forecasts the advent of a 'postnational global cultural economy'. Giddens (1994),
in his article on 'post-traditional society', argues that the traditional institutions of the nation-state have been disembedded and that they have been
replaced by institutions that follow the dictates of globalized communication
and outcomes. Sklair suggests the emergence of a new social class, a mobile
global bourgeoisie, which can change country and thus avoid the constraints
of national societies, and he defines it as 'an international bourgeoisie: a socially
comprehensive category, encompassing the entrepreneurial elite, managers
of firms, senior state functionaries, leading politicians, members of the
learned professions . . . plus the media, culture, consumption' (1995: 62; see
also Sklair 2001). This new bourgeoisie speaks English and has learned the
codes that operate within Anglo-American firms, universities, and consultancies;
it is developing a common global culture and particular consumption practices. This global society is apparently organized less on the basis of major
conflicts and more on the basis of professional networks, with norms and
models of excellence driven from within the professions by consultants, legal
specialists, managers, university academics, doctors, accountants, bankers, and
advertising executives. Proliferation of trans-national professional networks
is leading to proliferation of interactions and the development of models and
norms which may later spread. The media, by comparison, may have some
success in giving the impression that they are indispensable, as do international bodies, from professional associations to the World Bank, which give
their 'good practice' seal of approval or else shoot barbed remarks at those
who do not play according to the new rules. Discourse on globalization and
its benefits for the common good is obviously central to the legitimization
of these processes and to the domination of the above-mentioned social group,
or, to put it more accurately, to establishing the hegemony of this new social
class, which is principally a transatlantic bourgeoisie.

  This global society is, as yet, more potential than real, more a stage on
which actors interact than a system. Nevertheless, globalization processes are
destabilizing national societies and hierarchies. The nation-state can hardly
any longer claim the monopoly of culture or education. Flows and models
with sources elsewhere are making a wide variety of cultural models available to individuals and groups. In contrast, the proliferation of trans-national
networks is fostering the thesis that trans-national social spaces are forming
(Faist 1999; Hannertz 1996; Cesari 1994b; Smith and Guardino 1998). Tarrius
(1992) rightly mocks the enthusiasm for these elite trans-national networks;
in fact, immigrant communities have been playing this role for a long time,
in Mediterranean cities for example. Exchanges of goods, services, and ideas
take place within these spaces. For example, from such spaces, between immigrant communities that straddle several nation-states, real social spaces are
organized, with their codes, hierarchies, and practices enmeshed in national

societies. The literature on trans-national networks of immigration shows how individuals organize their practices according to their country of origin, and that this can be justified both in terms of social status and within the context of the host societies. These trans-national networks play a part in differentiating national societies, sometimes through the dynamic of exit:

Cultural hybridity, multi-positional identities, border-crossing by marginal 'others', and transnational business practices by migrant entrepreneurs are depicted as conscious and successful efforts by ordinary people to escape control and domination 'from above' by capital and the state . . . [but one has to] bring back into focus the enduring asymmetries of domination, inequality, racism, sexism, class conflict and uneven development in which transnational practices are embedded and which they sometimes even perpetuate. (Smith and Guardino 1998: 5–6)

The dynamism of such networks and the distance of these interactions seem to be growing constantly. The theoreticians of culturalism and mobility take the view that the dual impact of trans-national networks and of flows of images, information, and people are making national societies less capable of structuring the representations and social practices of individuals (Urry 2000). These trans-national networks increase interdependence between national societies. From this perspective, European integration is accelerating trends that can also be observed in other contexts.

These processes, however limited, have important repercussions for social groups within the cities, many of whom are simply not part of the story. By contrast, individuals and groups that have the resources to play the game on the European or global scale and develop different forms of competence, expertise, or specialized products see opportunities opening up.[4] These individuals and groups have a capacity for exit that, although partial and limited, exerts strong pressures on urban societies, and may potentially reduce interdependence between social groups within a national society or within a city, or may help to mobilize a spatial interest that reflects their interests: a city against the state, for instance. It could be in the interest of these elites to disengage totally or partially from national societies and to plot their individual or collective trajectory inside globalized professional networks and particular territories that are favourable to them.

Flows, Transnational Networks, and Forms of Cultural Differentiation: The City for 'City Users'?

The diversity of these flows and networks runs counter to the image of European cities as socially and culturally homogeneous. The argument valid for national societies—that flows and networks exert pressure on them and help

---

[4] This idea of a 'relativization' process is central to the literature of the sociology of globalization, in particular Robertson (1992). It is also present in the works of American geographers, such as A. Smith (1995) and Brenner (1998), on scales of organization of society and capitalism.

to differentiate them—is even more valid for cities. To that extent, flows and networks contribute to the fragmentation of urban societies. However, behind these general pressures the great diversity of European cities is re-emerging.

Europe is not a region of the world noted for large-scale immigration, and this is one of its key differences from American society. However, every European country has seen waves of immigration, frequently a long time ago, with their geographical origins often linked to colonial empire: Pakistan, India, the Caribbean, and central Africa for the UK; Indonesia and Surinam for the Netherlands; Italy, Poland, Spain, Portugal, then Algeria, Morocco, Tunisia and Black Africa for France; Turkey for Germany.

For the traditional countries of immigration in Europe, the percentage of the population from abroad varies from 5 per cent to 10 per cent in the Netherlands, Germany, France, the UK, Belgium, and Austria. More favourable legal provisions and an unemployment rate that remained low during the 1980s have made Sweden the European country with the highest proportion of people from abroad: 11.5 per cent. In contrast, immigration is a recent phenomenon in southern Europe, where the rate remains below 2 per cent. For the European Union, border closure policies have meant that the flow of immigration into Europe has stabilized at a level that is not very high and includes the immigration movements of highly skilled individuals, which somewhat blur the image of an immigrant.

Thus, immigration is not vast, but is now well-established in most central and northern European countries. In some cities, such as Mediterranean ports, this immigration took place a long time ago. The urban expression of immigration is well-known: ethnic minorities settle in very large numbers in big cities (Chenu 1996; Quassoli 1999; Body-Gendrot and Martiniello 2000). In the most centralized countries, France and the UK, more than half the immigrant population lives in the region around Paris or the region around London. The same holds good for Copenhagen, Stockholm, and Helsinki. There are then relatively sizeable percentages of ethnic minorities in the West Midlands (Birmingham), Manchester, and some large industrial cities, such as Bradford and Leicester in the UK, Lyons, Lille, and Marseilles in France, as well as some cities, like Nice or Grenoble, that are at a lower level in the urban hierarchy. In countries where urban organization is less focused on one large city, the distribution of immigrant populations is between major urban centres: in Italy, for example, they are distributed between Sicily—with its proximity to Tunisia—Naples, Milan, and Rome.

Consequently, although with some exceptions, the high density and wide variety of immigrant populations are more a distinctive characteristic of the largest European cities, notably Paris—8 per cent of the population in the Paris region is from abroad—or London, but also Frankfurt—25 per cent—Rotterdam—20 per cent—Brussels—just under 30 per cent of the city centre population—and Stockholm. However, immigrant populations in medium-sized European cities increased with the growth of European cities during the

TABLE 4.4. *Ethnic minorities in European cities, 1991–1996*

City	% of other EU nationals	% of non-EU nationals
Hamburg	3.1	12.9
Munich	6.4	15.2
Cologne	5.0	13.6
Frankfurt	7.3	21.0
Essen	1.8	7.5
Stuttgart	7.9	16.2
Leipzig	1.0	2.8
Dresden	0.6	2.1
Graz	1.3	9.8
Vienna	1.4	16.0
Antwerp	3.9	9.3
Brussels	14.5	15.4
Copenhagen	2.3	7.9
Madrid	0.5	1.4
Barcelona	0.5	1.3
Valencia	0.3	0.6
Seville	0.2	0.3
Saragossa	0.2	0.3
Malaga	0.3	0.5
Helsinki	0.4	0.4
Marseilles	1.1	5.5
Lyon	2.9	6.9
Toulouse	2.3	5.6
Nice	2.6	6.0
Strasbourg	3.4	10.5
Bordeaux	3.5	3.5
Nantes	1.0	3.4
Lille	1.6	8.1
Thessaloniki	0.3	1.1
Milan	1.0	4.1
Naples	0.1	0.7
Turin	0.3	2.2
Palermo	0.1	1.7
Genoa	0.2	1.6
Florence	0.1	2.7
Bari	0.3	0.9
Dublin	5.5	1.7
Cork	4.6	1.1
Luxembourg	43.8	6.7
Amsterdam	3.3	12.2
Rotterdam	1.8	9.4
Lisbon	0.5	1.3
Oporto	0.3	1.2
Braga	0.3	0.9
Birmingham	3.6	10.7
Leeds	1.6	4.0
Glasgow	1.4	2.5
Bradford	1.4	8.8
Edinburgh	1.5	3.4
Manchester	4.3	7.2
Cardiff	1.7	4.3
Stockholm	3.6	6.5
Gothenburg	2.8	7.7
Average of European Audit cities	3.0	5.8

Source: CEC (2001).

'thirty glorious years' from 1947 to 1976 and again from the 1980s, as well as with the increased diversity of their countries of origin. Chenu (1996) notes that cities in the west of France that had been little touched by immigration—for example, Nantes, Rennes, and Brest—saw numbers of people from abroad more than double between 1968 and 1990. This spread of immigration can also now be observed in most Italian cities. Therefore, although not a large-scale phenomenon, the presence of populations from abroad has become the norm for European cities, even though, of course, there are wide variations. Ports such as Liverpool, Rotterdam, Marseilles, Genoa, and Naples, for example, are cities that have long played host to immigrant populations. This means that, although cities that are now called 'global' are distinguished by a wide variety and high density of populations from abroad, medium-sized European cities are also affected, if to a lesser extent.

None of this takes place without tensions and conflicts. In Italian cities, illegal immigration has become a major issue in public debate, involving even the Catholic hierarchy. In French cities, from 1983 onwards the extreme right Front National party gained major electoral success by attacking ethnic minorities (Mayer 2000*b*). They even control the councils in a few cities in the south of France, such as Toulon. In Anvers, the nationalist Flemish party has done the same, and has made similarly large electoral gains (Kaika and Swyngedouw 2000): in 2000, it became the leading party in the city. In most European countries, some pockets of far-right activity—in some cases, large enough to be called movements—now exist, in relation to the issue of immigration. By contrast, if UK city councils and political parties have opened the door to ethnic minority representatives, that change has not been taking place in French city council, with limited exceptions (Garbaye 2002).

Within cities, cultural diversity is expressed in the existence of communities, organized within formal associations with representatives, and of whole districts, and the presence of schools, businesses, and shops. On a limited scale, the processes of social differentiation are increasing. Mosques have appeared in many European cities. This development caused rows in France and the UK in the 1970s, but has now become practically the norm. The example of religion is an interesting one: plurality used to appear to be a privilege reserved for very large cities or industrial cities of immigration, but now the movement is spreading. Muslim, Protestant, Jewish, Buddhist, and other places of worship can be found in European cities that have, until now, been dominated by medieval cathedrals and Baroque churches. An unexpected consequence of these changes is that local councillors in European cities seem to have become preoccupied with religious matters, to an unprecedented degree. Different religious groups inevitably make demands: to build places of worship, to be granted special dispensations for dietary practices or in the school timetable, to have festivals celebrated or associations recognized. These questions affect town planning, schools, and urban public spaces, and they inevitably cause conflicts of interest, tensions, and oppositions.

The diversity of populations can also be seen in the public space: festivals for Chinese New Year, Caribbean carnivals, Muslim or Jewish religious events. 'Ethnic' shops and restaurants are extremely widespread. Cultural events are just as much an opportunity to affirm this differentiation of urban societies. Issues relating to multiculturalism are also now being raised in European cities: the organization and representation of diverse communities, the questions of language, religion, and integration at school, transnational networks, job creation, and business start-ups (Body-Gendrot and Martiniello 2000). Beyond the policy issues raised by immigrants, notably in terms of political and social rights, economic integration through formal and informal networks is starting to take on forms similar to those seen in the United States: Turkish communities in Berlin and Frankfurt, thousands of immigrant entrepreneurs in Amsterdam, informal economic networks in Italy that are now hiring Albanian, Tunisian, or even Chinese workers, North African shopkeepers in French cities, and Chinese districts are all organized according to economic and community logics that are intermingling with the host societies in an original way.[5]

Moreover, changes of scale and the demands of internationalization are blurring the image and the representation of immigrants. In his comparative work on the people he calls 'the ants of Europe'—migrants, rich or poor—Tarrius (1992: 191–2) notes that

routes to exile have been transmuted into territorial and social—and therefore economic—networks, which have the status of real mechanisms of centralities, generating wealth and various types of protection . . . odd or outsider features, such as those displayed by groups and shaped on the basis of an asserted identity, and constraints on nomadism are all local determinants of opportunities for internationalization, globalization and new wealth . . . Migrant, occupational or ethnic cultural minorities possess the keys to decompartmentalization, and carry knowledge about movement and regrouping, and about social spaces, which those who have inherited the stories of states, who are the instigators and guardians of borders, measure only within the parameters of kilometres and hours . . .

Given the growth of urbanization over the last 30 years and the development of cities, it is not surprising that maps showing the movements of individuals, business people, tourists, students, professionals, and consumers of public and private services reinforce the positions of cities, notably the largest of them. Actors within cities now try to capture these flows.

In the UK, for example, students make a choice of three universities based on their grades and the university's prestige, but also on the reputation of the city. This consumer choice, which entails financial penalties for universities that do not attract enough students, has major destabilizing effects. Cities that have fashionable shops, football teams, clubs, and a music scene clearly

---

[5] Among a vast literature, see Neveu (2000), Aniello (2001), Tarrius (2000), Kesteloot and Meert (1999), Kloosterman, van der Leun, and Rath (1999), Hillman (1999), Kastoryanno (1996), Garbaye (2002).

attract more students. In Italy, the major universities of the north and centre retain more capacity to attract students, partly at the expense of some
southern universities such as Bari. Milan and Rome respectively attract 11
per cent and 13 per cent of Italy's 1.8 million students, followed by Naples,
Bologna, Bari, Palermo, Turin, Florence, and Pisa—between 3 per cent and 6
per cent each (Savino 1998). The universities also play a structuring role in
smaller cities such as Perugia, Urbino, Padua, and Pavia. Increased mobility
for teachers as well as for students means that hierarchies are being strengthened by choices made in favour of universities that benefit from a good image
within an attractive city, and those that allow international access.

However, mobility is only a part of the story. Above all, the development
of mass university education has given the universities a certain weight.[6] The
figures from Italy speak volumes: 200,000 students in Milan, 150,000 in Naples,
100,000 in Turin and Bologna, over 60,000 in Bari, Padua, and Florence, about
50,000 in Palermo, Catania, Genoa, and Pisa, 30,000–40,000 in Perugia,
Cagliari, and Messina. In France, regional capitals have also become great
university towns par excellence (Oberti and Le Galès 1995; Sauvage 1996).
In Rennes, Nantes, Bordeaux, Toulouse, Montpellier, Grenoble, Strasbourg,
Lille, and Rouen the student population varies from 30,000 to over 60,000.
Where the cities concerned have populations of 300,000–600,000, this
means students are nearly 10 per cent of the population; but in cases where
students are concentrated in the city centre, they can represent from 15 per
cent to 20 per cent of those living there. In the UK, the recent expansion
of mass university education is now rapidly putting cities there in a similar
situation. This analysis is probably valid now for most European cities, since
universities have undergone very major development since the 1960s. The
universities are again becoming a constituent part of European cities. A
Europe of universities and university cities is in the making, interacting with
American models. This should remind us of the dynamic of the European
universities in medieval cities, when exchanges and movements experienced
very little restriction by borders or by cultures, even though these were more
distinct than they later became.

Tourism provides another example. Home exchanges for holidays give
a good picture of how attractive cities are. Fragmentation of holiday
choices and distancing from conformist models of holidays have dislocated
previous practices. Flows of tourists are swelling continuously, leading to over-
exploitation of prestige destinations. Urban tourism is experiencing unbro-
ken growth. Viard (2000) draws attention to the phenomenon whereby the
cities that attract tourists and students are also the cities that attract economic activities. By contrast, cities that have acquired a less favourable

---

[6] On France, see Dubet (1994), the special issue of the journal *Annales de la recherche
urbaine*, 62–3 (1994); for Italy, see the special issue of the journal *Archivio di studi urbani
et regionali*, 60–1 (1997–8); for Great Britain, see Lewis and Townsend (1993).

image, notably crisis-ridden, old industrial cities and regions, have difficulty in capturing these flows.

Middle and senior managers in public and private organizations, those in the professions, consultants, and experts of all kinds provide the main body of the mobile populations that move between cities. Whether for business, conferences, official reasons, or simple everyday matters, this work-related mobility has taken on very significant proportions. The individuals involved represent the largest section of 'city users' identified by Martinotti (1992). They pass through, use the transport infrastructures, hotels, and restaurants, and may provide an audience for cultural events; but in fact, as well as using some of the city's facilities, they also contribute to the local economy and to city life. They get a picture of the city and contribute to its image outside, whether positively or negatively.

European cities do not avoid the increased mobility; flows and diversity are part of the picture. This in turn poses interesting questions about how to reassess their identity.

Identity

Values, identities, and culture form an intrinsic part of the differentiated national context within which European cities are now operating, and cities may be among those playing an increasing role in the formation of identity.

Most current research on the family and kinship, on gender, work, leisure, and consumption, on values, politics, religion, and education tends to the conclusion that society is undergoing processes of disorganization and reinvention. Concepts are springing up everywhere and going on to become more or less stable as attempts are made to account for the changes being observed: concepts such as de-institutionalization, fragmentation, reflexive individualism, postmodernism, hypermodernism (Lash and Urry 1993; Giddens 1994). Some points are relevant to the transformation of cities.

Individuals are distancing themselves from the large organizations that structured national societies, and this represents the continuation of a longstanding trend. The capacity of parties, trade unions, churches, armies, and large organizations to regulate the behaviour of individuals, to impose rules on them, and to mobilize them within the context of hierarchical ways of working is in decline everywhere. In the past, organized nationally, they provided a frame for social relations, representations, values, and norms; but now these organizations are subject to strong pressures to find new, different ways of functioning. The study of political mobilizations now places more emphasis on different forms of involvement, notably the role of social movements, which some call the advent of a social movements society (Della Porta and

Diani 1999; Meyer and Tarrow 1998). This decline can also be observed in the blurring of the major traditional socio-political cleavages in European national societies, namely, religion and class (Kriesi 1998). That said, other writers place more emphasis on the ability of the trade unions, the party political structure, and the traditional cleavages to resist individualism, changes of scale, and the transformations of capitalism (Esping-Andersen 1999; Mair 1997). Change takes place slowly, and the diversity of nation-states in Europe makes generalizations hazardous.

This individualization of behaviours and values can in fact be seen in all spheres of social life, from consumption to the family. Individualism is nothing new in western Europe, given the role of religion, and the medieval cities had already helped it to flourish (Dumont 1986; Gourevitch 1997). Individuals—or, to be more precise, some individuals—are now increasingly choosing and negotiating their own involvements in the family, at work, or within kinship networks, favouring certain bonds and certain continuities for emotional reasons and for reasons of identity and self-interest (Gullestadt and Segalen 1995; de Singly 2000; Barbagli and Saraceno 1997) The family, for example, has become more democratic and less stable (Schweisguth 1995). The traditional domination of men within the family, or patriarchy, strengthened by legal mechanisms and by economic and social organization—the breadwinner model in which the man works, earns the wages, and has the family benefits paid to him—has been seriously challenged by women's access to education and the labour market and by their gaining freedom and autonomy. The evolution of gender relations and identities, part of what Giddens (1994) calls the 'detraditionalization' of society, has carried forward substantial dynamics of social change and continues to do so (Walby 1997; McDowell 1997). The greater autonomy of individuals can also be seen in the field of social relations, where modes of negotiated cooperation seem to be supplanting hierarchical relations. The involvement of individuals in cities or regions is no exception to these trends.

The advance of individualism and mobility also has implications for cities. They are evidently no longer either communities or medieval cities, able to constrain and impose norms on individuals living in them. Individualism and technological innovation reinforce each other, giving individuals greater capacities of choice as to where they live or the political and social investments they make. These choices are relative, obeying, for example, labour market logics. This enables us to identify a first dimension of the paradox of territories. The growing autonomy of individuals within large organizations and social structures, such as class or family, is linked to growing material possibilities for mobility, and these considerably ease an individual's dependence on a territory, for example, on a city: the social and political construct containing the person's family, contacts, and friends, the reservoir of identity, the site of socialization. This distancing, including subjective distancing, from the city represents a powerful mechanism for 'de-territorializing' society, for potential mobility, which may vary over time and lead to instability for cities. However, the second element of the paradox is that, in societies where individuals are less likely to inherit roles and identities, where the game is more open because of distancing from the norms and rules of large organizations, individuals are led to attach more importance to the construction of their social identity and to their own experience (Dubet 1994). This social construction may form the object of individual strategies, particularly territorial ones. The city has become a central element in the experience of individuals, and that choice is taking on a growing importance, that is, a logic of selective re-territorialization of societies. Representations of cities or regions are being accentuated anew. The choice facing a computer engineer between spending his whole life in a Coventry, Salonique, or Aalborg and working in Silicon Valley for a few years has repercussions in terms of career, income, and prestige. For certain professions, symbolic places have acquired a particular legitimacy. This is nothing new as such, but Europeanization and globalization processes are increasing the number of possibilities and helping to create new hierarchies. In contrast, other territories or cities may find themselves even more marginalized.

In more differentiated, more individualized societies, which are party to globalization processes, national society, viewed from the perspective of the nation, no longer has a monopoly over structuring identities. This is leading to 'deregulation of the identity market' and the proliferation of alternatives on offer: ethnic, regional, religious, and sexual identities; so why not urban identities? In Europe, regional and urban actors take a willing pleasure in representing themselves as new 'imagined communities' (B. Anderson 1991; Smouts 1998*a*) in reconciling reinvented tradition with the future. In so far as cities have room for manoeuvre in national societies, where the groups and actors that make up the societies define themselves partly in relation to globalized processes—sanction, mobilization, resource allocation—cities could well become one space among many, a space for social regulation and for identity-based mobilization, subject to the same illusions (Bayard 1996).

Defining regional identity, Keating (1998: 86–7) highlights three dimensions:

The first element is the cognitive one, that is people must be aware of such a thing as a region . . . A second element is the affective one, that is how people feel about the region and the degree to which it provides a framework for common identity and solidarity, possibly in competition with other forms of solidarity . . . the third element, the instrumental one, whether the region is used as a basis for mobilization and collective action in pursuit of social, economic and political goals . . . Another issue concerns the creation and reproduction of identities. Regional identity may be rooted in historical traditions and myths, but in its contemporary form, it is a social construction, forged in a specific context under the influence of social, economic and political pressures.

Keating (1998: 86) rightly makes the point that regional identity belongs to day-to-day experience: 'Local identities, which predominate in many parts of

Europe, are typically based on personal experience, individual contact and the events of everyday life.'

Within the European context, cities have existed for such a long time that to assume they have a cognitive identity and, to a certain extent, an affective identity makes a lot of sense. These vary a lot, of course, from place to place, but one cannot fail to notice the whole enterprise being systematically undertaken by urban elites to re-establish or reinvent the culture and the identity of Naples, Turin, Sheffield, Nantes, Strasbourg, Munich, Innsbruck, Turku, Copenhagen, or Valencia, often in competition with regional entrepreneurs.

Mobilization within cities will be examined in the second part of the book. European cities are part of this wider movement of identity making; and urban elites are also political entrepreneurs attempting to mobilize this resource. Within this process, the rise of cultural policies over the past 20 years is, of course, no accident (Bianchini and Parkinson 1993). What is more, the renewal of historic districts and the renovation of monuments may be thought of as bringing to light again fragments of local cultures, translated into objects and services to be consumed.

Another interesting issue is that the current phase of promoting city identities leaves room for ambiguities. The traditional image does not suffice, yet successive waves of migration raise questions about the cultural unity of cities, which tie in with the issues raised by the presence of cultural minorities that have not been totally assimilated.[7] In cities in the UK, the Netherlands, Germany, Belgium, and France, multiculturalism and the cultural differences that can be accepted by a society have become central issues (Wieviorka 1997; Rex 1996; 1997; Jopke 1998). The same debate is now rocking Spain and Italy too (Quassoli 1999). Even the Scandinavian welfare states are not exempt. Thus, Finland, which has always been thought of as an extraordinarily homogeneous society, with the exception of the Lapp minority in the far north, is now astonished to discover that more than 1 per cent of residents come from abroad, mostly in Helsinki. The pluralization of identities makes the job of defining a collective identity more difficult but of concern to social and political actors.

Conclusion

In Europe, at least since the nineteenth century, modern society has meant national society, so that cities have been part of national societies, places where trends structured within the context of, and sometimes by, the nation-state have been accentuated. This national level of organization of the social is

---

[7] Todd (1994); Body-Gendrot and Martiniello (2000); Lapeyronnie (1993). See especially Crouch's (1999) penetrating analyses of the differences between the US 'melting pot' and the European way of producing unity by integrating different groups.

now being contested. However, differentiation and fragmentation do not mean disappearance: far from it. The examples chosen emphasize that European societies are not being differentiated and reshaped simply as a result of the transformations of capitalism. In his work on the advent of post-industrial society, *The Cultural Contradictions of Capitalism* (1976), Daniel Bell stressed the tensions between the polity, the culture, and the techno-economic order, which motivate our societies. He suggested that the period of mobilization of societies by the state in the name of economic progress is over, and that we ought to expect a growing disjunction between social and cultural logics which could, in their turn, partly reorder the economy.

European societies are being deeply disturbed by contradictory forces, such as de-industrialization, development of the tertiary sector, immigration, and social inequalities; and cities are not escaping these tensions. Less structured by the state and more differentiated, national society is characterized by greater autonomy for social actors. The latter can now apply their strategies through linkages between different scales in the direction of horizontal transnational networks: of regions and cities, of Europe and the world. But the effects are not the same, depending on the social groups concerned: 'Notwithstanding the exhilaration felt by globalized elites who are able to switch their consumption to the new Americano-centric opportunities and believe they are now globalized beings, probably the vast majority of the impacts around the world are corrosive of communities' (Lloyd 2000: 259).

However, despite processes of fragmentation, individualization, and pluralization, national societies are changing slowly. For most people, apart from the most privileged or dynamic groups, national logics of social mobility remain dominant (Breen and Rottman 1998).

Accounting for social structures in European cities requires consideration of this tension between networks, flows, and existing structures. Cities are relatively robust, diverse places of linkages between culture and different forms of exchanges. This conclusion echoes Hohenberg and Hollen Lees' analyses of the diversity of regional capitals and their relative stability over time (see Chapter 2).

Some social groups, individuals, and organizations within cities have a certain capacity for exit which can be exercised either against the city or against the national society of which it forms a part. In contrast, other groups have neither the resources nor the potential to escape their city or their district. Education, mobility, travel, occupational networks, and various social bonds give the former the possibility of partial exit, or exit for a time, from the social constraints associated with a city. On processes of social differentiation, Lagroye (1997: 100) has written of 'the appearance of social groups with new resources, tending because of these to organize and to promote their own interests in order to assert their ambitions in relation to the traditional power-holding elites, and thus able to act as support and stimulant for "modernizing" activity by, for example, those in authority'. A new transatlantic or

European bourgeois class may be in the course of forming, and could gain influence in cities and to some extent reinforce the discontinuity between territories, perhaps giving birth to a new Europe of cities: but so far this remains only speculation.

As for cities taken on aggregate, the interlocking of structures, scales, and networks is producing a 'denationalization' effect. The future of these cities does not depend only on the decisions and strategies of national social groups. Trans-national networks and flows of students, tourists, immigrant workers and their families, people in diasporas, middle and senior managers in the public and private sectors, experts, artists, sportsmen and women, and itinerant groups all have a major impact on the economic prosperity of the city and on local society and its future evolution.

Cities as local societies may be destructured and disorganized. Situations will be very diverse from one city to another. Cities may be no more than a receptacle for trends that essentially draw on resources from elsewhere. They may be no more than crossroads, or nodes on networks. However, the long history of European cities has taught us that social groups and individuals tend to take into account the destiny of cities. Although cities are 'partly denationalizing', strong pressures still exist for strategies to be developed that take into account these flows and these networks: filtering, forming, and structuring them, and making them instrumental in the development of the city, alongside strategies that promote the interests and prestige of one group or another. The linkages between groups and changing and unchanging logics may be the chance for the city to project itself onto the stage of European society, to take its place at the beginnings of societies that might emerge at the European or world level. These are important stakes, destabilizing but attractive to political and social entrepreneurs, who may derive advantage from a fluid situation, calling into question national hierarchies and social structures in order to propose different models that are partly involved in supra-national and trans-national logics.

This differentiation of spaces for interaction opens the field of the possible for individuals in terms of belonging and of negotiating their involvement in a given space. Individuals are to some extent able to choose or negotiate their belonging to one political or social space or another and their degree of investment and interaction. Mobility and individualization open the way to logics of choice. However, uncertainty and risk associated with changes also reinforce interdependence between individuals and groups. In that sense, one wonders whether cities might become a level at which interdependence is structured to prevent risk.

Some of the literature on cities emphasizes forms of mobility that render the classic image of the city obsolete (Ascher 1995; Urry 2000); but my conclusions do not tend in this direction. For example, sociologists of the family have shown that, although it has become more vulnerable and is the object of negotiation and selective investments on the part of individuals, the family remains 'robust'. It receives overwhelming support in all surveys of people's values, and remains a fundamental structure for socializing and integrating individuals. Less constrained by family, individuals invest in it by choice while retaining their autonomy. The more individualism gains ground, the more the family appears to be a refuge and an important structure. Similarly, European cities are no longer closed societies that constrain individuals. The issue of flows and temporary city users will remain very important. Cities may be seen and represented as passive spaces across which flows run or, at best, as nodes on networks, as major junctions where flows cross. Actors within cities, as well as coalitions, may also have an interest in trying to capture, steer, form, use, and structure these flows. This image of networks triumphing over places is, however, inadequate to account for European cities and how they are structured. The more mobile groups and individuals are, the more they may need, or choose, to benefit from the atmosphere of the city. European cities offer their monuments, their city centres, their public spaces, their public services, and their social and cultural diversity. There is nothing to say that groups and individuals will not come to combine forms of mobility and membership of networks with the roots they have put down in a city, all the more so because the city will be to some extent chosen—unless the choice is restricted because the labour market is transformed by globalization.

FIVE

Cities and Capitalism: Are European Cities Likely to Dissolve in the Networks of Globalized Capitalism?

Two changes, already mentioned in relation to the state, currently seem to be contributing to the dislocation of European cities—at least, those under consideration here: a technological revolution—that is, new information and communication technologies—and the globalization of the economy. The sheer volume of literature on these changes cannot conceal a degree of uncertainty as to their meaning and their spatial and temporal dynamics, not to mention their unexpected combinations and effects. Market logics seem to be openly pushing our societies towards what Marxists interpret as a new and deeper form of capitalism, a new round of 'commodification' that is allowing capitalism not only to reach increasingly distant spaces but, above all, to connect them in immediate time: in other words, time-space compression (D. Harvey 1989). Whatever the size or the novelty of the phenomenon, most social science research on these issues tends to suggest there are changes in state-market relations and social structures. For cities, this must also mean greater dependence on capitalism. For instance, geographers are pointing to the rise of mega-city regions all over the world, which may be the engine of the globalizing economy in Asia, Africa, North America, and South America (Scott 2001).

To the eyes of classical economists and social scientists fascinated by technologies, the future of European cities does not look glorious. For instance, in *The Rise of the Network Society*, the first volume in his trilogy, Castells takes us on a remarkable journey across five continents. Although he claims that he avoids falling into technological determinism, his approach mixes sociological analysis and a quasi-prophetic admiration with the information technology revolution. Globalization and the technological revolution are combining to form a network society whose powers of transformation are nothing short of colossal: 'The global economy emerging from informational-based production and competition is characterized by its *interdependence*, its *asymmetry*, its *regionalization*, the *increasing diversification within each region*, its *selective inclusiveness*, its *exclusionary segmentation*, and, as a result of all these features, an extraordinarily *variable geometry* that tends to dissolve historical, economic geography' (Castells 1996: 106). His whole analysis is centred around the triumph of flows over places. Like earlier forms, this new form of capitalism produces a type of city, in this case the mega-city, which is both form and process: 'a new spatial form, which develops in a variety of social and geographical contexts: megacities . . . They are the nodes of the global economy, concentrating the directional, productive, and managerial upper functions all over the planet; the control of the media; the real politics of power; and the symbolic capacity to create and diffuse messages' (Castells 1996: 403). In this account, Castells offers the explanation that the same forces produce the same effects, despite the fact that cities everywhere in the world are being restructured in ways integral to their particular stories. In similar vein, in a section titled 'The fading charm of European cities', he proclaims the marginalization of European cities, with the exception of London, as they are not among the 20 biggest cities in the world. However, after being momentarily carried away, the author does note that the processes and trends he is describing may take time, even if they are already dominant.

From a different angle, Krugman (1995) and Rogowski (1999) suggest another scenario, hardly more encouraging for medium-sized European cities. In Europe, dynamics associated with the making of the single market, coupled with the introduction of the single currency, arouse very serious concerns about future territorial inequalities. In many respects European integration processes are accentuating economic dynamics that can also be observed on the global scale, and the interesting issue is how things will evolve. On the basis of his theory linking the effects of growth in trade to regional specialization, Krugman anticipates a dislocation of European spatial dynamics, that is, a movement towards specialization on the part of large urban areas, in the wake of what has been observed in the United States.[1] Starting from the classic literature of economics, Krugman suggests that space is being reorganized by flows. Inspired by this literature, Rogowski has gone on to propose an exercise somewhat in the style of Zipf's Law, established in 1941, which pointed out that, on average and in a large number of countries, a country's second city had about half the number of inhabitants of biggest city, that its third city had about a third of the largest population, the fourth a quarter, and so on. After some decades of European integration and the continuous removal of trade barriers and state obstacles to the movement of goods and people, the European Union, with its 360 million people, should reach a spatial equilibrium; Rogowski suggests a period of 50 years for this. By applying Zipf's Law, he deduces that there will be a megalopolis of 21

---

[1] See Martin and Sunley (2000) for a closely-argued discussion of Krugman's theses.

million inhabitants, and several conurbations of 3 million people, as there are today; but above all—and this is the fundamental point—he predicts a decline by half in the number of conurbations with 1 million–3 million inhabitants and in the number of smaller cities. This law predicts both spatial organization on the exact pattern of what has been observed in the United States—and beyond—and the breakup of the core of urban Europe. As far as large European cities are concerned, he makes the following prediction:

Of cities like Amsterdam, Antwerp, Barcelona, Brussels, Copenhagen, Dublin, Frankfurt, Hamburg, Lisbon, Liverpool, Lyons, Manchester, Marseilles, Munich, Naples, Newcastle, Nuremberg, Stockholm, Stuttgart, Turin and Vienna, half must either grow or decline: expanding to become one of the six or seven European urban giants, or declining into provincial insignificance . . . The carnage will likely be most pronounced among the mid-sized cities of Germany and the United Kingdom. (Rogowski 1998: 16)

As is often the case with this type of work, the argument has the merit of the clarity and elegance of a mathematical model. Rogowski, however, pursues his intellectual exercise by a discussion of the economic and political factors capable of accelerating or hindering such a development: dynamics of concentration in the globalized economy, ethnic conflicts, and, above all, political pressures from European cities to avoid the consequences of this kind of change by attracting European subsidies, blocking immigration, or developing redistributive spatial policies. He concludes: 'Finally, as Europe overall becomes less urban but its few largest cities grow, the cultural divide between city and suburb will likely grow, and political support for the needs of cities generally may well decline—as has clearly occurred since the 1960's in the US' (Rogowski 1998: 23). *Here endeth the lesson*. Both Krugman and Rogowski position themselves within a neoclassical political economy perspective: social and political logics remain peripheral, being seen rather as constraints. It is easy to understand that the authors are interested in seeing the movement of goods and services eventually lead to Europe shedding any archaisms, including the heritage of its charming cities. The presuppositions of their analysis are the same as those found in the neoclassical view: namely, the superiority of market mechanisms and convergence towards an optimum equilibrium.

By contrast, the economic sociology-political economy tradition attempts to demonstrate linkages between social groups, forms of power, institutions, and beliefs, whether analysing economic or other phenomena. In Europe, conflicts are developing about both the level and the type of regulation of the various forms of capitalism and of society. Although we cannot deny the importance of the technological revolution taking place, its capacity to sweep all before it and, in particular, simply to dissolve history and geography is, at the very least, questionable. Historically, Europe is distinguished by institutionalized and territorialized forms of capitalism (Regini 1995; Crouch and Streeck 1996). A whole research tradition has highlighted various forms of institutionalized capitalism—in the sense of institutionalization through norms, rules, and procedures—framed by social compromises and integrated into national and sub-national territories. Since the late nineteenth century, Polanyi's 'great transformation' (1955)—the re-embedding of the economy in social and political structures in order to contain the destructive logic of the marketplace—has taken diverse forms in western Europe: consociational in Belgium and the Netherlands, corporatist—with variations between countries —in Scandinavia, Germany, and Austria, more statist in France. These national models of capitalism have gradually been institutionalized by inter-action and conflicts between states, economic interest groups, firms, and polit-ical forces. There is no doubt that the combination of information and communication technologies, associated with the forces of globalization—in particular, those powerful actors who most favour neo-liberalism, such as the financial sector—has produced a major shock for European economies and a destabilization of national models of regulation, whatever their variant of the Keynesian compromise. However, there are elements to suggest that actors within European cities have resources to adapt to the new economic environment.

This chapter examines the dynamics of economic globalization and their impact on European cities from two, inevitably partial, angles: first, in order to identify the dynamics and the forces of change and second, to demon-strate the paradoxes and contradictions, or least the uncertainties, of their impact. The economy of the city is not just a matter of location of activities, production, and services to firms: it includes the welfare state (see Chapter 4) and all the different infrastructures. I will concentrate first on the uneven dynamism of urban and regional economies, in order to identify restructur-ing on the US pattern—if there is any. Then I will examine the process of globalization and 'marketization' of urban services, firms, and networks, which is leading to pressures on cities. In both cases, the tension between globalized economic processes and existing territorialized social and polit-ical structures seems to be creating a mix that does not signal the end of European cities.

Interlocking Scales in the Economy, Fragmentation of National Territories, and a Mosaic of Territories

In most European countries, the development of certain territories in terms of economic growth has been subject to much research. As they clamber over the rubble of de-industrialization in their search for 'winner regions', many bold theoreticians have followed the trails of the industrial districts of Italy, or of embryonic Silicon Valleys, looking for the philosopher's stone that might produce the 'wealth of the regions' (Benko and Lipietz 1992). Beyond the

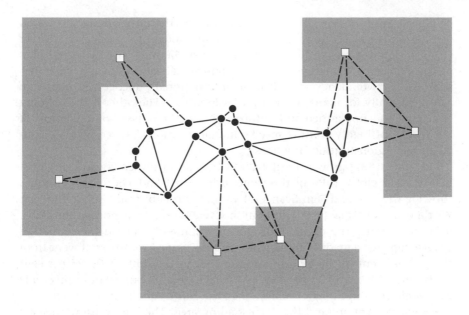

● Regional motor

□ Island of relative prosperity and economic opportunity

☐ Prosperous hinterland area

▨ Extensive economic frontiers of global capitalism

FIG. 5.1. Global mosaic of regional economies
Source: A. J. Scott (1998).

hierarchies-versus-districts debate, regional economists reveal a mosaic on a global scale in which local and regional economies are linked by horizontal and vertical networks, in what Veltz (1996) has called 'the archipelago economy'.

Territories of the European Economy and the Impact of Globalization Processes

It is first necessary to distinguish between globalization as a political project and globalization as a series of analysable and measurable processes. 'The space of flows' is a particularly thought-provoking economic and technological myth. In questioning the interactions between different types of economic flows, hierarchies, and territories, sociologists and economic geographers have helped to clarify and differentiate different types of processes: this is a vital step forward in departing from a view dominated either by the top-down story of globalization of flows and global cities or by the rather desperate search for flexible local economies on the Italian model.[2] In particular, Storper (1997: 191) has stressed the permanent tension between two types of forces in the globalized economy: 'One is the bureaucratization of capitalist enterprise, with its tendency to diffuse an internationally recognized matrix of rules, especially for managers and professionals . . . The other is the ongoing development—unplanned and unforeseeable at the outset—of new forms of knowledge of highly context-specific human relations.' Three points distinguish these globalization processes.

First, the strong growth in globalized trade, and the emergence of global markets and global rules of the game: using Hirst and Thomson's critiques showing the size and significance of various forms of trade before the First World War, Held *et al.* (1999) distinguish several historical periods in the globalization of trade. The classic indicator of volume of trade in the formation of GDP suggests a gradual acceleration. For developed countries, it went from about 8 per cent in the 1950s to 20 per cent in the mid-1970s, 25 per cent in the mid-1980s, and 30 per cent by the late 1990s. A large part of this trade was within the three major trading zones: the North American Free Trade Area, the European Union, and the Asian trading area. The big drop in transport costs has marked the end of the 'diktat of fixed costs'. The costs of communications, of air and—especially—maritime transport have fallen significantly, helping this expansion in several forms of trade. So economic actors have reorganized around focal points of trade: for example, areas of economic activity near airports, or development of agricultural produce around ports.

Second, the figures on globalization of finance are breathtaking, and this spectacular growth has caught the popular imagination. Technological resources now allow the movement of financial flows around the globe in search of the best possible returns. Held *et al.* give one simple indicator: total loans and financial securities, negligible in 1960, had risen to $US890 billion by 1997, with $7,635 billion dollars amassed at that date. The liberalization of financial flows in the 1980s, initiated in Europe by Mrs Thatcher, inspired innovation and stimulated this growth. Growth in these financial flows is even higher than growth in trade or production. It is now organized by an interconnected set of financial markets, actors, and rules of the game: pension funds, insurance companies, and banks make their effects felt in the capitalization of large firms or in states' borrowing capabilities.

Third, according to Veltz (1996: 116), and seen from the point of view of firms, 'globalization is imposing itself as a strategy for controlling the diversity of products, organizations and areas by internal or external co-ordination, concentration or dispersal'. In other words, it represents the other side of

---

[2] On these points and the various types of processes, see key works by Storper (1997) and Veltz (1996), the lively debate between Amin (1999) and Lovering (1999), the comparative work of Crouch *et al.* (2001), and a fair sample of the recent literature in Benko and Lipietz (2000).

differentiated mobility of the factors of production: rapid mobility of capital as compared with the limited mobility of labour—in Europe, in any case—and the relative mobility of technologies and knowledge, although some are very much anchored in territories (Storper 1997). For firms, globalization means the end of national oligopolies, destabilization through competition opening up, the pressure of demand and of customers, and the transformation of the logics of efficiency: 'modern competitiveness arises above all from the quality of organization of production units in the manufacture/creation stage, but also at the design and marketing stages; forms of performance are increasingly the result of *system effects*—of the relevance and coherence of chains of co-operation between multiple actors inside, and even outside, firms' (Veltz 2000: 100). The unceasing growth of mergers and acquisitions, of direct foreign investments—whose volume increased fourfold between 1984 and 1994—and of mega-mergers suggests that, in time and in different sectors, global oligarchies will form, with the largest firms controlling an ever more impressive part of the wealth, since the turnover of the largest firms is often larger than the GDP of average-sized states. Globalization means multiple forms of interdependence, differentiated between firms, markets, and territories, with the adoption of forms of cellular organization in networks to try to resolve these tensions.[3]

The importance of these phenomena is debated and contested, and varies according to sphere, territory, and sector. Some people stress the structured logic of the phenomenon as a new upsurge of capitalism, imposing its domination more and more intensely and widely across the globe, while others underline diversity and contradictions. Similar debates are driving urban research. The correlation recorded between the accelerated growth of metropolises and economic globalization processes has sharpened consideration of the contemporary logics of metropolization in Asia, in the Americas, and, to a lesser extent, in Europe.

One approach to taking this debate forward is to look at a small part of the economy, choosing one that seems to be a driving or dominant force in the economy, and then to examine the logics of globalization and the spatial implications. Sassen (1991: 3–4) does this in highlighting global cities:

. . . these cities now function [as centres] in four new ways: first, as highly concentrated command points in the organization of the world economy; second, as key locations for finance and for specialized service firms, which have replaced manufacturing as the leading economic sectors; third, as sites of production, including the production of innovations, in these leading industries; and fourth, as markets for the products and innovations produced.

---

[3] A point highlighted clearly by Castells (1996). Veltz (2000) distinguishes six forms of enterprise network: the classic large firm, which involves its subcontractors in a hierarchical relationship, networks of SMEs centred on one territory or around a 'conductor' firm, the hollow firm with a strategic centre, and other forms of looser and more limited networks.

Classic definitions of 'global cities' describe them in terms of their central role in exchange flows: flows of travellers and of merchandise, and as headquarters of the largest firms and of cultural and political institutions, banks, and insurance companies: in other words, on the basis of their functions and their power to exert economic and political influence. Thus, growth in exchanges of goods and persons, which has accelerated since the 1970s, gives cities at the heart of these exchanges a special position. The development of multinational and then global firms means the concentration of economic power within these firms, which establish their headquarters—and therefore the power of highly aggregated economic command—in a small number of very large metropolises. These metropolises are thus integrated into the most globalized part of the economy, which gives them a special role. Sassen (1991) goes further, first and foremost by stressing that the dynamic of economic globalization requires capacities for control and coordination, which are changing scale. Global cities are cities within which these modes of control and coordination are organized, giving such cities increasingly extensive influence. Above all, global cities have an original dynamic of producing innovations for the leading services of capitalism: financial and legal services, consultancy, and communication. The global city is a particular environment, producing specialized, innovative services that enable coordination and control of the globalized economy, thanks to the concentration of global firms' headquarters and of these services. For Sassen, the dispersal of activities increases the need in the global city for a social and economic environment that can produce its own codes and its own culture, thus contributing to coordination. She deduces from this that there is a new social structure, distinguished by the concentration of social groups involved in the global city dynamic, who need a whole set of professional and domestic services: hence the proliferation of low-paid, insecure workers cleaning offices, providing various domestic services, and staffing restaurants and cafés. This dual structure is characteristic of advanced capitalism and the global cities that are its command centres: New York, London, Tokyo, and, to a lesser extent, Los Angeles, Paris, and Frankfurt.

In these conditions, the global city could be said to constitute an original social structure. However, in this regard Hamnett's (1995) work on London and Préteceille's (1999) on Paris invalidate the thesis. Both confirm the dynamic of growth and of segregation of the most privileged groups, but do not detect either an accentuation of polarization or the decline of the middle strata. On the economic side, criticisms directed at this seductive thesis have started to bring into doubt the structuring effects of the part of the global economy Sassen is considering. The leading services she identifies are certainly important, notably in the financial sector, but are they the dominant part of the global economy, and what are the links by which they drive the rest? Others have pointed out that the economy of large metropolises includes many elements other than the one studied by Sassen, and that this reduces the significance of her analysis. Veltz criticises this way of linking globalization and metropolization, used by both Sassen and Castells. For him, although the cities that are being called global are the natural centres of services highlighted by Sassen,

the links between globalization and metropolization are both more complex and more general. (a) The concrete dynamics of metropolization result not from a top-down logic deriving from the most directly globalized processes in the economy —financial globalization . . . —but from the meeting between these dynamics and specific economic and territorial logics, a meeting on several scales—local, national, and regional . . . (b) Growing economic polarization results . . . from a much more general phenomenon, that of congruence between the metropolitan environment and the new dynamics of economic development . . . (Veltz forthcoming, 2002).

Others have also interpreted these globalization processes by stressing different economic changes, which interlock various scales.[4] This means the dynamics of metropolization can be used to account for both the growth of a good number of European cities, notably regional capitals, and the effects of acceleration and accentuation of these dynamics in the largest of them. Differences are of degree, not of nature, reflecting hierarchies of cities.

The dynamic of metropolization is conventionally explained by costs logic and by the effects of externality. The vertical and horizontal disintegration of firms (see above) and the development of various forms of cellular-network organization render the firm dependent on numerous externalities, with slightly higher transaction costs. These cost-related reasons explain the dynamic of firms clustering in metropolises (Scott 1988). Under the impact of competition, of new exchange and production organizations, and of the increasingly relational constituent element of competitiveness, firms may need the resources produced by territories—collective competition goods for Crouch *et al.* (2001)—yet they also need to integrate themselves into environments characterized by great diversity, by the production of innovations, and by varied forms of cooperation. In other words, they simultaneously need more market and more non-market relations and synergies. For Storper (1997), such non-market-led forms of interdependence are precisely a fundamental characteristic of certain industries and services and of certain territories, and this fosters the dynamic of territorialization. These competitive collective goods and these non-market-led forms of interdependence are situated and mobilized in different territories: however, cities, and notably the biggest cities, are the privileged terrain for their production and distribution. Destabilized by competition and changing forms of organization, firms are

---

[4] Jessop (2000: 340), in his precise manner, stresses the fact that he is attempting to analyse globalization as 'a complex, chaotic and overdetermined outcome of a multi-scalar, multi-temporal and multi-centric series of processes operating in specific structural contexts, and to assess the implications of the emergence of the global as the ultimate horizon of action in the economic and political systems'.

looking for territories within which they can quickly alter their strategies and their forms of cooperation. Cities offer 'flexibility guarantees', to use Veltz's (1996) expression, in that firms can find partners for sophisticated competition-cooperation games there, as well as services and sizeable, differentiated labour markets. However, should the need arise, firms want to be able to pull out as fast as possible and without any difficulty.

These authors have put their finger on a major contradiction that should prevent us from taking too naive a view of local development. On the one hand, firms need competitive collective goods and non-market-led forms of interdependence, such as a large, trained, highly differentiated workforce, research centres, networks for the production and dissemination of innovations, learning capacity, knowledge, services, roots in globalized networks: all things that require a lot of time to produce and organize, and which are not often the result of pure market logics (Crouch *et al.* 2001). On the other hand, firms increasingly obey short-term logics, which push them to use these goods without helping to produce them in the medium or the long term. In other words, the more firms obey short-term market logics, the more dependent they are on non-market goods and services produced by the territories on which their competitiveness depends. This argument demands a caveat, however: untraded forms of interdependence are not stable, and an increasing volume of collective competitive goods is also produced by the market on a global scale.

In Europe: National Spaces Fragmented into Regions, Metropolises, Cities, and Local Systems

The localization of economic activities is the object of impassioned debates in Europe. States used to be the guarantors of national unity and of economic and social cohesion within their borders. In each country, urban dynamics were oriented towards strengthening capital cities and, in some cases, frequently other cities as well. In all countries, major economic crises involved state intervention, which was called regional policy or, in the more proactive French version, *aménagement du territoire*: a combination of carrot—subsidies—and stick—setting limits on the most prosperous areas. During the Fordist period, states had to mobilize all their viable forces, including peripheral regions, for economic development. Since the beginning of Italian unification, the *Mezzogiorno* has remained one of the horizons beyond which Italian politics and policies seem unable to move. Regenerating large industrial cities in the north of England, modernizing the west of France, and maintaining economic activities in northern Sweden or northern Finland are ongoing themes. The enlarged European market and globalization appear as threats to local societies, cities, and regions that have seen, or fear, the power of capitalism's creative-destructive mechanisms. Contrasts between periods do not make analyses any easier. During the 1970s, the accentuation of de-industrialization, the economic crisis, and demands for quality of life seemed to be leading towards 'the end of cities'. In contrast, the second half of the 1980s, which corresponded to the rediscovery of a European Union dynamic and the take-off of economic globalization processes, was accompanied by rediscovery of a dynamic for cities.

In Europe, the way activities have localized since the 1970s reveals the following changes: the decline of old industrial regions, the growth of cities, and the growth of local systems of production.

1. The relative or absolute decline of the most industrial regions, particularly the oldest, and of industrial ports: the Ruhr, Wallonia—Liège—Limburg, north-eastern France—Lille-Roubaix-Tourcoing, Metz, and Nancy—Saint-Étienne and Le Creusot, Marseilles, Bilbao, the industrial triangle of North-western Italy—specifically Turin, Genoa, and the small industrial cities—Naples, Cork, the Midlands—Birmingham, Coventry, and Wolver-hampton—Liverpool, Manchester, Sheffield, Newcastle, Glasgow, Essen, Düsseldorf, Bremen, Dresden, and Leipzig. The decline is more pronounced still in small industrial cities. Most of these have experienced the effects of de-industrialization, the urban crisis, loss of population—especially the most highly-skilled people—and the departure of firms, followed by attempts to renew the fabric of enterprise, either by attracting businesses or by creating them. Some have been revived, whether in economic terms—these are more likely to be conurbations—or in terms of population, notably large cities such as Birmingham, Manchester, Barcelona, and Milan (see Commission of the European Communities 2000).

2. Concentration and dispersal into metropolises that combine political power and economic might. Since the mid-1980s, cities—those that are not old industrial cities—and above all the largest cities have felt the full benefits of growth. In centralized countries, it seems to be mainly the region around the capital city that absorbs the strongest forces and the economic dynamism: this is true not only of London, Paris, Rome, and Berlin, the capitals of the leading EU member states, but also of Madrid, Dublin, Stockholm, Helsinki, Copenhagen, and Lisbon. In the lower echelons of the hierarchy of cities, some regional capitals and other medium-sized European cities have also experienced strong growth: Bologna, Strasbourg, Lyons, Grenoble, Nice, Montpellier, Toulouse, Bordeaux, Nantes, Rennes, Munich, Cologne, Frankfurt, Geneva, Valencia, Seville, Saragossa, Norwich, Bristol, Swindon, Leicester, Turku. In some cases, however, economic dynamism has actually combined with population losses to release the grip previously exerted by certain metropolises, a development that has been particularly spectacular in northern Italy, where medium-sized cities from Milan to Venice have seen very strong growth. A new feature has been that a number of cities have undergone economic development discon-nected from the regions surrounding them. The movement of concentration-dispersal of activities favours smaller cities and rural spaces around cities.

By contrast, others, especially smaller cities, which, from a French point of view, might be described as medium-sized cities, are experiencing changes that tend more towards decline, as if regional metropolises in their turn are largely absorbing the economic dynamism of their region, as in Tuscany, Emilia-Romagna, Languedoc-Roussillon, and Midi-Pyrénées.

3. Relative heliotropism: economic activities have more of a tendency to become established in the south: in Germany, in south-east England, on the French Mediterranean rim, in Finland, and to some extent in Sweden and Denmark, although not in southern European countries.

4. The spectacular economic growth of local systems of SMEs: in districts in central and north-eastern Italy, then spreading both north to the area around Milan and south to the area around Naples or Bari; in Baden-Württemberg; in Jutland in Denmark; and in the Arve Valley and Oyonnax in France. The north-east region of Italy has seen, in recent years, the strongest growth of any European region (Crouch *et al.* 2001).

5. In terms of growth in per capita GDP by region—a contested measure—the period of convergence between regions within states seems to have gradually come to an end between the late 1970s and the late 1980s, depending on country. Since then, strong differences have arisen, with both increasing inequalities and greater convergences in terms of incomes.

Economic growth has tended to become an urban phenomenon, with local economic dynamics playing a part. Rather than unreservedly espousing the space of flows thesis, Europe over the last 30 years has offered more an image of linked cities and flows that respect existing urban structures. The urban framework seems to be robust, while the national economic territory is suffering from discontinuities and from accentuated inequalities. Metropolises and cities that have not been over-industrialized are the major winners. There is also some discontinuity in the productivity of territories. Davezies (1998*c*) has calculated that the productivity of London and Paris took off during the 1980s, and these two metropolises now function as points of articulation between the national economy and the European or global economy. London and Paris massively accentuate the fluctuations of the national economy, whether this shows growth or decline. On a lesser scale, French regional capitals have experienced higher productivity than their regions (Rousseau 1998; Davezies 1998*b*).

This emphasis on metropolises must not lead us to ignore analyses such as that of Rodriguez-Posé (1998) in considering the economic growth of European regions from 1960 to 1991, he examines the growth differentials between the UK and France on the one hand, and between Italy and Germany on the other. Like Cheshire and Gordon (1996), he puts forward the hypothesis that, for the period under consideration, too much economic centralization could have been harmful to growth. More balanced, less hierarchical urban systems such as those in Italy or Germany have allowed stronger growth because of competition between cities and innovations in the governance of urban economies.

All this is moving more in the direction of the meta-stability of the European system, as described by Cattan *et al.* (1999). The current dynamic seems more to strengthen existing urban hierarchies, especially to the advantage of the biggest metropolises and a large number of medium-sized European cities. Without prejudging trends, we should note for the moment that the space of flows is strengthening rather than dissolving the existing hierarchies, and some of the literature, notably Cattan (1995) on air travel flows, demonstrates this. The robust framework of European cities seems to be bearing the shock and able to take advantage of economic changes, although the largest metropolises in Europe are the big winners in recent developments.

Urban Networks and the Building of Cities: The Globalization of City Industry

The economy of the city cannot be seen solely from the point of view of firms' strategies in deciding where to set up. By virtue of its materiality, the city is also a site for the construction, management, and production of services that are an important vector for capitalist accumulation. The role of banks and of property developers in the building of cities has long been well-known. Once fairly much confined to the public domain, the construction of facilities, infrastructures, and technical networks is now at stake for the major service sector groups that have formed in Europe and elsewhere.

In these troubled times, with uncertain identities, interlocked scales, virtual reality, and proliferations of powerful images, cities epitomize this new world—for instance, in the science fiction of Philip K. Dick or William Gibson—but they also represent something reassuring: buildings, houses, streets, squares, monuments, and shops, not to speak of the hidden tangle of pipes and cables that enable water, power, communications, and information to circulate: the city of engineers, town planners, development planners, and architects. The materiality of cities is expressed through buildings and services: water management and distribution, construction of housing, offices, and industrial or craft premises, property development, planning, waste collection and recycling, energy supply, cables needed for communications and information, transport infrastructures and networks—roads, traffic, tramways, buses, underground transport, airports, parking, railways, stations, cycleways—urban district heating systems, shopping centres, museums, conference halls or sports stadiums, parks and open spaces, prisons, hospitals, cemeteries, schools, and universities.

Organized mainly in a public-sector context, or tightly controlled by the public authorities, the production and management of such housing, facilities, and services have now become subject to the logics identified earlier: technological revolution, globalization, European integration, deregulation/re-regulation, and changing scales of actors. In this story, cities can partly escape from the hold of the state. They are becoming dependent on major global firms in the urban services sector, but they are able to retain some political leverage to control certain developments. European cities are not just nodes on privatized trans-national networks.

Globalization of Firms

European cities have been constructed gradually. Princes, bishops, and burghers financed and built palaces, districts, and squares. The European's imagined picture of the city has been handed down through this legacy of monuments, squares, and districts, which still structure most European cities today. Property developers and bankers played a central role in building cities. In the nineteenth century, working-class districts were hastily flung up in the centres of industrial cities, and small houses and large buildings were located rather anarchically on their peripheries. Gradually, however, most facilities and services came to be organized and funded by public authorities, state services, or local authorities. The appalling living conditions of the working class and public health concerns led to the development of modern networks—water and gas for all—to the building of housing, and gradually to the development of facilities and services. State development in the twentieth century took the form, in part, of such housing, roads and bridges, technical networks, facilities, and infrastructures.

Production of services and facilities developed in a national context, whether directly linked to the state in a public or quasi-public form, or, more rarely, in a commodity form encouraged or framed by the state. Therefore, they have taken varied forms in Europe, according to the development of the welfare state—in the case of housing, for example—or according to the distribution of powers between local and central levels. The predominantly public-sector logic and the national context are now being called into question. Thus, in his survey of social housing in Europe and the United States, Harloe (1995) traces four major phases in the building of social housing in Europe. The first two were before the First World War in the social reform era—a little later in France—and the inter-war period, notably when Sweden was laying down the foundations of its welfare state. He then contrasts the golden age of post-war reconstruction and the 'thirty glorious years' with the decline and marginalization of social housing since the 1970s. He demonstrates the particular nature of housing and the role it has played in capitalist development, since it lies at the core of issues of ownership, financial networks, and industrial strategies. Consequently, large-scale social housing has developed only in particular social, economic, and political conditions, during periods of crisis or post-war reconstruction and Keynesian compromise. In every country, major construction groups, in close cooperation with the state, played a key role in the large-scale building of public and private housing (Dunleavy 1980; Topalov 1987). In the Netherlands, Germany,

Scandinavia, and the UK, city councils are responsible for building and maintaining social housing, in cooperation with the central state, sometimes under the control of the state and large construction firms. In France in the 1950s, senior civil servants in the Ministry of Finance used the *Caisse des Dépôts et Consignation*, a state-owned savings and loan group, to create subsidiary organizations responsible for planning and development in French cities, at the height of accelerated urbanization. Today, in all countries, non-market-led production of housing has again become limited, even residual.

Another example is that of technical networks:

networks for the distribution of water, for drainage, electricity, heating, transport, telecommunications . . . they are 'networks' because each is an arrangement of lines and points—rather than a movement of flows— equipped with certain functions in relation to the services it delivers—rather than an infrastructure, which is just an aid; and they are 'technical networks' because each is a physically present network equipped with facilities and a layout, exerting a hold over the ground into whose space it has inserted its own concrete devices. (Offner and Pumain 1996: 21)

These networks are at the core of thinking on cities and urban planning (Tarr and Dupuy 1988). Specialists distinguish three dimensions: network infrastructure, service to the end-user, and the command network that steers the whole thing. These networks and their infrastructures were once the pride of modern cities: power stations, pumping stations, and water towers were a salient feature of the urban landscape before modern technical networks were, with an equal flourish, able to conceal the physical reality and the socio-political arrangements that enabled them to function, making them seem to some extent natural (Kaika and Swyngegouw 2000).

The organization of these services resulted in a mix between state, local authorities, and private firms, each country having its own mix (Lorrain and Stoker 1996). In Britain, the main urban services were all originally organized by local authorities and some private firms, until some—electricity, gas, telecommunications, and railways—were nationalized. Such a movement 'from city councils to state' can take various forms. In France, the state took control of operations very early, except in the case of water, which, surprisingly, was entrusted, on long-term concessions, to private firms or to local publicly controlled enterprises created in the nineteenth century. Managed as quasi-public enterprises, the *Société Lyonnaise des Eaux* and the *Compagnie Générale des Eaux* were to develop gradually and unobtrusively, without any spectacular nationalization such as that of *Électricité de France* (Lorrain 1996b). In Germany, on the other hand, after a period when the city councils entrusted long-term concessions to private firms for the supply of gas and heating, for example, they went on to bring services under direct management on the eve of the First World War: water, gas, electricity, urban district heating systems, and tramways (Reidenbach 1996). Despite conflicts—between adherents of the free market and those of municipal socialism, for example—the city councils created the *Stadtwerke*, managed either by direct control or as subsidiary bodies to the city councils to run these services, but with differences between one *Land* and another. Italy had a system of large public enterprises for energy and railways, while water remained the responsibility of the city councils under the close supervision of the state; but the extraordinarily high number of operators gave rise to many difficulties. Finally, some Italian city councils, particularly in the north, also had generalist municipal enterprises in charge of urban transport, water distribution, waste collection, and urban district heating systems. Consequently, the European countries offer a very diverse panorama of institutional arrangements and forms of organization, with, despite everything, a classic contrast between the powerful Nordic local authorities, which often have broad spheres of competence in terms of service management, and those of the south, where discrepancies in the development of these services combine with a low level of municipal autonomy in management terms.

Technical networks and associated technical expertise can therefore be viewed as powerful instruments for unifying territory, for social cohesion (Offner and Pumain 1996), and for control, and this holds good for the national territory—with the telegraph, for example—for the city, and the conurbation. The technical network also has another face, since it can move freely, thumbing its nose at political and administrative borders. 'Challenging spatial proximities, it creates, through its connections, a map made up of individual points, far removed from the continuity and exhaustivity that form the basis of territory' (Offner and Pumain 1996: 22). For cities, the ever-increasing power of interlocked scales and networks represents a risk of being dismantled.

Despite the variations mentioned, a sizeable part of the infrastructures and technical networks, while managed in the public or quasi-public sector—thus bringing city councils face to face with the state or with nationalized public enterprises—had its own rules and funding, its political legitimacy, and its own expertise. This is no longer the case. Some technical networks—in particular, telecommunications, information, energy, and water—have been privatized over several years and transferred to the market sphere, which has public forms of regulation distanced from politics. This is a background wave whose effects are still difficult to measure. Carried forward by firms and political authorities, this deregulation movement takes varied forms:

it combines three processes: the transfer of property rights from the public to the private sector—*privatization*; the opening-up to competition of previously monopolistic or narrowly oligopolistic markets—*liberalization*; finally the modification in the regulatory mechanisms implemented to control these markets—*de*regulation, which it would be more precise to call *trans*regulation, so as to signify that it is not a case of deposing but of transposing a regulatory practice and device. (Curien 1996: 43)

This shift during the 1980s related to some spheres, some states, and some cities more than others; yet the background wave extending market logics in this sphere has remained no less impressive. Lorrain (1996*a*) has highlighted two key variables that explain the diversity in this extension of the market: the type of concern existing at the outset—public, quasi-public, or private—and the strength of the political project—radical Thatcherism as against local public management. He suggests several reasons that might explain this change, which affects not just Europe but every continent: fiscal arguments for cities, financial arguments, the economic sciences literature on regulation and the optimum,[5] and the movement to decentralize and create contracts between public policy and firms. Above all, Lorrain has decisively highlighted the dynamic of markets and of firms. Focusing on urban services enterprises rather than cities, he has shown how enormously major firms have changed. British regional water and electricity companies, newly privatized, have set out to take the world by storm, and were bought by American, German, and French companies; conglomerates, around Fiat in Italy or the now-dismantled Trafalgar House and Hanson conglomerate in the UK, include construction, engineering, gas turbines, and property development among their many activities; French water management groups, over ten years or so, have become worldwide groups with markets of global size, diversifying by drawing in increasingly varied activities: funeral directing, urban transport, motorways, major projects, waste collection and recycling, and energy, moving on into new information and communication technologies, and even Hollywood studios; Italian holding companies and French public enterprises, such as *Électricité de France*, seek a foothold in new markets, as EDF aggressive bid to buy Montedison, in alliance with Fiat, demonstrates, as do both old and new Japanese, Korean, Hong Kong, and American groups.[6] Some examples can better illustrate the size of these groups, the extent of their activities, including spectacular bankruptcies, and their global strategies (see Fig. 5.2).

The same dynamic has taken hold in the construction sector. In most countries, this sector was most often dominated by a myriad of small firms, which created close ties with local officials, whether these worked for the state or for the city council. With post-war rebuilding and the new wave of urbanization, bigger firms came into being: however, these were years that saw everything accelerate, and a subsequent movement of concentration led to the formation of large national construction groups. Since the 1980s, these have

[5] By way of example, John Vickers, the new Director-General of the UK Office of Fair Trading, which regulates competition, is a former Oxford economist who has worked with political scientists on issues of regulation and privatization. The director of the electricity regulation agency is also an economist.

[6] See the company profile of the world leaders that D. Lorrain writes for each issue of the journal *Flux*.

- Suez (formerly Société Lyonnaise des Eaux, merged with the construction group Dumez and then the Franco-Belgian financial group Suez). Turnover: €20.614 billion. €12.868 billion in energy, €4.769 billion in water, €2.662 billion in cleaning, and €314 million in communication (figures for 2001).

  In the first six months of 2001, it won 30 new large contracts, including (1) a €150 million contract over 30 years to manage water in Shagai, together with Hong Kong new world company and a Chinese state-owned firm, Shanga Pudong Spark Development zone United; and (2) a €275 million contract over 25 years to produce energy for new Airbus industrial site.

  It fails to buy leading French firm Air Liquide, but buys two engineering firms: GTI Dutchà and Sulzer (Swiss), each with a turnover of €1 billion a year. Last but not least, it plans massive investment in the production of energy; it buys Cabot LNG in the US and a unit to produce energy and make investments in Mexico, for instance to supply energy-hungry Californians.

  Main subsidiaries: Tractebel (energy), Sita (waste, cleaning), Ondeo (water).
- Tractebel: Distribution and trade of natural gas, electricity, and services; electrical engineering; electrical plant; air-conditioning systems; industrial maintenance; urban district heating systems; facilities management; electricity and compressed air supplies. Turnover: €8 billion. 60,000 employees.

  Privatisation in the UK has transformed this market into a vast hunting ground for major energy companies.
- Innogy/Powergen (UK), electricity generation, now building an energy retailing business in competition with Centrica (formerly British Gas). Now controls 25% of the electricity and 8% of the gas market in the UK, in particular in the Midlands, Yorkshire, and the North.
- Centrica is also offering telecoms and financial services (it has gained 1 million telecoms customers). It is considering buying a water company. Northern Electric belons to Mid-American Energy.
- Électricité de France wants to become a world leader in the electricity business but also in the environment.
- Dalkia Holding Company (Vivendi with EDF's service centre) is to buy firms in Asia and Latin America. It has bought London and South West Electricity.
- Other large players in Europe include RWE (Germany), Endesa (Spain), EON (Germany), ENEL (Italy), and also smaller groups such as Essent (Netherlands) and Fortnum (Finland) which are entering the newly liberalized German market.
- In water, by contrast, the Scots have moved cleverly to unite the three privatized operators: East, North, and West of Scotland. Thames Water, the largest water company in the UK, which has been very active, was bought in 2000 by the German utility firm (electricity) RWE. Vivendi owns three British water companies.
- Vivendi: *La vieille dame de l'eau*, formerly the Compagnie Générale des Eaux, lost very large sums in the property collapse of the 1980s, especially its subsidiary, SAARI-SERI, which specialized in combined conference hall, housing, and office developments and was deeply involved in developing the Défense district of Paris during the 1980s.

  Purchase of British and US water management companies, development of the environment branch and massive investment in communication (Universal Studio). Now, turnover for Vivendi environment: €14 billion.

FIG. 5.2. Examples of the scale of large utility firms and their developments

Source: *Financial Times*, 2001.

- Vinci GTM: now the world leader in construction and associate services Turn-over in 2000: €16.4 billion. Net income: €400 million. 115,000 employees.
  Activities: Building and public works, very strong position in road building, production of road-building materials, waste recycling. Diversification through concessions (Cofiroute for motorways, the Stade de France stadium, bridges in Europe and Canada, tunnels, 25 airports).
  Parking: 740,000 parking spaces, 8,600 impoundment places.
  New project: A 40-year concession (with Miller Group) to build and oper-ate the Newport new road and bridge (PFI system), €92 million. New roads in the US too.
- Construction and property developments have seen spectacular success and bankruptcies over the past 20 years, for instance, giant property developers such as SARI-SEERI, Trafalgar House, Olympia and York, Rosehaugh.

FIG. 5.3. Construction firms

Source: *Financial Times*, 2001.

undergone further changes of scale, becoming large worldwide construction groups, their strategies closely intermingled with those of other major groups in the urban services sector. A few examples should be enough to give an idea of the size of these groups today, and of their diversified activities (see Fig. 5.3).

For Campagnac (1992), the major construction groups' change of strategy has its origins in the petrol crises and the end of major prestige projects financed by petrodollars. They found themselves back in Europe with different markets, cities at the height of expansion with complex urban projects, and an enlarged European market in the making, with consequent changes in the rules of the game, in contracts, and in the division of roles between public and private sectors, because of the EU, or institutional reforms such as decentralization or privatization in the UK. Some construction groups therefore linked up with other large groups in the urban services sector, as in France, or even with conglomerates. Some of these groups were led into the property development collapse of the late 1980s. They underwent profound restructuring, as in the case of French firms, and some firms went bankrupt, such as the Trafalgar House conglomerate in the UK. The boom in financial markets and property markets in the 1980s especially encouraged a wave of speculation in the world's largest cities.[7]

These firms and their allies—banks, consultancies, legal specialists—are vigo-rous actors in the scenario being played out: redefinition of the boundaries

---

[7] In her book *The City Builders* (1994), Fainstein traces and analyses the dynamic of property development in New York and London in the 1980s, up to the reversal of the dynamic and the sensational collapse of some groups, including Olympia and York, as a result of the Docklands development.

between public and private, or, more precisely, very strong interlocking between the two. Technology is not neutral in this story: technological advances have been integrated into traditional activities, and are also helping to redefine markets and economic models. The telecommunications and energy sectors offer excellent examples of this. Lorrain's works have shown the dynamic of social and political construction of markets by trial and error and through consultation between cities and large firms. The UK thus became a laboratory for experimenting with new rules of the game. However, the behaviour of water and electricity regulatory agencies has not yet stabilized these rules: in fact, nowhere near. British legal firms, consultancies, and 'financial engineering' specialists are now selling their know-how to the whole world. Large French firms have made the moves by taking over markets and buying up firms so that they too can benefit from this know-how, all the better to counter it in the Asian and South American markets or in the battle for influence between the different construction and management models set up within the World Bank by the Anglo-Americans and the French (Lorrain 1996a; Barraqué 1995). Public-sector actors, at whatever level, have frequently found it rather difficult to keep up with the dynamic of these firms, whose legal and financial services and lobbyists work unceasingly at the level of international bodies, in the European Union and its major regions, and with national governments from Indonesia to Brazil or Belgium; it should also not be forgotten that firms have a very strong historical understanding of cities and their elected representatives. In setting out to conquer the electricity market in Ivory Coast, the water market in Sao Paulo, to build Hong Kong airport or a toll motorway in Malaysia, these major groups are learning new techniques, including legal and accountancy techniques; they are coming into contact with partners and competitors; they are learning, sometimes painfully, the local political and social conditions: the influence of extreme left trade unions in some transport networks, the state-family form of organization in Asian capitalism, the instability of the rules laid down by British regulatory agencies, the particular conditions for funding political life in France, Italy, or Belgium. On the strong basis of their national markets and supported by their governments, these firms come into confrontation on the great world markets—and, at the same time, negotiate with cities for their services.

These groups have become major actors in European cities. Up to a certain point, they have the resources to impose types of contract and types of technology on cities. Firms bring technical and financial solutions to cities, whether to solve their technical problems or to carry out major facilities projects. The confrontation between cities and states is becoming one game among several, and the dynamic of relations between firms and representatives of cities is moving to centre stage (Lorrain 1993; 1996a).

Cities and Large Infrastructure Firms: Social and Political Contests

Large firms, supported by state and EU regulations, play an increasing role in organizing services and infrastructures within European cities. However, actors within cities have the resources to mediate these effects and to negotiate political priorities.

Technical networks represent important economic stakes. Globalization, information and communication technologies, and deregulation are changing the scales on which these stakes are found. Marxist writers have long ago demonstrated that a 'commodification' movement—a movement transferring activities into the market-led sector—can obviously be in no way politically and socially neutral. Social relations and power relations influence and frequently determine these processes, and are themselves profoundly altered at the end of the day. A lively debate about the effects of these trends on cities is now running through the research community, and also involves experts and those responsible for policy and administration. From the firms' point of view, things are clearer: the debate is more about forms of action. For them, liberalization of markets requires stable legal and financial settings to allow ambitious investments at limited cost to the public purse. Those who construct and manage networks have developed, with their bankers, multiple versions of sets of legal and financial arrangements in order to allow private initiatives to take on constructing and managing various services and facilities. Encouraged by the European Union, toll roads and bridges, such as the Vasco da Gama Bridge in Lisbon or the Dartford Bridge in England, have started to become more widespread in Europe. The British have institutionalized this model in their 'Private Finance Initiatives', which entrust the building and management of hospitals and other public facilities to the private sector. Technical networks are subject to strong pressures to open up to competition, and from privatization and deregulation; this movement developed on a large scale in the UK, supported by big firms and encouraged by the European Commission. The telecommunications sector is emblematic of this revolution, but transport, energy, and water are also involved.

Long confined to technical specialists and economists, the debate on the social effects of these changes in cities is now of concern to social scientists.[8] There are two opposed interpretations of these changes: for some, mostly the Italians and the British, globalized, deterritorialized, and increasingly commodified technical networks are organizing the physical breakup of the city and strengthening social inequalities. For others, notably the French and the Germans, the interweaving of different networks and the diversity of their modes of organization—still linked to the state—in European cities makes

---

[8] See the journals *Flux* and *Journal of Urban Technology* on these issues.

political control problematic, but does not lead to such distinct social polarization effects.

Graham and Marvin (1995*b*) have developed a critical analysis of the changes in progress. From their research into the development of water and electricity networks in Newcastle and then their book on telecommunications and cities, these two British writers first put forward the idea of a paradigm shift in the organization of networks, that is, a transition from urban hierarchies in a national context to a 'space of hubs and spokes'.

A diagram of this type privileges interconnections and heavy investments in big cities, with the tunnel effect that is the concentration on major routes guaranteeing the use of these advanced networks. Given the mass of different forms of information, goods, and people moving around in these networks, distance loses its relative importance, with nodes structuring the space, as airports do for economic activities. This development also benefits the most mobile social groups and the most privileged large users of these technical networks, as well as the major operators, who can target their investments on the most profitable segments of the market, thumbing their noses at the constraints of social responsibility or the inequalities created by access to high-performance, high-cost services such as cable television or mobile phones. Thus, Graham (2000: 185) distinguishes 'premium networked spaces: new or retrofitted transport, telecommunications, power or water infrastructures that are customized precisely to the needs of the powerful users and spaces, whilst bypassing less powerful users and spaces'. This logic of network differentiation entails powerful logics of social differentiation between cities and within cities.

Next, in line with Dematteis'(1997) work in Italy, they go on to stress the breakup of the city into small fragments divided by networks. Frequently closer to postmodernist writers such as Lash, Baudrillard, or Virillio, Graham, and Marvin (1995*a*) offer a vision of the 'telecommunication-based city' that differs from the 'old notion of the integrated, unitary city'. Finally, they put forward a third argument: the reconfiguration of technical networks is increasing polarization and social segregation in cities. Here their argument is twofold. It is markedly the case that access to advanced networks is the exclusive preserve of the most advanced groups. The increasingly sophisticated and market-led supply of telecommunications and transport is aimed at, and benefits, these groups. Physical access to connections, control, and the ability to purchase the services offered on the network are all creating new, cumulative social inequalities: disadvantaged groups are physically, economically, and socially excluded from these services and networks, and thus from cultural capital. For more traditional services, Graham and Marvin (1994) analyse the strategies of UK companies privatized after the dismantling of monopolies, which they sum up in the elegant phrase 'cherry picking and social dumping': deriving profits from better-off customers while cutting the costs of providing services to the least well-off customers. In other words, liberalization has led firms in the urban services sector to stop treating their customers as citizens forming a homogeneous group and entitled to established rights, in order to view them as a heterogeneous group of consumers, distinguished on the basis of the profits to be made from them. Competition and privatization have now led profit-centred firms to look much more closely at the profitability of different segments of the market and to concentrate their efforts in the most profitable domestic and industrial markets, while trying gradually to disengage from marginal, low-profit markets. (Graham 2000: 160)

This is expressed in the restructuring of tariffs and services offered and the introduction of 'intelligent metres' and prepayment meters. In Newcastle, Graham and Marvin have shown low rates of telephone connection—under 30 per cent—in certain districts, as well as falling consumption of water and electricity, and even cut-offs, among poor families: in other words, 'social disconnection' phenomena, symptomatic of the growing social inequalities in British society. By contrast, privatized regional water, gas, train, and electricity companies made record profits, and payments to directors and shareholders reached such peaks that even John Major's Conservative government was agitated by what seemed to be a pillaging of collective goods, given the chronic under-investment these sectors suffer from. Since then, things have become more balanced, but the collapse of the train system in the UK illustrates this trend.

These arguments are the subject of debate. One group of French researchers has contested the validity of some of them: that is, not of the UK examples, but of generalizing from them. Criticizing Castells'(1996) technological determinism, especially the myth of the end of territories, and generalizations about networks, Offner (2000) stresses the variety of confrontations between territories, networks, and types of network management. In his eyes, the coexistence of several types of qualitatively very different universalism of services and the interweaving of different technical networks discredits the movement to de-territorialization presented above: he sees it as more a matter of transition from one type of diversity to another. The power of networks does not engender a unique phenomenon of end of territories or abolition of distance, but a situation in which different systems of measurement coexist or become nested together (Offner 2000): a situation that poses serious problems for political regulation. As far as impact in terms of social fragmentation is concerned, Lorrain (1996b) proposes a different interpretation of firms' interests: for reasons of economy of scale, image, competition, and diversity of services offered, firms have no interest in playing the 'social disconnection' game since relations with customers and shareholders are mediated through long-standing trust relationships, as the examples of France and Scandinavia have shown.[9]

---

[9] For France, there is the example of Électricité de France in Coutart (1998): free water and electricity for minimum income claimants; water and electricity charters to guarantee access for everyone; Poupeau (2001) and Offner (2000); and Lorrain's (1995) comparative analysis of water company profits in the UK and France.

Finally, the newly-acquired visibility of the economic and social stakes of these technical networks itself provokes reactions. The social actors cannot but react, lobbies and coalitions are created, and political stakes are set. Independently of the private or public origin of ownership or operation of the network, there still exists a broad political consensus in western Europe to avoid the worst effects of social dumping. European-level discussion on universal service obligations for operators is an example of these developments. The existence of inequalities at a given moment can also mask other dynamics, whether of generalized access to a network or of the growth of negative inequalities.

At the end of the day, city councils are not without resources and capacity to make choices. Private firms need public spaces, access to refuse collection, and coordination for carrying out works: in short, if there were open conflict with a city council, network operators might find themselves in a difficult position. There again, Lorrain and Coutart plead for consideration of the political construction of these markets, the interplay of the actors in the legal context, and different forms of conflict and cooperation between different types of actors in different circumstances. Deregulation may lead to new rules, and the content of these new rules is open to negotiation and to political contention. Lorrain (2000*a*) has particularly emphasized the time dimension of these phenomena. At the end of the nineteenth century, political choices were made in different countries and in different cities, which had considerable, lasting effects on the organization of services. Nowadays, local authorities and mayors in most European cities (see Chapter 7) still enjoy considerable legitimacy to organize services and to lobby in Brussels. Rehabilitating politics in that field, Lorrain concludes on the conditions of the importance of politics (2000*a*: 175–6):

The business of construction—of an urban service model—is not only due to large firms; it would appear to depend upon the involvement of many actors . . . entrepreneurs, engineers, legal experts, politicians and users' movements . . . Development is over a long period . . . the political actors must be able to adjust to two different time-scales: one involving the handling of crises, the other incremental action . . . Intervention has no meaning unless it occurs at every level of the edifice: technologies, framing, principles and values . . . Within this role (general steering) is the function of devising the procedures for action and the instruments of control . . . urban political actors are entitled to say what is legitimate or not, what is allowed or forbidden, and to create a space of legitimacy which may thereafter serve as a basis for the actors. Under this role, political actors are the guardians of ethics and norms.

Lorrain's optimism about the balance between large firms in the city industry and city councils is questionable. The UK example provides substantial evidence of redistribution of resources in favour of the middle classes and firms after privatization. Technologies which allow detailed knowledge of customers give firms some room for manoeuvre in offering incentives to their best customers. The logics which guarantees some minimum services to the poor—in EU jargon, 'universal service'—and differentiates between other customers is clearly a market logics, which increases inequalities. It may be true that privatization sometimes offers opportunities to develop innovations and the dynamics of firms or to help reduce costs. It is also true that many city councils have political resources and expertise to negotiate with firms, so they are more aware of what is at stake. But there are cases where City councils have not fulfilled that role and where the commodification of a number of services has clearly indicated a change in favour of market logics, including its social implications for growing inequalities and limited access to some services.

Conclusion: Relativizing Scales, Linking Spaces and Flows

This chapter has stressed the extension of market logics and a new up-surge of capitalism, expressed, for example, through mobility of firms and the introduction of market logics into urban services. Cities have become more dependent on market logics: their futures, their job markets, and their resources depend more on decisions taken by private-sector actors than they did in the 1980s, whether they relate to localization of activities or to management of particular urban services. The interplay between the strategies of firms, cities, states, and the European Union has become a game with several dimensions.

European cities are directly involved in this large-scale, structuring phenomenon. The approach adopted in this book does not share with Marxist sociology the aim of developing a general frame within which to interpret the effects of this transformation of capitalism. Marxist writers have been more successful than others in stressing the importance of these globalization dynamics, transformations of capitalism, linkages between state and cities, and the influence of production in social structuring. Although often agreeing with their analyses, the avenues they follow, and the critical dimensions of their reasoning, I reject the determinism of their explanations. The balance of power has unquestionably changed in favour of market forces over the last 20 years or so; but that is not the end of the story. Conflicts at different scales about regulating these forms of capitalism may yet modify market logics—or reinforce them. Such forces must come to grips with political, social, and cultural logics that do not inevitably allow themselves to be governed by market forces.

This difference of interpretation reveals the terms of the political debate that exists at all levels, independently of firms and of technological developments. In societies and cities racked by logics of social exclusion, but where privileged social groups are an integral part of new scales, what can be done to keep society together? Technical networks and public services, and their different constituent elements, are a part of this broader political debate. The logics of firms naturally push them towards making profits and helping to organize European regulatory frameworks that will support this. Entrusting the organization of collective advantage and the common interest to firms, as is frequently suggested by the adherents of self-regulation of these services, clearly relates to the old belief in the beneficial effects of the market for society. Although, in certain particular conditions, the market can contribute to social cohesion and cement the social bond, capitalism has rather the habit of destroying society and its institutions. Although globalization clearly corresponds to a disembedding of market forces, it is better not to forget the lessons of Marx and Polanyi. The United States and the UK, the societies most favourable to the free play of market forces, are also the societies where social inequalities are greatest. In this context, technical networks are organized in a way that increases inequalities. However, the extension of the market does not happen all on its own. Partisans of its logic also come into conflict with forms of resistance, interest groups, social actors, and cities opposed to the liberalization that the European Commission seems to defend. Cities are actors in this game, both in their relations with firms—contract negotiations—and as actors of European governance.

The logics of firms may be contributing to the fragmentation of cities, imposing uniform logics without taking other criteria into account. As Storper (1997: 239) has put it: 'A global economy is emerging then, but it is not a global space of flows. It is instead a complex meeting of new kinds of globalized flows and new kinds of territorial economies. Castells' theory takes one side of this complex process and elevates it into a highly misleading metaphor for the whole.'

Cities are not merely the product of economic logics to which they submit passively. Although pressures, of which we are aware, can produce this effect in certain circumstances, cities also have their own role to play. The analyses presented in this chapter have stressed the territorial dimension of capitalism and the linkages between logics of firms and the resources of cities that produce the 'externalities' especially crucial for firms. Firms are never totally de-territorialized. Harvey (1985*a*; 1989) has long since demonstrated the need for the spatial fixing of capitalism. Cities are finding a new legitimacy and a role in terms of economic development, and the globalization of flows and exchanges means their economies are no longer so intrinsically bound up with what happens in the national economy. They are becoming— in some cases, not for the first time—privileged sites for the accumulation of capital and the production of wealth. Rather than thinking homogeneously and from the top down about the effects of globalization processes imposing themselves on cities, my approach has been to reflect on linkages; and rather than thinking in terms of absolute novelty, I have considered the initial conditions and the possible forms of interlocking that will permit change, for example, through conflict, or through learning and the renegotiation of social relations and power relations. European cities that are not global cities are not inevitably the ones most disadvantaged by the processes outlined above. 'A diversified economic base, a broad portfolio of activities, a socially diverse population, and the existence of an urban job market in the etymological sense of the term, that is to say, allowing exchange of all ranges of skills, are the least risky assets for managing increasingly uncertain environments' (de Roo 1993: 13).

In some cases, these pressures provoke reactions. Cities are made up of social and political actors and organizations that play a role in these processes; so, in a fragmented way, at the level of their constituent elements—or in some cases in a more integrated way—cities may be viewed as actors in these processes.

Finally, as far as relativizing scales is concerned, the analysis presented in this chapter on globalization processes and cities has shown the ways scales interlock and the complex relations between actors interacting at the same time on different scales: a signal theme of critical economic geography (Brenner 1998; 2000). Thus, national modes of regulation of the economy inherited from the Keynesian compromise no longer function. The search for methods of regulating capitalism operates on different levels: the global level, the level of transnational entities—the European Union—nation-states, regions, and cities. These are not separate scales: they are interlocking. More limited forms, not embedded in economies but inserted in economic and social entities in a more limited way, have emerged (Brenner 1998; Hollingsworth and Boyer 1997). The dynamic of capitalism is destabilizing existing scales, and battles are being joined to organize different levels and modes of regulation. On the industrial relations front, for example, firms are decentralizing collective bargaining in order to escape the existing balance of power at the national level, in branches where the trade unions have a strong presence; this decentralization aims to strengthen flexibility and weaken the unions. The latter are reacting by trying to strengthen organization at the level of the employment region, but also by trying to help develop European rules. The reshaping of economic interests and confrontation between them is being played out on different scales, and the same dynamic holds good for industrial disputes. Cities, like other sub-national territories, form one of the possible scales for reshaping and for regulation of interests. Nevertheless, such an intermediate level can be ambiguous since it is impossible to know if this is an original level of structuring and regulation of the political or the social, or simply a level into which macro- and micro-logics have both penetrated, simply becoming more visible on this scale. However, this is not an insignificant factor: increasing the visibility and legibility of regulations that have their origin elsewhere may also allow us to identify both mechanisms of change and crises. Therefore, this 'intermediate' or 'meso' level of analysis has some virtues. It may make it easier to apply some analytical divisions and to account for the ways political and social logics become enmeshed and for the inter-play of political and social actors. This can be even more useful if it can be demonstrated that the intermediate level exists as a unit of analysis with some meaning for institutions and for collective actors, structuring their interaction. This poses formidable methodological problems, since one of the dimensions of the 'complexity' of the social aspect is precisely the impossibility of estab-lishing clear boundaries between sectors, territories, or networks.

As far as relativizing distance and time is concerned, distance is clearly not nullified by networks, history and geography do not vanish into a virtual space, and the virtual city is not replacing the material city. All the processes in train are more complex and contradictory than was foreseen, and combina-tions between these trends and existing structures, which have their own dynamics, must form the object of future research. Space-time compression includes more dimensions, whose logics and mechanisms must be dissected in more detail. Networks as a category do not dissolve actors and structures, or their interests. Castells (1996) is solely preoccupied with networks, which he sees everywhere, and has lost sight of the fact that the elements consti-tuting the strength of weak links, such as the network, also often contribute to their weakness. Actors and organizations can easily negotiate their mem-bership and their withdrawal from within these networks. Sometimes, in par-ticular conditions, the dynamic of what is being exchanged becomes the structuring one, primarily in relation to actors and their interests: it can help to redefine their expectations, their practices, and their interests. This dimension has been highlighted in structural analysis of networks. But it is not always the case: the fact that a network exists does not prove these processes are primary. In many cases, the network is secondary; it is only one type of belonging among others, and has formed for a particular type of activity, which can change rapidly, become obsolete, and contribute nothing to actors' strategy and their interests.

The confusion that has reigned around networks of cities in France illus-trates this point. Cities can be dissolved by technical networks, by social net-works, or by public policy networks; but they can also be instrumental in activating such networks, bringing them together, or helping to differentiate them, while not destroying any of their structuring characteristics. Associat-ing determinism with networks can be a methodological error and display considerable naivety in regard to certain social interests, interest groups, and power groupings. By contrast, the analyses presented here lead more towards work on the linkages, contradictions, and nestedness of different flows and places.

Analysis of the evolving growth of cities and the evolving localization of the economy in several European countries suggests that, despite metropol-ization, the diversity of local and metropolitan economies has every chance of persisting. Urban economies combine private and public sector resources. More generally, can we not envisage that Europeans will succeed in finding new forms of institutionalization and territorialization of the economy, which will permit them to change everything while still remaining themselves? The social and political actors, including states, still have resources. In the new urban context (Healey 1995), cities are both territorial systems and nodes on global, European, national, regional, and local networks.

Part II Conclusion: Cities Are Dissolving, Dismantling, Sprawling, and Dematerializing: But Must This Mean the End of the Model of the European City?

European Cities: An Idea that Makes Sense?

We should recall some of the arguments put forward about the strengths and weaknesses of European cities.

The relative long-term stability of the European urban system has been noted, as has its original structure—with a concentration of medium-sized cities—and the remains of its physical form.

A second point worth mentioning is the fact that European cities, although they are gaining more autonomy, are still structured and organized within European states: in particular, welfare states. The state and Europe protect the city. The ongoing restructuring process does represent a threat, but, for the time being, European cities are supported and to some extent protected by the state, including in terms of resources.

European cities are becoming more European in the sense that the institutionalization of the EU is creating rules, norms, procedures, repertoires, and public policies that have an impact on most, if not all, cities. Politically and institutionally, this category makes more and more sense. The EU also is a powerful agent of legitimization. By designing urban public policies and agreeing, under the influence of city interests, to mention the idea of 'a Europe of cities' as one of the components of the EU, it is giving a boost to cities to act and to behave as actors within EU governance. This also, to some extent, leads other actors—firms, for instance—to take European cities more seriously. Now part of an increasing number of trans-national networks, European cities are being recognized as such.

Another point relates to their economic and social structure. European cities are characterized by a mix of public services and private firms, including a robust body of middle class and lower-middle class public-sector workers, who constitute a firm pillar of the social structure. Despite increasing social tensions, inequalities, even riots at times, European cites have resources, identities, and political legitimacy, and it is not appropriate to describe them as dual cities. More will be said about this in the third part of the book.

There is a further point that I will examine in the third part: the continuing representation of the city as a whole and the increased legitimacy of political elites in sustaining and re-inventing this presentation. As noted by Jaillet (2001), the idea of urban secession is more or less irrelevant in European cities in political terms, although this does not mean that processes in some way similar to social urban secession are not taking place (as indicated in Chapter 4).

The conclusions of the previous chapters already signal conflicts, tensions, problems, and debates that cannot just be solved at the state or EU level. Issues of social and political regulation and of urban governance are on the agenda. Cities may be fragmented by networks. However, questions of linkages between different networks and of conflict resolution have been raised. The second part of the book has argued that many governance issues are now more visible within European cities, as are interdependence and interrelation between different actors and organizations: all things that used to be represented and made visible on the national scene. This new-found visibility of interdependence gives opportunities to social and political actors to be involved in modes of urban governance or, by contrast, to increase the fragmentation and dislocation of European cities. My argument so far is that European cities have not—yet?—been dislocated and that they have considerable resources which they can draw on in adapting to or resisting the new frame of constraints and opportunities.

The End of the Model?

This, however, only makes sense if the model of the European city is not on the point of collapse. Many authors evoke the end of cities, the post-city era of the global mega-city, or the end of city unity. This book does not discuss in detail the logics of urban sprawl or the dissolution of the city, but a few points are worth mentioning at this stage.

Whatever the aspect under consideration, it now seems well established that globalization processes mark a resurgence in the movement of city growth and of metropolization. The dynamic of trans-national economic flows, reinforced by the movement for liberalization of trade, reduces states' capacities to organize the distribution of economic activities in space—although it does not remove them. It is completely natural that attention has been focused mostly on the biggest cities, which are the main beneficiaries of this trend. The metropolization movement—concentration and dispersal of activities— affects most European cities. Figures from the late 1990s reveal that even some of the industrial cities and regional capitals harshly affected during the 1970s and 1980s, such as Leeds, Birmingham and Manchester, Lille, Liège, and some cities of the Ruhr, found a new dynamic of growth in the 1990s. The whole core of urban Europe has been affected by this growth, which has been accompanied by sprawl and dispersal around cities.

Several arguments contribute to the thesis of the breakup of cities. The 'old, integrated cities' of Europe are said to be subject to several logics of dis-aggregation, which render any attempt to consider cities as structures or as categories obsolete: technical networks and urban sprawl, strengthened by globalization, are said to be leading to the end of European cities.

Perhaps cities are tending to be dismantled, to de-materialize; but these are only trends. In such complex dynamics, the temporal dimension and the initial conditions should not be neglected. Except in the case of telecommunications, as yet, the majority of facilities and technical networks in European cities are still managed within public or semi-public settings. The UK has spearheaded extreme liberalism: on the scale of European cities, the figures shown for Newcastle and for other large British cities no longer constitute an exception—that would be putting it too strongly—but they are still in a minority. The vast majority of citizens of European cities, including the poorest, have access not only to water and electricity but also to urban transport and television; and the rapid spread of the mobile phone is following the same pattern. The initial situation is not one of feigned universality in provision of these services in a public context, but of different types of generalized provision within diversified regulatory frameworks, with private—as has applied to water in France since the nineteenth century—public, and semi-public operators. In regard to network operators and gradual opening-up to competition, the extension of market logic is incontestable; and the rules of the game are wide open. Yet the growing weight of consumer opinion in decision-making by regulatory agencies in Britain must frequently have led some directors to feel nostalgic for the time when public monopolies, even nationalized ones, largely escaped the control of the state. Coutart (1998) rightly points out that the growth of poverty in cities requires special measures on the part of operators. For the moment, it is difficult to claim that, among all the factors producing inequalities, technical networks are the major one, even though they are certainly contributing to the differentiation of urban bourgeoisies, and even though we cannot discount the fact that this contribution is increasingly important.

The theme of the physical breakup of the city has become a classic one in the American literature because of the exodus into residential suburbs and the decline of the centres of big cities. This vision of breakup has been strengthened by the political marginalization of cities, the creation of fortified districts on the margins of cities, and the development of secessionist movements, for example in Los Angeles or Toronto (Keil 2000). In the American experience, privately owned, fragmented technical networks have promoted urban sprawl and the breakup of cities, giving rise to urban regions with several focal points defined in contrast to the city centre.

In Europe, too, geographers have highlighted both the concentration processes identified above and spatial dispersal processes around these cities, which give rise to vast urban regions with a dense fabric of medium-sized towns around the capital, as in the south-eastern region of Great Britain, Lombardy —around Milan—and the Paris region. These can vary from country to country: in Italy or France, for example, urban centres with a population of 50,000–150,000 are considered true cities, which is not the case in Germany, the UK, or the Netherlands. The way these few large urban regions are forming confirms a model of dispersal, breakup, and fragmentation of social interests. Working-class suburbs lie cheek by jowl with residential suburban developments, so like some American suburbs as to be indistinguishable.

The second model of dispersal is that of the city network. Italians writing about Turin and Milan, such as Dematteis and Camagni, have clearly demonstrated the breakup of Milan and the existence of networks of small and medium-sized towns (Dematteis 1997). Up to the 1960s, Milan was a regional and economic capital. However, the old governing elites are still present, the influence of old families, notably Catholic ones, structures a governing elite, and its conflicts with other groups is an organizing factor in politics and culture. In other words, Milan can still be analysed to some extent as a local society. The remarkable economic growth of the 1960s and later years led to a change of scale: the development of a conurbation that includes Bergamo, Brescia, Pavia, and Alessandria, then the diversification and internationalization of its economy, the end of the hegemony of great families, the proliferation of different economic interests and their fragmentation— with the rise of non-material capitalism and the new economic bourgeoisies of the tertiary sector, such as Berlusconi, as highlighted by Bagnasco (1996) —and the breakup of local society, a breakup strengthened by political fragmentation. Taking the examples of Randstad and the Ruhr, Dematteis (1997) visualizes the strengthening of this model—once held up as a public policy aim for French cities—in Europe, which also signals the end of the regional capital-type model.

The third model of breakup of European cities is the development of residential peripheries around regional capitals. In German cities such as Frankfurt (Keil and Ronneberger 2000) or French cities such as Toulouse (Jayet 1993) or Lyons, rapid economic development has been accompanied by the formation of a periphery. Shopping centres, industrial zones, and leisure centres all play a role in this dynamic (Hannigan 1998).

Yet, despite technical networks, global cities, urban sprawl, and city networks, European cities remain fairly robust, although less dominant and more uncertain because of the rise of more or less integrated city-regions. In going on to discuss the thesis of resistance by regional capitals, Dematteis (1997: 91) admits it as possible, but regretfully stresses that, in fact, metropolization is set to become the major phenomenon:

It does not seem that these issues—of metropolization—can be avoided simply by looking to the lower levels of cities, and in particular to medium-sized cities that appear to have better preserved their role as local and regional territorial co-ordinators . . . In fact, images of European urbanization clearly indicate that medium-sized cities do not escape—or will not escape for much longer—the 'catastrophe' of metropolitan globalization.

Perhaps; but it must still be remembered that (1) announcements of the demise of regional capitals go back a long way; (2) the 'metropolitan catastrophe' may be characterized and managed in different ways, without, for example, leading to the ending of the attraction and meaning of the centre; and (3) even in large urban conurbations small cities are not dissolved in an undifferentiated space: some of them retain the characteristics of cities, and this is even more true in regions of network cities (Béhar and Estèbe 1998). The aim here is not to reify European cities as fixed in history and unchanging to the end of time. Changes are in progress, including in the physical organization of the city, and one need only take a walk on the outskirts of a European city to see the pressures and the changes. However, must we infer the breakup of European cities from this? In many cases, their dispersal and their breakup has not led to any marked decline of the centre. The metropolitan dimension has linkages with the 'old city' dimension, deriving certain characteristics from it. Social groups and elected representatives have not inevitably renounced this city dimension. Of course boundaries are more uncertain, of course the structure of the city and its degree of integration should be viewed relatively. This is certainly so. At the same time, however, I have attempted to demonstrate that relativizing scales, boundaries, or degrees of integration is becoming the norm as far as the state, firms, or networks are concerned; yet it does not mean their end or their dissolution. As Beauregard and Haila (2000: 24) put it:

First, new and old process join together in complex and over-determined ways and do so in particular places at particular points in the history of these places. The consequences are not easily traced back to one or a single cluster of forces operating together across time and space. Second, the actors who control the built environment are not simply puppets dancing to the tune of socio-economic and political logic but rather relatively autonomous agents. Third, the spatial form of the city inhibits rapid and large-scale transformations. Capital is 'frozen' in fixed structures and people have political and social commitments to places that cannot easily be dismissed forms. The relative fixed form of the city enables and constrains current and future investments, modes of living and cultural meanings. Consequently, new processes enter a world that is resistant yet malleable.

III

SOCIAL AND POLITICAL
ACTORS WITHIN EUROPEAN
CITIES AND THE MAKING OF
URBAN MODES OF GOVERNANCE

SIX

Cities as Incomplete Societies: Actors and Regulations

THIS chapter is about actors, organized interests in European cities, and the extent to which their forms of compromise, aggregation, and representation produce something original. The main thrust of the chapter is that the diversity of groups, organizations, and interests is accompanied by processes, strategies, and diverse modes of regulation that lie beyond the paradigm of competition. The issue of unity, of the whole, of how far the city is complete—or, indeed, incomplete—remains especially fundamental to European cities. Despite diversity of neighbourhoods, differences between the centre and the outlying suburbs, and the existence of stigmatized districts, forms of regulation can be identified. The issues of integration and redistribution have not been wiped off the map. These cities are, to some extent, local societies. Their diversity of interests does not prevent the structuring of local forms of regulation and modes of governance, which not only result from the aggregation of actors at a given moment, and are not only an intrinsic part of a locality in the sense of social structures, organizations, and political choices that are reshaped over time—but also impose modes of doing, representations, and norms of cooperation.

Any study of cities must steer a course between the Scylla of representing the city as a separate unit, thus risking its reification, and the Charybdis of showing it to be infinitely diverse and complex. Avoiding the first of these risks means taking into account the diversity of actors, groups, and institutions that make up the city. The city is also by its very nature fluid, confused, full of movement, and made up of individuals who live, work, have fun, trade, and participate.

However, tackling this diversity presupposes that we will not fall into the trap of '*l'émerveillement du tout collectif*',[1] which amounts to marvelling at the diversity of a multitude of actors, their interactions, and their contradictory discourses, while conveniently ignoring the constraints, institutions, power relations, conflicts, and resources of these actors—and the relations of domination. This view of the world stresses interactions, contingency, change, and the instability of social relations. It is legitimized by the role of associations

---

[1] The phrase is from J. C. Thoenig.

or by political authorities anxious to achieve consensus and a harmonious vision of urban development: for example, of partnership as disseminated by the European Commission. It frequently carries within it an idealized view of civil society and of a democracy undefiled by politics.

Cities do not simply develop on the basis of interactions and contingencies: groups, actors, and organizations oppose one another, come into conflict, coordinate, and produce representations in order to institutionalize collective forms of action, to implement policies, to structure inequalities, and to defend their interests. Therefore, they can, to some extent, be studied as local societies. So the risk of reifying the city as collective actor may be avoided by analysing the different organizations and groups that comprise it, then highlighting the logics of conflict and cooperation between those groups, as well as the arrangements, combinations, and ideas that help to shape a collective actor and/or a locality.

European cities are incomplete societies: they constitute only one of the levels at which social actors interact, represent themselves, and are mutually interdependent. In the face of the fragmentation processes highlighted in the second part of this book, the issue that always used to be key for sociologists—that of social differentiation and integration—is coming to a head again in cities. The metropolis is a clear representation of the prospect of mosaic, fragmentation, and differentiation. It is hard to see, for example, how the concept of collective actor or local society could have any meaning for Paris or London. In medium-sized European cities, on the other hand, the concept is often meaningful, providing that we disaggregate this collective actor and analyse the interplay of social groups and organizations in such cities. Lovering (1995; 2000) has vigorously criticized the drift towards this kind of analysis of actor cities, which he refers to as the risk of 'new localism': privileging local strategies, the capacity of local actors, and local forms of regulation. According to him, the strategies of groups and actors cannot come to fruition independently of broader changes: that is, in the terms used in this book, changes to the structure of constraints and opportunities, the reshaping of the state, and economic restructuring. The way this book is constructed represents an attempt to consider cities—in the sense of localities or incomplete urban societies—in relation to these changes; but this does not exclude consideration of cities as local societies.

Local societies are also the result of interaction between multiple actors working at different levels, some of whose actions are guided by local society and take on a particular direction over time. They draw stability from a whole set of organizations, linked in varying degrees to the public sector: hospitals, schools, universities, harbours, and social and cultural centres. Social movements, associations, and sometimes even families are deployed in different organizations and take part in shaping—although always partially and with only occasional stability—a degree of coherence, a certain local social and political order.

The initial shaping and the subsequent trajectory of each national society has produced a particular relationship between society and territory, especially in cities. Bagnasco and Trigilia (1993) have shown that, in 'the Third Italy', the market has been integrated into local societies. In these regions, market mechanisms are deeply intertwined with local communities, family structures—the most significant in Italy—and political subcultures, because 'reciprocal trust between the actors is the *sine qua non* of participation in a co-operative market game' (Bagnasco 1994: 16). 'Neo-localism'—in our terms, a mode of governance—is defined as 'a particular division of labour between the market, the social structures and, increasingly, the political structures, a division which allows a high degree of flexibility in the economy and rapid adjustments to market variations, but also a redistribution of social costs and real benefits from development within the local society' (Bagnasco and Trigilia 1993: 95).[2]

In France and in the UK, for example, apart from 'community studies' following the American tradition and stressing the stability and continuity of more or less idealized local communities, analyses of French or British 'localities' have attempted to stress the social construction of localities, the social relations noted over time in the city, the conflicts, the dynamics—which are not isolated from the rest of society—and the localized social practices of the actors, and to highlight autonomy and capacity for innovation.[3] In the tradition of Weber recalled in the Introduction, the city as local society is analysed in terms of aggregation, integration, and representation of groups and interests. The three pillars of these local urban societies are: investment of resources by groups, interests, and organizations in cities; reciprocity; and relative stability over time.

This chapter aims to present the two faces of the city through the set of issues raised by the locality: that is, on the one hand, the different interests, groups, and organizations present in European cities and, on the other hand, the mechanisms of coordination and the forms of regulation that contribute to integration. To put it another way, in the perspective adopted in this book, the study of local actors, interactions, and diversity is not enough on its own: it must be accompanied by research into the mechanisms for integration and the modes of cooperation that help to construct an urban social and political order, fragile and ephemeral though this may be. Consequently, this chapter starts by identifying the forces present, the associations, private interests,

[2] Of course, this neo-localism has a particular social and historical context: the urbanized countryside and the legacy of Renaissance city-states, the absence of major industrialization, the influence of family structures—domestic group and kinship network—the absence of polarized class structures, and the existence of political subcultures—some Catholic, some Communist—which are maintained thanks to a closely woven network of institutions: trade unions, mutual aid societies, associations, cooperatives, town councils, political parties.

[3] Lautman (1981); Observatoire du Changement Social (1986); Benoit-Guilbot (1991); Stacey (1969); Cooke (1988); Harloe, Pickvance, and Urry (1990).

and social movements that form the fabric of European cities; it then goes on to highlight the forms of regulation that are, or are not, linked together in these cities. Cases and examples may be mobilized in different ways. The choice was made not to develop a small number of deeply researched case studies but rather to provide illustration of the arguments through cases taken in different countries, taking into account the bias indicated in the introduction.

European City Actors Outside Government

At the scale of European cities, social movements, associations, and private interests are most often highly visible and identifiable. They fall within different temporalities, sometimes long-term ones. They deploy to organize the defence of their interests, to accumulate legacies, and in distinctive social strategies—schools, housing, cultural practices, clubs—in political groups, in public policy networks, in property and commercial investment strategies. In general, they are divided rather than integrated into a single organization or under a legitimate leadership. All these private interests have long been organized into a political and economic system, most often structured at the national level, which has taken very different forms from one country to another (Crouch 1993). Contrasting with the logic of local or 'community' studies, Marxist urban sociology of the 1970s showed the importance of local and national private actors, supported and framed by the state. Relating more to convergence phenomena explained by the dynamic of capital, this sociology gave rise to a proliferation of detailed empirical studies which eventually revealed local regularities and original political scenarios (Pickvance 1995a).

The following sections contrast two principal forms of interests within cities: associations and private sector interests, which represent two different forms of organization and interaction within European cities, varying over time. However, both types provide evidence of territorialization and institutionalization within cities.

Associations and Social Movements: a Dialectic of Protest and Cooperation with Public Authorities

Cities are obviously a part of European societies where the old boundary between institutionalized politics and social protest movements has become blurred (Tarrow 1994; Della Porta and Ziani 1999). Most research work has highlighted the diversity of forms of involvement in groups or associations in Western societies (Klingemann and Fuchs 1995; Perrineau, 2001). It is estimated that over half of all Europeans belong to an association or a group. In France, where the 1901 legislation makes it easy to form an association, it is estimated that there are about 700,000 members of associations or groups, of whom between 15 per cent and 20 per cent are inactive. Except in sports associations, associate professionals represent between 20 per cent and 35 per cent of members, clerical workers between 20 per cent and 25 per cent, and managers and professionals between 10 per cent and 15 per cent (Barthélémy 2000). Social movements and protest have become permanent elements of our societies, involving both disadvantaged groups and the middle classes.[4] Cities are no exception to this. Apart from electing the mayor and councillors, citizens mobilize politically in all sorts of ways, through their social practices and their mobilization. The forms of collective action adopted by city-dwellers are crucial to understanding cities as a local society, their dynamism, and their development.[5] Social movements were first analysed in the context of the urban protests of the 1970s, but they now form part of a variety of organized interests that have become more institutionalized within cities.

Protest: The 1970s Onwards: Social Protest Versus Nimbyism

European cities are the place where actors and social movements have been shaped: from those with their origins in the trade unions, through the social movements of the 1970s demanding collective facilities, the squatters' or

---

[4] A definition of social movement society: '1) that social protest has moved from being a sporadic, if recurring feature of democratic politics to a perpetual element in modern life; 2) that protest behavior is employed with greater frequency by more diverse constituencies and is used to represent a wider range of claims than ever before; 3) that professionalisation and institutionalisation may be changing the major vehicle of contentious claims, the social movement, into an instrument within the reach of conventional politics; 4) that state strategies have shifted from reliance on repression towards facilitation and that police practices have moved towards more sophisticated and subtle forms of the latter' (Meyer and Tarrow 1998: 15).

[5] Drawing on the research tradition mentioned above, Balme and Chabanet (2001: 4) define collective action as 'all the behaviours—engagement, mobilization, representation and negotiation—through which social interests are constituted, and through which their political influence is exercised. Thus, this is a complex range of behaviours, with differences between individual and collective actors, most often bringing together co-operation and conflict, identification and transaction. The social dimension of these interests contrasts them with more specific political mobilizations, such as the vote or partisan commitment. Their nature may differ according to how diffuse or concentrated the interest is, how material or ethical, how particular or attached to a definition of the common good, how private or public, and according to how far it is a separable good or a collective good, to use economic terminology. Repertoires for promoting interests—whether based on protest or instituted—and the interpretative focus of stakes, actors and procedures define the mode of involvement of mobilizations in the political field, as well as the relational dynamics of public policy during the phases when it publicizes issues and draws up timetables for decision-making and implementation'.

students' movements, the women's movements in Italian cities calling for a different way of managing time in the city, to citizens' committees . . . the list is a long one—and immediately gives the lie to any consensual, harmonious vision of the city as a single actor.

What was once called 'the new urban sociology'—that is, the innovative Marxist and neo-Marxist urban sociology of the 1970s—demonstrated the importance of these social movements in structuring the city, the dynamic of social relations, and urban changes (Castells 1983). Urban social movements have generally been defined as collective mobilizations—as distinct from political parties—of urban populations, directed to changing policies and to defending their interests, involving widely diverse actions and repertoires not institutionalized in political parties (Walton 1998). However, few writers now, unlike those of the 1970s, accept the idea that urban social movements are necessarily progressive. The urban dimension means, apart from the scale, that these movements relate especially to (1) issues of collective consumption and of public services, (2) issues of quality of life in the neighbourhood, and opposition to planned physical changes, and (3) demands for transparency and for democratic participation in urban government, and challenges to elected representatives and parties (Pickvance 1995*b*: 199).

Urban social movements became famous in the context of the urban struggles of the 1970s, when the many politicized—left or extreme left—members of the new middle strata, together with sections of the working class, challenged major planning projects, demanded the transformation of cultural policies, or demonstrated in favour of opening up collective facilities. In Germany and northern Europe, squatters' movements set up in districts destined for demolition and renewal, mobilizing young radical students and immigrants.

Repression by the public authorities provoked broader mobilizations of district associations: for example, of tenants in Frankfurt. The radicalization of some movements, changes in local policies and modes of interaction with these mobilizations, and the institutionalization of movements all contributed to the decline of this first wave, in the context of an economic crisis that delegitimized major urban planning operations. However, Margit Mayer (2000*b*) has shown that in Germany, as well as in Amsterdam and Zurich, other squatters' movements developed during the 1980s, helping to maintain an alternative urban culture strengthened by environmental associations and the peace movement.[6]

Actions by various groups challenging urban projects have not disappeared. Campaigns by young radicals against urban prestige projects still exist alongside more conservative ones. In Naples, the renovation of the main square and other regeneration work started by the mayor, Antonio Bassolino, in the

---

[6] Unlike in the 1970s, local governments began to make use of this dynamic and helped to organize some groups: for housing renewal, for example.

mid-1990s came up against bitter opposition, especially mobilizations by shop-keepers (Sebastiani 1998). In Bologna, when mayor Vitalli undertook a major urban project to renovate the main railway station, he came into conflict with associations on both left and right, determined to protect their living environment (Jouve and Lefèvre 1999), and this led to his losing the 2000 elections. In France, in the late 1980s, when the mayors of Strasbourg and Rennes committed themselves to building a tramway and a metro respectively, they had to face bitter opposition from residents of the districts concerned and from shopkeepers. In the UK, urban projects have aroused less opposition, but the environmental protection and animal rights movements have become radicalized. Movements of the unemployed and housing movements have not disappeared from European cities (Péchu 2001).

From north to south across Europe, mayors and economic elites complain about the unadventurous nature of residents and about systematic opposition to their major projects: stations, airports, shopping centres, property complexes, leisure parks, regeneration activities, and, last but by no means least, the construction of service networks. Councillors and economic elites must systematically compromise with district associations, tenants' committees, environmental groups, and groups protecting their living environment, all more or less institutionalized and taking part in numerous types of activity: demonstrations and petitions accompany systematic legal appeals, brawls with the constabulary, or heckling of councillors.

The literature has popularized this type of movement under the title of 'Nimbyism'—'not in my back yard': that is, residents organizing to protect their district or their home from what they experience as external aggression imposed, via elected representatives, by forces they view as hostile—the forces of capitalism, the state, or other districts. Moreover, these movements relate to various groups: frequently they are progressive, in the tradition of the 1970s movements against property developers—especially those with little respect for residents—but others, in contrast, may be very conservative and motivated essentially by defending purely private interests under the banner of mutual defence.

Diversification in European cities can be discerned through associations that represent immigrant or sexual minorities. Especially in British and French cities, the effects of urban restructuring and economic crisis and the reinforcement of exclusion processes have re-established a taste for more violent forms of mobilization, such as riots (Benyon and Solomos 1987; Body-Gendrot 2000). In a single given city, movements and associations may exist over a long period, though some disappear. Among individuals and economic or political elites, cities are the place where numerous groups are mobilized, and these are frequently better studied at the scale of the district. For a quarter of a century, in Leeds, the dynamics of mobilization in the multi-ethnic district of Chapeltown has been characterized by recurrent local mobilizations and campaigns, followed by long pauses: school campaigns, anti-drugs campaigns, riots, anti-racist campaigns, campaigns for recognition of minority rights (Farrar 1999). Social tensions and exclusion processes have become visible, thanks to movements and associations tackling poverty and social exclusion.

Apart from these movements defending living environments, all European cities contain different types of groups, among them parents' associations working for schools, immigrant community associations, anti-poverty associations, housing associations or associations fighting social service cuts, many and varied cultural associations, women's movements, family associations, churches, groups defending the rights of sexual minorities, pacifist, Third World and anti-racist associations, movements of illegal immigrants or of unemployed people. Leisure associations have also proliferated: sports clubs, pensioners' associations, associations linked to a particular hobby. In some cities, more original mobilizations have been organized, such as anti-mafia mobilizations in Palermo (Andretta 1999) or, in contrast, mobilizations against an influx of immigrants, such as those in Turin and Florence described by Della Porta (1999). Bobbio (1999) and Sebastiani (1998) suggest distinguishing four types of citizens' groups: (1) residents' movements: the Nimbys; (2) movements of independent professionals, craftspeople, and shopkeepers, whose activities are linked to city development: the petty bourgeoisie; (3) movements and associations that form an intrinsic part of a broader perspective, which they call 'cosmopolitan', made up of people who are interested in economic issues, the environment, sociability, culture, and the common good; and (4) citizens who act as volunteers in relation to their various interests and hobbies.

Changes of Scale and Institutionalization

Turku provides a succinct example of a dynamic that has been quite common in many European cities, particularly in central and northern Europe.

Turku is one of the three oldest and largest cities in Finland. Dominated by an imposing fortress, it has a population of 170,000 (Jauhianen 1997). From the 1960s onwards, a small group of Turku managers organized the development of the city: this involved ambitious urban projects in keeping with the canons of modernity and of 1960s and 1970s property development. This group included the mayor, chief town planners, an architects' practice, the proprietor of the region's newspaper group, the bosses of two huge building and public works firms, and some bankers. The complicities within this group and the outcomes for the city acquired a certain reputation in Finland, known as 'Turku disease'. From the early 1980s, activists from environmentalist groups organized to challenge large urban planning projects and town hall practices. These groups were made up of young people, and the university provided large bodies of protesters—left-wing students and teachers. Protest became professionalized, and all of Turku's urban planning was called into question during the 1980s. In parallel, groups of young squatters appeared in disused factories. Conflicts between these different groups and the dominant coalition in Turku proliferated. Then, the city, in the wake of the whole of Scandinavia, was belatedly but brutally affected by the economic recession of the early 1990s. A group association, 'Our Turku', was created in 1993, bringing together all those who opposed the town hall, especially urban environmental movements. This group put forward an alternative vision of Turku's future, proposing a car-free city centre and the development of forms of public transport. In particular, it mobilized against new plans to destroy old districts and create city-centre car parks and shopping centres. This challenge made use of legal avenues, which led to the mayor being dismissed for corruption. A new Social Democratic-Green coalition was elected in 1996.

Some associations and movements have become institutionalized, moving from protest to contractualization, participation, and service provision. Public policies increasingly call on various groups, which are frequently brought together under the title of 'third sector' or the ambiguous 'civil society', which seems to cover indiscriminately the family, churches, associations, the extended family, the local community, non-market organizations, and so on. These groups actively help to implement public policies and local initiatives, for instance in the sphere of public management of the drugs problem or AIDS (Kübler and Wäjti 2000; Borraz and Loncle 2000). Urban governments have, moreover, developed programmes of cooperation with associations and informal groups. Margit Mayer (2000*b*) takes the example of the Social Democratic Munich city council, which from 1984 onwards created a programme known as 'the Munich concept for supporting self-help groups and self-organized projects in health and social services'. The municipalities tried to involve their leaders and play a role in the 'third sector economy': direct local government control in districts, job creation enterprises, social policy associations, and increased assistance to individual or collective projects. Social movements have been transformed into not-for-profit organizations. More generally, district committees and other groups linked to particular districts or sections of the population have acquired strong legitimacy and are getting funding from local government, the state, or the European Union, which is encouraging this development.

In European cities, this myriad of movements and associations cannot be interpreted only in terms of diversity and as contributing to the fragmentation of urban societies. In fact, they help to structure urban society. The involvement of numerous groups and associations in public policy activities or in service provision requires frequent interactions with the legitimate political centre of cities: that is, with councillors and officials. This is probably where the novelty lies: not in the mere existence of urban social movements and associations, but in the way these groups claim to be actors in the city and are recognized as such by urban governments, which have developed various techniques for dealing with them—relations of cooperation, which, however, do not prevent recurrent conflicts and opposition. Protest movements also help to clarify another issue: they are evidence of the existence of a city centre. Contrary to visions of flux and of the city as disorganized, demonstrations in Bologna, Copenhagen, Nancy, and Sheffield have taken place in the main square or outside the town hall, almost in natural fashion. The urban public space of these European cities remains relatively legible and codified.

Social movements, in their turn, reflect the paradox of territories. Following in the footsteps of Tilly, who demonstrated the shift of social movements from the local to the national in nineteenth-century policy repertoires, many writers have dealt with the shaping of trans-national, European, and global repertoires. On the other hand, local and regional social movements have also gained in importance, and this has led to the relative decline of the national level as the main level on which repertoires are structured. One example of this can be found in Rucht's (1998) study of the territorial dimension of German social movements from 1950 to 1989, in which he demonstrates precisely this strengthening of local and regional movements.

In medium-sized European cities large mobilizations leave traces, producing leaders and actor networks. In Frankfurt, Helsinki, or Rennes, the exceptional learning experience of 1968 left traces in the form of networks or oppositions, which endured at least until the 1990s. Some associations have been present throughout, and have been sites of socialization for new generations. In mobilizing against the arrival of an extreme right-wing leader, most large associations have met in regional capitals and thus have been able to bring the associations and their networks together quickly. Behind the diversity, structuring logics can be identified. In Germany, some local social and political innovations were first initiated within the urban counter-culture, then within the German Green movement, whose impact in German cities since the 1980s has been enormous: for example, in Frankfurt (Roth 1991), it has ensured that the environment and the social organization of the city are at stake. In Italy, associations and cooperatives still find themselves partly caught up in the classic divisions between Catholic, Socialist, and ex-Communist spheres of influence. In Bergamo, a city north of Milan that is dominated by the small business people of the Northern League, the left's minority networks are organized into a myriad of cultural, economic, and political associations. In this case, the locality is clearly structured between ideological spheres of influence, which lie at the origin of networks of associations and organizations clearly identified with one another. Conflicts and opposition between families, social groups, and political organizations have been relatively stable over the medium term, and these organize the dynamic of the locality. In European cities, beyond the logic of integration, there are often, though not always, more or less marked structuring principles: principles that are also evident in the organization of political conflicts. In the city of Grenoble and its surrounding conurbation, the left-wing middle classes, working in research establishments, the university, or the hospital, and in the cultural industries, swell the ranks of a very lively network of associations, underpinning a more environmentalist and managerialist left than can be found elsewhere. In Strasbourg, religious allegiances still mark the social dynamics of the city, while the working classes of Liverpool and Glasgow have been divided between Catholics and Protestants for a long time.

These social and political forms of structuring social movements and associations are not immutable or stable. The large-scale, rapid growth of urban social movements in the 1970s put paid to any vision of cities as single, consensual units, especially in Europe (Fainstein and Hirst 1995). Social movements interact with the urban restructuring context, with processes that exclude young people, women and immigrants, with the blurring of social classes and identities, and with local governments that are increasingly disposed to consider the movements' demands, if only to strengthen the effectiveness of their own policies and/or legitimacy. To a great extent, these observations relate back to Chapters 3 and 4. Even in those countries such as the UK, Scandinavia, or France, that are, in their different ways, the most centralized, cities reveal a particular social dynamic, with differing degrees of linkages to the outside. In this interplay of movements and associations, their dynamism cannot be interpreted only as a function of national variables, but, on the contrary, is linked with the individual pathways, networks, and institutions rooted in a given city. This is also true for business interests.

Economic Interests: European Cities as a (Minor) Scale at which Business Interests are Being Restructured

The extension and the deepening of market logics, highlighted in Chapters 4 and 5, are having repercussions in cities. City development and mobilizations within cities are once again being seen less from the perspective of collective consumption (Harding 1997). Instead, European cities are characterized by a mix of organized business interests with quasi-public status becoming more involved in urban coalitions and city strategies, in contrast with other business actors who are becoming less territorialized: another paradox of territory. Overall, the role of economic interests in structuring and governing cities has increased, but it still cannot be described as central (Jouve and Lefèvre 1999).

Organized Interests Are Becoming More Territorialized: Chambers of Commerce and Industry are Looking for a Role

In capitalist economies, private interests do not inevitably have to organize, since they can influence society and politics either through the market or through the individual contacts that their resources and positions bring them (Offe and Wiesenthal 1980). Even though their role is considerably reduced, some great families still have an important position based on their heritage and their economic activities: the Agnelli in Turin, the Antinori in Florence, the Benettons in Treviso, and the Illys in Trieste. In some cases, local and regional newspaper groups organize public debate and have a strong political presence, like the Hutin family with *Ouest France* in Rennes, the Baylet family with *La Dépêche du Midi* in Toulouse, and *La Stampa* in Turin. 'Company towns' seem to have had their day, but this does not prevent certain financial or industrial groups from remaining important in certain cities, like Philips and DAF in Eindhoven, Mercedes-Benz in Stuttgart, Airbus in Toulouse, British Aerospace in Bristol, Nokkia in Helsinki/Espo, and Michelin in Clermont-Ferrand. In many cases, individuals or groups are involved in the development of the city, especially in carrying out major projects or in organizing representation to the outside world. Managers of the firms most inclined to intervene in city policies are not inevitably those whose firms are most dependent on the local economy. Social prestige, identity, and capacity to influence strategic choices are equally powerful motivations. Involvement in urban government networks can contribute to individual opportunities as well as to potential economic openings for the firm (Le Galès 2000).

Organized interests constitute a primary type of economic actor in European cities: chambers of commerce and industry, trade and craft associations, shopkeepers' and employers' organizations, business creation and professional associations have all formed a dynamic pillar of European cities for a long time. This situation was sustained well after the Middle Ages, until the two forces of economic liberalism and the nation-state removed their privileges and rearranged the scales of economic development at the national level (Black 1984). Although British economic liberalism and the French Revolution proved particularly effective in reducing the influence of corporations and chambers of commerce to almost nothing, the same did not apply in Germany or the Netherlands. The belated making of the nation-state in Germany and Italy has enabled associations of this type to prosper for a very long time at the local and regional level.

Chambers of commerce and industry (CCIs) are often first and foremost representative of associations of shopkeepers, while a chamber of trades tends to represent craftsmen. These groups are important in a city because they are numerous and were often set up a very long time ago; they have a heritage, and they play a role in the life of districts and of the city centre. Although employers' associations vary according to the cities and their different situations, they play a coordinating role in the private sector, and this generally leaves the CCIs with a minor role: although sometimes the opposite is true. As bodies, they rarely get involved in business start-up or activities related to information and communications technologies. In the UK,

CCIs are a sort of businessmen's club, used as agencies for government programmes but often competing for this role with another government agency, the Training and Enterprise Councils (TECs), especially for economic development programmes. Their participation in local development issues is often limited to an interest in car parks, roads, shops, and golf courses. Lines of cleavage frequently run through both CCIs and TECs. In Norwich, the CCI has traditionally represented local shopkeepers and the big shopkeeping families, like the Jarrolds, or the more traditional local bourgeoisie, while more industrial or more recent firms have had more of a presence in the TECs. In Birmingham, the CCI has played an important part in the city's history. When, under the leadership of Labour's Richard Knowles and Albert Bore, the city council decided to abandon its highly bureaucratic past in order to embark on European competition and import 'city boosterism' from the United States, the CCI became a weighty ally in favour of major flagship projects like the International Convention Centre, the National Indoor Arena, or the renewal of the city centre (Loftman and Nevin 1998). In Manchester, business interests were dominated by a group of powerful business leaders, 'the Manchester Mafia' (Peck and Tickell 1995). Partly through central government pressure, individuals and employers' representatives were appointed to numerous agencies in order to inject their values, objectives, and ways of working. However, assessments of the capacity of local business elites to direct cities' strategies remain variable (Peck and Tickell 1995; North, Valler and Wood 2001; Bennett 1998).

In Austria and in Germany, CCIs play a rule- and norm-generating role in the local economy, and their legitimacy and the scope of their activities are strengthened by large budgets. When during the 1980s German cities, like cities elsewhere, became an integral part of economic development logics, CCIs provided them with partners of undisputed influence. In Hamburg (Dangschaft and Ossenbrügge 1990), Stuttgart (Hoffmann-Martinot 1995), and Dortmund (Voeltzkow 2002), the CCIs supplied ideas, threw all their weight behind major redevelopment initiatives, and got involved in urban redevelopment. In France, in Belgium and in Italy, CCIs have a public status inherited from Napoleon, which gives them a dual role as state representative and representative of local private interests. When the city of Anvers was plunged into economic crisis, the renewed thinking about its economic future was an initiative of the mayor and the CCIs. The undisputed representative of private sector actors, and especially of the harbour, the CCI was co-founder, in the early 1990s, of the Association for the Renewal and Promotion of Anvers (Van den Berg, Braun, and Van der Meer 1997*b*). In Italy, CCIs and business associations form very influential networks. Protected for a long time by the Christian Democrats—who had effectively colonized the state—craftsmen, small businesses, and shopkeepers still have an exceptionally high level of influence in the Italian social structure, an influence that is also found in cities via the various institutionalized associations. The 'old' petty bourgeoisie remains an active group in the cities. In the early 1990s, the first wave of elections for mayors by universal suffrage, during a period of legal upheaval, saw the emergence of left-wing mayors with an atypical profile. The CCIs then provided candidates for the right. In Bologna, the sensational defeat of the left in Spring 1999 enabled Guazzaloca, former president of the CCI and the Association of Shopkeepers and Business Services, to take control of the town hall with the support of shopkeepers and small businesses (Baldini and Legnante 2000). In Milan, too, the CCI, in the person of Albertini, took over the town hall. Having long been just a subsidiary of the Christian Democrats, Italian CCIs were reformed in 1993, cutting their party links, transforming themselves into active territorial actors and agents of economic development involved in the regulation of local economic activity, and drawing their resources from providing services to firms. With the great diversity characteristic of Italy—although, on this point, the same also goes for France—CCIs have become actors in urban policies and cities' development strategies (Perulli 1999*b*).

Apart from CCIs, whose status is linked to a sub-national territory, employers' associations do have a presence in cities, but they are more rarely actors in the city's development. The territory—as far as we are concerned here, the city—enables the heterogeneous interests of the members of these numerous associations to be managed, while still providing a frame for interaction that allows exchange, proximity, and identification (Streeck 1992). Except in the case of firms whose business is directly linked to the territory—building and public works, for example—employers' associations are generally not very active in the strategies of cities, though there are notable exceptions in German cities and in Barcelona. However, employers' organizations, following the lead of the trade unions, are also redeploying their activities onto different scales, and attempts are being made to 'territorialize' employers' associations. In France and in Italy, changes in their leaderships in the late 1990s and the internal reforms of MEDEF and CONFINDUSTRIA had a similar outcome.

Fragile Urban Coalitions

Economic actors in cities are very diverse, from the organized interests of small artisans to the conglomerates that manage and build whole districts, and so are their roots and investments in this territory. Like any other actors, they mobilize on various scales, helping to strengthen some levels at the expense of others. Greater mobility—at least for some of them—allows them room for manoeuvre, linked to their nomadic behaviour, and situates their relationship to the territory in a more uncertain, more negotiated logic. Their role in cities is not new. The progressive bourgeoisies of the late nineteenth and early twentieth centuries were the originators of public facilities, social housing, and social policies. Even during the period after the Second World

War, bosses, shopkeepers, and property developers never disappeared from their localities.

For example, Matejko (2000) recalls that in Lille, which is both an old Flemish town and an industrial city, there was a vigorous confrontation between Catholic employers and the socialist labour movement in the early twentieth century. The employers declined as the textile industry did, but guarded their independence long and jealously until the public-sector interventions in Lille and Roubaix in the late 1970s, which also saw some consultations around the university. The decline of textile industry employers and of Lille's old industrial families contrasted with the increasing power of the city, and above all of the Communauté Urbaine de Lille, notably after the 1973 crisis and Mauroy's becoming mayor. He took many more initiatives, which anticipated the decentralization laws and introduced economic development as a perceived stake for the conurbation and for private actors. And when the mayor of Lille became prime minister, he did not forget the textile employers of northern France, who benefited from generous state aid for managing decline and modernizing, even though this was contrary to European regulations. The rigorous turn taken by the Mauroy government in 1983 and the decentralization reforms, from1982 onwards, changed the context for the mayor of Lille, who tried to mobilize both public sector and private sector actors to achieve the economic conversion of a city very severely affected by industrial decline. The prime minister-mayor's pragmatism and economic modernism were as much vaunted as his project for Lille. Local employers were not insensitive to this, and the Chamber of Commerce and Industry then elected as president a businessman who did not belong to any of the traditional major families. A period of cooperation began, expressed in the creation of the *Association pour la promotion industrielle de la Métropole Nord*, the emergence of a discourse on the northern French metropolis in European competition, the work of the town planning agency, and cooperation with the CCI and the Employers Union on major issues, such as the coming of the TGV Nord high-speed train. The mayor gained state support for major projects and negotiated employers' support to achieve the economic transformation of Lille. Exchanges, visits, and meetings proliferated, notably in preparation for Euralille, the city-centre flagship project for a new mainline high-speed rail station-shopping centre and office complex. The Employers' Union of the Northern French Metropolis mobilized, developed projects and ideas, and participated in urban government and in developing public policies: all part of the idea of international status for the Lille metropolis. The Greater Lille Committee, an informal club of economic and political decision-makers, steered by businessmen—in particular, Bonduelle —and involving university academics, was formed. This committee worked on the Olympic Games bid, the Greater Lille Charter, the Euroregion—with Courtrai and Tournai—the Charter for Territorially-based Business, 'La haute borne', a European science park project, European specialist subject centres, and the museum, in close liaison with the town planning agency and the strengthened authorities of the conurbation. In the 1990s, however, tensions arose within employers' organizations between the section most interested in the metropolization of Lille and the section made up of the traditional CCI and some employers, which was opposed to the mayor as he came to the end of his career (Cole and John 2001).

Other private interests also construct and manage city networks: property developers, construction firms, managers of services and of networks. They provide some of the services the population needs, on a private or delegated basis. The changes of scale and perimeter undergone by these groups have already been presented in Chapter 5. Supported by banks, insurance companies, and other financial institutions, the great 'city builders' (Fainstein 1994) have a presence in real-estate activities in the biggest cities. At the scale of medium-sized European cities, these big developers have less of a presence, though there are some exceptions. Each state has developed a system of urban planning rules and property markets, of which private actors form an integral part (Berry and McGreal 1995). Beyond the role of the city government and of the state in urban planning, private actors obviously play an essential part, frequently acting brutally, in cooperation with the state, to drive out ordinary people so that they can carry out lucrative building work.

Big international operators frequently get involved in the development game, bidding for specific operations in regional capitals, but it is still most often national or local operators who are active in European cities. The Europeanization process is under way, but institutions and territories are not disappearing into the space of flows. Everywhere in Europe, varied forms of public-private partnership have been developed for the renewal or development of strategic urban sites, against a background of challenges to the most normative forms of planning (Heinz 1994). These developers are capable of carrying out operations on an ambitious scale as part of cities' development strategies, especially where the cities are undertaking economic transformation. In Düsseldorf, the development of a high-tech business park, Wahler Park, was the work of a single developer, Calliston (Dieterich and Drangsfeld 1995), working closely with the local authorities. However, it would be a mistake to see these changes only from the angle of the relationship between councils with limited resources and increasingly Europeanized and globalized developers, who run the same type of operations everywhere with a few local variations. The property development sector as a whole, like the construction industry, still includes a very large number of very active small and medium-sized firms. There are strong tensions everywhere, however, and property developers are creating a proliferation of shopping centres and of operations mixing leisure, shops, and entertainment, all in an apparent logic of public space which is, in fact, becoming harder and harder to perceive behind commodified, more or less privatized spaces. In the wake of what has been observed in American cities (Zukin 1995; Hannigan 1998), culture and consumption increasingly often come together in urban renewal activities. This is first and foremost true of the biggest metropolises, but is also the case in medium-sized European cities: Glasgow's 'merchant city', the docks in Liverpool, the fashion district in Milan, the old districts of Copenhagen preserved as a museum for visitors and the Nyehaven district with its nightlife, Amsterdam's Red Light District, or Dublin's Temple Bar. The big names in clothing, like the Scandinavian group H&M, the American Gap, and the Spanish firms Zara and Mango, have been inspired by the Italian firm, Benetton, to invade the streets of European cities beyond the capitals. Gucci's luxury boutiques and those of the wealthy LVMH conglomerate are multiplying. Carrefour or Rinascente shopping centres, Hard Rock Cafés, and other record-book-video game shops like Virgin or Fnac are spreading rapidly beyond their national boundaries. These groups are becoming Europeanized and globalized and are investing in European cities, which welcome them with open arms as part of their own window on the international world. The same trend holds good for hotels. What European city does not want to welcome a luxury hotel which will serve as a marker of prestige, promoting tourism in the city, and as a conference centre? In this sense, it seems that European cities are converging under the auspices of major European or American commercial companies.

This brief description would be incomplete if it did not take into account trade unions and cooperatives in the Italian case. In the nineteenth century, trade unions originally evolved on the basis of occupations and were strongly territorialized at the level of 'travel-to-work areas' or labour exchanges (Crouch 1993). Trade unionism later organized at the national level, alongside the centralization of the state and the economy, just about everywhere, although to a lesser extent in southern Europe. In Italy, trade unionism has remained rooted in the territory, generating specific social relations. In most countries, the creation of new linkages between different scales lies at the heart of their strategy: finding modes of articulation for interests and for the collective game at the European level so that they can play a role in the creation of a social Europe; involving, or not involving, local trade unions in cities' strategies—for example, through development committees or *conseils de développement*; seizing the opportunities offered by European Union policies—Structural Funds and employment policy—to exert pressures on urban public policies; using regional organization to question the influence of both local branches and sub-regional levels of union organization. Trade unions also have a strong presence within public bodies. Studies of specific cases, particularly in Belgium, Germany, Italy, and France, have demonstrated the role played by trade unions in cities, their involvement in collective activities for city development or youth training, and the part they play in regulating the employment market. However, comparative research has tended to show that trade unions, rightly or wrongly, still have a fairly low presence as actors of cities' strategies: their role in local societies remains a difficult one, despite forms of reorganization that seem to be increasing their presence (Geddes 2000; Regini 1988).

In all European cities, these organizations and these individuals represent conflicts and multiple interests. Forms of opposition based on cleavages can structure a city over a long period; these may be social, political, district, or religious cleavages, or those rooted in large mobilizations. The political work of elected representatives consists of naturalizing these interests, shaping them, and integrating them into a whole, likely to represent something that can be presented as 'the local interest' (Fontaine and Le Bart 1994): a concept often reinterpreted in reference to local development. Beyond the political dimension, relationships between organizations, between groups, and between individuals are an intrinsic part of organizations and institutions.

Integration and Representation: Has Competition Become the Organizing Principle for Social and Political Actors Within European Cities?

In the Europe of the Middle Ages, city-states were in mutual competition. They used their military might, bought the services of mercenaries or *condottieri*, grew rich through their banks, and tried to monopolize certain trade routes. In fifteenth-century Italy, Florence, Venice, Milan, the Vatican, and the Kingdom of Naples were powers who cooperated or came into confrontation according to alliances and reversals of fortune. The consolidation of nation-states did not remove all forms of competition, but it did mean that war was no longer a means of regulating conflicts between cities. Within centralized states, competition between cities was regulated by the state. We have seen in Chapter 2 that the urban bourgeoisies mobilized their cities, small or large, to become the headquarters of a bailiwick, a parliament, a university, a bishopric, or, later, a *préfecture* or a mainline railway station. In Great Britain, the Industrial Revolution transformed the urban map and fuelled conflicts between the new cities. Thus, Briggs (1962) gives an account of the failure of the proud city of Bradford to win the central main-line railway station for the north-east of England, which was created 15 kilometres away in Leeds. Bradford's leaders still bemoan this decision, in their eyes a tragedy, which guaranteed the preeminence of the rival city. The building of large town halls, the planning of railway stations, the organization of universal exhibitions, and the construction of new districts enabled local bourgeoisies to confirm their wealth and power. In more recently formed nation-states, such as Germany and Italy, rivalries between cities have never ceased.

The 1960s offer us no shortage of examples of competition within the state. In the Scandinavian countries, some city councils were at the forefront of developing social services and were good at capturing the resources needed for their experiments. The creation of new universities, the electrification of the railways, and the building of modern hospitals, airports, museums, and research centres formed the objects of claims and rivalries between local governments: between Glasgow and Edinburgh, Bristol and Cardiff, Turin and Milan, Manchester and Liverpool, Bordeaux and Toulouse, Lisbon and Oporto, Munich and Stuttgart, Düsseldorf and Cologne, Eindhoven, Utrecht, Amsterdam and Rotterdam, Bilbao and San Sebastian, Le Havre and Rouen. This competition between cities is, therefore, not a new phenomenon but it used to be contained within a national space restricted by boundaries and regulated essentially by the state. This is no longer the case.

Competition has clearly become an organizing principle for actors within European cities. One of the first examples was Hamburg (Dangshaft and Ossenbrügge 1990), a port city, but also a centre for the media and the insurance industry. In 1983, the Social Democrat mayor, Dohnanyi, threw himself into an economic development strategy based on new technologies, the university, the media, and the service sector, relying particularly strongly on local business leaders. This coalition and this cocktail went on to be imitated in many places, and was characterized by Harvey (1989) as an indicator of the rise of 'urban entrepreneurialism'. However, this argument has been exaggerated and is only partly relevant to European cities. The following section takes a critical look at the argument and its limits.

The Pressure of Competition: Its Disciplining Effects on the Entrepreneurial City

Representations of competition have the aim of mobilizing and integrating different organizations. Local development and competition with other cities act as a form of urban common interest, developed by various groups within the city. Urban research has seized on this. After all, American social scientists have long since demonstrated the influence of private sector interests in the United States, notably property developers conniving with local politicians to organize city development. The whole urban history of the United States is set in this dynamic of competition (Sbragia 1996; Peterson 1981; Banfield 1961). The neo-Marxist urban sociology of the 1970s gave a new impetus to this literature, with a proliferation of monographs (Feagin and Smith 1987; Davis 1990) culminating in the major work by Logan and Molotch, *Urban Fortunes* (1987). This explains the organization of cities through conflicts relating to the development of, and variations between, different 'urban growth coalitions' formed in various cities between business people acting to amend town plans and resist political construction of the market, business people anticipating growth, and fortunate landowners carried along with the general movement, in an American context of powerful market dynamics in relation to buildings and land, with little structure imposed by public policy.[7]

The decline of state regulation of economic flows has, in general, made European cities more directly dependent on firms for jobs, taxes, and development. Neo-liberal ideology and the strengthening of market forms of regulation have made their mark on European cities:

competition has become the dominant model for relations between individuals. Competition now shapes our representations and models our ways of acting . . . today, when the market economy has everything in its grip, there is no longer anything to distinguish goods from shams and commodities from representations of them . . . Competition, once limited to a few kinds of commodities on one market involving a small number of proactive participants—merchants—now appears to be a normal mode of social regulation and even a life ethic. (Thureau-Dangin 1995: 8)

There is general agreement that competition between European cities is growing, but the concepts of interurban competition and urban success remain diffuse. Interurban competition basically is rivalry between cities in the European urban system for the creation or attraction of economic activity which produces income. The capacity to generate income is in turn related to other aspects of urban economy and society such as levels of service, size of the tax base, infrastructure, quality of life, and educational and cultural facilities. (Jensen-Butler 1997: 3)

The drift of this is that cities—this time in the sense of the coalitions that govern cities—have an interest in getting involved in these dynamics, that is, in improving their position on the scales of prestige, wealth, and political influence in international competition between cities. Harvey (1985a) has identified the different dimensions of this pressure in terms of competition to attract investments, well-off social groups, and visitors, and in terms of its implications for urban policy. Cities are trying to strengthen their positions as consumption centres, with shopping centres and leisure complexes, entertainment, major urban projects, and culture, and as command centres— as headquarters of big firms and public bodies. They are implementing policies to make themselves attractive to investors and people: urban planning, social policy, image, and culture can all be reviewed and measured against the demands of competition; and this is not a benign process, since it

---

[7] In the American context, the urban crisis of the 1970s was accompanied by a withdrawal on the part of the state, which took the form of restrictions on social and urban policies and precipitated serious financial difficulties for cities already impoverished by the mass exodus of the middle classes to the residential suburbs. American city councils reacted by doing everything they could to increase their two main sources of revenue: business and the better-off social classes. The urban elites to some extent set aside the classic functions of local government under this financial pressure and threw themselves headlong into the competition to attract managers and firms. In this process, the sphere of urban government and urban policies was restructured in the direction of the entrepreneurial city: resources were mobilized in favour of competition, and actors acted according to that imperative and that constraint.

involves social transfers, policing of the poor, and redistribution towards favoured groups. Harvey focuses on the mode of regulation involved in competition and stresses: in particular, that discipline is imposed from outside and the sanctions threaten those who do not play the game. This competition is codified by agencies and the media which develop classifications, performance indicators, and 'good business climate' indexes, helping to make this logic of competition seem natural and desirable. This allows housing and exclusion problems and social conflicts to be denied or, at least, to disappear from the political agenda, with lower taxation—compared with other cities—being seen as a good indicator of 'healthy management'. Success in competition is gradually imposing itself as the legitimizing principle of public policy: it is made to seem a natural, unavoidable constraint. The negative mirror image of this is that the spiral of economic decline and the failure to attract populations and incomes lead to impoverishment, departure of the better-off, and accentuation of the crisis, except perhaps in rich suburbs isolated from the city. The image of the city is measured and qualified as a response to the demands and requirements of the groups concerned. Refusal to play the game can contribute to negative effects on image, with anticipated consequences for prosperity.

So how far have things gone in European cities? The power of globalization processes is leading, directly or indirectly, to convergence of the strategies of urban elites as they respond to the pressures of capitalism. Cities, formerly structured by the Keynesian state and industrial capitalism, are perhaps becoming more 'entrepreneurial cities', adapting simultaneously to the requirements of globalized capitalism, to forms of mobility organized within the European Union, and to the discipline imposed by the 'competitive state', to pick up on the expression used in Chapter 3.

For European cities, the basis for discussion of this argument should be to distinguish the scale and scope of the discourse of competition to attract investments from that of urban policies. Starting when the state ceased to guarantee the economic prosperity of cities—a fact distressingly confirmed during the 1970s and after—the issue of economic development has burst onto the urban policy scene. The stake is now to attract outside investments and, therefore, jobs and revenues, along with certain populations: business people, tourists, students, new residents. Factory closures have lent urban economies a sense of vulnerability and risk; and since unemployment has become the highest-priority worry for city-dwellers, councillors cannot treat it as an abstract. What is more, discourse on urban competition holds a lot of attractions for urban elites (Jessop 1997*a*). It justifies the promotion of the city in terms of innovation, competitive dynamic, identities, assets, and positioning in an international space that removes the city from confrontation with the state: in short, a whole set of things that validate the elites who sustain this discourse. What is more, this competition acts at different scales: regional, national, European, and even global. Therefore, it gives elites a chance to situate themselves, to travel, to refer to foreign examples, and to try to attract the attention of the most prestigious media.

Analysis of trans-national flows of private investment and the mobility of firms provides ambiguous indicators of the real burden of this constraint. The UK, under tight government control, has pushed this logic of competition furthest, through heavy reliance on forms of regional assistance, a favourable tax regime, low labour costs, and labour flexibility, which have enabled it to capture 40 per cent of trans-national flows in Europe. Other countries have followed this lead.[8] Although this does not constitute the unique key factor for an urban or regional economy or an insurance policy against all future risks, it is true that investment in the car industry in crisis regions— Nissan in Sunderland or Toyota in Valenciennes—high-tech investment— Sun Microsystems in Grenoble or Microsoft in Cambridge and Stockholm —investment in leisure complexes or tourism in Barcelona and Dublin, the big logistics firms that have invested in Genoa and Anvers, and Aventis in Strasbourg all represent major stakes for these cities; and this explains the proliferation of bodies involved in locating or attracting firms. States, regions, cities, consultants, and public and private bodies have launched themselves into the race to attract investments. Moreover, this competition has gradually become professionalized, codified, and institutionalized as a result of European competition rules and of indicators drawn up by the big consultancies and major firms. These organizations often bring together property developers, planners, communication agencies, banks, and consultancies.[9] Big firms have adopted the habit of negotiating their new locations through private international organizations, which contribute to a powerful trend towards standardizing practices, defining location criteria, and organizing the rules of competition between cities—none of which can be taken for granted. In the UK, France, Scandinavia, and Germany, consultants have developed skilful evaluation grids which they use to situate particular cities 'within European competition' or even international competition, applying criteria and methods as complex as their principles are uncertain. Nevertheless, in modern societies, the production of a myth requires tools that are, or appear to be, scientific; and one can still marvel at the wealth of imagination deployed in aggregating economic data, opinion polls, and the findings of panels of experts or image studies.[10]

[8] Including France, which had long been reluctant because foreign investment was seen as a competitive threat for national firms until the 1980s. Those investments represented in 1999 and 2000 between 30,000 and 35,000 jobs, around 500 projects.

[9] D.Yull from the Strathclyde University has estimated that, in Europe in 1994, attractiveness policies employed over 3,000 people in several hundred organizations.

[10] On that point, see Neveu (2000). Economic, political, and social criteria are rolled together to reveal 'an international city'—this means a city open to numerous foreigners, as long as they are 'good', highly educated foreigners, with resources and a skilled job —'a European city', or 'a competitive city'. These criteria are often devised with the support of university academics, who are active members of the business elites in their cities, following in the footsteps of some of their American colleagues; and competition

The metaphor of the 'entrepreneurial city' has three characteristic elements: (1) the discourse of competition and of the market, including that of image and identity; (2) the political priority given to the stakes of economic development and attracting favoured investments, flows, and social groups; and (3) changes in local government towards organizational forms of a public-private partnership type, which give private-sector actors a major role in defining the common good of the city, its priorities, and modes of management, as well as in designing and implementing projects. Discourse on the metropolis is at the heart of a new urban dynamic of economic development, heritage development, and the search for new identities (Biarez 1990). This could pass for a modern version of civic mercantilism: the patriotism towards their city felt by merchants of old. Yet the metaphor also carries with it the usual batch of ambiguities and multiple, even contradictory, definitions (Hall and Hubbard 1998; Painter 1998).

'Good management practices'—those indispensable complements to the measurement of competition—arise in their turn from seeing the world in terms of optimal balance and of competition. The systematic re-processing of promotional and urban policy documents by different European cities has provided a document base synthesizing good advice to urban elites anxious to make their own city competitive:[11]

- Cities must have a strategic vision of how to face new challenges and global economic uncertainties.
- A strategic style of planning must be established, directed towards the needs of clients and consumers—essentially business people, residents, and tourists; planning must serve market logics.
- Policies implemented and programmes planned must be of very high quality if the city is to be competitive. This quality is achieved through the mobilization of competencies and of specialized professionals capable of creating competitive advantages.
- The economic base must be diversified so that it can adapt to the constraints and fluctuations of the flexible economy.
- The city's entrepreneurial characteristics must be developed: management; encouragement of dynamic employers; an open, welcoming social structure; easy access for firms to risk capital; competitive banks; a skilled, well-motivated labour force; support structures for business start-up; innovative research centres; good quality of life.
- Above all, the city government must be transformed into an entrepreneurial government: replacing public servants with managers and marketing

rages between different academics to produce indicators that will help to impose their own measure of competition and of these symbolic and real sanctions. Here I should mention, for example, the work of the EURICUR group in situating and classifying the Randstadt and then other European urban regions.

[11] On this point, see also the edifying marketing literature—for example, Koter, Haider, and Penn (1993).

people; providing very high-quality, innovative, competitive services; developing a business culture; changing citizens into consumers of, and shareholders in, the city; having a flexible bureaucracy; bringing together the public and the private sectors; making local officials dependent on private-sector decision-makers; and, finally, devising clear, original responses and strategies, articulated around a strong, identifiable leadership with good professional advice.

• In terms of public policies, urban entrepreneurial government must reduce taxes, implement policies to attract public and private investments, promote the city's image through culture, urban flagship projects, festivals, spectacles, conferences, and so on, reorganize social services, borrow on the international financial markets—and get itself noticed by agencies that assess financial risks—and reduce the burden of the local public sector.

• Last but not least, the city's interests in economic development must be sustained by a clearly identified leader, who gives coherent and legitimate responses to economic development issues and blots out any conflict.

This anthology of clichés drawn from business management or inspired by the crudest form of neo-liberalism is somewhat absurd. No European city strategy could be reduced to these so-called good practices, not even in the UK, where Conservative governments did impose some of these changes. Nevertheless, these prescriptions and the representations associated with them are commonly put forward in publications all over Europe, and serve as a basis for many consultancy exercises. The discourse and practices of urban competition have now been internalized by the urban elites of Europe, who have the ability to adopt this language and use it whenever the need arises. However, several points must qualify this presentation of competition: the reality of economic pressure, ambiguities in the concept of 'entrepreneurial city', and the permanence of the state.

The Metaphor of the Entrepreneurial City and its Limitations

Economic development represents a high stake from an economic point of view, but the future of the urban economy also depends on public investments and on infrastructures. However, the way in which cities have seized on competition and its expected effects masks very diverse preoccupations: 'Territorial competition thus combines the concerns of traditional property-oriented growth machines, the newer city marketers oriented both to image manipulation and the repackaging of a place product, New Left urban authorities pursuing industrial restructuring in the social interest and French or Japanese planners of regional technopoles' (Cheshire and Gordon 1996: 385). The literature on economic competition between cities highlights a whole set of factors that contribute to local economic development, the diversity of factors and processes, and the fact that the notion of 'competitive city' does not make much sense from a strictly economic point of view (Veltz 1996;

Jensen-Butler 1997; Cheshire and Gordon 1996). Comparison accentuates the contrasts between cities and between economic sectors. Competition works very differently from one city to another, according to the sectors of the economy represented there, the type of firms, their size, their development, and the volume of outside investments—which is actually only one factor among many. In Europe, even though the single market accentuates the dynamic of competition, national logics remain strong, including in the urban regions— the scale that economists mainly use—most engaged in this competition: London, Paris, the Randstad, the Ruhr, Milan, and, to a lesser extent, Stockholm, Copenhagen, Rome, Brussels, and Madrid. For others, this logic exists but it does not call their existence into question.

Drawing on Schumpeter, Jessop looks at the image of the entrepreneurial city from a somewhat different angle. Schumpeter's entrepreneur takes risks, uses technologies, mobilizes people and different forms of capital, opposes any resistance he meets, and implements a strategy to develop the enterprise and its profits: he does meet resistance, so he must mobilize his forces. Taking this comparison to its logical conclusion, and requiring us to set aside the imposing volume of material produced by the discourse on competition and entrepreneurialism, Jessop (1998: 79) rightly stresses that

there are few cities which are systematically oriented to securing sustainable dynamic competitive advantages through continuing economic, political and social innovations that are intended to enhance productivity and other conditions of structural and systemic competitiveness . . . Weaker forms of competition are usually more concerned with modifications in formal and substantive regulatory, facilitative or supportive measures aimed at capturing mobile investment (a deregulatory race to the bottom) as well as simple image-building measures with the same purpose (boosterism).

Most of the time, as far as cities are concerned, the reality of competition translates into public policies presented in the language of competition. So there are contradictions and uncertainties associated with the metaphors of the 'entrepreneurial city' or the 'competitive city'.

A third, somewhat different, angle will serve to reinforce this point. The state has not disappeared from European cities, but is reshaping itself. State expenditure translates into redistribution and public investment in a context where urban governments also have resources for public intervention. There is some dependence on privileged social groups and firms who are mobile and somewhat inclined to quit the city. However, there has been no accelerated decline over the short term, and, other than in exceptional cases, no collapse. The elites of medium-sized European cities, however clearly aware of the stakes of economic development and of the benefit that they can derive from such mobilizations, also know that their city does not just come down to that.

There are two final comments to be made on the logic of competition and the organization of cities. The first relates to the term 'actor city'. All interpretation of competition tends to promote this picture of the actor city: of the entrepreneur with a unified leadership vision, with social conflicts euphemized or even ignored, contradictions set aside, and the social issues at stake subordinated to logics of mobilization in the name of a local common good expressed in terms of economic competition. This logic can have the effect of legitimizing forms of pragmatic, or so-called apolitical, public policy, thus privileging public-private partnerships and networks of economic and political elites. Padioleau (1991) has rightly denounced the risk of seeing new 'urban oligarchies' getting hold of the entrepreneurial rhetoric in order to better criticize the state and promote more flexible forms of public policy, more in line with their own interests.

Second, although this configuration can now be observed in European cities, this is only part of the story. Associations, social movements, and public organizations remain very active. Although, within this nebulous picture, some of them seem to be behaving more according to market logics imposed by their financing, most of them remain firmly anchored in the logics of action of local groups or even in a relationship with the state. In European cities, cases where elites have succeeded in imposing a predominantly entrepreneurial logic without meeting strong resistance are rare. Conversely, some neo-Marxist literature has too rapidly adopted a bias that suggests a 'natural' mobilization of private interests in the direction of inter-urban competition. As far as the majority of European cities are concerned, such collective action is not a given. These cities are not exactly swarming with the kind of economic interests that can benefit from this competition, and their territorial interest in it remains partial (Cheshire and Gordon 1996). It must also be remembered that some of these private interests are fairly strongly opposed to more competition in their own territory, for land, labour, and even public aid. Competition is unquestionably one element of the discourse and a constraining factor for European cities, but it does not erase all the rest; it can, with varying degrees of difficulty, be linked with other priorities such as integration, security, or sustainable development.

The Making of Urban Coalitions?

Two examples will serve to illustrate European cities in entrepreneurial terms: Leeds and Bilbao.

Leeds benefited from the creation of its main-line railway stations and gradually established itself as the administrative and financial capital of north-east England. Leeds is now a city with a population of 700,000, governed by the Labour Party. Since the mid-1980s, there have been several noteworthy changes in urban policies and in the organizations responsible for government (Haughton and Williams 1996; Cole and John 2001). After some initial hesitation and resistance, the Labour leader, Jon Trickett, and his team entered wholeheartedly into the competitive game organized by the British state so that they could transform the city. The turning point was marked by the creation, in 1990, of a public-private partnership in the UK sense, that is, of a real urban policy agency with powers and budgets. The Leeds Initiative brings together the Chamber of Commerce and Industry, the council, the police, the Training and Enterprise Council (TEC), that is, the local semi-public agency in charge of employment and training, the Urban Development Corporation, that is, the property development agency required by the state, and the university. The Leeds Initiative was tasked with implementing policies that would make the city an international competitor: policies for transport, land use, European programmes, and the environment—and, evidently, little social policy. Under the guidance of the Director of the CCI, a partner in the firm Coopers and Lybrand, consultants rushed to help the city renew its image and promote Leeds as a financial capital in order to attract insurance companies and banks wanting to leave London and thus strengthen an existing Leeds tradition. One university academic, a friend of the council leader, produced a proliferation of studies and reports. The Leeds Business Environment Forum brought together business elites and council leaders in order to improve the business environment. Leeds' image has been the subject of numerous campaigns, and the council has succeeded in attracting the most fashionable clothing store in England—at the time, this was the only instance of a branch being established outside London—which is said to have led not only to a change of image but also to a flood of applicants to the university. In short, in a few years, a traditional Labour council has been transformed into a neo-elitist government, mainly concerned with economic development, the success of financial bodies, and the activities of property developers in renewing the city centre: all in the aim of making Leeds a European city.

Leeds is not an isolated example. The strong, or authoritarian, state of the Thatcher years imposed a regime of privatization, reduced credits, and competition rules on British cities, which MacLeod (2001) has called 'the political shaping of privatism'. After a period of revolt and stalemate, exemplified by the confrontation between the 'New Urban Left' and the government (Gyford 1985; Harding 1991; Le Galès 1990). Labour's urban elites, under financial and political constraints, adapted to their new environment (Quilley 2000). They worked closely with the private sector in the context of public-private partnerships, they embarked on responding to UK or European invitations to competitive tenders for urban policies such as City Challenge, and they assiduously pursued promotional strategies by trying to organize major sporting and cultural events of international repute, like Glasgow, which was one of the first European Capitals of Culture in the 1990s, Birmingham, and Manchester, which launched campaigns to host the Olympic Games, or Sheffield's bid for the Commonwealth Games. The term 'entrepreneurial city' has gradually come to be used to account for this shift of urban policies and of urban government to promote economic development, often on the basis of property development projects, towards completely revitalized aims and through thoroughly revitalized modes of governance.

In Bilbao, to take a different example, culture and identity are at the heart of the project to revive the city by transforming its image (Gomez 1998; Plaza 1999; Chadoin, Godier, and Tapie 2000). An industrial port in crisis, undermined by unemployment and poverty, Bilbao has experienced fairly spectacular development over about ten years, although it is far from solving all its social problems, has been striking. In the late 1980s, business elites and local political circles drew up a strategic plan to revitalize metropolitan Bilbao, which brought together the City of Bilbao, the Basque government, and the Province of Biscay, and led to the 'Bilbao Ria 2000' plan. Four hundred people came together to develop a representation of the city and a strategic plan rooted in the revitalization of metropolitan Bilbao, especially the river banks that had formerly been the city's industrial core. In 1991, the 'Bilbao Metropoli' association was created, bringing together private sector actors, the public authorities, and the university. Three strategic plans became more or less enmeshed. Consultants manufactured an image, carried out benchmarking with other European cities, strongly inspired by what had happened in Glasgow, and put forward ideas. The 'Bilbao 2010' renewal project—about €2 billion of investments, including, in particular, European funding from the URBAN programme—included a metro system with stations built by Norman Foster, a conference centre, the rehabilitation of the docks, and, above all, the Guggenheim Museum, built by Frank Gerhy, which has been exceptionally successful in attracting visitors. The 'Bilbao Metropoli' association adopted the language and modes of action of European city competition: publishing its own indicators, mobilizing to get into the vanguard of the knowledge society, astonishingly measured, and initiating a promotional campaign based on the bewildering slogan 'tomorrow sings out in Bilbao, the city where everything is possible'. In 1998, the association initiated a strategic rethink, in the city project mould, by appealing to over 320 national and international experts who, it was supposed, would give their blessing to Bilbao's success.

Similar combinations of issues have emerged elsewhere in Europe. States have encouraged the strengthening of economic capitals through urban policies that go beyond welfare and aim to promote big cities in international competition, as when Denmark, in 1992, developed a National Plan that gave cities a role in national economic development. The example of Barcelona has been used innumerable times by Europe's entire stock of urban elites and consultants. The joint activity of urban restructuring and organizing the 1992 Olympic Games has led to a view of the city as a model of success to be copied and envied.

Policies to promote and enhance the image of cities have become unavoidable. City marketing has seen two decades of continuous expansion, relying on the classic recipes of marketing: identifying targets and strong and weak points, and gaining knowledge of the competition.[12] In the general cacop-

---

[12] Neil, Fitzsimons, and Murtagh (1995) for Belfast.

hony, slogans have proliferated: 'Glasgow's miles better', 'Belfast is buzzing', 'Birmingham means business', 'Montpellier la surdouée', all accompanied by a welter of consumer products marketing the city. Culture has been used to attract attention, customers, investors, and tourists. Cultural attractions have been created by the private sector—giant aquariums, amusement parks, water sports centres, shopping and leisure centres—or by the public sector—museums, opera houses, theatres, symphony orchestras, ethnic districts—all good for attracting tourists and making the city a space for consumption, in the wake of what has been observed in the United States. Some European cities, like Florence or Amsterdam, have already felt the effects of this transformation into a space for cultural consumption, but this is not inevitably the case everywhere. Where there is a lack of cultural heritage to exploit, shopping centres have provided a favoured substitute: for example, in the north of England—in Sheffield and Sunderland—or in Belfast. Large, sanitized, privatized, supervised consumption spaces seem, in some cases, to be gradually replacing public spaces (Hannigan, 1998).

Urban elites have also launched themselves into various economic development policies, from local neo-Keynesian policies compensating for market failures through to supply-side policies aiming to socialize firms' costs or to attract firms. These policies were 'invented' during the 1970s, when unemployment grew rapidly in most European cities. Councillors began by intervening in the aim of defending local industries. They made a point of getting close to company heads, commissioned studies, developed expertise capacities in the local economy, and created bonds with different economic partners. Then they launched into economic interventions that were increasingly diverse in form, such as indirect aid to firms or land purchase. These economic development policies were oriented mainly in three directions: active training policies and defending jobs; taking part in developing enterprises—creation, modernization, networks of firms, financial support; and improving the business environment in order to attract firms and managers—image, culture, property development, planning, and so forth (Eisenschitz and Gough 1996; Harding 1991; 1997; Le Galès 1993). Policies of this type spread across the great majority of European cities, from north to south, and were supported by national policies.

Following the American example, these policies entailed redefining the legitimate actors of public policy and urban government. Organized forms of cooperation between the public and private sectors developed everywhere in Europe: Urban Development Corporations in the UK, similar forms in Copenhagen from 1992 onwards, and others in Bilbao. In addition, associations that give a lot of room to business have been observed from the late 1980s onwards. As always, the UK pushed these developments to the extreme: for example, with the role played by the Urban Development Corporations or the Training and Enterprise Councils responsible for employment, almost competing with local authorities for economic development or urban renewal.

Legitimization of these public-private partnerships was presented in terms of capacity for action, flexible public policy, and decentralization. In the UK situation, they clearly represented a transfer of power from elected local authorities to networks of elites and urban oligarchies (Peck 1995; Quilley 2000). Although public-private partnerships proliferated in Europe, they were very different from those in the UK (Peck and Tickell 1995; Cole and John 2001), and different models exist (Newman and Thornley 1996). In Italy, attempts to develop partnerships were blocked and the implementation of projects thwarted for a long time by the near-impotence of local authorities opposed to the dynamism of firms and cooperatives, major families, and charitable associations. During the 1980s, public-private partnership projects, such as the Association of Metropolitan Interests (AIM) created in 1987 to draw up Milan's development project of 1987–91 and including big firms like Pirelli, Italtel, and Mondedison, were revealed as powerful forces for corruption. Generalized corruption can hardly be described as a growth coalition. But, as mayors and councils changed, things in Italy began to alter. In Finland, public-private partnership meant, primarily, the introduction of some private sector actors into the most important project, which related to the relocation of Helsinki's harbour. The tradition of strong public administration has remained throughout northern Europe, including Germany (Heinz 1994). In France, Verpraet (1999: 105) has noted

the importance of relations woven between partnerships and municipal policies (in Hauts-de-Seine, Euralille, Nantes, Poitiers). The capacity of councils to negotiate depends on their local resources (taxes, or the market in office space) as well as on their political competence in building and asserting a public policy, in initiating a process of squaring different negotiations in a society where exchanges have become wider.[13]

Flagship projects have also proliferated: to renovate the old docks in Marseilles or Liverpool, or to build the bridge between Copenhagen and Malmo and the new district of Orestadt to the south of Copenhagen, near the motorway link to the bridge. This consists of a district with services, housing and, above all, economic activities intended to shape a new urban region, 'Oresund', extending from Copenhagen to Malmö and containing 3.2 million people. The elites are already actively working to create an image, a labour market, a festival. Airports have become a major stake, and conflicts over them

---

[13] This analysis is particularly valid in the case of ports. Port cities have attracted attention in Europe since they are often both old trading and commercial cities—for example, around the Baltic Sea and the North Sea in the north, and around the Mediterranean in the south—and the site of industry, which has caused their major difficulties over the last 30 years, as in Gothenburg, Copenhagen, Hamburg, Bremen, Rotterdam, Anvers, Le Havre, Nantes-St Nazaire, Bilbao, Barcelona, Marseilles, Genoa, Naples, and Athens. Often, the port authorities, which represent the interests of either firms and shipowners or the state—or, in the case of Chambers of Commerce and Industry, both—are actors in devising and implementing development and economic conversion strategies.

are multiplying, both with residents and in terms of rivalry between airports. Major projects now form part of the mobilization of cities from north to south, from the new opera house in Edinburgh to the bridge over the Tagus at Lisbon, from Oslo airport to the renewal of Naples.

All these cases show both the dissemination of public-private partnership models and the limits of the exercise: that local government remains dominant, although local voluntary groups have the resources to block them, and that these partnerships relate mostly to large-scale operations.

The movements and organizations described above are not fixed for all time, but it is frequently the case that a number of them are present over a medium or even a long period of time. Within a city, relations and interactions between these organizations are not only typical of specific, ad hoc exchanges. First and foremost, they fall within a frame that is in part determined by national institutions. However, the way this frame has been called in question now constrains many organizations to reconsider their relationship with the territory—in this case, the city—of which they form an integral part, whether in order to escape it or to revise their mode of investment in this territory. In other words, loosening state constraint leads organizations to reconfigure their relations and their interactions in cities. In some cases, this reinforces the fragmentation and the dislocation of sub-national territories and of very weak modes of coordination. In contrast, in other cases—and especially in European cities—it has led to a strengthening of local logics and the making of a collective actor city. Given the spectacular strengthening of market logics—which can be observed, for example, through privatization movements in energy production and supply, and through globalization processes—the logic of competition has emerged as a structuring principle of coordinating social and political actors. This competition is accompanied by production of discourse, strengthening of social groups, and modification of linkages between politics and policies, as well as by the exclusion of other groups, policies, and ideas: in other words, there are strengthened forms of entrepreneurial governance that favour the domination of new urban oligarchies. However, cities cannot be likened to firms: at these scales, many other things come into play, including the strengthening logics of territorialization and the making of a kind of collective actor not inevitably directed towards urban competition.

Beyond Competition: Diverse Forms of Regulation Within European Cities

Industrial cities were produced by business and by members of the working class, and industrial relations structured these cities for a long time. Until recently, it was impossible to think of Liège, Coventry, Sheffield, Turin,

Düsseldorf, Saint-Étienne, or Lille without thinking first of the working class. Particular forms of bourgeoisies—in varying degrees commercial, intellectual, industrial, or based on inheritance—directed the evolution of many European cities: Edinburgh, Marseilles, Le Havre, for example. Although social relations are now less legible in European cities, they are still, in renewed forms, an important structuring factor. Social groups, organizations, and the behaviour of actors within cities are partly shaped by pressures, interactions, and incentives from the outside world. However, they also defend their sectoral or spatial interests, and this helps to institionalize urban forms of collective action. Models of locality and modes of governance in European cities are not only organized around competition. They are linked to organizations, local cultures, and social groups, which in certain cases produce relatively coherent models. The political influence of cities comes partly from their being perceived as a democratic space, as a political stage—and as a whole. This does not just mean falling back on some kind of pacified view of the city as a community. However we should emphasize that modes of integration of urban societies are always partial and incomplete. It remains that the picture that is put forward of a relatively discrete unit has a meaning in the imagination of Europeans.

To provide evidence of every kind of integration process and mode of social and political regulation within European cities would be a near-impossible task. The following examples have been selected as presenting forms of regulation that reveal the social and political dynamics of European cities and the extent to which they contribute to the making of local society, beyond the logic of competition. They demonstrate the outcomes of forms of regulation within European cities, and include anti-poverty strategies, the development of lower- and middle-class strata employed in the public sector, political regulation of the property market, cultural mobilization, and the rise of strategic planning. All these examples demonstrate the density of horizontal relations and the logics of linkages between—even sometimes the actual integration of—the various actors at work in European cities who structure localities, direct behaviours, work collectively, find ways to solve conflicts, and promote long-term investments in the city: in short, what Bagnasco (2001) has elegantly called '*Tracce di communità*'.

Anti-Poverty Strategies

European cities are subject to severe pressures that can lead to rifts in the social fabric and to multiple processes of social exclusion. They are faced with forms of poverty that were thought to have disappeared in the 1960s under the joint effect of economic growth and social policies. Beyond national model of welfare states, studies of poverty and modes of poverty management in cities demonstrate strongly the influence of localities and of local regulations integrating different organizations into coherent, stable policy models, at least in relative terms (Saraceno *et al.* 1998; Oberti 2000; Benington and Geddes 2001).

In European nation-states where the welfare state had not stopped expanding, anti-poverty strategies first arose under the auspices of national social policies, implemented by local authorities. Nowadays, anti-poverty strategies are more likely to be organized by, and take their direction from, local forms of regulation. Yet most research has been based on national policies and welfare state schemes, even European programmes: for example, public-private partnerships encouraged by the European Commission (Benington and Geddes 2001). Urban governments are now at the forefront of those affected by these issues. In most European countries, they do something other than simply apply national policies. Councillors are subject to daily pressures that mean they attempt, if with difficulty, to coordinate and adapt public policy in collaboration with other groups, since anti-poverty strategies mobilize the associative sector including, for example, humanitarian groups and religious or charitable associations as well as associations combating exclusion.

Comparative research conducted by Saraceno *et al.* (1998) reveals remarkable differences within the same country and the influence of localities. Comparison between Milan and Turin shows that the latter has a strong social assistance tradition, that there is clear identification of what is at stake, and that the council has a presence; in Milan, on the other hand, poverty is viewed as marginal, and responsibility for this sphere is largely taken by religious institutions. In Saint-Étienne, in the context of an industrial city in crisis, with rigid industrial relations, the city council has not become very involved in strategies to combat exclusion, which has left state services in the front line and involved associations less. In Rennes, in contrast, local public intervention and the dynamism of associations have produced an original model of regulation of poverty, which instrumentalized national policies within its own logic. Specific local systems of poverty management were apparent in twelve case studies: these were sometimes fragmented, but often revealed a territorialized mode of linkages between state bodies, the council, and various associations: a mode of poverty governance rooted in a particular city. Each case revealed its own pattern in relation to existing organizations, the city's social and ideological divide, the role of family, the division of labour between organizations, and the institutionalized mode of horizontal and vertical cooperation over time. Oberti (2000) suggests that local welfare systems are in the making, reorienting national and local programmes within a system whose logics are organized and regulated at the urban level: norms, values, and the policies of anti-poverty policy networks have, in most cases, been rooted within urban society, as in Bremen, Gothenburg, or Saint-Étienne.

In most European cities, anti-poverty strategies have become a priority. For various reasons, from combating poverty to maintaining social order—not to mention decentralizing the welfare state, which may mask a withdrawal of public intervention—urban social and political elites and the associative sector have created more and more programmes and initiatives in these cities. Incentives for experimentation, along with the fact that conventional national policies have run into blind alleys, are leading to strong pressures towards fragmentation. In reaction to this, political and social actors within a good many European cities are mobilizing to territorialize public policies, institutitionalize local regulations.

Middle-Class University Cities: Taking Charge of Development

In European cities, left-wing parties have undergone major changes. The working-class base of the social democratic and communist parties has most often given way to the new, post-1968 middle strata: better educated, more feminized, closer to the public sector, and more concerned about the environment and culture. These developments have been more clearly marked in states where the welfare state, especially health, education, and social services, were the most developed: northern Europe and central Europe. These social groups have mobilized in social movements, associations, and left-wing and environmentalist parties, and can draw on the network of organizations mentioned in the first section. Local urban societies, however incomplete they may be, have therefore been marked and organized by these groups, and this is all the more true in cities that are non-industrialized or, at least, not heavily industrialized.

In those European cities that were little affected by industrialization and subject to only a low level of organization by the bourgeoisie, the university has remained an institution: a pillar of the city's social and political structure. Many modestly sized European cities commonly have about 50,000 students among their population. Thus, in Bologna, Padua, Leicester, Sheffield, Turku, Tampere, Odense, Utrecht, Amsterdam, Montpellier, Grenoble, Valencia, Seville, Fribourg, and Heidelberg, the university trains large numbers, including members of the political and intellectual elites, many of whom will stay on in the city. These people constitute a reservoir for associations, political parties, and special interests, and the making of urban social and cultural networks. Thus, the university contributes directly or indirectly to the city's vigour and to its cultural life.

Comparing the structures and policies of what he calls 'university cities'— those with significant medical and university communities—in Europe and in the United States, Sellers (2001) highlights types of political and social interests and of political priorities oriented more towards the quality of life typically valued by the middle and upper classes working in the public sector or close to it; this may take the form, for example, of a correlation between the presence of a university in a medium-sized city and the environmental vote. In Fribourg, for example (Sellers 2001), the university has historically played as central a role in the city as the hospital and the health-care and tourism infrastructures. Formerly governed by conservatives, the city was taken over by Social Democratic elites in association with the Greens, who became a sizeable force during the 1980s. The dense associative network has opposed major projects and over-vigorous urban growth. All these groups have exerted pressure to achieve pedestrianization of the city centre, sensitive restoration policies, environmentally friendly forms of urban development, sustainable development, public transport, energy saving, area conservation, and cycleway development. They are able to mobilize quickly and effectively against major planning projects, such as a business centre or a leisure complex, put forward by big property development companies. These groups are particularly powerful and well-organized in Germany and the Netherlands. In the wake of what has frequently been observed in San Francisco (De Leon 1992), some of these university towns are characterized by the mobilization of coalitions opposed to urban growth or new developments. When, in the late 1980s, a major shopping and leisure centre project was proposed, with the support of central government, for Norwich, county town of Norfolk, the council worked with associations—notably, though not solely, environmental groups—the intellectual elites of the University of East Anglia, and political figures to exercise strong constraints on the developer. They were finally successful, and a smaller, underground centre was created so as not to destroy the landscape of the city centre and the old cobbled lanes that surround the hill overlooking the cathedral.

Even in old university or cathedral towns that later became heavily industrialized, renewal or development projects allow a lot of room for these perspectives. In Duisbourg in the mid-1990s, the integrated renewal project in Marxlogh, to the north of the city, brought together the *Land* government and the municipalities, as well as schools, churches, committees and districts, associations, and a whole host of intermediate organizations (Kürpick and Weick 1998). The project associated perspectives ranging from economic development to improvement of districts, housing, and inter-ethnic relations with issues relating to the environment and quality of life in the district and to the role of associations. Spreading beyond what seems to be a medium-sized university city model, the concerns felt by these groups have moved into wider European societies, where they are expressed in terms of government and public policies. Concerns about the environment and the quality of life are present in most cities. In Scandinavian cities, there are significant conflicts between those who stress economic development and major infrastructure projects and those who give priority to sustainable development and collective transport, who want to limit road-building, and who oppose transport privatization or systematic attempts to increase the speed of trains, planes, and cars. These conflicts may be local, but often they also set cities and local groups against a central government more concerned with economic competition. In Stockholm (Wijmark 1997) until the 1980s, the city council was very reticent about the idea of attracting new businesses, and budgets for this were low. All this changed with the recession in the early 1990s, and with the economic stakes of European integration and the globalization of information and communication technologies identified with Ericsson's success. When the issue of economic development and tourism became central, the creation of the urban region of Mälar was justified in these terms. Moreover, environmental and cultural priorities were reaffirmed, and Stockholm sought to be a 'green and blue' city: a slogan marking its concern for the environment.

These university cities have also become privileged locations, second only to Paris and London, with flourishing information and communication technologies employing the middle classes in a mix of private sector and public sector bodies: in Cambridge, Oxford, or Pisa, for instance. Similarly, in Toulouse and Grenoble, there is pride in prosperity based on scientific and technical complexes: aeronautics in Toulouse and information technology in Grenoble. They did not appear spontaneously: Grossetti (1995) has made a study of the formation of these complexes over nearly 100 years. They are the result of pioneering work in the universities, scientific movements, business, and local groups, which have combined their forces to develop organizations gradually, in a 'spirit of place', with cooperation between scientific research and economic environments. When the French state devolved major scientific facilities and research centres during the 1960s, interaction between urban society, key political leaders, and state elites enabled significant development of local research potential, which subsequently led, 20 or 30 years later, to an economic development boom. The formation of a local scientific system requires mobilizations, entrepreneurs, strategies, and local forms of cooperation, which must be present over the medium or long term and which, once in place, form a structuring principle for the city's social groups, networks of actors, and culture. Every round of municipal elections demonstrates the influence of the aerospace industry in the Toulouse conurbation and of information technology researchers and engineers in Grenoble. These cities are now structured by these complexes and by the interplay of relations between social groups, shopkeepers and the professions, the middling strata of the public sector, researchers, and the firms' managers and engineers, not to speak of the disadvantaged strata in the large social housing districts of Mirail and La Villeneuve. These social relations are legible in space and internalized by residents; they form the social bases of the politics and logics of coalition-building and of the logics of integration or exclusion, according to the situation.

Regulating Property Markets

The extraordinary dynamic of property markets during the 1980s exemplifies the strength of capitalism in cities, with its procession of immense urban renewal operations, like London Docklands. These have often been brutal,[14]

---

[14] Neil Smith (1996) uses the expression 'revanchist city' to convey the brutality of gentrification in New York districts. See Fainstein (1994).

and colossal profits have been amassed by the biggest developers—followed by no less spectacular bankruptcies. For example, in Berlin, urban development, organized with foreign investors and with the support of the *Senat* during a period of financial upheaval, has generated an explosion in the property market (Strom 1996). These logics are also at work in those medium-sized European cities that are particularly attractive to capital, such as Frankfurt, Leeds, Edinburgh, or Nice. However, this logic of property capital acts in different ways depending on locality and planning rules, so it does not give a complete picture of property markets in European cities.

Housing and the market in office space are classically seen as providing an excellent indicator of the dominant forms of regulation, in which the state, local authorities, private firms, and, to a lesser extent, associations are intermingled (Harloe 1995; Charney 2001). European comparisons show the diversity of situations and the contrasts between large-scale public interventionism in northern Europe, with housing policy used to combat social segregation, the inheritance strategies of Italian families, and the market-led form of regulation framed and encouraged by the state in the UK. State and urban governments use a whole range of public policy instruments: town planning codes, city plans, financial incentives, taxation, public land ownership—very prevalent in Scandinavia and the Netherlands, as it used to be in Labour-controlled cities in the UK—and consultation procedures. European urban governments still use a range of housing policies, up to and including those that favour immigrants, as in Rotterdam (see Kloosterman 1997*a*).

The element of public regulation has not disappeared from European cities. The councils of cities as far apart as Copenhagen, Utrecht, and Nantes are pursuing urban policies according to an agenda of mixed housing, social housing in the city centre, controlling the prices of newly built housing, opposing the formation of ethnic ghettos, and controlling the spatial distribution of disadvantaged categories. The regulation of the property market in Rennes offers one example of this. The council has a long tradition of intervention and urban planning, which is an intrinsic part of a progressive local Catholic culture that does not much favour property speculation (Le Galès 1993; Cole and John 2001). During the 1970s, in contrast to previous decades, the ageing mayor invited Parisian developers in to create a prestige district in the city centre, an initiative which led to the electoral defeat of his party. In 1977, the council was taken over by the left. During the years of sustained growth in the 1980s, the council institutionalized cooperation with a network of property developers, thus creating an urban public policy community. Strongly legitimized, councillors used all their regulatory resources and their expertise to maintain the social balance of different districts of the city, to avoid speculation and gentrification of the city centre, and to attract new populations. On the public side, they developed observatories, semi-public bodies—town planning agencies; companies on a *société d'économie mixte* basis—and tools of expertise that enabled them to manipulate national policies to their advantage, thus strengthening their capacity for negotiation with private developers. Since the 1960s, apart from briefly during the 1970s, the council has worked with a small number of property developers, notably four main Rennes firms, and, at most, about 30 other smaller ones, including cooperatives. For these developers, their Rennes operations form either the core or else a stable part of their business, and this enables them to take risks on other markets. In addition to the strict application of highly interventionist town planning rules, councillors and local planning officers have gradually developed a set of written and unwritten rules and standards with local developers, and these organize the Rennes market: methods of consulting residents, building and environmental standards, a balance between different types of building, and a good practice charter. When a developer wants to build offices or profitable upmarket housing, he generally undertakes to build social housing, whether at the same time or later, in the city centre or on the outskirts. In exchange, the council—or the inter-municipal structure—protects developers from the effects of competition in two ways: on the one hand, they are each guaranteed a minimum number of operations and, on the other, they are protected from outside competition. While this sphere is open to competition, the formal and informal rules make costs of entry to the Rennes market very high for an outsider, all the more so because over 80 per cent of work during the period in question has gone to the local network, and the risks of failure are high. This exchange protects local developers, but at the same time it constrains them: if one of them does not respect the rules of the game, he will be excluded in future. The system has proved fairly effective: an attempt in the mid-1980s by a major national estate agency—selling office space to open a branch in Rennes ended in failure. This case was not isolated in France—see Strasbourg—but in the case of other cities, such as Rouen, Toulouse, or Nice, local and national developers were not under the same constraints; this gave rise to speculation and, by the time the crisis came in the early 1990s, to over-supply. In Rennes, by contrast, not one developer went bankrupt, and prices remained relatively stable despite continuous growth of the city.

This local regulation of the property market requires politicians to take an active role in defending the mixed nature of any development and legitimizing a form of urban production supported by housing tenants and associations. The regularity of exchanges between local actors presupposes not only procedures for exchange but also respect for norms produced by the local actors over time, which structure behaviours in the locality. These norms frame negotiations and constrain developers from outside Rennes—failing which, they at least serve as a starting point for any negotiation (Verpraet 1999).

This case, when set alongside other policy spheres, also suggests that there is considerable overlap between policy networks within a city, with the role of key organizations and urban elite policy networks helping to institutionalize collective action and to create a relatively stable mode of governance (Le Galès 2001).

Reinventing Culture and Identity

How can unity, a bond, and a sense of belonging to local society be created in the face of diversity, fragmentation, conflicts, and the infinite field of interactions in everyday life and lived experience? Culture has been widely called upon to rescue European cities. The loss of meaning of national symbols, the proliferation of cultural producers, and the state's loss of capacity to monopolize or control cultural production have opened up new fields of activity (Négrier 1998). The locality, the city, and the region have again become image-enhancing codes for expression of identities, although they are not the only ones.

Most evident on first reading is the instrumental dimension of culture, where it is at the very least a resource mobilized and articulated within political and economic projects. Anthropologists have long stressed the importance of the production of the imagined picture, the mobilization of tradition, and the manipulation of symbols in the appropriation or preservation of power (Balandier 1980; Edelman 1964). The context of 'redistribution of authority' favours any attempts to invent or mobilize local or regional culture. Even though regions seem most involved in this dynamic, cities are not isolated from it. Culture is mobilized by local elites trying to create a sense of belonging and unity, to go beyond social cleavages and conflicts, and to mobilize the resources needed to develop an urban common good. Culture is, therefore, made instrumental to the purposes of political control: this can be seen, for example, in the role of cultural facilities that not only enable young people or ethnic minorities to express themselves but also exert social control (Loncle-Moriceau 2001).

Beyond such social control, culture is put forward by elites who are trying to create a sense of solidarity and of interdependence, especially in relation to the outside. Individuals and groups are subject to multiple influences, which to a large extent rule out the existence of a stable local culture passed down from one generation to another. For European cities, culture has become a key element in the city's image and its representation. The educated middle strata in European cities, who have become the majority in left-wing and Green parties, are particularly sensitive to this cultural stake: it adds value to resources and represents social capital in the Bourdieu sense, supporting their political influence, especially in the face of economic elites. In Coventry, Amsterdam, Frankfurt, Florence, or Montpellier, these highly educated, left-wing middle strata have carried forward cultural policies. Seen from this instrumental angle, a city's identity consists in 'an implicit or explicit venture, developed by particular local actors who consider it to their advantage or convenience to pursue mutual action. This rules out neither conflict nor competition but it does imply a relatively stable context in which to interact, with schemes generated by several actors, investment in the local society with deferred returns and the creation of common assets and collective goods' (Bagnasco and Le Galès 2000: 24). For the reasons given in Chapter 2, European cities have immense cultural resources, which can be mobilized to create identities and can facilitate mobilizations and collective action: heritage, universities, and museums still shape a particular type of relationship to urban society, one that it is not too hard to mobilize.

The pursuit of culture in cities at this scale and scope means that culture has also been mobilized for economic development. Urban research into the economic development of cities has clearly stressed the linkages between culture and the economy in order to account for processes of gentrification and social segregation (Zukin 1995; Savage 1995) and in the pursuit of economic development of the city as such or of the major firms that create private leisure spaces. The symbolic, cultural dimension of the economic development of cities is visible in what they are doing to attract tourists and consumers, as well as managers and firms (Judd and Fainstein 1999). In the case of European cities, these trends may be interpreted in terms of competition between cities, the commodification of spectacle, and flagship projects or projects to create major sites of consumption. But in European cities, cultural policies also serve to recreate a sense of belonging, to assert an identity, to bring life back to public spaces, to provide a sense of locality, and to mobilize and integrate social groups (Bianchini and Parkinson 1993).

In order to achieve this, heavy investments have been made in culture. During the 1980s, French cities almost doubled their cultural spending, which now represents about 15 per cent of their expenditure. In the 1990s, the new Italian mayors tried to revive cities through culture, festivals, and the renewal of architectural heritage. Sporting contests, festivals, and museums have proliferated everywhere. Images of the city, visions, symbols, and imagined pictures have been mobilized in all their forms, both to mask conflicts, violence, and exclusion processes and to recreate shared representations, norms, people's desire to live together, a sense of the public space, common good, and solidarity. The most ambitious buildings are emblematic of these two dimensions: for example, the Kuursal, a conference centre and auditorium in San Sebastiàn, 'for the Basques of the Province of Guipùzcoa and especially of the capital, symbolizes a necessity . . . in a difficult political and social environment marked by terrorist violence and deindustrialization, the future edifice expresses the new alliance between economy and culture, the spirit of enterprise, and the pride of a society sure of its cultural identity' (Chadoin, Godier, and Tapie 2000: 99). For Bologna, Jouve and Lefèvre (1999) explain that the metropolitan city project forms an intrinsic part of the reinterpretation and mobilization of local culture by the city's modernist, managerial left. In Italian cities, the rejection of the old political class has made culture all the more essential to the remobilization of different sections of urban society in collective projects: a dynamic that is also particularly significant in the case of Naples.

Beyond the instrumental dimension, any reference to culture suggests that we should think in terms of relations with others and with the rest of the world. The example of Zurich emphasizes the dimension of resistance and opposition that also mobilizes culture in a city. Hitz, Schmid, and Wolff (1996) identify the contradiction between, on the one hand, the desire of the local Zurich bourgeoisie and middle classes to keep it as a kind of provincial city, with traditions, hierarchies and codes, and a certain quality of life, and, on the other hand, the attraction of the headquarters of major firms and the pressures from groups of young people. There were riots in Zurich in 1980 and 1981, and the city was one of the centres of urban social youth movements demanding cultural openness. The Movement for an Independent Youth Centre mobilized these movements and precipitated the cultural opening-up of the city, which went hand in hand with economic development. A coalition of environmentalists, squatters' groups, anti-nuclear groups, and younger Social Democrats more oriented towards cultural liberalism gradually increased in influence, until, in 1990, it came to form the majority on the council. At the same time, and in opposition to the opening-up of the city, right-wing parties adopted themes that were more oriented towards identity and towards public security issues. They were strongly against any symbols of opening-up, and were anti-foreigner; they demanded the suppression of liberal attitudes towards drugs; they promoted local culture. This story echoes what has been said about the rise of right-wing parties and racism in European cities, where tensions between local residents and immigrants occasionally lead to fights, killings, and riots, as was the case in Lyons, Hanover, Bologna, and Bradford.

Going beyond these linkages between urban culture, politics, and economics, the whole 'cultural studies' tendency has stressed the logics of deconstruction-reconstruction of the social game, including in cities, and has made an attempt to seek a globalizing culturalist paradigm. Opposed to the classic idea of the city, this research current has concentrated on differences and on the enmeshing of particular identities, which are, moreover, partly produced by processes of domination and processes that shape inequalities:

Growing emphasis is being placed on the intersection of differently scaled processes in the construction of identity . . . an apparently 'local' urban public square is also at the same time situated in a liminal space of a global city and may consequently play a more pivotal international role in the production and dissemination of social identities or mythologies, than entire regions or nations in other parts of the world . . . Local spaces are not limited to their relationships to local identities. (Fincher and Jacobs 1998: 21)

This perspective analyses gender differences and the high stakes of multiculturalism in cities, calling into question the usual categories and prompting us to think about the diversity of cities. The perspective taken in this book both privileges the way culture is linked up with society and the economy, and tries to stress the dynamism of integration processes in cities.

The Urban Strategy to Mobilize Local Society

How can the different groups in cities be mobilized? One final example will serve to illustrate another mechanism common to many European cities, and now widespread: the development of an urban strategy (Pinson 2001). Although no one contests the view that fragmentation and diversity are prevalent in European cities, there is no suggestion that groups, actors, and elites are not reacting. Cities are not merely passive spaces. The metaphor of the city as actor suggests that actors mobilize within the city to produce strategies, stabilized contexts for interactions, norms, and collective choices, and that these have an impact on the city's fate. The revival of strategic urban planning probably represents one of the developments most symptomatic of this change. Faced with the changes identified in the first part of this book, the urban elites of European cities, always—or almost always—under the direction of elected politicians, try to organize to develop strategies, to create reciprocity, and to institutionalize dynamics in the form of a city strategy. Pinson (forthcoming, 2002) defines it thus:

urban policy activities that link together, on the one hand, a forecasting and identity aspect—mobilization in a context of collective thinking, more or less institutionalized around the city's particular 'vocations' and strengths, and in a context of economic development strategies that can improve the city's image and help to position it internationally—and, on the other hand, an operational aspect—one or several large urban transformation projects and/or economic activities, mobilizing a plurality of resources and types of actors, and carried out using fresh methods and techniques, based especially on partnership, negotiated objectives and modes of implementation, and iteration between the different phases of the project.

Unknown or exceptional until the mid-1980s, these urban projects illustrate the revival of strategic spatial planning in Europe (Healey *et al.* 1997; Newman and Thornley 1996). They have become the chief form of mobilization for local societies in European cities. They aim to strengthen horizontal interactions within the city between all the city's actors—so that they will have a shared representation—and to regulate complex, enmeshed systems of action, but without forgetting concerns of efficiency, management of the territory, manufacture of a consensus between urban elites, development of an urban common good, building capacities for action, and renewing power relations. Because they are developed collectively, they give a stronger legitimacy to elites imposing specific projects such as public transport or major public investments—media libraries or conference centres—and overcoming any resistance.

City projects and strategies such as Barcelona's strategy or Lyon 2010 have served as reference points for other European cities. In Lyons, about 4,000 people took part in working groups, and the project developed an image of a pleasant, balanced European metropolis, with a social economy, major facilities, and an urban environmental charter. Italian cities, faced with the territorialization of their social actors and the difficulties of traditional urban government, have been particularly keen to develop this approach. The new urban planning laws of 1990 and 1996 gave shape to ideas of negotiated programmed planning, diversity of interests, dense horizontal relations in place of hierarchies, and the need to integrate different actors (Balducci 2001; Gelli 2001). In Turin, Naples, and Milan, urban strategies and projects brought forward by the mayors and university academics have aimed specifically to mobilize coalitions of actors to define and implement strategies. In France in the early 1990s, the newly elected mayor of Nantes involved the city in a metropolitan project that took in a social aspect—social housing; strengthening collective transport, including creating a tramway—an environmental aspect, and an economic development aspect, establishing major urban social strategy objectives and redefining a city identity to make Nantes an Atlantic metropolis (Verpraet 1999, Pinson (2002—forthcoming)). Negotiations and political exchanges between actors were legitimized by discourses and representations that were always somewhat fragile, together with physical projects: the rapid regeneration of derelict industrial sites and the extension of the tramway system. The creation of a metropolitan government in 1991 aimed to organize transport and economic development policy at the level of the urban area. There was a policy of targeting city centre housing at the middle classes through price controls. Alongside this redefinition of urban municipal strategy in social terms, there was an active policy of investment through borrowing supported from taxation, and culture was mobilized to give a sense of a common fate and future.

Conclusion

European cities are not only assemblages of multiple identities and of individuals. Associations, political elites, and organizations mobilize to adapt to the changes outlined in the first part of the book, especially the fragmentation of society. Some of these reactions can also be analysed in relation to the dynamics of competition, but that is only a part of the story. Groups, interests, various organizations, and individual actors coexist in European cities and invest themselves in them to varying degrees. This diversity does not challenge interest in the collective actor or the local society approach. The chapter has highlighted the—always incomplete—ways in which interests are structured and in which the social and political dynamics that institutionalize collective action help to formulate priorities and normative frames and to orient the investments made in the locality by outside actors.

Tensions and conflicts are present, and contested priorities are manifest: Utrecht as a 'clean, complete, safe' city, Copenhagen as a 'redistributive' city, or Birmingham as 'more entrepreneurial'. One of the objectives of this chapter has been to demonstrate both the strong impact of the stakes linked to urban competition and the limits of the argument: issues of violence, pollution, redistribution, culture, and public services always combine, and they frequently dominate cities' strategies. In various examples, we have seen emerging attempts to link priorities that bring together the four dimensions of social integration, culture, economic development, and the environment.

All these elements have been shown through examples presented in compressed form, and they come out more strongly in monograph studies of European cities, which are starting to become more extensive (Houghton and Williams 1996; Cole and John 2001; Borraz 1998). This does not solve all the problems of the local society approach. Local society, following the pattern of society analysed at other levels, remains relatively ill-defined, first of all because even the idea of society reflects less an order created by classes and the state than, today, a contested reality that depends partly on both the investments and the representations of actors (Dubet and Martucelli 1998). In addition, the issue of autonomy of these local societies, and of how to measure this autonomy, remains difficult to define precisely, given the links and forms of interdependence between different levels, and variations from one sphere to another.

Linkages between social dynamic and political dynamic are especially evident in our examples. The political, which is moving in the direction of integration, is always very evident in European cities, and this gives meaning and direction, however limited. This dimension has become apparent in the cities of southern Europe, but is also true for northern Europe, and increasingly so. Focusing on social and political forms of regulation and then moving on to integrate them into modes of governance enables me to highlight changing forms of political regulation within a context of horizontal interdependence, identity-making strategies, and the legitimization of social actors and interests, whether among themselves or in relation to public and private actors at different scales.

In this chapter, politics has appeared first in terms of exchanges between groups in the pluralist tradition. But it has also appeared in governance, less in terms of domination and more in terms of mobilization and organization of interests in order to define new forms of regulation within the frame of a collective project to counter risks of dislocation and exclusion processes. European cities are at the heart of these logics and of attempts to link together political and market forms of regulation, the city-society, and the creation of a mix: that is, at the heart of modes of governance. These issues require us to look beyond the actors presented in this chapter and to consider the transformations that governments of European cities have undergone.

SEVEN

Dynamic Mayors and Restructured City Councils

I N the previous chapter, cities appeared as incomplete urban societies within Europe, where social and economic regulation interact, contributing to the emergence of local societies and modes of governance. Politics and city councils seemed closely bound up with social actors, and this should come as no surprise. City councils have a long history and long-standing legitimacy within European societies, and politics has always been a key component of European cities. Despite problems of definition and of administrative boundaries, city councils—in the sense of elected councillors and local officials—as heirs to the communes and corporations, at first played this role, representing and articulating a 'common good for the city'. However, city councils were gradually absorbed by nation-states and then reorganized on the basis of rules and norms defined by central governments.

Another important point is that cities are still organized within nation-states, which themselves remain major political institutions; so cities still perform functions on behalf of the state, even deriving more responsibilities from the decentralization, restructuring, and differentiation of the state and the fragmentation of public policies. Furthermore, if the city is increasingly becoming a site of aggregation and representation of different interests, then the task remains of bringing them together to organize a mode of governance of the city, to institutionalize collective action, and to integrate them within a more or less shared cognitive framework: a set of priorities which may seem to represent the city's common good.

All the processes of making collective choices, choosing, linking, aggregating, and representing interests within a territory, and taking and implementing decisions are inherently political. Therefore, within European cities, city councils and elected politicians are under pressure to deal with a set of problems that used to come within state control: economic development, law and order, social exclusion, representation of the city in Europe.

The aim of this chapter is to analyse the transformation of city councils in Europe and the increasing/changing role of urban mayors. These changes bear witness to the fact that, in most European cities, city councils play an important role in the structuring of modes of governance (see Introduction). The importance of politics for European cities is being reassessed, as it is the principal form of regulation that could provide integration and a sense of unity. Mayors, in particular, are in the forefront of the dynamics that are leading to the making of cities as collective actors in European governance. The restructuring of city councils in order to aggregate interests, implement collective strategies, and deliver public policies indicates that they are becoming a crucial resource in the making of a collective actor.

Modes of governance were defined in the Introduction as the outcome of linkages between market regulation, large organizations, the state, and civil society. Political regulation was classically viewed in terms of hierarchy, control, and the exercise of coercion in a territory. In European cities—and the argument is equally valid for regions—the lessening of state coercion has been expressed through movements to decentralize powers and to strengthen subnational levels of government (Sharpe 1993; Keating and Loughlin 1997; Balme *et al.* 1994; Jeffrey 1997; Le Galès and Lequesne 1998). The strengthening of market regulation can be seen both in movements towards privatization or quasi-privatization of services and in the introduction of private management models into public service management, frequently brought together under the vague title of 'new public management'.

This chapter aims to discuss changes in the government of European cities in order to understand the role these changes are playing in shaping a mode of governance for cities. The constraints and opportunities identified in the first part of the book form a context within which actors at different levels are likely to transform their modes of action, their repertoires, and their world view. Within the urban governance perspective, government, even contested government, offers stability, legitimacy, and durability. Tocqueville has long since drawn our attention to the importance of local government as a locus of citizenship and the exercise of democracy

After the wave of major studies comparing the making of states in Europe, comparative literature on local government began to proliferate from the 1980s,[1] contributing to the understanding of nation-states and of their transformation. This chapter does not aim to give a detailed presentation of changes in local government in Europe. However, the subject has become central. The goal is not to review the issue of European local authorities' autonomy, nor to discuss interpretations, theories, and typologies in detail, but primarily to answer the question of what is becoming of the government of European cities, in the context of the challenge to the nation-state analysed in the second part of the book. In fact, nation-states remain very interventionist in

---

[1] See especially Mény and Wright (1985), Page and Goldsmith (1987), Dente and Kjellberg (1988), Page (1991), Batley and Stoker (1991), Pickvance and Préteceille (1991), Hesse and Sharpe (1991), Bennett (1993), Sharpe (1993), Keating (1991) Goldsmith and Klausen (1997), and, more recently, Gabriel and Hoffmann-Martinot (1999) and John (2001).

restructuring the rules and procedures under which city councils are organized. This point is, however, not central to my argument, and is merely mentioned in passing.

Different Models of Local Government Within European States: The Classic North-South Divide

City council can be understood through three dimensions: (1) a representative democracy dimension, involving the political participation of citizens; (2) a service delivery dimension, involving the supply of collective goods and the definition and implementation of public policies; and finally (3) a dimension that legitimizes state management of the territory and the political order. The functions of city councils vary from one state to another and within states: transport, town planning, housing, education, social services —nurseries, benefits, sheltered housing for the elderly and disabled— security, rubbish collection, supplying water and energy, consumer protection, parks, and, more recently, economic development, culture—libraries, museums, festivals, leisure pursuits—the environment (Agenda 21), and sustainable development. Looking at cities in terms of local government presents numerous difficulties. Local divisions between different city councils do not correspond to boundaries between cities, which in itself has been found to pose formidable difficulties. Therefore, this chapter has a definitional bias, since the perspective adopted emphasizes division into political and administrative units. Cities form only one part of local government, and it is often difficult to isolate data that relate only to cities. In southern Europe, and most especially in France and Italy, as a result of the large number of small city councils, the issue of inter-municipal activity to try to limit the effects of political fragmentation is at the centre of debates.

European cities have a long tradition of local government, and the free administration of city councils is part of the European political tradition in most states. However, it was not until the 1970s that political conflicts, reorganizations, social movements, and research interest began in earnest.

The principles by which local governments are organized depend on national rules. The rights of local government are usually broadly defined in national constitutions, except in the UK, and the city council, in particular, figures as one of the pillars of European democracy. Consequently, despite diversity of systems, local governments in all European countries have been organized within states, and councillors and local public servants are constrained by national rules, even subject to sanction when necessary. Conversely, in no case are councillors and local government officers passive agents of the state; they are actors with room to manoeuvre, whether to initiate or implement public policies, or to gain access to the central state in order to defend the interests of their territories. Local government is by nature ambiguous within the state (Sharpe 1970).

During the 'nation-state cycle' identified in an earlier chapter, local government became institutionalized within the state, in a logic that continued towards greater uniformity within the welfare state. In contrast, recent changes suggest differentiation of city governments.

Functional Restructuring in the 1960s and 1970s

Alongside the growth of the state and its democratization, local governments formed an integral part of the trajectories of nation-states. Comparative literature started to emerge in the 1970s, highlighting distinctive features and changes in local government, mostly from a centre-periphery perspective. Comparison was made easier by the movement to restructure local authorities in the 1960s and later. From north to south across Europe, in the name of rationalization and the search for an elusive optimum, local authorities were regrouped, abolished, and set up, with varying degrees of success. In the British case, cities, especially metropolitan county councils, were at the core of the issue. In Germany more than anywhere else, cities enjoyed special status, although the situation varied from one *Land* to another. Elsewhere, the universalist perspectives of the welfare state in northern Europe lent uniformity to the status of cities: in Scandinavia, cities gradually moved to a universal local authority model, notably when local government was functionally restructured. In Belgium, France, and southern Europe, the Napoleonic organizational model provided for municipal institutions to become more uniform.

The restructuring of local government occupied the minds of reformers during the post-war period. In southern Europe, reforms were limited. Italy went back to 8,000 *comuni*, equivalent to the number of *municipios* in Spain. In contrast, the impossibility of reducing the number of French *communes* has been the despair of generations of senior civil servants, even though various forms of cooperation have been developed on a large scale to manage water, waste, and transport, in close liaison with large firms in the urban services sector (Lorrain 1991*a*). The country's 36,600 *communes* remain the symbol of a certain republican notion of France. The most spectacular reorganizations took place in northern Europe. Even Scandinavian local government, powerfully organized and strongly legitimized, with the right to regulate its own affairs under state control written into law, was subject to reorganization. During the 1960s, committees met, frequently over periods of several years, in order to arrive at consensus on reducing the number of city councils, an objective that was viewed as a priority if the management of social services and education was to be improved so that they could be developed further. This approach produced radical results: the small centralized countries of northern Europe have few city councils: just under 300 both in Sweden and in Denmark, 460 in Finland. Local government structures in Germany vary between north and south, from one *Land* to another. Broadly, between 1965 and 1975, the number of *Gemeinden* was reduced from 25,000 to 8,500. City councils form part of the *Länder*, which guarantee their rights to deal with issues that affect the local community. Obviously, all this gives us only a general idea of the situation, since political and administrative organizations with formal and informal structures have proliferated (Delcamp 1994).

Once levels of analysis have been established, a lot still remains to be done: comparisons between spheres of competence, staff, policy areas, and funding: income and expenditure, especially taxes. These elements tend to vary in two dimensions: (1) within nation-states, which seem to be increasingly differentiated, and (2) over time, since reforms have been pursued almost uninterruptedly in search of new, non-fixed rules of the game between different levels of government. All this underlines the wide diversity of local government in Europe, including within nation-states themselves.

In the 1960s, reforms were linked to the search for the management optimum. The context of the post-war decades was characterized by a new phase of accelerated urbanization in Europe, especially in the south and west, and by the rapid expansion of the welfare state, especially of social services, hospitals, schools, and universities. The rapid economic development of states generated ever more striking inequalities between centres and peripheries, and this was one of the reasons for the creation and strengthening of regions. During the 1960s in particular, reforms were guided by the search for an optimum level of local management, to enable more efficient functioning of management of services—education, social services, transport, service delivery —under 'functional, rational motivations', as Sharpe (1993) put it for Britain. In many European cities, urban expansion took the form of increased numbers of city councils around the historic city. City council boundary reforms also aimed to rationalize such divisions, so as to integrate a significant part of the peripheral city. Cities were at the heart of this process of rationalization since the tradition of local political participation and the meaning of community clearly conflicted with bureaucratic desires for rationalization into large-scale metropolitan systems or even into city regions (Bennett 1993).

This somewhat functionalist, management-related argument was especially crucial in northern Europe and Britain, since local government there developed essentially to deliver services as decided by the state. These urban local governments underwent very strong bureaucratic growth during the post-war years, playing the vanguard role in the expansion of the welfare state. In doing so, they became an arm of the central state, one public body among several responsible for the organization of services, without any clear-cut political legitimacy. In Sweden, for example, a reduction in the number of rural districts in 1952 was followed by the 1969–74 wave of mergers, which gave a minimum number of 8,000 inhabitants in each of 284 city councils. In Scandinavia, the dual process of welfare state expansion and restructuring municipal government led to a relative decline in citizen participation in local affairs, to the advantage of powerful bureaucracies and professional organizations that were supposed to increase administrative efficiency and reduce costs (Lane and Magnusson 1987; Bogason 1987).

The universalist, egalitarian ideology of the welfare state, which motivated the states' modernizing elites, runs counter to the specific nature of cities. In northern Europe, including in the Netherlands (Zidjerveld 1998), the development of the welfare state was accompanied by powerful mechanisms of centralization and increased uniformity—in professional networks, public service norms and indicators, budget allocation—created at the expense of cities' political autonomy and of their status as sites of urbanity.

In the UK, this state of affairs was coupled with a separation between 'high politics' and 'low politics', in the form of the country's elites' deep distrust, even scorn, of local authorities, and of city councils in particular (Bulpitt 1983). Nowhere was the 'functionalist' logic of local government pushed so far, particularly in the 1972 reform of local government structures. The broad functions exercised by local governments gave them a great deal of room for manoeuvre, although in a constraining legislative context —the *ultra vires* rule— and with only weak political legitimacy. This logic, in which local government is a bureaucratic quasi-agency of central government within a system described by Rhodes (1986) as 'interdependent asymmetry', made the reorganization advocated by central government, which was also seeking its own optimum size, through the Redcliffe-Maud Commission for example, relatively easy.

In a context of growth, the central state, local authorities, and, to a certain extent, the leading political forces all shared general objectives of improving social services and public utilities, and city councils also derived advantage from this growth in services. When cost control became the priority, central governments were well-placed to encourage the more or less voluntary reorganization of local government. In a crisis, on the other hand, the balance of power favoured the central state, which was able to impose restructuring and budget cuts or to 'decentralize penury' (Mény and Wright 1985). In southern Europe, by contrast, local government reorganization was more limited, especially because of the political influence of territories and their representatives in national political systems (Tarrow 1977). The development of regions in Italy and France and of federated autonomous or quasi-States in Spain and in Belgium to some extent played an equivalent role (Sharpe 1993).

Typologies of Local Governments In Europe

Various patterns of classification have been developed to account for different forms of government in Europe (Leemans 1970). From a legal point of view, Marcou (1999) suggests analysing local autonomy through four elements:

the right, recognized by the state, of local authorities to administer themselves; the general power to deal with local affairs—including financial autonomy; the degree to which local authorities are democratic—with the norm being councils elected by universal suffrage; and the degree of state control. Beyond this, taking into account public policies, most typologies tend to draw more or less sophisticated contrasts between countries where local authorities are city councils of a traditional kind and countries where rationalization movements have created vast bodies with a more established functional purpose.

Generally speaking, two types of criteria can be brought into play in evaluating the autonomy of sub-national authorities. First, local governments, including those of cities, can be analysed only in relation to other levels of government. All the literature on relations between 'the centre and the periphery' has shown the wealth and diversity of interactions and forms of interdependence[2] between the state and local authorities, and the diversity of resources mobilized: financial, legal, technical expertise, political, constitutional, cultural. The consolidated form of this diversity, frequently referred to under the title 'meso'—between city council and state—can only reinforce this point, as the development of intergovernmental relations has shown. Second, the autonomy of local authorities can be measured through broader economic and social processes, which partly determine their room for manoeuvre (Gurr and King 1987; Pickvance and Préteceille 1991). At one time, the theoretical debate about changes in city governments opposed political scientists, who combine institutional and organizational approaches with political logics—parties, elites—to Marxist or neo-Marxist writers, who are more concerned to link restructuring, social dynamics, and transformations of capitalism. The latter are especially pertinent in analysing tensions and contradictions affecting the welfare state in the 1970s and the ensuing transformation of class relations (O'Connor 1987; Offe 1984; Jessop 1990). The neo-Marxists have made important efforts, linked to significant quantitative research, to theorize and bring to light normative dimensions, the issue of the hegemony and naturalization of certain interests, and the dynamics associated with conflicts and collective mobilizations, as well as the linkages and conflicts between social groups, organized interests, and city councils. Even if these linkages have not always been subjected to sophisticated thinking— far from it—they have enabled reflection on the political beyond traditional political institutions and organizations and have emphasized policy outcomes, especially in terms of inequalities (Pickvance 1995*a*). These writers were the first to emphasize the devolution and decentralization of the management of the welfare state during the 1970s, noting that these enabled the state to shed responsibility for the implementation of budget cuts or rationalization

---

[2] See the classic literature from the Centre de Sociologie des Organisations in France, by Rod Rhodes in the UK, and especially Bruno Dente in Italy.

of hospitals and social services (Pickvance and Préteceille 1991; Tonboe 1991).

Within the scope and scale of 'orthodox' political science, various attempts to account for the types of local government in Europe have tried to move away from a purely legal and institutional view, such as that of Vandelli (1991) and others, who essentially distinguish between unitary states and federal states. All these writers refer to the history of the making of European states, while stressing the endurance of the small city council, which represents a cornerstone (Bennett 1993; Page 1991). All of them emphasize the late nineteenth century as a key period, and stress the different situation of those northern countries where the centralized state was able to achieve strong integration rapidly because they were Protestant and therefore not subject to Catholic influence, unlike Germany and, especially, the Catholic states of southern Europe. Even today, at the institutional level, this longevity of cities and political and administrative structures still offers us some keys to understanding changes in local government, especially in cities.

The most systematic comparative analysis has been Goldsmith and Page's (1987; 1991), based on the first wave of in-depth research into local government in different European countries. These two writers suggest a distinction based on three criteria of autonomy: (1) the role of local government, its spheres of competence, and its functions; (2) legal status and political legitimacy; and (3) the capacity of locally elected representatives to gain access to and influence central government, and to shape public policy.

In European states, local government is intrinsically linked to the state and does not have complete autonomy. Especially where the welfare state, involving universal services with parameters and funding determined at central level, has grown to a significant size, some local governments, previously autonomous and separate from the centre—self-governing—have become, in part, agencies of the state, with financial resources and bureaucracies developed to carry out these agency tasks, leaving locally elected representatives little political legitimacy or autonomy. Conversely, especially in southern Europe, elected political representatives are powerful and legitimate, and have access to the centre through the *cumul des mandats*—multiple office holding—whereby local politicians hold another elected office at national level, or through parties; however, local government here tends to have few resources and little expertise, which gives a more 'territorialized' national political system.

This typology combines institutional aspects with the dynamic of power relations and the behaviour of political actors. Above all, it emphasizes the contrast between northern Europe and southern Europe, thus bringing back into play the classic literature on the making of nation-states in Europe and 'frozen cleavages' (Lipset and Rokkan 1967). This paradigm has retained a good deal of its relevance, even though various writers have suggested expanding the differentiations to include a separate 'Anglo-Saxon model'— Ireland and Britain—that is closer to the North American or Australian one, as well as a 'Germanic model'—Germany, Austria, and Switzerland (Hesse and Sharpe 1991; Bennett 1993; Newman and Thornley 1996). By comparison with the Scandinavian countries and Finland, local government in the UK does not by any means enjoy the same institutional recognition—it is a creature of Parliament—and is not in any way an integral part of the nation-state model structured by the universalist welfare state (Esping-Andersen 1990). The absence of general local authority powers recognized by the constitution, or de facto, represents another way in which Britain is an exception: for even the Republic of Ireland, another centralized country, has now given them some recognition.

The limits of this 'dual polity' model, with separation between central government and local government, have been demonstrated during the periods of confrontation leading to the near-breakup of British local government, in the classic sense, over the last 20 years (Stoker 1999; 2000). Hesse and Sharpe (1991) stress that the differences of the German model lie in the longevity of German City councils, the constitutional protection they enjoy within the Länder, and their involvement in the complex interplay of German intergovernmental relations (Benz and Goetz 1996).

Yet all this literature on local autonomy falls essentially within the field of comparison between states. Posed in these terms, the question of local government autonomy now seems somehow both obsolete and increasingly crucial: obsolete, because the end of a particular phase for the state, such as that outlined in the second part of the book, transforms the interplay of constraints and opportunities for local governments, especially cities. The question is no longer simply what autonomy actually is for local authorities within the state, but rather what capacity territories have to become collective actors of European governance. What can local governments do to improve their citizens' living conditions? What is their capacity to exert pressure on their own future evolution, especially as far as their development is concerned? Can they restore coherence and social integration? All this reflects different types of autonomy (King and Pierre 1990), not only in relation to the state but also to other levels of government, to other territories, and to the actors of the market and civil society. In this context, the issue of local government and its autonomy in relation to the state is one piece of the jigsaw among many, even if it is a piece that remains important. The issue of autonomy has no meaning unless it is linked with the issue of cooperation between actors and between levels, including the state.

Urban Mayors Take the Lead

By contrast to the committee model of organizing city councils, the urban mayor model is becoming more popular in European cities, thus making

political leadership more visible in cities. Therefore, mayors and city councils have political resources with which they can try to engage actors within
cities in the making of collective strategies. They are keen to see their cities
becoming political actors in Europe, despite the uncertain shape of electoral
participation in politics.

The Uncertain Development of Electoral Participation

Even though European cities were the crucible of democracy—after Athens,
of course—the same cities have also been the object of all kinds of anxieties.
In their book on urban democracy in twelve European countries, Gabriel and
Hoffmann-Martinot (1999: 5)[3] note that

> we seem to have seen a real, large-scale crisis of democracy in several countries,
> mainly since the 1980s, manifesting itself in numerous ways: fewer people are
> voting, there is a decline in the legitimacy of municipal councillors, a growing
> complexity in the expectations and demands of social groups that have become
> increasingly heterogeneous, a relative de-vitalization of city centres in favour of
> suburban municipalities, strengthened social segregation, increasing financial
> tensions between growing responsibilities and shrinking resources, and a gener-
> alized withdrawal of state actors.

In short, these writers conclude, the spectre of decline that stalks American
metropolises is threatening European cities. We have already seen that the
worst does not appear inevitable for those European cities that demonstrate
a certain robustness and so have not yet disintegrated; in most cases, they
face financial tensions, but the tensions of social segregation within them
have not yet led to US-style ghettos. Rather, city councils have been strengthened over the last 25 years, a picture that contrasts with the difficulties of
large American cities.

Everywhere in Europe, election specialists have scrutinized developments
in political participation carefully and have raised questions about the
imperfections and illusions of democracy (Gaxie 2000; Przeworski, Stokes, and
Manin 1999). Whatever the level under consideration, representative government is being partly called into question: mechanisms of direct citizen
participation and procedural mechanisms have been mobilized to keep
democracy alive. In fact, representative government is not synonymous with
democracy: Manin (1995: 236–7) has studied the paradox by which 'Conceived in explicit opposition to democracy, today it is seen as one of its forms
. . . Representative government has undeniably a democratic dimension. No
less undeniable, however, is its oligarchic dimension.' At one time, the local
seemed to provide an answer to the challenges of modern democracies, as
an ideal site for democracy where its two key principles, of control by the
people and equality between citizens, had the greatest chances of becoming

---

[3] Hence Dunleavy and Hood's question (1994) '. . . can government be "best in world"?'

concrete (Beetham 1996); however, this is a normative point of view and has often been contradicted by fact, whichever countries are concerned. Questioning democracy and the uncertainties surrounding representative government is as pertinent at the local level as elsewhere, particularly in cities. Representative democracy requires the active participation of citizens, whether in elections or by other means.

In their investigation into participation in local elections in Britain, Rallings, Temple, and Thrasher (1996: 64) particularly emphasize the role of electoral competition between the parties in explaining changes. They show average turn-out in European local elections in the mid-1990s ranging from 90 per cent in Sweden to 40 per cent in Great Britain; turn-out in cities tended to be a little lower. In most European countries, the figures are around 60–70 per cent. The figures for Canada and the United States are about 33 per cent and 25 per cent respectively, so the difference between Europe and North America is immediately apparent. This shows a trend towards territorialization of European societies and especially towards the political being focused on the city council in European societies; this is less true in Britain, which, as always, lies somewhere between the other 'Anglo-Saxon' countries and Europe. Thus, turn-out in local elections, including urban ones, remains high across Europe, from north to south.

Change over time has mirrored these national differences fairly closely; that is, in the long term there has been no really clear 'crisis in participation' but, at given points and in the short and medium term, there have been quite a lot of examples of falling turn-out in local elections, especially since the 1980s. One example is that the turn-out in municipal elections in the twelve large German cities studied by Gabriel (1999) remained stable from 1975 to 1997 at between 66 per cent and 67 per cent: a stability that masks variations between cities and higher turn-out in northern cities. Hoffmann-Martinot (1999: 124) has demonstrated a net decline in turn-out in large French cities from 1971 to 1995; decline is less marked in the case of the Netherlands for the same period, but more spectacular if the comparison is carried as far back as the 1960s.

Initiatives to Improve Citizenship and Residents' Participation

In the area of direct democracy—apart from the spread of the elected mayor model, which uses a wide variety of methods—mechanisms have been introduced to try to achieve greater participation by citizens.[4] Different forms of political involvement and participation in democracy are the objects of differing initiatives: 'citizen conferences', popular initiative referendums, petitions, court actions. Democracy is viewed more and more actively,

---

[4] I am leaving aside here the issue of organized political forces in cities; on this point, see Gabriel and Hoffmann-Martinot (1999) for numerous examples.

whether in terms of consultation or of mobilization, social movements, and collective action, so various forms of participation are developing. More generally, mechanisms for citizens to be consulted and to participate in decision-making processes have become the norm in political discourse, despite difficulties and unequal degrees of willingness to translate this into practice. More powerful but also more vulnerable than they used to be, councillors make unceasing attempts to mobilize residents, if only to increase their own legitimacy. A very wide variety of experiments has been set up across Europe, such as Scandinavian 'free local government' with its neighbourhood committees. The spectrum covers all possible varieties and nuances, and its constant revision clearly emphasizes the difficulty of questioning relationships between elected representatives and citizens.

More active participation by citizens has also justified the internal decentralization of municipal governments. In Scandinavia, the greater autonomy given to local governments to organize themselves has been accompanied by recommendations suggesting greater decentralization in the organization of services and neighbourhood councils, in order to compensate citizens for the loss of power they have suffered as a result of the earlier mergers. In Denmark, Finland, and Sweden, most city councils, especially in cities, have established neighbourhood committees and have embarked, though not without difficulty, on a trajectory of devolving services. Similarly, in France, since the 1970s the ideology of self-management and, later, the need for councillors to increase their own legitimacy have led to numerous experiments, not always conclusive, with neighbourhood committees, elected neighbourhood representatives, and devolution of budgets and services. That said, the chief characteristics of the French case have been the weakness of these initiatives, the centralization of power around the mayor and his deputies, and increasing reservations about local referendums, except perhaps for the urban transport projects—tramways and metros—that have cost some mayors their seats. Britain has gone further in this direction, allowing associations, including neighbourhood associations, to take on some of the tasks that once fell to the municipal services: the principle of the 'enabling authority'.

Increasing Role and Legitimacy of the Political Executive—Collectively, and the Mayor in Particular

European mayors have made their voices heard over the last decade, and this is a new political phenomenon. In Germany, in 1994 urban mayors produced a high-profile leaflet about the risk of decline in city centres and the need to mobilize resources to help them deal with their cities' social and economic problems. In the midst of the Italian institutional crisis of the mid-1990s, a 'mayors' political party' came briefly to prominence, bringing together Italy's new generation of popular, directly elected mayors. Later, in France, urban mayors seceded, for the first time, from the local government assembly and organized a national association of urban mayors, which has become very active. Among other activities, they publish books and brochures lobbying for the interests of French cities. The urban mayors are back in town.

Within Europe's mosaic of local governments, a classic division contrasts those which are essentially run by specialized executive committees, as in Sweden or Britain, with those run by mayors elected through direct universal suffrage or by their councils—in southern Europe, parts of Germany, and France—although there is a whole range of slight differences between and within countries.

According to the hypothesis I outlined at the outset, the organization of cities as collective actors is a political process. The actors organize and react in order to combat fragmentation, challenges to representative government, and the confusion related to European integration. Elected representatives, and especially the most visible of them, are charged with solving these problems. What Duran (1998) has called 'the paradox of consequences' and Scharpf (2000) 'output-oriented legitimization' are becoming important factors for elected representatives. Legitimacy is no longer acquired just by getting elected, but partly also through public policy and through performance. In the realignment between state, market, and civil society, reaction to pressures towards fragmentation is, paradoxically, leading to a form of return to the political, which is expressed in various ways, including through demands for social and political integration and for representation: demands addressed to elected representatives and to leaders, to mayors in particular, that they should define shared objectives, values, and representations, structure interactions, institutionalize collective action, and make accountability visible. Although the management of discrepancies lies at the core of policy work (Borraz 1999), elected representatives, especially mayors, can develop their role in the direction of linking different interests and different temporalities and scales in public policy.

Such reasoning lies directly at the origin of reforms. In Italy, Germany, and Britain, the debates of the last ten years have led to the development of models for electing mayors by universal suffrage. The reasons put forward relate to mobilizing groups and organizations against the fragmentation of territories, to strengthening the political role of elected representatives so as to revive local democracy, and, finally, to increasing 'leadership capacities'. Everywhere, elected municipal representatives—'part-time amateurs', to use the British term—have gradually given way to professionals, who are increasingly engaged in politics. In some countries, such as Sweden under the 1991 Act, elected representatives are paid. Debate on the status of elected representatives has taken place everywhere. Writing on France, Borraz (1998) has clearly shown the investment made in city government not just by the mayors but also by deputy mayors. In Italy, apart from mayors, whose recent role I have already stressed, deputy mayors, or *assessore*, are most often engaged full-time or nearly full-time in their duties, even when they are not professional politicians.

The election of urban mayors and the strengthening of their political influence constitute two trends that demonstrate the importance of cities as places for structuring conflict and orientations in European societies. In several countries, rules have changed significantly in order to promote the election of the mayor by universal suffrage. There are major changes in progress in Germany, Italy, and Britain from this point of view. In countries where mayors were already important, whether elected—France—or not—Scandinavian countries—their political influence within the national policy-making system is increasing.

In Italy, direct election of mayors by universal suffrage—a democratic revolution in the context of the country's crisis—has gone hand in hand with change in the method of electing municipal councils, favouring the more stable dynamic of majority voting. The 1993 Act provides for direct election of mayors by universal suffrage in towns with over 15,000 inhabitants. The new law confirms the role of the mayor as leader of the city council, able to appoint his deputy mayors—*assessori*—without reference to the municipal council (Vandelli 1997) and to choose the equivalent of the chief executive—*segretario comunale*—within certain limits. According to the mayor of Rome, Rutelli, quoted by Vandelli—himself at one time *assessore* in charge of Bologna's metropolitan city plan—the new system can be described

in just a few words: personal accountability is recognized as devolving onto one individual, who forms a team which takes responsibility for running this experiment in government, linked with a political majority but also autonomous in relation to that majority; the electorate has been asked about a clearly recognizable programme and can then check that it is being carried out, and go on to give it a stable mandate. (Vandelli 1997: 15)

At the height of the regime crisis, elections in the early 1990s saw the emergence of 'new mayors'. Some, in the spirit of renewal that accompanied the *Mani Pulite* or 'Into Clean Hands' move, were newcomers to politics, while others were seasoned politicians who jumped at the chance to confirm their status. All of them dreamed of transforming Italian politics, starting with the government of cities.[5] This new generation of mayors was organized within an ephemeral mayors' party, launched in September 1995, and for a time it seemed to herald a movement of renewal in Italian political life—until the major parties were able to regain their strength. Some mayors still have conflict relations with the parties. Indeed, in several cases—Palermo, Venice, Turin, Trieste—they were chosen because they represented an alternative to

[5] Their testimonies are interesting, such as Castellani's (1996), quoted by Pinson and Vion (2000). The most important were Enzo Bianco in Cattagna, Massimo Cacciari in Venice, Leoluca Orlando in Palermo, Antonio Bassolino in Naples, Ricardo Illy in Trieste, Valentino Castellani in Turin, and Francesco Rutelli in Rome.

traditional politicians, even though the limits of this renewal of the political class were quickly revealed.[6] Several of them were ministers—Antonio Bassolino, mayor of Naples, in the D'Alema government, Enzo Bianco, mayor of Cattagna, in the Amato government—and were confirmed as regional leaders after two terms as mayor: Massimo Cacciari in the Veneto, Antonio Bassolino in Campania. Francesco Rutelli, former mayor of Rome, was the defeated as the centre-left leader in the 2001 elections. This generation of mayors, most of them on the left or centre-left, somewhat recalls the dynamic of the socialist mayors elected in France in the 1977 elections, of whom several went on to become pillars of the Mitterrand governments in 1981. Even years later, opinion is still divided, and the outcome of this dynamic is contested. It cannot be denied, however, that this generation of mayors gave cities fresh impetus in terms of modernizing administration, town planning, and city plans, and representing the city's interests to the outside world. This brief account marks a clear change from the previous period. Mayors have acquired considerable room for manoeuvre, organizationally and in their budgets. They have, above all, gained political visibility outside the gigantic machine of the Italian party system. They exist politically as mayors of Italian cities, taking on responsibilities in the organization of local society, in city government, and in the representation of the city's interests to the outside world: in other words, they are leaders of territories.

Although more limited as yet, the increasing power of leading urban elected representatives in Britain is significant. Local authority leaders have not traditionally played such a major role as French mayors; they have been subject to strong public servants, weak political legitimacy, and government by specialized committees. The sustained conflict between leaders of the new urban left and the Thatcher government in the 1980s—which turned to total victory for Mrs Thatcher after she won a third general election in 1987—brought to the fore political figures who played a key role in some British cities, including, in particular, Livingstone in London, Blunkett in Sheffield, and Stringer in Manchester. Conflict did not prevent the breakup of the classic model of British local government. However, it did lead to the emergence of political leaders who abandoned the traditional role of Labour local authority leader as apparatchik, a committee man or woman, even though many of these had helped, in collaboration with other cities, to articulate an urban common good and a defined urban strategy against central government. Labour's long period in opposition gave many Labour politicians good experience of city councils, which they transferred into their roles in John Smith's team and later, to a lesser extent, in Tony Blair's. Many became MPs, others ministers: David Blunkett, Margaret Hodge, Hilary Armstrong. When Blair was elected in 1997, he embarked on the first raft of institutional reforms

---

[6] See Vandelli's (2000) somewhat disillusioned comments on 'disaffection with dilettantes' and the return of the parties after 1996.

in Scotland, Northern Ireland, and Wales. Another innovation involves the election of a London mayor by universal suffrage—which saw the spectre of Ken Livingstone winning, against the official Labour candidate, in May 2000—and the development of a new system of local government, probably including the election of the mayor in some British cities.

In Germany, local political and administrative arrangements are the domain of the *Länder*, while also forming an integral part of the constitutional framework that guarantees the rights of city councils. The situation varies a great deal from one *Land* to another. City mayors used to be elected only in Bavaria and Baden-Württemberg. The East German democratic revolution of 1989 enabled institutional innovations such as the election of mayors: an innovation that then spread to West German *Länder* in the 1990s (Gabriel 1999), so that the direct election of mayors has become the norm in Germany.

In other countries, election rules have either not changed or changed very little; but the role of the city mayor and his influence in the political system have increased significantly. In the case of France, mayors of large cities did not enjoy any special position until the 1970s. During the 1950s and 1960s, some leading politicians combined the role of mayor of a large city with a position such as *Président du conseil* or prime minister, as did Pierre Pflimlin in Strasbourg or Jacques Chaban-Delmas in Bordeaux. Then, in 1977, French town halls went over to the left, presaging Mitterrand's 1981 victory. The governments of Pierre Mauroy, himself mayor of Lille, clearly demonstrated how much the power of the mayors of large cities had increased within the left, a phenomenon that even went on to affect the neo-Gaullist party, the RPR (Knapp and Le Galès 1993). This phenomenon has grown, since most prime ministers in the last 25 years have been or have become mayors of medium-sized cities or—a new phenomenon—of large cities. For example, Pierre Mauroy in Lille and Raymond Barre in Lyons were mayors until March 2001, while Alain Juppé is the mayor of Bordeaux. Among the heavyweights of the Jospin government —Jospin himself is an exception from this point of view—Martine Aubry was elected mayor of Lille, though Elisabeth Guigou failed in Avignon. Finally, we cannot forget the role played by the mayoralty of Paris in the political career of President Jacques Chirac.

The powerful city councils of northern Europe were remarkable more for their political legitimacy within the state than for the political influence of their leaders. Since the committee structure was the most general form, either there was no mayor as such, because local government was organized on the basis of specialized committees, or the mayor was barely first among equals. Local government functioned on an essentially collective, consensual basis. In Finland especially, the leading figures in municipal committees did not have great political prestige. A lot of them had alternative careers at the centre, or even locally, through their close links with party bureaucracy. Now things are in the process of changing: the increased autonomy of Finnish city councils since the late 1980s has given them room for manoeuvre in managing financial crisis, and opening up to Europe has changed the rules of the game. Helsinki has suddenly found itself not just the capital of a small social democratic country on the fringes of Europe, but the focal point of the Baltic Sea, an advanced eastern outpost near St Petersburg and the Baltic states, and prospering as an economic region thanks to the remarkable success of the firm Nokia. This change of scale has led to a shift in direction, and the dogma of universalism has begun to crack. Well aware of what is at stake in the European integration project, Finnish elites have rapidly seized the initiative. Gradually, the anonymous politicians who ran the city council of Helsinki and its related organizations have turned towards Europe, and they now stress the city's position in Europe, renovation of the docklands, and competition with Stockholm. Politically, Helsinki has become a much more sensitive stake: even though the term had no meaning in Finland, Mrs Eva Riitta-Siikonen soon began to present herself at European conferences as the 'mayor' of Helsinki. For the first time, the political role of mayor of Helsinki has gained consistency in terms of leadership and of building links with a project inside Europe. It is now a truly political role, which goes beyond internal party logics to issues of power, and which aims to articulate a plan, a special interest for Helsinki.

This tension is equally strong in Stockholm, where the mayor is not an anonymously interchangeable politician but a major political figure, transforming local government management, spearheading privatization. This mayor has also initiated local management reforms, introducing market logics into the provision of public transport; he wants to make his city the European information and communications technology capital and is playing an active role in European networks of cities, devising and defending a development plan for Stockholm that runs counter to the universalist principles of the Swedish state.

Finnish, Norwegian, Swedish, and Danish chief executives, traditionally a fairly homogeneous group, have all changed profoundly, moving in the direction of a greater capacity for leadership and for managing links between different interests and groups (Klausen and Magnier 1998). Traditional administrators are gradually giving way to managers motivated by management efficiency and by politics, in the sense of positioning the city council within a set of vertical and horizontal relationships, whether intergovernmental or not, and in the sense of articulating a common good and a plan for the city council.

In the Netherlands, reshaping of the welfare state and of the 'pillars model' has favoured greater autonomy for cities. Even though, conventionally, mayors were chosen and controlled by their parties, changes in the 1990s favoured the emergence of mayors who had gained strong autonomy from their party, capable of launching ambitious territorial strategies and becoming national political figures, like the Labour mayor of Rotterdam, Bram

Pepper (Vergès 1999). As in Scandinavian countries, some urban mayors have undermined traditions of equality and collegial authority in order to assert a political form of leadership and a strategy of territorial mobilization in the European context. There are also some leanings in this direction in Belgium, where several politicians have chosen to manage cities rather than pursue their careers at another level, in Portugal, where President Sampaio is the former mayor of Lisbon—and his successor there, too, has other ambitions—and in Spain (Botella 2000).

These different examples do not suggest the development of independent city-states in Europe. On the contrary, the political trajectories of mayors and urban leaders clearly show their involvement in national political systems, within which their influence and visibility have become even greater, expressing the growing importance of cities in European governance.

Local Governments Restructured for Action

Although the system of constraints and opportunities for European cities is now less structured by the state—a point I attempted to demonstrate in the second part of the book—two trends should be emphasized: (1) greater internal differentiation within countries, especially of cities—as was also shown in the second part; and (2) processes of convergence between states and between cities in different states. Nevertheless, the state remains active in shaping the parameters for and the forms of city council.

Within European governance, local governments, as representative governments, experience the same difficulties and uncertainties as other levels of government: fragmentation, challenges to representative democracy, changes in the ways administrations function, and uncertainties and changes in the role of elected representatives. In most cases, local authorities have gained areas of autonomy in terms of internal organization, management of services, and implementation of policies, even though financial monitoring and audits have also tended to become stronger. In other words, they have more autonomy, but in a more difficult and, in terms of various forms of interdependence, a more constraining environment. 'The end of city council' has no meaning in Europe, although at one time the Thatcher and then the Major governments officially considered this unhappy fate for Britain.

European integration, decentralization, state restructuring, and devolution are processes that mostly have to do with the reorganization of scales of government and the development of different forms of interdependence. The same causes also produce effects on the government of cities. The issue of size and boundaries remains and takes two forms: that of metropolitan government, frequently of the city region, and that of neighbourhoods or districts. Everyone is looking anxiously at North America and the secessionist desires that are leading to disintegration of the city there, such as those appearing in Los Angeles (Keil 2000*a*).

Metropolitan Government: Reorganization and Conflict

Even though, in the 1960s, the issue of size was buried under the superficial search for optimum management—with good reason, since different services and different public policies do have different optimal sizes—the specific issue of the size of city government has now re-emerged with increased vigour. This redefinition of scales is anything but neutral, since it results from conflicts between groups and interests, is accompanied by reorganization of powers, and alters the parameters of conflicts between social groups and the parameters of domination (N. Smith 1995; Brenner 1998). Groups and organizations mobilize to extend scales of city government, citing better management of major services and claiming to combat fragmentation in public policy; they also justify this mobilization either by citing efficiency in economic competition between territories or by claiming they will implement policies directed towards sustainable development: for example, transport policies. Others oppose these changes. Yet others mobilize in the name of local democracy and citizen participation, claiming to bring citizens closer to levels of government and pleading the cause for decentralization of city government to neighbourhoods as well as opposing the more technocratic logic of city regions. Politically, positions vary according to national and local situations: metropolitan government has long been encouraged by social democratic reformers in the name of equality, solidarity, and management efficiency, while the neo-liberal right has tended more to defend division into small competing units, strengthening possibilities for citizens to choose.

Sharpe has identified the ideal type of metropolitan government through three dimensions, which have, in fact, rarely been found together: political legitimacy, autonomy—in various spheres of competence—and the scale of the city region, functional to varying degrees (Sharpe 1995). Attempts at creating metropolitan governments have, in most Western countries, ended in failure and contested experiences: British metropolitan districts, French *communautés urbaines*, the metropolitan corporation of Barcelona, Scandinavian experiments, and Dutch endeavours. Lefèvre (1998) has highlighted two factors that explain these setbacks: failure to consider issues of legitimacy, favouring a rational functional approach instead, and the authoritarian way in which states have acted to enforce forms of reorganization that were detrimental to populations and to well-embedded basic local authorities.

After a decline during the 1980s, metropolitan plans came to the fore again, and with greater vigour, in the 1990s. Lefèvre (1998) has called this '*the trompe l'œil renaissance*' of metropolitan governments, referring in particular to plans for Italian metropolitan cities, Spanish plans for Madrid, Barcelona and

Valencia, Portuguese plans for Lisbon and Oporto, German plans for Stuttgart, Dutch plans for Rotterdam and Amsterdam, French plans—the 1999 Voynet and Chevènement Acts, communities formed from built-up areas—British plans, primarily for London, and Scandinavian plans for Stockholm and Copenhagen. Several factors governed this renaissance: the strengthening of metropolization, which heightened the issues involved in managing the peripheries of historical cities, and processes of Europeanization and globalization. At the point when, in a fairly assertive manner, cities redrew the shape of the playing field and began to try to exist politically, culturally, and economically on the European level or even beyond, the issue of scale became central again. Discourses and logics of economic and political competition (see above) are not the only things being called into question. Individual states and the European Union are actively pushing in this direction: changes in urban and regional policies make it almost vital to strengthen institutional capacities in order to obtain resources and implement public policy programmes. Metropolitan governments are very much part of a dual logic, a logic, on the one hand, of mobilization through groups and organizations able to act on the European playing field and, on the other hand, a logic of reshaping states, which have adapted their policies and their modes of action in territories in response to the imperatives of economic competition and financial constraint: in neo-Marxist terms, adapting to the conditions of contemporary capitalism (Jessop 1997a; Brenner 1998; 1999).

Nowadays, more active consideration of the logics of competition between cities frequently reverses these positions: the most fervent partisans of economic competition between cities plead the cause of metropolitan government—for Toronto, see Keil (2000)—particularly because it enables greater efficiency in cutting or privatizing public services. In Europe, employers' groups and Chambers of Commerce and Industry have often been very active in promoting metropolitan governments, as in Bordeaux, Lille, or Stuttgart (Hoffmann-Martinot 1995), hoping that they will help to achieve better performance in this competition. On the other hand, the left, and the Greens in particular, have set more store by local democracy and by the stability of institutions that are more open to the influence of civil society; in Germany, for example, they have opposed major urban flagship projects and loose coalitions that they perceive as part of a competitive technocratic logic.

The new wave of metropolitan plans, guided less by 'functional optimum' imperatives, has met with similarly diverse fortunes. Some took account of the two factors that had led to the failure of the first wave of such plans. Lefèvre (1998), comparing the European and North American experiences, emphasizes that authoritarian approaches to reorganization were replaced by negotiation, partnership, and more flexible mobilization. The issue of legitimacy was also frequently tackled—though not in France—in one of two ways: either by providing for a referendum to legitimize the new form of organization or by challenging the city centre—taking away its powers or partitioning it—in order to avoid conflicts between city-centre councils and metropolitan government. However, referendums failed spectacularly in Amsterdam (Terhost 2000) and Rotterdam (Toonen 1997) precisely because residents refused to allow the city centres to be broken up. The electoral defeat of Walter Vitali, the mayor of Bologna, historic bastion of the Italian Communist Party and its reformers (Baldini and Legnante 2000), further dampened the ardour of those who had conceived this metropolitan city as the beacon example for Italy, and other metropolitan plans were blocked (Dente 1990; Jouve and Lefèvre 1996). Many mobilizations of actors have run out of steam, except as far as local technocracies and, sometimes, employers' associations are concerned (Jouve and Lefèvre 1999).

As these examples show, there is a point at which the simple application of economic logic in coordinating activities at the scale of a more or less identified city region, in order to deal with competition from other European cities, comes into conflict with other logics, especially with the political logic of cities and their longevity. Therefore, it is useless to identify a level and a depoliticized model of 'good governance', as if this would guarantee some fantasy version of economic efficiency. Reorganization of scales has more to do with the changes identified in the second part of the book: it is a political process that is neither predetermined nor linear. It has linkages with existing structures, with group and organizational strategies, and with political entrepreneurs at different levels: levels determined in the context of European unification and the transformation of capitalism. This kind of reorganization occurs in all cities where there is simultaneous experimentation with different scales of proximity in service management: the municipal scale, the inter-municipal scale of the conurbation, and beyond these to the scale of the city region, which extends urbanization. This last scale, in general, uses a fairly light touch in coordinating things, but it may be the place where coordination of public policy—transport, the environment, or to attract business—is learned; it is rarely a site of democracy (Leresche and Joye 1995). Thus, the Danes and the Swedes attempted to invigorate a city region, Öresund, linking Copenhagen and Malmö with a new bridge and including the city region of Copenhagen—with a population of 1.8 million—Greater Copenhagen—19 city councils, with 1.2 million inhabitants—and the city council of Copenhagen—population: 490,000. The same issues arise when one looks at Lyons, the Urban Community of Lyons, and the city region of Lyons, or at Lausanne, Geneva, and Montreux, which could be integrated into a Lake Geneva metropolis (Joye and Leresche 1999).

Local Government Reorganization: Increased Differentiation Within Countries and Transnational Convergences

Given that local government forms an intrinsic part of the state picture, any reshaping of the state must be sensitive to sub-national levels. This is the case in all European countries, but opinions on how to interpret what is happening diverge, and the way phenomena combine makes it difficult to measure change through detailed quantitative surveys—although it is not impossible if certain limited areas are considered.

For writers inspired by rational choice theories, these changes are clearly part of the end of the bureaucratic Keynesian welfare state. Bennett (1993: 11–17) celebrates what he calls 'two themes' or 'two dimensions' of decentralization: 'intergovernmental decentralisation' and 'market decentralisation'. Within this perspective, which generally corresponds politically to the neo-liberal right, consideration of 'good governance' is very much part of a classic economics perspective, depoliticized and aiming to identify the most cost-effective practices. Always on the lookout for a major paradigm that might turn the world upside down, other writers have looked at variations of what has been called 'the new public management', that is, the application of enterprise management approaches to the public sector. The famous work *Reinventing Government* by two Americans, Osborne and Gaebler (1991), is looked on as the bible in this area. Determinism is no more acceptable here, since in local governments, urban ones especially, the ideas that circulate and the 'cognitive and normative frameworks' (Surel 2000) serve both to direct practices and to legitimize endogenous changes.

There is no need to detail the changes in local governments, especially urban ones. For the purposes of my argument, we need only introduce empirical factors that justify the importance of city councils as sites of conflict and regulation. Then we need to bring together factors precise enough to demonstrate the dynamic of change in local government: resistance to change would invalidate my initial hypothesis. Finally, these changes should be re-situated within the perspective that concerns us here: the making of the city as collective actor.

Narrower Financial Constraints

Financial criteria are a convincing indicator of local authority autonomy. If local governments have an independent ability to tax, with a significant part of their revenues coming from local taxes, this generally contributes to establishing their autonomy. In contrast, strong financial centralization generally goes with local authorities having little room for manoeuvre in terms of public policy. This is not always the case, however. In the Netherlands, extreme financial centralization does not prevent powerful city councils from having a strong policy-making capacity and a large burden of local expenditure. While taking into account the disadvantages of low financial autonomy, Kloosterman (1997b) shows that there can be advantages to the situation: (1) reduction of inequalities: since the resources of city councils are not dependent on their populations' incomes, they are not penalized for concentrations of poverty; and (2) the greater possibility of cooperation

TABLE 7.1. *Percentage of fiscal revenue by level of government, excluding social security*

	Federal or central administration	State	Local authorities	Social security
Austria	52.7	9.3	10.2	27.8
Belgium	36.7	23.3	4.9	35.1
Germany	29.4	22.0	8.0	40.6
Denmark	64.9		11.9	44.1
Finland	52.6		22.2	25.2
France	43.6		10.6	45.8
Greece	68.8		1.1	30.1
Ireland	86.8		2.0	11.2
Italy	58.8		11.7	29.5
Luxembourg	68.1		6.3	25.6
Netherlands	56.5		3.0	40.5
Portugal	67.0		6.1	26.9
Spain	48.0		17.0	35.0
Sweden	58.1		30.8	11.1
United Kingdom	63.0		13.3	23.7

Source: OECD (2001: 200).

between city councils that are not competing, or competing very little, for financial resources.

Northern countries are characterized by both strong autonomy and a large burden of local expenditure, while in Ireland, the UK, and federal states local authorities have little autonomy and a low burden (Tables 7.1 and 7.2; see also Table 3.2). Not everything in this table is gloomy; it gives a more subtle picture than the usual interpretations of change in local government, which always seem to start by asserting that there is generalized financial crisis. In France, the true picture is well-known: 'All in all, the financial autonomy of French local authorities seems to be extensive, effective, strongly supported by decentralization, and guaranteed by the political influence that local politicians have within national elected representative bodies' (Gilbert 1999: 159). This is not an assertion of general expansion in public finances; also, of course, some northern European countries faced severe crises in the early 1990s. However, in Italy, for example, laws introduced since 1989 have moved in the direction of increased fiscal autonomy for city councils, especially through the major 1993 innovation of creating a municipal tax on land ownership. The financial situation of French cities and conurbations in the 1980s was little short of glorious, and became only a little more strained in the 1990s.

The financial autonomy of local authorities is subject to harsh pressures. In the context described in Chapter 3, European states have developed a financial framework within the European Union, which limits deficits: the famous Maastricht, and then Amsterdam, 'convergence criteria'. The fact that local authorities fall within the definition of public authorities therefore constrains them, directly or indirectly. In many cases, European states have been able

TABLE 7.2. *Local fiscal autonomy*

EU member state	Local authority spending as % of GDP (1995)	Degree of local fiscal autonomy (relationship of tax to total non-borrowing income)
Denmark	33.0	49.0
Sweden	28.7	60.0
Finland	23.0	43.0
Netherlands	19.1	8.0
Italy	13.7	25.0
Spain (excl. autonomous regions)	7.2	30.0
Austria	12.0	5.0
Luxembourg	11.7	32.0
Germany	10.0	20.0
United Kingdom	10.0	14.0
France	9.2	54.0
Belgium	7.4	35.0
Ireland	5.4	16.0
Portugal	3.7	7.0
Greece	2.1	

Source: Gilbert (1999: 163).

to share out constraint: in other words, to make local authorities take on part of the effort towards financial constraint. This was true in Germany in the context of reunification, in Italy under the Prodi government, and more recently in France with the Jospin government. In Italy, regions and local authorities have even signed a pact with the state to take on a proportional share of reduction in public sector deficits (Porla 1999). This has strengthened other, older trends, that is, the state's tendency to 'decentralize penury' to sub-national levels of government. In the early 1990s, at a time of major crisis in northern Europe, the Swedish, Danish, and Finnish states implemented forms of financial reorganization that moved towards constraining local authorities through centralization (Mouritzen 1993; Letho 2000). Last but not least, the British state's pincer movement of centralization and introduction of market logics under Thatcher and Major was accompanied by abandonment of local taxation of firms—nationalization of business tax—and massive reduction in the financial autonomy of local authorities, which from then on became the most severely constrained in the whole European Union. The pursuit of equality and transparency has also pushed in the direction of limiting financial autonomy: everywhere in Europe, starting with Germany, complex systems of financial adjustment have been developed in order to limit the divergence of territories. Without exception, these mechanisms have invariably moved in the direction of nationalization and strengthening the controlling function of the state, frequently by strengthening the role of central government grants in spending resources taken from local taxes. The search for transparency is often accompanied by an increased demand for control over the use of public funds, which can lead to strong centralization, as in Ireland (Coyle 1997).

The complex mosaic of financial relations between levels of government has retained all its rich variety, despite the processes of European unification. Constraints unifying some financial criteria at the level of states and at EU level mean that more innovations and diversity are needed at the sub-national level, just in order to face up to new constraints and their effects. In this process, cities are attempting to play the game to their advantage. In Germany, Ireland, Denmark, Sweden, and the UK today, cities are organizing more and more actively to demand financial support from the state in order to deal with the pressures of economic competition and the management of social problems. Local government figures overall conceal differentiated sub-national developments within each country. Everywhere, city councils must face additional responsibilities: for example, in Italy, because of the decentralization of functions once assumed by the state, there is now a context of greater autonomy and tighter control.

Public Management and Politicization: Action-Oriented Municipal Administrations

Recent European research on senior local public servants—*secrétaires-généraux de mairie*, chief executives, city managers—whom Klausen and Magnier (1999) call 'anonymous leaders', has highlighted those changes in municipal administrations that are less organized by clientelist logics or simple service management approaches.[7] The professionalization of local government administration reflects the north-south contrast outlined earlier. In the north, including Britain, where local government took charge of a large part of the management of public services and policy implementation, local administrations underwent a massive professionalization movement. Moreover, the different occupations concerned were organized within powerful associations at national level: an important centralizing factor in guaranteeing territorial equality in Scandinavia and in Finland, for example. In the south, this movement took longer to emerge. In France, where state services claimed a monopoly on expertise and resources, it was not until the 1960s that a dynamic of professionalization in city government was set in motion by pioneer local authorities such as Grenoble, Strasbourg, and Rennes. Lorrain (1989) has made a study of the way this movement spread in the 1970s, first to large cities and then more widely, until today, when it has provoked a crisis of legitimacy in the external services of the state, which often see their expertise surpassed by that of city councils or of regions. In

---

[7] UDITE (Union des dirigeants territoriaux d'Europe) Leadership Study coordinated by P. O. Mouritzen. First work to appear: *The Anonymous Leader* by Klausen and Magnier (1998).

Spain or Portugal, the movement to professionalize local government administration developed only after democratization.

Italy probably experienced its biggest upheaval ten years ago, when the 1990 Municipal Autonomy Act and the two Bassanini Acts strengthened local executives. Italian city councils had been fragmented, with no financial autonomy, and closely controlled by central government, which led to local administrations being renowned for their inefficiency. The city council, an extraordinarily fragmented organization, was divided into *assessorati*, each functioning as a small political fiefdom for a deputy mayor. In practice, everything it did was determined by the interplay of political parties, their clienteles (Bettin and Magnier 1992), and legal formalism. The reforms also changed the deal for those who were once quiet public servants—the *Segretari Comunale*—responsible for external monitoring and acting as local representatives of the Ministry of the Interior within the city council. In Italy, mayors elected under the new legislation complained bitterly of lacking an even remotely efficient local public service. It took some, like Francesco Rutelli in Rome or Antonio Bassolino in Naples, a long time to achieve reform of their inefficient administrations, the effect of years of *malgoverno*. Vandelli (1997: 74) compared this task facing new mayors to the torments of Sisyphus, for municipal bureaucracies had built up successive layers dominated by resistance to change, clientelism, and a total lack of initiative:

Antonio Bassolino—in Naples—found a monstrous machine made up of 19,000 employees—27,000 counting the individual municipalities . . . a machine inflated by great waves of hirings, by Achile Luaro in the 1950s, by the Christian Democrat and multi-party councils in the 1970s and 1980s—a gummed-up, elephantine mechanism, directed at self-preservation and conditioned by the widespread conviction that a job with the council was just a quiet sinecure . . . And Valentino Castellani's first impressions were not too different, when he found that the city council of Turin had 17,000 employees, subdivided into 87 working sections, badly arranged, all at the same level of mediocrity, and drowning in a surfeit of formal and legal provisions . . . Not to speak of Cacciari's reactions in Venice . . . to an unchanging machine, mistrustful up to the highest levels, resigned to the commonplace, and operating perverse procedures where 26 signatures were needed to get a building permit . . . a paralysing tangle of vetoes, obstacles, and labyrinths—futile difficulties that sometimes made it heroic just to carry through any plans or initiatives.

The 1997 Bassanini Act satisfied these complaints by creating, alongside the post of *Segretario Comunale*, chosen by the mayor, the post of Director-General of the city council. In some cases, the latter had certain similarities to a real city manager, tasked with setting municipal administration on a new path, as in Milan. Gamberruci and Magnier (1998) have described the 1997 Bassanini Act as a revolution in the organization of city councils because it involved legislative redefinition of the running of local authorities and probably heralded major decentralization of powers.

In the countries of northern Europe, city councils have major responsibilities for high levels of service delivery: schools, social services, nurseries, housing for the elderly, health, and culture. The cities of northern Europe were the first cities to become especially concerned with issues of quality of life and environmental conservation. The dominant approach of these city councils to organization has now become that of experimenting with deregulation, since the Scandinavian city council is heavily regulated (Rose 1990; Baldersheim and Stava 1996; Montin 2000). Broadly speaking, city councils have acquired greater organizational and management autonomy despite increased financial control from the centre. The best-known of these experiments has been 'free local government' in the Nordic countries—or 'free communes' (Rose 1990; Baldersheim and Stava 1996)—which has been tried by about 10 per cent of city councils.[8] Other experiments have involved the way city councils were actually organized, devolution into neighbourhoods, committee organization, the role of the mayor, and the role of senior public servants. Some of the ideas underlying these changes relate to a variant of management frequently known as 'new public management'. These city councils were, first and foremost, intrinsically tied to the context of unitary, centralized states, with homogeneous populations, within which increasingly high levels of welfare state provision had developed. Senior public servants made their careers within local government administration. Councillors functioned on a highly collectivized, closely linked basis, and their careers were within the major parties. Any differentiation between city councils within these states was limited, and could be only a matter of degree: the dynamic of the system drove towards homogenization.

The 1992 economic crisis posed a particular challenge to existing practices, and precipitated local government management reforms. In Finland, for example, implementation of budget cuts was accompanied by increased freedom for some 400 city councils to organize themselves as they saw fit. Decentralization of powers, autonomy, and flexibility, including the introduction of principles that fall partly within the sphere of management, whether 'new public management' or not, have led to strongly differentiated practices in organizing and running city councils in Finland (Sandberg 1998) and Sweden (Haglund 1998). Despite the existence of sizeable structures for cooperation—gathering statistics; performance indicators; target norms—particularly directed at tracking the development of social policies, there are very strong pressures within the system towards increasing autonomy for cities. And, despite resistance, political leaders, as well as the part of the state

---

[8] For Baldersheim and Stava (1996), the free local government experiment differs from traditional approaches in five ways: the initiative comes from the grass roots; solutions to problems are sought through alternative local solutions; central government supports these initiatives rather than controlling them; local government is autonomous; and the central-local relationship is characterized by partnership rather than by relationships of dependency or hierarchy.

bureaucracy inside the ministry responsible for cities and regions, are increasingly tending in their public policies to recognize differentiation between cities.

Britain has experienced the most spectacular upheavals in local government over the course of the two last decades, at one time to the point of risking its total disappearance. Any assessment of the impact and importance of these reforms should start from more general changes to the British state and to public policy, since local authorities have been an integral part of the model brought in by the Conservatives and pursued by New Labour. Britain has experienced a shift towards what is called 'new public management' (Massey 1997; Hood 1995). Consequences for cities are vast:

1. *Systematic introduction of competition in service delivery, or purchaser-provider-service user split.* In a large number of spheres, especially health, education, and other services run by local authorities, a whole range of legal and financial mechanisms profoundly transformed public policy.
2. *About 1,200 quasi-autonomous non-governmental organizations (quangos)— agencies dependent on central government—have been created or developed.* At the local level, there are now over 4,500 organizations of this type, that is, financed by central government. Some of their senior staff are appointed directly by the government and others according to criteria drawn up by central government, with a high proportion of private-sector input. This has been accompanied by a movement towards increased autonomy: hospitals and schools, for example, can 'exit' the existing system. The 'quango state' has profoundly challenged the role of local councillors in public policy, favouring instead a non-elected 'new magistracy' and consumers.
3. *Privatization of a broad section of the economy and a large number of services, such as railways, airports, and social services.* This also involves privatization of public investment, since the radical 1992 Private Finance Initiative reform provides for public infrastructures, including hospitals and schools, to be funded by private capital in exchange for long-term or medium-term income, on the model of what has already been done with motorways and bridges.
4. *Far-reaching alteration of mechanisms for control and coordination in the direction of formalized rules, use of budgeting tools, and subtle differentiation between organizations and services offered.* The introduction of 'market testing' allows different agencies within ministries, or even different local agencies, to compete to take on responsibility for one programme or another. More spectacularly, various series of indicators have been systematically developed to measure performance and the efficiency of organizations and programmes. The publication of league tables of schools, universities, hospitals, and social services represents a very strong constraint for these organizations, since those that come out in the low categories will be subject to sanctions, that is, budget cuts, resulting in job losses.

British local authorities, which had a key role in the provision and organization of public goods and services, found they were easy targets when Conservative governments from 1979 onwards ruthlessly mounted a profound challenge to the existing system. The breakup and subsequent reorganization of British municipal government were effected within a context of tough political conflict and imposition of a new set of rules of the game from the centre (Stoker 1999; John 2001). Briefly, the first step in reorganizing British local government was through fiscal reforms and budget cuts, which radically altered its environment and reduced its room for manoeuvre. The introduction of competitive tendering mechanisms, the close tracking of different services through performance indicators, the possibilities offered to some local institutions for exiting local public services—'opting out' for schools; and especially in housing (Pollit, Birchall, Putnam 1999)—and the introduction of personnel management, not to speak of privatization and other market mechanisms, have disrupted modes of organization in these bodies (Lowndes 1999). Set in competition with a proliferation of other quangos—for example, Training and Enterprise Councils—local government has been placed in the permanent position of having to fight for survival within the framework of rules imposed by central government: rules based on 'value for money'. Local authorities trying to maintain or increase their budgets and areas of involvement now find that their core activity is the preparation of responses for competitively organized government programmes. These targeted programmes—for example, anti-crime or environmental protection programmes—may be 'won' by associations or public bodies.[9]

Britain has acted as a real public policy laboratory for the last 20 years, combining political radicalism with various pragmatic experiments in managerialism, and this probably explains why there is debate about the unity of the 'new public management' model strongly disparaged by Vivien Lowndes and Christopher Hood. As a result of this, it is easy to pinpoint which elements of reform have been inspired by the same vague grouping of corpus and ideology, either in favour of reforms or to legitimize marginal changes. Beyond the precise examples given above, the municipal governments of Belgian cities and Dutch, German, French, and Spanish cities have shifted their approaches in the direction of managerialism, policy coordination, strategic thinking on the economic development of the territory, and greater budgetary transparency: in other words, towards the professionalization of

---

[9] In drawing conclusions from a five-year research programme on 'new British local governance', Stoker (1999; 2000) stresses not only the importance of changes in local government in the direction of private enterprise, but also what he calls 'new community governance', that is, the mobilizing and coordinating role of associations and neighbourhood groups in charge of local programmes. In other words, British local authorities have moved beyond the bureaucratic management of services, developing public policy tools—including, in particular, contractual ones—and a role in promoting the common good of the territory and creating coherence between groups and public policy: 'the politics of creative autonomy' (Atkinson and Wilks-Heeg 2000), which is now being encouraged by the Blair government.

management and involvement in a more political approach to developing the city. This process means that certain practices have spread rapidly, whether through European associations or consultancies—management or urban planning consultants—or through the shared development of public policy instruments. One example of such practices is that of contractualization: one of the key dimensions of change in public policy, this relates both to local authorities and other levels of government; indeed, local authorities play an essential role in linking the latter together (Gaudin 1999). In European governance in the making, accentuated fragmentation and various forms of interdependence between different types of actor are becoming core characteristics of public policy. Contractualization has become a central instrument of cooperation between actors, whether between actors at different levels (Marcou, Rangeon, and Thiébault 1997) or between public and private actors. Contracts take different forms: they are frequently inspired directly by company law, and have helped to introduce market mechanisms into public management in the UK or Flanders. Conversely, they frequently act against the momentum towards institutionalizing collective activity within the public sector to coordinate the different elements of the state with local authorities, as in the Netherlands or in France.

Urban Privatization

Last but not least, in most European countries, for fiscal, ideological, and technological reasons, direct management of urban services as well as of civil engineering and public works by city councils, the regulatory framework, and fiscal mechanisms have all undergone major changes (see Chapter 5) which also leading to a changing role of city councils.

According to Lorrain (1996a), the dynamic of change in European urban services can be explained through two major variables: the strength of political planning of local utilities—very strong in northern Europe and in Germany, less so in southern Europe—and the extent of management by private actors, especially in the UK and France. These changes also reveal a consequent reshaping of local power and the introduction of market logics into the delivery of services such as water, electricity, housing, heating, transport, and parking.

In Italy, for example, local government reforms, especially the 1990 Act, and the newly strengthened status of mayors have given them the chance to embark on privatization of some municipal enterprises. This act has opened up the field to municipal holding companies that have traditionally been responsible for the direct production of services and for running these enterprises. This challenge has marked a relative withdrawal of city councils from direct management of services and a move towards concessions, which tend to act more at the level of the conurbation—encouraged by Act 142, 1990—sometimes even through privatization: Jouve and Lefèvre (1999) give

TABLE 7.3. *Changes in the organization of the main urban services, 1880s–1990s*

Service	Dominant provider		
	Early development and municipal provision (1880s–1930s)	Nationalization and expanding welfare state (1930s–1970s)	Privatization (1970s–1990s)
Water and sewerage	Local authorities	Ad hoc agencies	Private company
Electricity	Local authorities	Nationalized industry	Private company
Gas	Local authorities and others	Nationalized industry	Private company
Telecommunications	n/a	Nationalized industry	Private company
Education	Local authorities and others	Local authorities and others	Separately managed schools and colleges
Public rented housing	Local authorities	Local authorities	Local authorities and others
Social services	Local authorities and others	Local authorities	Local authorities and others
Social security	Local authorities	National administration	National agency and contractors
Ports	Local authorities and others	Mixed	Private companies
Regional airports	n/a	Local authorities	Private companies (by end of decade)
Rail transport	Private companies	Nationalized industry	Private companies (by end of decade)
Bus transport	Local authorities	Local authorities and other public bodies	Private companies
Refuse disposal	Local authorities	Local authorities	Local authorities and contractors
Police	Local authorities	Local authorities	Hybrid national administration
Fire	Local authorities	Local authorities	Local authorities
Health	Local authorities	National administration	Locally managed providers in national administration

Source: Lorrain and Stoker (1996: 64).

the example of pharmacies in Bologna. In many cases, services have been transformed into limited companies under municipal control, as in Turin; however, mayors from Berlusconi's party, especially where they have been threatened with electoral defeat, have frequently pushed the logic of privatization further forward.

Conclusion

City councils have not disappeared from cities in Europe. Major reshaping is taking place in many of them, directed towards diversifying modes of management of different services, confirming the role of mayors and their deputies, and professionalizing the management of local government. The city council and the city remain fundamental political institutions in European societies (Marcou 1999). Moreover, even though city councils may be at risk of fragmentation and de-territorialization, we should note that the principles of local government have been confirmed and codified at the European level, guaranteeing the rights of local authorities. The Council of Europe's 'European Charter on Local Autonomy' (15 October 1985) has made local autonomy one of the shared values of European states, and this despite considerable differences of political and administrative organization (Marcou 1999). This document has been signed and/or ratified by most European states, including the UK, and thus it marks the institutionalization of the principle of local autonomy. The Charter, with its strongly normative content, was taken up as a reference document by the Committee of the Regions, and is playing a similar role for the democracies of eastern Europe now negotiating to join the European Union (Delcamp 1999). So this Charter, which was drawn up over a long period, has set in motion a dynamic of institutionalization involving monitoring its implementation, networks of independent experts, and negotiations with national governments and the European Union: in other words, 'gradually establishing an international system for monitoring its application' (Delcamp 1999: 148).

In organizational terms, the developments outlined above reveal both a blurring between the usual models and an increase in internal differences, moving away from hierarchies and towards horizontal, contractual relationships. In relations between elected representatives and citizens, and between political regulation and civil society, something is shifting towards more autonomy for the various actors, increased legal control over relationships and conflicts, and more consultation. However, city councils retain a strong presence, and their political expertise and influence are also tending to increase. By comparison with American public-private partnerships, which frequently vest most power in the private sector, European public-private partnership experiments remain fairly limited, except in the UK, and city councils still have strong capacities for initiative and control. City councils have developed their mode of action in two directions in particular: consideration of group, neighbourhood, and residents' demands, and management of urban services.

The system of constraints and opportunities for cities has changed. The pressures exerted by the state, and by the whole society, towards uniformity and homogenization have become less distinct. At the same time, local authorities have to face changes brought about by European integration, economic globalization, individualization, metropolization, state restructuring, and competition. Within cities, problems and priorities are beginning to be articulated differently from those that exist for the rest of the country. Actors' interests, perceptions, and strategies are diverging. Redrawing the boundaries of the political playing field has the direct or indirect effect of repositioning cities, especially the largest of them, within states. Close links, developing transversely with other European cities and vertically with the EU, have impacts on the way city councils organize. Elected representatives—especially the most important of them, the mayor or equivalent—are being given a more important role in representing the city to the outside world and in building links between interests. Cities' political and administrative elites are benefiting from their increased autonomy, creating more innovations and experiments in organizing and running services. The key words are now: experimentation, managerialism, leadership, governance; but all this is happening within nation-states that have not in any way abandoned their highly developed welfare state foundations, retaining high levels of taxation and social services. This should prevent any over-hasty comparisons or suggestions of strong convergence with Britain and its fundamental reforms: neither Sweden nor Finland is Britain, and one has only to look at the influence of city councils and their essential role in managing the welfare state—particularly social services—rates of poverty, or educational standards, to be convinced of this.

There are pressures on actors within cities to express the city's common good, to define strategies for relating to the EU, firms, the state, the region, or other cities, and to manage social and cultural conflicts within the city; but mayors and city councils in European cities do have the resources to play a major role in the making of modes of urban governance. In some countries, where the city council has been more politically enshrined within society—in terms of clientelism, for instance—or where the city council has been viewed as a functional agency of the state, moving in this direction may prove more difficult.

EIGHT

Conclusion

E UROPEAN cities were originally mostly cities that represented points of articulation between trade, culture, and forms of political autonomy. Then, when the nation-state gained a monopoly over organizing culture, political power, and different forms of exchange, European cities became integrated into this national whole. Integration meant that the nation-state, which organized the economy, became the main force influencing the future evolution of cities. The more the city was integrated into the state, the more dominant 'those who made it their business to serve the state' became. Robust European cities now have to cope with more competition, more market regulations, and more networks. Again, all this is not entirely new. Lepetit (1988: 121) suggests that, by the end of the eighteenth century, images of dynamism and flows crossing cities, related to economic development, had already become dominant, contrasting with older representations of the immutable city. However, the last hundred years of the nation-state phase have brought European cities back to a situation, if not of resistance to change, then at least to limited movement within centre-periphery relations. But now the field is opening up again, as was shown in the second part of the book.

A preliminary conclusion of Part II suggested that the relative robustness of European cities, related to the legacy of the past, represents a remaining strength which still partly structures the shape of cities and their citizens' expectations as well as the strategies of actors within cities. Most monographs on cities highlight an awareness, especially on the part of councillors and organized interests within cities, of a sort of European city standard organized around a mix of public and private sector activity, public intervention, economic development, culture, and anti-poverty policies. In the conclusion to his book, Crouch (1999: 402) expresses himself elegantly on the subject of European cities: '. . . much of the long history of that very distinctive concept of intermediation between private and public lies in the emergence of the autonomous urban systems of the great European commercial city belts . . . There is still a Durkheimian sense of there being something distinctive and valuable about the public arena. With the probable exception of the armed forces, it is difficult to make such a statement about public authority in the USA'.

This book has argued that European cities constitute a fairly general category of urban space, relatively original forms of compromise, and aggregation of interests and culture, bringing together local social groups, associations, organized interests, private firms, and urban governments. The pressures created by property developers, major groups in the urban services sector, and cultural and economic globalization processes provoke actors within European cities to react and adapt in defence of the idea of a fairly particular type of city, not yet in terminal decline. The modernized myth of the European city and its identity remains a very strongly mobilized resource, and is strengthened by growing political autonomy and transverse mobilizations. The research perspective adopted in this book has favoured a view that stresses the integration of urban society and the representations that unite the city as an actor, based on the reshaping and strategies of groups and interests within cities. It has enabled me to emphasize the originality of the European city in contrast to postmodern theoreticians, like Rose (2000), who see in all this only a mixture of illusion of unity and a neo-liberal ideology of reshaping the state.

Many of the finer points have revealed the limits of the arguments put forward here. Changes and pressures are taking place and the situation varies from one city to the next. A detour enabled me to isolate a series of variables, so eluding the traps of localism: relations with the state, degree of involvement in a certain type of capitalism, embeddedness within national societies. Several objections to a priori use of the category of 'European city', corresponding here to medium-sized European cities, were mentioned: objections relating to fragmentation, 'metropolitan catastrophe', globalization processes, changes resulting from information and communication technologies, mobility, and networks. Processes of exclusion, strengthening and transformation of inequalities, segregation, and domination are also unfolding in these cities. The development of residential suburbs separate from the city and of polycentric cities, the isolation of disadvantaged districts, the development of cultural complexes, leisure facilities and shopping centres, as well as diverse cultural models and migrations, all clearly demonstrate the pressures exerted on the European city. Their impact seems to be more contradictory than was expected, and actors within cities resist, adapt to, and instrumentalize those changes, producing combinations which are rather complex to grasp. The result is that, although mobility and networks are growing, their impact on the social structure, on the making of society, and on the governance of European cities is not absolutely decisive.

Factors to be considered, again, are the robustness, strength, inheritance, and dynamism of European cities and the actors within them. Unity is also an illusion, a representation, or the result of a strategy. At the same time, cities do not succeed in everything they attempt: examples of recent anti-poverty mobilizations and their ambiguous outcomes demonstrate the limits of what can be achieved by cities. Following what Marcuse and Van Kempen (2000) have emphasized, hasty generalizations on globalization probably reveal too strong a degree of American tropism. Similarly, in Europe, announcements of the demise of local government and the triumph of public management and of public-private partnerships probably reveal slightly too much of a British tropism. Over the long term the UK, with Ireland, can still broadly be looked on as a special case in Europe, whether from the point of view of its chief mode of urbanization, of what cities represent in British culture, of the Conservative reforms breaking up local government, or of the burden of spending on public infrastructures and the welfare state. This does not prevent the country serving as a reference point for reforms on the Continent; nor will it, in the long term, prevent the European neo-liberal turn from being accentuated. Obviously, the meaning of such a proposition depends on the level of abstraction with which one views it. In relation to other criteria, the north-south divide inside Europe may be more pertinent, although certain changes in the making are rather tending to blur that distinction.

Local Societies and Collective Actors

This book has attempted to show why European cities could, in certain conditions, be analysed as local societies. Cities everywhere are characterized by a myriad of small groups and micro-projects, of which only some have been gradually institutionalized or aggregated. Now, in the context of the European Union, pressures to put forward collective strategies and to mobilize different actors within the city are mounting, and the political and social actors of European cities are reacting to this. Frequently, they are given responsibility for acting in such a way as to get in on the game of European governance. The examples mentioned in the third part of the book illustrate the active strategies of individual and collective, public and private sector actors, and of organized interests: within cities, these contribute to the—often incomplete—making of a collective actor, with varying degrees of success. This idea of actors within cities helping to create a collective actor-city expresses the notion that cities are not passive spaces suffering the indiscriminate exercise of top-down logics. Obviously, a given city, faced with a big trans-national firm, may have limited room for manoeuvre, and generally neither actors within cities nor cities themselves play much part in defining the firm's strategies. But European cities are not the cities most exposed to the trends commonly associated with globalization: their resources and actors are located within their territory; they are broadly recognized by public and private sector actors at different levels; and they are still protected by states.

The analysis of cities as local societies requires in-depth monograph treatment, and there is not a great deal of this. With the exception of Italy and the—now out-of-date—programme on localities in France and Britain, research of this type is relatively limited. Political scientists go in for in-depth analysis of governments, parties, and elections, while sociologists tend to concentrate either on the micro or on the macro level. Both come out with interesting findings on social movements, collective actions, and the relationship between political and social forms of regulation. This is not surprising, given the ambiguities and uncertainties associated with the concept of society—mentioned in Chapter 4. The same applies to the analysis of Europe as a society or to the comparison of European societies. In contrast to political scientists, who have more bases on which to analyse the making of a European polity, sociologists are far from convinced that a European society is in the making. Comparative data on social structure and values reveal only a small part of the story; yet generalizing about social regulation and dynamics within cities seems hazardous. I have made a few points in this area: there are growing cultural tensions resulting from the presence of ethnic minorities; increasing social, economic, and cultural inequalities between groups; strong middle strata; increased poverty; middle classes in an ambiguous situation, some excluding themselves by moving to expensive neighbourhoods in and outside the city, while others remain firmly within the more diverse social fabric of the city centres; the relevance of the city centre as a symbolic place for protest, identity, and culture. A more sophisticated argument suggests three points that require more work. The first, and easiest, of these is that, because more public policies are under the control of city elites and groups, cities play a more important role in the making of society or in answering the demands of various groups. For instance, business interests—chambers of commerce, for example—anti-poverty associations, and environmental groups have 'territorialized' their strategies, raising demands, contesting policies, mobilizing residents in collective or specialized protest, and entering the game of governance through regular interactions with other groups in the city. Second, this idea of cities as sites for resolving conflicts and problems is accentuated by the relative withdrawal of the nation-state. Cities, and especially their mayors, are increasingly in the front line of mediation between cultural and economic forces and the population. Conflicts about religion and the use of public space illustrate that point. Examples relating to growing concerns and mobilizations around crime and law and order, which have not been addressed in this book, would also enhance this argument. Third, the city is now a more visible place in which to identify interdependence between social groups, between firms and institutions, and between organized interests. Cities have become the locus for interdependence in terms of water, waste disposal, pollution, and crime, for instance, and policy networks tend to be set in opposition or brought together at that level. Again, the blurring of boundaries between private and public sectors, on the one hand, and the interdependence between different levels, on the other, tend either to increase social and political fragmentation or to strengthen the city as a site of governance. Politics remains very important and visible in these processes; but its close links with social and market forms of regulation must be made apparent if we are to understand how a particular combination is formed and expresses itself through a mode of governance.

Another way to move forward is to combine the analysis of local societies with the concept of collective actor, while keeping in mind all the difficulties related to that term. Can a European city really constitute a collective actor? Despite the risks of instrumental drift and reification, and despite the illusion of unity present in the term itself, even though the reality is one of diversity, analysis of this perspective is not without interest provided its terms are carefully defined. From this point of view, the five dimensions that form Pichierri's (1997) model of the collective actor still provide a safe, useful framework:

1. *Common interests within the city, and those perceived as such.* This dimension has never really been a problem for Italian cities, where it is the state rather than the city that has found it hard to be seen as guaranteeing the common good. In other countries, many factors have created pressures for cities: the changing scales of politics, of the economy, and of social organization, and the reshaping of the state, with the erosion of the protection it offered to cities and their constituent actors. Moreover, pressure from higher authorities also comes to bear on the issues of common interests, the future, and which strategies should be used: these authorities most often act within a logic of 'God helps those who help themselves', and this constrains actors to develop their thinking towards a strategy, towards something that resembles a common good of the given city or given region. This change is particularly marked in Scandinavian cities, in Finland, and in the Netherlands, since it calls into question welfare state egalitarianism and universalism. Common interests are now most often the interests broadly perceived to be 'common' by elites and organized interests, and have frequently been promoted to the point of saturation. The proactive stance expressed in strategies, projects, and various plans reflects this attempt to give shape to, and bring into existence, a common good for the city. However, we should not be deluded by this form of inflation. The question of whether the population of a city recognizes a common good remains wide open. In fact, this perception is uneven, is more likely to exist where there is a strong local identity—and must be proved in each case.

2. *Collective decision-making.* The political dimension of European cities is central in the long term, and will remain so. Cities represent a specific level of aggregation of the private, public, and associative interests that, in some cases, gradually go to make up a collective actor. In developing certain examples in this book, I have tried to show both the relevance of this proposition and it limitations. Once masked by the triumph of the nation-state,

the political dimension never completely disappeared, and has now come out into the open again. The chapter on government showed how important local governments have remained and how far elected representatives, mayors in particular, retain a key political role. Several factors were mentioned as leading to the institutionalization of forms of collective action and decision-making: the renewal of strategic urban planning, forecasting, and urban projects; the proliferation of partnerships, public-public or public-private; the development of consultation processes and the consideration of diverse interests; flourishing contractual procedures; experiments in reviving public debate and deliberation; the obsession with transverse and global approaches. Local governments have never been completely isolated from their environment. This does not mean there is unity or coherence between collective choices. The political dimension involves conflicts, controversies, and power relations—and has very diverse outcomes. At worst, collective choices and decision-making in cities may be used to justify a disturbing drift in the wrong direction. A small group of actors can monopolize the mechanisms of choice in the name of efficiency and competition between cities; they might then succeed in imposing their plan and legitimizing the domination of a sort of urban oligarchy, as denounced by Padioleau (1991). For example, the emphasis placed on efficiency and performance by supporters of 'new public management' is in no way encumbered by a concern to respect representative democracy.

3. *Internal and external representation.* Elites in European cities are anxious to situate themselves in relation to outside actors, either in order to gain a position in economic competition or in order to encourage outside actors to become involved, over time, in playing the city's game. The development of a whole arsenal for promotion and for shaping forecasting and strategy and the development of both vertical and horizontal ties contribute to this representation. Most European cities launched themselves on this trajectory in the early 1980s, and have not stopped since then. Moreover, we should note that mayors have played an essential role as both internal and external representatives in these processes. The popularity of the term 'leadership' and the revival of research work on these issues are good indicators of this development (John 2001; Smith, Genyès *et al* 2001). Mayors shape and animate the local scene, and cases where the role of the mayor as internal and external representative of the city is seriously contested are rare. On the contrary, the dissemination of models of mayor, however varied, is most often legitimized with reference not just to the coherence of public policy but, more especially, to internal and external representation. Consequently, any detour through issues of governance will lead to questions based in traditional political sociology, and not to setting the representation aspect on one side.

4. *Integration mechanisms.* A whole set of mechanisms is at work in cities, combining culture—festivals, images—the political—contracts, elections,

social policy—the market—labour market—and, to a lesser extent, the more social mechanisms—family, community, district, religion. It remains difficult to generalize about these or to disentangle urban processes from more general processes. Both the theoretical and empirical debates on these questions raise many difficulties, and that constitutes one limitation of the argument put forward here. One approach I have used is to give examples of the institutionalization of collective action, examples of the making of collective strategies and of policies aiming to prevent growing social exclusion, examples of social forms of regulation, and examples of the institutionalization of conflict-resolution mechanisms. The interdependence between social and political groups or interests, which has been apparent in various cases, is also an indication of the strengthening of cities as sites of integration mechanisms. But it remains far from obvious what 'an integrated society' means nowadays.

5. *Capacity for innovation:* this criterion is easily satisfied in many European cities, whether it is a matter of public policy innovations—the many examples of social or environmental policies, which are still spreading—of the institutionalization of collective action, or of the integration or exclusion of groups and populations. Cities in Europe seem once again to be becoming an important locus of cultural, social, economic, and political innovation. The examples put forward in this book are evidence of the vigour of these experiments.

Analysing European cities as collective actors seems justified, therefore. However, two subtleties need to be brought into the analysis. First, this statement does not mean that all European cities are collective actors: each case must be studied precisely and measured by specified dimensions. Then, each time such an analysis is applied to a particular case study, we must analyse the actors and their interplay within the city in order to construct the collective actor, which cannot be taken for granted. This does not mean that everything relates back to the actions of individual actor—this approach falls within another type of analysis, which has its own logic. European cities can mostly be described as 'collective actors in the making', but this is by no means inevitable.

The uncertainties linked to the status of actor in contemporary societies were mentioned in the Introduction. In a situation where all groups, organizations, and even individuals claim to be actors, most will fear or suffer not being recognized as such by others, though without knowing exactly what that might mean. Meyer (2000) emphasizes the consequence of such a paradox as being a craving for norms, models, and modes of doing, to serve as reference points and as legitimization; and he deduces that this will lead in turn to strong mobilization, for example within organizations. This analysis certainly holds good for European cities. Encouraged by external sources—consultants, university academics, journalists, the European Commission, officials of trans-national associations of cities—the elites of European cities, and of most sub-national territories, have seized on the rhetoric of the actor city. It validates the role of councillors, puts them centre stage, and enables a strong degree of instrumentalization to mobilize groups internally. Once having claimed the status of 'European actor city', they still have to give it content. Gradually, and especially under the influence of the above-mentioned external actors, a sort of 'European standard' of the actor city has emerged over the last two decades. In turn, the dissemination of this model justifies a strong mobilization within cities. The pressure is twofold. Elites, including councillors, use this rhetoric as a discourse of legitimization, to organize consultation between different interests, and to develop a discourse and a strategy for building a dominant local common good and compelling actors to mobilize within the city. Some of these actors feel the pressure of internal concerns. Chambers of commerce and industry, for example, are often outside or opposed to municipal strategies, and they 'territorialize' their own strategies, claiming to be actors of local development and defenders of interests that must inevitably be aggregated at the level of a city so as to bring it into international competition. In another example, anti-poverty associations call on firms and officials in the city to develop urban policy systems without expecting everything to come from the central level. This kind of mobilization is also effected internally, to enable adaptation and, often, to legitimize external pressures (Jouve 1998). Claiming to be an actor city leads to mobilization on different levels, both internally and in relation to the outside, in order to shape and present the various elements that appear important: promotion policy; participation in horizontal European networks or vertical ones involving the European Commission and Parliament; defining a forecast and a strategy; shaping and displaying an identity.

This makes it possible to identify the following mechanism: the claim of a city as actor in European governance leads to a profound uncertainty and a mobilization within the city towards recognition as such by outside actors—from the European Union through Eurocities to the *Financial Times*—who provide models and legitimation. This mobilization then contributes to the making of the city as collective actor.

This concept of the city as an incomplete collective actor in the making— which others might describe as 'systems of action in the making'—manifest in European cities, is structured on the basis of the traditional legacy of the classic concept of the city of citizens, of local government in the collective sense.[1]

---

[1] Contrary to Demesteere and Padioleau's (1990) suggestion, this collective actor cannot be reduced to an instrumental view of a city-enterprise aiming for maximum efficiency. The critique that reduces this whole development to a simple institutional evasion favouring the market, in the wake of the evolution of American strategic planning, does not relate, other than in exceptional cases, to European cities where local governments remain important—although this does not exclude drift in this direction.

Dimensions of Modes of Governance

Each city represents something unique, the result of an individual history— made up of a type of integration and external representation, a type of social relations, a type of culture, and certain political elites—which is difficult to grasp. Particular combinations of social, political, and economic forms of regulation have been institutionalized and transformed. The examples given have suggested that cities are spaces for the regulation of conflicts and for developing compromises between social groups, as well as spaces of cultural conflicts, and that because of this they contribute to the regulation of European societies as a whole. Following the avenue of research into cities as local societies has enabled me to highlight their strategies for adapting while still preserving a certain originality based on their particular arrangement of heritage, relative unity, and mode of managing diversity (Mendras 1976).

Every city is characterized first and foremost by structural conditions that relate to the market, to the state, or to civil society, as well as by a culture and identities that are more or less established and congruent. To avoid the stumbling block of fetishizing the local requires, for example, consideration of the situation of each city in relation to the market and to conditions of economic development, which will vary according to period (Harding 1997). As we come to the end of our journey, having highlighted different variables along the way, it is useful to differentiate between modes of governance of European cities, along four dimensions: (1) variables in the structure of local society; (2) the institutionalization of collective action; (3) political orientation; and (4) results or outcomes.

Dimension 1: Conditions for Modes of Governance, Local Society, and Political Institutions

Modes of governance of European cities first depend upon characteristics of the structure of local society. These are objective conditions, which do not determine the making of a mode of governance but which make it more or less likely and contribute to the form it will take. Classic dimensions of local societies include:

- institutional and political resources; type of urban government; relationships to other levels of government, to the state, and to the European Union; horizontal relations in general and specifically with subject-based networks of cities; degree of fragmentation of local government, financial autonomy;
- economic situation, market pressures, organized economic interests, relations with large firms, structure of firms in the territory, relationship to firms running networks and services, labour market, industrial relations;
- social structure: social groups, influence of the middle classes in the public sector, extent of segregation and exclusion processes, domination by elites; and

• influence of the associative sector, organization of civil society—religion, family, district, communities—organization of different interests, including trade unions and political parties.

Weak local government, lack of organized interests, financial constraints, and large-scale poverty are usually conditions that contribute to the making of a particular mode of governance. In contrast to what has sometimes been assumed in the classic comparative institutionalist literature, the political institutional framework is only one element among several (Cole and John 2001).

Dimension 2: Coalition and the Institutionalization of Collective Action

A mode of governance has its characteristic forms of coalitions of actors and institutionalization of collective action in order to respond to demands and to solve collective problems. It depends, first, on the actors involved in the process and, second, on the type of arrangements and the way collective action is institutionalized between them.

These issues have been explored by American sociologists and urban political scientists since the 1970s. However, importing the concepts of 'urban growth coalition' (Logan and Molotch 1987) and 'urban regime' (Elkin 1987; Stone 1989; 2001) into European cities is not without problems (Harding 1997; John 2001; Le Galès 1995; Stoker and Mossberger 1994; Keating 1991). In both cases, American writers have taken as their central factor the dependence of urban governments on private sector actors, given the high priority placed on carrying out projects and, thus, on having the right conditions to implement public policy: that is, having the power of so doing. However, these conditions, which are central for American cities, do not correspond to the European situation, where cities' resources depend first and foremost on local taxes and state subsidies. Dependence on firms and developers is structurally much lower, except perhaps, to some extent, in the UK. Consequently, in the case of European cities it is essential to take into account the public sector element, including various sections of the state present in the territory. The concept of 'urban regime' has proved valuable, but it is strongly oriented towards economic development as a priority and concentrates on politicians and bureaucrats (Dowding 2001). My preference for the term 'mode of governance' can be explained, therefore, by three concerns: one is to differentiate between the dimensions outlined above; the next is to cover types of arrangements that cannot be analysed solely as a function of economic development or of dependence on private sector interests; and the last is not to take the centrality of political regulation for granted, since examples from Italy have shown that the combination of market and community forms of regulation can dominate a city and produce a particular mode of governance weakly related to politics. However, the two concepts are close.

This dimension of a mode of governance can be analysed primarily on the basis of organized interests, actors, mobilizations, protests, organizations in a city, and their interactions, institutionalized over time—this does not imply resistance to change, since the stability of a mode of governance is always fragile and remains subject to conflicts, concurrent coalitions, electoral defeat, and so forth. The degree of fragmentation or, alternatively, the degree of integration of groups and organizations within the city varies over time. The stabilization of a coalition produces repetitive, visible effects on public policy and the behaviours and expectations of actors: a different issue from that of efficiency. The formation of a coalition can be analysed politically in terms of compromise, competition, control, power relations, and leadership.

Key elements are, therefore, the scope and organization of actors involved in the making of a mode of governance; the degree of institutionalization of collective action and conflict-resolution mechanisms; the combination of political, social, and market forms of regulation; the strength and stability of mechanisms to aggregate and represent interests.

Dimension 3: Political Orientations, Collective Choices.

Modes of governance of European cities are oriented by values and by collective choices. It is well beyond the scope of this book to identify all shades of politics in the European Union, but it is useful to highlight a few of the main dimensions. Within the European Union, the opposition most likely to have some relevance is the one between social democratic and neo-liberal orientations.

Neo-liberal orientation prioritizes economic development, which can be expressed in terms of public policy by playing the game of competition between cities; attracting firms, jobs, and favoured social groups; reducing taxes; privatizing urban services; favouring the game of the market and of property developers—fewer town planning rules, labour market flexibility; introducing market mechanisms into management of local services; giving priority to promoting the city, to major urban projects, and to prestige events.

Social democratic orientation prioritizes economic development and social cohesion via public services—urban services, education, social services, housing, health—and combats inequalities and risks—income, labour market, gender, immigration, access to various services, social segregation.

However, these two political orientations are not the only ones. Thus, in German, Dutch, Scandinavian, French, and Italian cities, the Greens are attempting to make the environment and sustainable development the main priorities, especially in terms of public transport, urban sprawl, energy consumption, waste management, protection of natural spaces, anti-pollution strategies, and democratic procedures, such as consultation with residents and associations. In other cases, nearer to or on the extreme right, other groups plead the causes of rejecting foreigners, of law and order, security, and rejecting the European Union and globalization. Although in very different forms, some politicians in Toulon, Anvers, Piacenza, Hanover, and Bradford have given voice to these sinister themes, and have gained electoral successes. The far right is stalking some cities and generating violence against ethnic minorities.

Dimension 4: Outcomes

Traditional American pluralist and neo-Marxist analyses have long since taught us that the issue of results—of losers and winners in terms of resources and of power—is fundamental. Modes of governance can also be analysed according to results. From the point of view of the city as collective actor, the main outcome that merits study relates to its capacity to extract resources in the medium term, whether from the European Union, the state, the region, firms, or large organizations, and whether in cooperation or in competition with other cities. Next, results can be analysed on the basis of the type of action carried forward—or not—of the coherence of a particular policy, and of the capacity to implement policies that will modify the behaviour of outside actors and their involvement in the territory, like building social housing, strengthening the skills of the workforce, improving air quality, or trying to prevent retailers from leaving the city. Last, and internally, outcomes can relate to processes of selection-exclusion of actors, to winners and losers in terms of redistribution and of projects, or to social and political innovations.

These four dimensions could serve as the basis of a typology of modes of governance of European cities. The aim of my whole analysis has been to highlight globalization processes, not to suggest a single model of some kind of entrepreneurial city, organized essentially around economic development, challenging local government, and restructuring social policies (Harding and Le Galès 1998; Harding 1997). The four dimensions remain analytically separate, since the degree of institutionalization of collective action tells us nothing about political orientation or the type of regulation that dominates the city as a result of the influence of one economic sector or another, of religious traditions, or of the city's relationship to the state. One critical view of the representation of cities as collective actors challenges the idea of linking the unity of cities with the fact they are becoming actors, given that the whole of the present situation (see Chapter 4) suggests that fewer conditions for unity actually exist (Bourdin 1998). However, in very divided or fragmented cities groups and elites are frequently successful in creating the dynamics for the making of a collective actor, directed outwards, which may have a low capacity for internal integration, but be perfectly capable of mounting a strategy. Diversity, fragmentation, and conflicts of various kinds must now be accepted as given in the structure of European cities: it is useless to dream of an idealized unity. As indicated in Chapter 6, the analysis of locality is not the analysis of community (Tiévant 1982; Benoit-Guilbot 1991; Frazer 2000). Actors, organizations, and social groups may be integrated into or excluded from coalitions that are trying to produce collective action, to represent the city to the outside, and to give meaning and coherence to policies.

Some examples may be provided. Lille's mode of governance is characterized by the domination of the urban government and its mayor, the institutionalization of collective action, social democratic orientations—with a mix of entrepreneurial and Green—lack of concern for ethnic minorities, and a strong capacity to mobilize actors and obtain resources.

Birmingham: until the mid-1990s, a sort of growth coalition between the city council, business leaders, and state agencies; included ethnic minorities, but excluded left groups and many associations. Strong institutionalization of collective action between the council and business interests, and between the council and ethnic minorities. Under typical UK constraints, mainly oriented towards economic development and obtaining extra financial resources: a mix of entrepreneurial and social democratic. Weak capacity to steer outsider strategies.

Turin: strong social regulation and institutionalization of collective action are in the making, with an increasing role for the mayor. Weak capacity to solve problems and gain resources, social democratic orientations—some Green—medium capacity to control development and steer the strategies of outsiders within the city.

Caen: weak institutionalization of collective action, to some extent of local government. Weak to medium problem-solving capacity; fragmentation dominates. conservative orientation, weak capacity to extract resources, to mobilize actors, or to modify external actors' strategies.

In European cities, if the existing structural conditions are not entirely unfavourable, then it is not impossible to create the right combination of conditions in which to structure a relatively integrated mode of governance. Institutional and political barriers are often hard to overcome, notably in terms of financial resources, expertise, legal autonomy, and political fragmentation. For a long time, Italian cities have been largely paralysed by the dual influence of an institutional straightjacket on their autonomy and of municipalities colonized by political parties. In Portugal, legal and financial constraints still weigh heavily, even though mayors are now political figures of the first order. In Finland, rural interests in peripheral regions defend the universalist vision of the welfare state and try to block the creation of an urban policy that increases resources for Helsinki, whether these relate to social policy or to major economic investments.

A second series of barriers to the making of a mode of governance originates in the social and political dynamics within cities. Coalition-building and the institutionalization of collective action in a territory are always, when they exist, fragile outcomes, never completely stabilized. Social, cultural, or political conflicts, powerful logics of exclusion, the lack of interest of some social groups, or the departure of firms may all be contributing to fragmentation and frequently to economic and social dislocation in the city. Conversely, well-organized social groups or a prosperous economic fabric tell us nothing about capacities for collective action, about conflicts that have been institutionalized, about processes of adaptation to external pressures, or about the capacity to resolve conflicts.

This underlines, if there is still any need to do so, the point that European cities cannot be a priori viewed as collective actors. The thesis defended in this book seeks to highlight the fact that, against a background of transformation of constraints and opportunities for cities, actors within them react by trying to organize a mode of governance that gives the city a status as actor. This is not a 'natural' activity. Such mobilizations give rise to the production of ideas and discourse on governance, which justify and legitimize certain social interests and certain political entrepreneurs at the expense of others. The marked obsession in public policy with global, transverse, integrated, partnership, collective, and coherent approaches is a sign of both the pressures on and the strategies of the actors in charge of public policy and the political management of territories. Anyone who can demonstrate, or convince others, that he or she is the 'most global' will legitimately be able to pursue his or her own strategies for control, to capture resources, to strengthen his or her own power at the expense of other actors, to create coalitions, to set up the city as collective actor in European governance, and to derive economic, social, and political advantages from this, whether individually or collectively. Discourse on governance, instrumentalized by the political actors, offers a whole set of registers in which collective constructions can be legitimized, while presenting the city as an actor who, equipped, inevitably, with a strategy, can constrain or direct the behaviour of internal or external actors.

The diversity of situations in European cities does not, however, exclude some forms of convergence, in terms of the direction of developments, largely in a neo-liberal direction, given the pressures exercised by large firms, banks, states, and the European Union: a convergence that can be seen in the importance relatively recently accorded to economic development. Without sharing the more deterministic argument of Jessop or Brenner, who write on the reorganization of scales in society, I should point out that debate on the direction of, and explanation for, these developments remains open.

These modes of governance are structured in the aim of organizing a social order within the context of the institutionalization of the EU. Here we see again the political dimension of the European city and issues of power. While political scientists stress coercion and control in a territory, Chazel (1992: 223) recalls that 'as Parsons made efforts to establish, in an institutionalized political system, with power comes a capacity to co-ordinate social units around the achievement of collective goals: it is in the name of collective goals that legitimacy is claimed for decisions of a political order'. In these modes of governance, power combines the logics of coercion—which have not disappeared—with the problems of legitimization—all the more thorny in a context of institutional instability—and with a capacity for coordination and mobilization. Governance has not succeeded government as a mode of managing public affairs, from either an analytical or a normative point of view, as detailed in the Introduction. Governance does not push the issue of politics to one side. As Jean Leca (1973: 24) recalls, 'the landmark that essentially situates the political, therefore, is its function—social regulation, a function that is itself born of the tension between conflict and integration in a society'.

I also want to exclude another risk: that of being too ready to assimilate the government-governance debate to the two perspectives distinguished by Leca (1996) in his analysis of the crisis of democratic control:

the 'exchangist' perspective constructed from notions that the aggregation of individual preferences produces collective actions through processes of rational bargaining, negotiation, exchange, and coalition-building; and the 'institutional' perspective, which stresses the role of institutions in defining the terms of rational exchange on the basis of any conceivable way of painting reality and identities so as to establish which behaviours are to be deemed appropriate.

Governance cannot be reduced to a perspective that privileges collective action, any more than the concept of government comes down to the institutional approach. On the contrary, both concepts try to create linkages between these two approaches: in this respect, combining them opens the way to conceptual renewal (Borraz and Le Galès 2001; Montagné 2001). Although I have not taken it up within the scope of this book, the way has been opened by others for rethinking the classic issues of democracy, of linkages between partisan politics and public policy, of political regulation, of local democracy, and of citizenship. Against the background of change, emphasized in the first part of the book, cities have become a laboratory for the reshaping of the political in Europe. However, in his study of issues of democracy and citizenship in the cities he calls 'Anglo-American'—in North America, Australia, and New Zealand—transformed by two decades of neo-liberal reforms, Isin (2000: 157) concludes incontrovertibly: 'Modern city government is increasingly like an empty shell, whose territory marks out the once-meaningful boundaries of the political.' In this context, seeing things in terms of moving from government to governance—in the neo-liberal sense, combining community and the market—seems appropriate. In contrast, all the analyses presented in this book stress the strength of the political in the governance of European cities, the complex relationships between government and governance, and the importance of issues of public policy and of the power of doing. Questions remain about 'who governs?' and about transformation of local democracy, constituting a vast field for future research (King and Stoker 1996).

A further question remains, about the direction of the European Union. Although Europe is, for the moment, an enlarged market and a political form that is perhaps not too different from what some states used to be, fears about the future of this entity are strong. Hooghe and Marks (1999) have suggested representing the dynamic of European integration as the result of conflict between two political projects, one spread by neo-liberals and the other by supporters of regulated capitalism, the social democrats. In the face of the dynamic of liberalization of energy, transport, or public utilities, of stronger and increasingly strictly applied competition policies, and of monetary integration, the postponed Social Europe project cuts a pale figure—although this does not exclude some interesting experiments. Of course, the social actors need more time to reorganize at the European level than do firms and their representatives, who have the advantage of mobility. For the moment, except in cases that are, ultimately, fairly few in number, European integration is leading to the free movement of goods and people, the making of an enlarged European market, and the shaping of a set of rules that are rather favourable to the smooth functioning of markets. Advances in the sphere of work or of the environment cannot conceal the absence of any perspectives on their social consequences and on inequalities.

The question posed at the outset also remains: are Europeans going to invent a new form of institutionalized and territorialized capitalism, with European cities as one of its pillars and one of its actors? Failing that, the effects of changing scales—of the processes of de-territorialization and re-territorialization analysed in the first part—could be expressed as profound transformations of the European urban model. Harloe (2001) is right to emphasize that the language of urban competitiveness, social cohesion, and governance, along with the implicit connections between them, which has now spread to all corners and all levels on both sides of the Atlantic, reveals 'a new liberal formulation' of the urban question. Crouch (1999: 408, 406) adds that:

In the words of the Swedish sociologist, Gøran Therborn (1997), Western Europe might become to the world what Scandinavia has been to Europe: a Northern corner of strong social citizenship and relative equality. However, and as Therborn fully recognizes, this process clashes completely with another one: the 'Americanizing' trend towards greater inequalities and a more finance-driven capitalism . . . Overall it is perhaps the more rigid European form of combining diversity with overall order which has most difficulty with contemporary trends towards fragmentation and individualization. On the other hand, it is necessary to place this fragmentation in perspective as occurring around a core of institutional stability that survives in reduced form.

The medium-sized European city model identified at the end of the second part shows capacities for adaptation and resistance—capacities that are still usually enhanced by states—for diversity structured by institutions, and for generating public authorities worried about social exclusion processes and as much concerned with culture and integration as with economic development. However, there is nothing to say that the continued extension of the European market and the reshaping of welfare states cannot, in the end, produce a different structure of organization and of territorialization of interests.

In a period when we are 'under the sign of the interim' (Anderson 1997)—between radical change and slow evolution over the long term, experiencing the reshaping of scales in a Europe that is seeking itself—all bets are still open.

BIBLIOGRAPHY

Adriaenssens, S. and Geldof, D. (1997). 'La polarisation sociale et spatiale d'Anvers', in A. Maertens and M. Vervaeke (eds), *La polarisation sociale des villes européennes*. Paris: Anthropos.

Agier, M. (1999). *L'invention de la ville, banlieues, townships, invasions et favellas*. Amsterdam: OPA.

Agulhon, M. (ed.) (1983). *La ville à l'âge industriel* (Histoire de la France urbaine, iv). Paris: Le Seuil.

Albaeck, E., Rose, L., Strömberg, L., Stahlberg, K. (eds) (1996). *Nordic Local Government*. Helsinki: The Associations of Nordic Local Authorities.

Amin, A. (ed.) (1994). *Post-fordism: A Reader*. Oxford: Blackwell.

—— (1999). 'An Institutionalist Perspective on Regional Economic Development'. *International Journal of Urban and Regional Research*, 23/2: 365–78.

—— and Graham, S. (1997). 'The Ordinary City'. *Transactions of the British Geographers*, 22: 411–29.

—— and Thrift, N. (1995). 'Globalisation, Institutional "Thickness" and the Local Economy', in P. Healey *et al.* (eds), *Managing Cities: The New Urban Context*. Chichester: John Wiley.

Amna, E. and Montin, S. (eds) (2000). *Towards a New Conception of Local Self-government*. Bergen: Fagbokforlaget.

Andersen, H. T. (1991). 'Urban Policy: from Welfare Planning to Business Development'. *Scandinavian Housing and Planning Research*, 8: 25–30.

—— and Jorgensen, J. (1999). 'Institutional Change in Globalizing Cities: Urban Politics Between Growth and Welfare' (manuscript). Copenhagen: University of Copenhagen, March.

Anderson, B. (1991). *Imagined Communities* (revised edn). London, Paris: Verso.

Anderson, P. (1974). *Lineages of the Absolutist State*. London: Verso.

—— (1994). 'The Invention of the Region, 1945–1990' (EUI European Forum Working Paper, 94–2). Florence: European University Institute.

—— (ed.) (1997). *Under the Sign of the Interim*. London: Verso.

Anderssen, H., Jorgensen, G., Joye, D., and Ostendorf, W. (eds) (2001). *Changes and Stability in Urban Europe, Form, Quality, Governance*. Aldershot: Ashgate.

Andretta, M. (1999). 'Sistema politico locale e protesta a Palermo'. *Quaderni di Sociologia*, 43/21: 68–9.

Angiolini, F. and Roche, D. (eds)(1995). *Cultures et formations négociantes dans l'Europe moderne*. Paris: EHESS.

Aniello, V. (2001). 'The Competitive Mezzogiorno (Southern Italy): Some Evidence from the Cothing and Textile Industry in San Giuseppe Vesuviano'. *International Journal of Urban and Regional Research*, 25: 517–36.

Appardur"i, A. (1996a). *Modernity at Large: Cultural Dimensions of Globalization*. Minneapolis: University of Minnesota Press.

—— (1996b). *The Social Life of Things: Commodities in Cultural Perspective*. Cambridge: Cambridge University Press.

Armstrong, W. (1995). 'The Role and Evolution of European Community Regional Policy', in B. Jones and M. Keating (eds), *The European Union and the Regions*. Oxford: Clarendon Press.

Arnaud, A. J. (1998). 'La régulation en contexte globalisé', in J. Commaille and B. Jobert (eds), *Les métamorphoses de l'action publique*. Paris: LGDJ.

Ascher, F. (1994). 'Le partenariat public-privé dans le "re-développement": le cas de la France', in W. Heinz (ed.), *Partenariats public-privé dans l'aménagement urbain*. Paris: L'Harmattan.

—— (1995). *Métapolis ou l'avenir des villes*. Paris: Odile Jacob.

Ashworth, G. and Voogd, H. (1990). *Selling the City: Marketing Approaches in Public Sector Urban Planning*. London: Belhaven Press.

Asquith, A. and O'Halpin, E. (1998). 'Power with Responsibility: The Role of the Manager in Irish Local Government', in K. K. Klausen and A. Magnier (eds), *The Anonymous Leader: Appointed CEOs in Western Local Government*. Odense: Odense University Press.

Atkinson, H. and Wilks-Heeg, S. (2000). *Local Government from Thatcher to Blair: The Politics of Creative Autonomy*. Cambridge: Polity Press.

Atkinson, T. (2000). 'Agenda social européen: comparaison des pauvretés et transferts sociaux', in Conseil d'Analyse Économique, *Questions européennes*. Paris: La Documentation Française.

——, Glaude, M., Freyssinet, J. and Seibel, C. (1998). *Pauvreté et exclusion*. Paris: Conseil d'Analyse Économique, La Documentation Française.

——, Glaude, M., Olier, L., and Piketty, T. (2001). *Inégalités économiques*. Paris: Conseil d'Analyse Économique, La Documentation Française.

Augé, M. (1992). *Non-Lieux*. Paris: Seuil.

Autès, M. (1995). L'exclusion', *Lien Social et Politique*, 34: 43–54.

Avenel, C. (1999). 'Les exclus de la banlieue, Étude d'un quartier et des rapports sociaux de dépendance' (Ph. D. thesis). Bordeaux: University of Bordeaux II.

Axtmann, R. (ed.) (1998). *Globalization and Europe*. London: Pinter.

Aylmer, G. (1996). 'Centre et périphérie: définition des élites du pouvoir', in W. Reinhard (ed.), *Les élites du pouvoir et la construction de l'État en Europe*. Paris: PUF.

Bache, I., George, S., and Rhodes, R. A. W. (1996), 'The European Union, Cohesion Policy and Subnational Authorities in the UK', in L. Hooghe (ed.), *Cohesion Policy and European Integration: Building Multi-Level Governance*. Oxford: Oxford University Press.

Badie, B. (1995). *La fin des territoires*. Paris: Fayard.

—— (1999). *Un monde sans souveraineté*. Paris: Fayard.

—— and Birnbaum, P. (1994). 'Sociologie de l'État revisitée'. *Revue Internationale de Sciences sociales*, 140: 189–201.

Baechler, J. (1995). *Le capitalisme*, 2 vols. Paris: Gallimard.

——, Hall, J., and Mann, M. (eds) (1988). *Europe and the Rise of Capitalism*. Oxford: Oxford University Press.

Bagnasco, A. (1986). *Torino: Un profil sociologico*. Turin: Einaudi.

—— (ed.) (1989). *La città dopo Ford: Il caso di Torino*. Turin: Einaudi.

—— (1994). *Fatti sociali, formati nello spazio*. Milan: Franco Angeli.

—— (1996). *L'Italia in tempi di cambiamento politico*. Bologna: Il Mulino.

—— (1999). *Tracce di comunità*. Bologna: Il Mulino.

—— and Le Galès, P. (eds) (2000). *Cities in Contemporary Europe*. Cambridge: Cambridge University Press.

—— and Negri, N. (1994). *Classi, ceti, persone*. Naples: Liguori.

—— and Trigilia, C. (1993). *La construction sociale du marché*. Paris: ENS Cachan.

Bairoch, P. (1985). *De Jéricho à Mexico: Villes et économie dans l'histoire*. Paris: Gallimard.

Balandier, G. (1967). *Anthropologie politique*. Paris: PUF.

—— (1980). *Le pouvoir sur scènes*. Paris: Balland.

Baldersheim, H. and Stahlberg, K. (eds) (1994). *Towards the Self-Regulating Municipality: Free Communes and Administrative Modernization in Scandinavia*. Aldershot: Dartmouth.

—— —— (1999). *Nordic Region-building in a European Perspective*. Aldershot: Ashgate.

—— and Stava, P. (1996). 'Free Communes, Pilots and Pathfinders: A New Vocabulary of Local Government Reforms in Scandinavian Countries, the Case of Norway', in N. Ben-Elia (ed.), *Strategic Changes and Organizational Reorientations in Local Government: A Cross National Perspective*. Basingstoke: Macmillan.

Baldini, G., and Legnante, G. (1998). 'Dal Sindaco dei partiti al partito dei sindaci', in L. Bardi and M. Rhodes (eds), *Politica in Italia* (Edizione 98). Bologna: Il Mulino.

—— —— (2000). 'Le elezioni comunali del 1999 e la "disfatta" della sinistra a Bologna', in M. Gilbert and G. Pasquino (eds), *Politica in Italia* (Edizione 2000). Bologna: Il Mulino.

Balducci, A. (1999). 'Pianificazione strategica e politiche di sviluppo locale. Una relazione necessaria?'. *Archivio di Studi Urbani e Regionali*, 64.

—— (forthcoming, 2002).*The Decline of Statutory Planning in Italy and the Long Search for a New Effective Approach*.

Balme, R. (1996). 'Pourquoi le gouvernement change-t-il d'échelle?', in R. Balme (ed)., *Les politiques du néo-régionalisme*. Paris: Economica.

—— and Chabanet, D. (2002). 'Action collective et gouvernance de l'Union européenne', in R. Balme, D. Chabanet, and V. Wright, *l'action collective en Europe*. Paris: Presses de Sciences Po.

—— , Faure, A., and Mabileau, A. (eds) (1999). *Politiques locales et transformations de l'action publique locale en Europe*. Paris: Presses de Sciences Po.

—— and Le Galès, P. (1997). 'Stars and Black Holes, French Regions and Cities in the European Galaxy', in M. Goldsmith and K. Klausen (eds), *European Integration and Local Government*. Cheltenham: Edward Elgar.

—— , Garraud, P., Hoffmann-Martinot, V., and E. Ritaine (1994). *Le territoire pour politique, variations européennes*. Paris: L'Harmattan.

Banfield, E. (1961). *Political Influence*. New York: Free Press of Glencoe.

Barbagli, M. and Saraceno, C. (1997). *Lo stato delle famiglie in Italia*. Bologna: Il Mulino.

Barca, F. (ed.) (1997). *Storia del capitalismo Italiano dal dopoguerra a oggi*. Rome: Donzelli.

Bardet, F. and Jouve, B. (1999). 'Entreprise politique et territoire à Lyon'. *Sociologie du Travail*, 41/1: 41–61.

Barel, Y. (1975). *La ville médiévale, système social, système urbain*. Grenoble: PUG.

Barnekov, T., Boyle, R., and D. Rich (1989). *Privatism and Urban Policy in Britain and the USA*. Oxford: Oxford University Press.

Barraqué, B. (ed.) (1995). *Les politiques de l'eau en Europe*. Paris: La Découverte.

Barthélémy, M. (2000). *Associations: un nouvel âge de la participation*. Paris: Presses de Sciences Po.

Bartolini, S. (1993). 'On Time and Comparative Research'. *Journal of Theoretical Politics*, 5: 131–68.

Bartolini, S. (1998). 'Exit Options, Boundary Building, Political Structuring' (EUI Working Paper, SPS 98/1). Florence: European University Institute.

Bassett, K. (1996). 'Partnership, Business Elites and Urban Politics: New Forms of Governance in an English City'. *Urban Studies*, 33: 539–55.

Bassolino, A. (1996). *La Repubblica delle città*. Rome: Donzelli.

Batley, R. and Stoker, G. (eds) (1991). *Local Government in Europe*. Basingstoke: Macmillan.

Bayart, J. F. (ed.) (1994). *La réinvention du capitalisme*. Paris: Karthala.

—— (1996). *L'illusion identitaire*. Paris: Fayard.

Beauregard, R. and Body-Gendrot, S. (eds) (1999). *The Urban Moment*. London: Sage.

—— and Bounds, A. (2000). 'Urban Citizenship', in E. Isin (ed.), *Democracy, Citizenship and the Global City*. London: Routledge.

—— and Haila, A. (2000). 'The Unavoidable Continuities of the City', in P. Marcuse and R.Van Kempen (eds), *Globalizing Cities: A New Spatial Order?*. Oxford: Blackwell.

Beck, U., Giddens, A., and Lash, S. (1994). *Reflexive Modernization: Politics, Tradition and Aesthetics in the Modern Social Order*. Cambridge: Polity Press.

Bédarida, F. (1990). *La société britannique*. Paris: Seuil.

Beetham, D. (1996). 'Theorising Democracy and Local Government', in D. King and G. Stoker (eds), *Rethinking Local Democracy*. Basingstoke: Macmillan.

Béhar, D. and Estèbe, P. (1998). 'Des petites villes en Île de France: de la cité équilibrée à la ville éclatée', *in* N. May *et al.* (eds), *La ville éclatée*. La Tour d'Aigues: Éditions de l'Aube.

——, Epstein, R., and Estèbe, P. (1998). 'Les détours de l'égalité: remarques sur la territorialisation des politiques sociales en France'. *Revue Française des affaires sociales*, 52/4: 81–94.

Bell, D. (1973). *The Coming of Post-Industrial Society*. New York: Basic Books.

—— (1976). *The Cultural Contradictions of Capitalism*. New York: Basic Books.

Belloni, M. C. and Bimbi, F. (1997). *Microfisica della cittadinanza, Città, Genere, Politiche dei tempi*. Milan: Franco Angeli.

Benassi, D., Ghezzi, S., and Mingione, E. (1997). 'La restructuration économique et la pauvreté urbaine dans les pays européens', in A. Maertens and M. Vervaeke (eds), *La polarisation sociale des villes européennes*. Paris: Anthropos.

Bendix, R. (1978). *Kings or People: Power and the Mandate to Rule*. Berkeley: University of California Press.

Ben-Elia, N. (ed.) (1996). *Strategic Changes and Organizational Reorientations in Local Government: A Cross National Perspective*. Basingstoke: Macmillan.

Benevolo, L. (1993). *La ville dans l'histoire européenne*. Paris: Le Seuil.

Benington, J. (1994). *Local Democracy and the European Union: The Impact of Europeanisation on Local Governance* (Research Report 6). London: Commission for Local Democracy.

—— and Geddes, M. (2000). 'Exclusion sociale et partenariat local, la dimension européenne'. *Pôle Sud*, 12: 79–94.

—— —— (eds) (2001). *Local Partnership and Social Exclusion in the European Union*. London: Routledge.

—— and Harvey, J. (1999). 'Networking in Europe', in G. Stoker (ed.), *The New Management of British Local Governance*. Basingstoke: Macmillan.

Benko, G. and Lipietz, A. (eds) (1992), *Les régions qui gagnent*. Paris: PUF.

—— —— (eds) (2000). *La richesse des régions. La nouvelle géographique socio-économique*. Paris: PUF.

Bennett, R. (ed.) (1993). *Local Government in the New Europe*. London: Belhaven Press.

—— (1998). 'Explaining the Membership of Voluntary Local Business Associations: The Example of British Chambers of commerce'. *Regional Studies*, 32: 503–14.

Benoit-Guilbot, O. (1991). 'Les acteurs locaux du développement économique local, y a-t-il un "effet localité"?'. *Sociologie du Travail*, 4: 453–59.

Benyon, J. and Solomos, J. (eds) (1987). *The Roots of Urban Unrest*. Oxford: Pergamon Press.

Benz, A. and Goetz, K. (eds) (1996). *A New German Public Sector? Reform, Adaptation, Stability*. Aldershot: Darmouth.

Berengo, M. (1999). *L'Europa delle città. Il voloto della società urbana europea tra Medioevo ed Età moderna*. Bologna: Einaudi.

Berglund, S. and Persson, L. (1997). 'La restructuration du marché du travail et les processus ségrégatifs à Stockholm', in A. Maertens and M. Vervaeke (eds), *La polarisation sociale des villes européennes*. Paris: Anthropos.

Berry, J. and McGreal, S. (eds) (1995). *European Cities, Planning Systems and Property Markets*. London: E&FN Spon.

Bettin, G. and A. Magnier (1992). *Chi governa la città*. Padua: Cedam.

—— —— (1995). 'I nuovi sindaci: come cambia una carriera politica'. *Rivista Italiana di Sociologia*, 1: 91–118.

Bianchini, F. and Parkinson, M. (eds) (1993). *Cultural Policy and Urban Regeneration in European Cities*. Manchester: Manchester University Press.

Biarez, S. (1989). *Le pouvoir local*. Paris: Economica.

—— (1990). 'Le discours sur la métropole en France, nouvelle communication et nouveaux rapports dans le cadre de la décentralisation'. *Revue Internationale des Sciences Administratives*, 56: 1635–95.

—— and J. Y. Nevers (eds) (1993). *Gouvernement local et politiques urbaines*. Grenoble: CERAT.

Bigo, D. (1996). *Polices en réseaux, l'exemple européen*. Paris: Presses de Sciences Po.

Birnbaum, P. (ed.) (1997). *Sociologie des nationalismes*. Paris: PUF.

Black, A. (1984). *Guilds and Civil Society in European Political Thought from the Twelfth Century to the Present*. London: Methuen.

Bleitrach, D. *et al.* (1981). *Classe ouvrière et sociale-démocratie: Lille et Marseille*. Paris: Éditions sociales.

Blockmans, W. (1988). 'Princes conquérants et bourgeois calculateurs. Le poids des réseaux urbains dans la formation des États', in N. Bulst and J.-Ph. Genet (eds), *La ville, la bourgeoisie et la genèse de l'État moderne*. Paris: Éditions du CNRS.

Bobbio, L. (1999). 'I processi decisionali nei communi italiani'. *Stato e Mercato*, 49: 39–66.

Body-Gendrot, S. (1992). *Ville et violence*. Paris: PUF.

—— (2000). *The Social Control of Cities*. Oxford: Blackwell.

—— and Martiniello, M. (eds) (2000). *Immigrants in European Cities*. Basingstoke: Macmillan.

Bogason, P. (1987). 'Denmark', in E. Page and M. Goldsmith (eds), *Central and Local Government Relations: A Comparative Analysis of West European Unitary State*. London: Sage.

—— (1996). 'The Fragmentation of Local Government in Scandinavia'. *European Journal of Political Research*, 30: 65–86.

Bongers, P. (1992). *Local Government in the Single European Market*. London: Longman.

Borraz, O. (1992). 'Intégration et régulation: la crise politique à Lausanne'. *Sociologie du Travail*, 34/1: 23–45.

—— (1996). 'Représentativité, sociabilité et pouvoir dans quatre municipalités suisses et françaises'. *Revue Française de science politique*, 46: 624–49.

—— (1998*a*). *Gouverner une ville, Besançon, 1959–1989*. Rennes: Presses Universitaires de Rennes.

—— (1998*b*). *Les politiques locales contre le SIDA*. Paris: L'Harmattan.

—— (2000). 'Pour une sociologie des dynamiques de l'action publique locale', in R. Balme, A. Faure, and A. Mabileau (eds), *Politiques locales et transformations de l'action publique locale en Europe*. Paris: Presses de Sciences Po.

—— (forthcoming, 2002). 'Le leadership institutionnel', in Smith et Genyès, *Le Leadership local*. Paris: L'Harmattan.

—— and Le Galès, P. (2001). 'Gouvernement et gouvernance des villes', in J. P. Leresche (ed.), *La gouvernance des villes suisses*. Paris: Pedone.

—— and Loncle, P. (2000). 'Action publique et matrices institutionnelles, les politiques locales en lutte contre le SIDA'. *Revue Française de Sociologie*, 41/1: 37–60.

——, Bullman, U., Hambleton, R., Page, E., Rao, N., and Young, K. (1994). *Local Leadership and Decision-Making: France, Germany, the US and Britain*. London: LGC Communications.

Botella, J. (2000). 'Local Government in Spain: Between Centralisation and Regional Decentralisation', in E. Amna and S. Montin (eds), *Towards a New Conception of Local Self-government*. Bergen: Fagbokforlaget.

Boudon, R. (ed.) (1992). *Traité de Sociologie*. Paris: PUF.

Bouinot, J. (ed.) (1987). *L'action économique des grandes villes en France et à l'étranger*. Paris: Economica.

Bourdieu, P. (ed.) (1993). *La misère du monde*. Paris: Le Seuil.

Bourdin, A. (1998). 'Le gouvernement des villes institue autant qu'il coordonne ou les limites des théories de la gouvernance', in N. May *et al.* (eds), *La ville éclatée*. La tour d'Aigues: Éditions de l'Aube.

—— (2000). *La Question locale*. Paris: PUF.

Bourgois, P. (1995). *In Search of Respect: Selling Crack in El Barrio*. Cambridge: Cambridge University Press.

Boyer, R. (1986). *Théorie de la régulation*. Paris: La Découverte.

—— (2000). 'The Political in the Era of Globalization and Finance: Focus on some Regulation School Research'. *International Journal of Urban and Regional Research*, 24: 273–321.

—— and Drache, D. (eds) (1997). *States against Markets*. London: Routledge.

Braudel, F. (1979). *Civilisation matérielle, économie et capitalisme, XVème–XVIIIème siècle*. Paris: Colin.

Breen, R. and Rottman, B. (1998). 'Is the National State the Appropriate Geographical Unit for Class Analysis?'. *Sociology*, 32/1: 1–22.

Brenner, N. (1998). 'Global Cities, Global States: Global City Formation and State Territorial Restructuring in Contemporary Europe'. *Review of International Political Economy*, 5/1: 1–37.

—— (1999). 'Globlization as Reterritorialization: The Re-scaling of Urban Governance in the European Union'. *Urban Studies*, 36: 431–52.

—— (2000). 'The Urban Question as Scale Question: Reflections on Henri Lefèvre, Urban Theory and the Politics Of Scale'. *International Journal of Urban and Regional Research*, 24: 361–77.

Bridge, G. (1995). 'The Space for Class: On Class Analysis in the Study of Gentrification'. *Transactions of the Institute of British Geographers*, 20: 236–47.

—— (2001). 'Estate Agents as Interpreters of Economic and Cultural Capital: The Gentrification Premium in the Sidney Housing Market'. *International Journal of Urban and Regional Research*, 25: 87–102.

—— and Watson, S. (eds) (2001). *The Blackwell Companion of Cities*. Oxford: Blackwell.

Briggs, A. (1958). 'The Study of Cities'. *Confluence*, 7/Summer: 107–22.

—— (1962). *Victorian Cities*. London: Penguin Books.

Brotchie, J., Batty, M., Blakely, E., Hall, P., and Newton, P. (eds) (1995). *Cities in Competition*. Melbourne: Longman.

Brunet, R. (1989). *Les villes européennes*. Paris: Datar-Reclus-La Documentation Française.

Brusco, S. and Paba, S. (1997). 'Per una storia dei distretti industriali italiani dal secondo dopoguerra agli anni novanta', in F. Barca (ed.), *Storia del capitalismo Italiano dal dopoguerra a oggi*. Rome: Donzelli.

Bulpitt, J. (1983). *Territory and Power in the UK*. Manchester: Manchester University Press.

Bulst, N. and Genet, J.-Ph. (eds) (1988). *La ville, la bourgeoisie et la genèse de l'État moderne*. Paris: Éditions du CNRS.

Burgel, G. (1993). *La ville aujourd'hui*. Paris: Hachette.

Burke, P. (1988). 'Republic of Merchants in Early Modern Europe', in J. Baechler *et al.* (eds), *Europe and the Rise of Capitalism*. Oxford: Oxford University Press.

—— (1974). *Venice and Amsterdam: A Study of Seventeenth Century Elites*. London: Temple Smith.

—— (2000). *La renaissance européenne*. Paris: Le Seuil.

Burteshaw, D., Bateman, M., and Ashworth, G. (1991). *The European City: A Western Perspective*. London: David Seldon.

Butler, T. (1995). 'Gentrification and the Urban Middle Classes', in T. Butler and M. Savage (eds), *Social Change and the Middle Classes*. London: UCL Press.

—— and Savage, M. (eds) (1995). *Social Change and the Middle Classes*. London: UCL Press.

Cacciari, M. (2000). *Veneto, proviamoci insieme*. Venice: Il Poligrafo.

Caillosse, J. (1989). 'Réflexion sur un processus aléatoire: l'émergence d'une capitale périphérique, Lyon?'. *Revue de droit public*, 6: 1635–95.

—— (1991). 'La modernisation de l'État: variations sur le modèle juridique d'administration'. *Actualité juridique. Droit administratif*, n.11: 755–64.

—— (1999). 'Le droit administratif contre la performance publique?' *Actualité juridique. Droit administratif*, n.3: 195–211.

—— (2000). 'Le droit administratif français saisi par la concurrence?'*Actualité juridique. Droit administratif*, n.2: 99–193.

Cammelli, M. (1993). 'Eletto del popolo: il sindaco tra ruolo nuovo e vecchi poteri'. *Il Mulino*, 4.

Campagnac, E. (ed.) (1992). *Les grands groupes de la construction, de nouveaux acteurs urbains?*. Paris: L'Harmattan.

Caporaso, J. (1996). 'The European Union and Forms of State: Westphalian, Regulatory or Post-Modern'. *Journal of Common Market Studies*, 34/1: 29–51.

Carradine, D. (1990). *The Decline and Fall of the British Aristocracy*. London: Picador.

Castel, R. (1995). *Les métamorphoses de la question sociale*. Paris: Fayard.

284 *Bibliography*

Castellani, V. (1996). *Il mestiere di sindaco*. Milan: Cantiere Italia.
Castells, M. (1983). *The City and the Grassroots*. London: Edward Arnold.
—— (1996–98). *The Information Age: Economy, Society and Culture* (3 vols). Oxford: Blackwell.
—— (1977). *The Urban Question: A Marxist Approach*. London: Edward Arnold.
Cattan, N. (1995). 'Attractivity and Internationalisation of Major European Cities: The Example of Air Traffic'. *Urban Studies*, 32: 303–12.
——, Pumain, D., Rozenblat, C., and St-Julien, T. (1999). *Le système des villes européennes* (2nd edn). Paris: Anthropos.
Cavallier, G. (1999). *Défis pour la gouvernance urbaine dans l'Union européenne* (rapport pour la Fondation européenne pour l'amélioration des conditions de vie et de travail). Dublin.
CEC (Commission of the European Communities) (1990). *Green Paper on the Urban Environment*. Brussels: CEC.
—— (1992). *Urbanization and the Functions of Cities in the European Community* (Regional Development Studies). Brussels: CEC.
—— (2001). *Urban Audit*. Brussels: CEC.
Cerny, P. (1990). *The Changing Architecture of Politics*. London: Sage.
Cesari, J. (1994a). *Être musulman en France: associations, militants et mosquées*. Paris: Khartala.
—— (1994b). 'Les réseaux transnationaux entre l'Europe et le Maghreb: l'international sans territoire'. *Revue européenne des migrations internationales*, 13/2: 81–94.
——, Moreau, A., and Schleyer-Lindenmann, A. (2001). *Plus marseillais que moi tu meurs! Migrations, identités et territoires à Marseille*. Paris: L'Harmattan.
Chadoin, O., Godier, P., and Tapie, G. (2000). *Du politique à l'œuvre, Bilbao, Bordeaux, Bercy, San Sebastian*. La Tour d'Aigues: Éditions de l'Aube.
Chapoulie, J. M. (2001). *La tradition sociologique de Chicago, 1892–1961*. Paris: Le Seuil.
Charney, I. (forthcoming, 2002). 'Three Dimensions of Capital Switching Within the Real Estate Sector: A Canadian Case Study'. *International Journal of Urban and Regional Research*.
Chauvel, L. (1995).'Valeurs régionales et nationales en Europe'. *Futuribles*, n.200: 167–200.
—— (1998a). *Les destin des générations*. Paris: PUF.
—— (1998b). 'Clivages politiques, culturels et religieux dans les régions européennes', in B. Cautrès and P. Bréchon (eds), *Les enquêtes Eurobaromètres*. Paris: L'Harmattan.
Chazel, F. (1992). 'Pouvoir', in R. Boudon (ed.), *Traité de Sociologie*. Paris: PUF.
Chenu, A. (1996). 'Les étrangers dans les agglomérations françaises', in D. Pumain and F. Godard (eds), *Données Urbaines 1*. Paris: Economica.
Cheshire, P. and Gordon, I. (eds) (1995). *Territorial Competition in an Integrating Europe*. Aldershot: Avebury.
—— —— (1996). 'Territorial Competition and the Predictability of Collective In(Action)'. *International Journal of Urban and Regional Research*, 20: 383–99.
Chesnais, F. (ed.) (1996). *La mondialisation financière*. Paris: Syros.
Chevalier, B. (1982). *Les bonnes villes de France du XIVème au XVIème siècle*. Paris: Aubier Montaigne.
—— (1988). 'L'État et les bonnes villes en France au temps de leur accord parfait (1450–1550)', in N. Bulst and J.-Ph. Genet (eds), *La ville, la bourgeoisie et la genèse de l'État moderne*. Paris: éditions du CNRS.

Chevallier, J. (1994). *L'État de droit*. Paris: Montchrestien.

Chevallier, L. (1958). *Classes laborieuses et classes dangereuses à Paris pendant la première moitié du 19ème siècle*. Paris: Plon.

Chiarello, F. (1997). 'Travagli urbani a Bari. Trasformazioni sociali e governo locale in una città del Mezzogiorno'. *Quaderni di Sociologia*, 41/14: 21–41.

Christopherson, S. (1994). 'The Fortress City: Privatized Spaces, Consumer Citizenship', in A. Amin, *Post-fordism: A Reader*. Oxford: Blackwell.

Ciciotti, E. (1994). *Competitività e terriorio*. Rome: NIS.

Cini, M. and MacGowan, L. (1998). *Competition Policy and the European Union*. Basingstoke: Macmillan.

Clark, T. N. and Hoffmann-Martinot, V. (eds) (1998). *The New Political Culture*. Boulder, CO: Westview Press.

Clarke, M. (1997). 'Governance and the European Union', paper presented to the EU conference hosted by the Dutch presidency in Rotterdam, 28–30 May.

Cloulas, I. (ed.) (1990). *L'Italie de la Renaissance*. Paris: Fayard.

Cochrane, A. (1993). *Whatever Happened to Local Government?* Milton Keynes: Open University Press.

——, Peck, J., and Tickell, A. (1996). 'Manchester Plays Game: Exploring the Local Politics of Globalisation'. *Urban Studies*, 33/8: 281–302.

Cohen, E. (1996). *La tentation hexagonale*. Paris: Fayard.

Cole, A. and John, P. (2001). *Local Governance in England and France*. London: Routledge.

Commaille, J. and de Singly, F. (eds) (1997). *The European Family: The Family Question in the European Community*. Boston: Kluwer Academic Press.

—— and Jobert, B. (eds) (1996). *Les métamorphoses de l'action publique*. Paris: LGDJ.

Cooke, P. (ed.) (1988). *Localities*. London: Unwin and Hyman.

Coppola, P. (ed.) (1997). *Geografia politica delle regioni italiane*. Turin: Einaudi.

Corfield, P. J. (1982). *The Impact of English towns, 1700–1800*. Oxford: Oxford University Press.

Coulson, A. (1999). 'Local Business Representation: Can We Afford TECs and Chambers?'. *Regional Studies*, 33: 269–88.

Coutart, O. (1998). 'Le "droit" à l'eau et à l'énergie en France', in N. May *et al.* (eds), *La ville éclatée*. La Tour d'Aigues: Éditions de l'Aube.

Cox, K. (ed.) (1997). *Spaces of Globalization*. New York: Guildford Press.

Coyle, C. (1997). 'European Integration: A Lifeline for Irish local Authorities?', in M. Goldsmith and K. Klausen (eds), *European Integration and Local Government*. Cheltenham: Edward Elgar.

Crosta, P. L. Politiche (1998). *Politicche Publique Quale Conoscenza per L'azione Territoriale*. Milan: Franco Angeli.

Crouch, C. (1993). *Industrial Relations and European States Traditions*. Oxford: Clarendon Press.

—— (1999). *Social Changes in Western Europe*. Oxford: Oxford University Press.

—— and Streeck, W. (eds) (1996). *The Diversity of Capitalism in Europe*. London: Sage.

——, Le Galès, P., Trigilia, C., and Voelzkow, H. (eds) (2001). *Local Industrial Systems in Europe, Rise or Demise?* Oxford: Oxford University Press.

Crouzet, F. and Furet, F. (eds) (1998). *L'Europe dans son histoire. La vision d'Alphonse Dupront*. Paris: PUF.

Curien, N. (1996). 'The Economics of Networks', in D. Lorrain and G. Stoker (eds), *The Privatization of Urban Services*. London: Frances Pinter.

Curien, N. (2000). *L'économie des réseaux*. Paris: La Découverte.

Cutler, C. (1997). 'Artifice, Ideology and Paradox: The Public/Private Distinction in International Law'. *Review of International Political Economy*, 4: 261–85.

Czempiel, C. and Rosenau, J. (eds) (1991). *Global Changes and Theoretical Challenges*. Lexington: Lexington Books.

Daalder, H. and Irwin, G. (ed.) (1989). *Politics in the Netherlands: How Much Change*. London: Frank Cass.

Dahl, R. (1961). *Who Governs?* New Haven: Yale University Press.

—— (1967). 'The City and the Future of Democracy'. *American Political Science Review*, 61: 953–70.

—— (1978). 'Pluralism Revisited'. *Comparative Politics*, 10/2: 191–201.

Damette, F. (ed.) (1994). *La France en villes*. Paris: La documentation française.

Dansgshaft, J. (1994). 'Concentration of Poverty in the Landscapes of Boomtown, Hamburg: The Creation of a New Underclass?' *Urban Studies*, 31: 1133–47.

—— and Ossenbrügge, J. (1990). 'Hamburg: Crisis Management, Urban Regeneration and Social Democrats', in D. Judd and M. Parkinson (eds), *Leadership and Urban Regeneration*. London: Sage.

Davezies, L. (1998*a*). 'L'autre main invisible. La dépendance des régions et des villes à l'économie hors-marché'. *Pouvoirs Locaux*, 37/II. 39–45.

—— (1998*b*). 'Le poids des fonds publics dans les revenus des villes et des régions', in D. Pumain and M. F. Mattei (eds), *Données Urbaines 2*. Paris: CNRS/INSEE, Anthropos.

—— (1998*c*). 'Ville éclatée ou société éclatée?', in N. May *et al.* (eds), *La ville éclatée*. La Tour d'Aigues: Éditions de l'Aube.

Davis, M. (1990). *The City of Quartz*. London: Verso.

Dear, M. (2000). *The Postmodern Urban Condition*. Oxford: Blackwell.

—— and Flusty, S. (1999). 'Invitation to a Postmodern Urbanism', in R. Beauregard and S. Body-Gendrot (eds), *The Urban Moment*. London: Sage.

Degenne, A. and Forsé, M. (1994). *Les réseaux sociaux*. Paris: Colin.

Dehousse, R. (1995). *La cour de justice européenne*. Paris: LGDJ.

—— (1996). 'Les États et l'Union européenne, les effets de l'intégration', in V. Wright and S. Cassese (eds), *La recomposition de l'État en Europe*. Paris: La Découverte.

Delanty, G. (1995). *Inventing Europe*. London: Macmillan.

—— (2000). 'The Resurgence of City in Europe? The Spaces of European Citizenship', in E. Isin (ed.), *Democracy, Citizenship and the Global City*. London: Routledge.

Delcamp, A. (ed.) (1994). *Les collectivités décentralisées de l'Union européenne*. Paris: La Documentation Française.

—— (1999). 'La charte européenne de l'autonomie locale et son système de contrôle'. *Annuaire des collectivités locales*, 19: 139–70.

De Leon, R. (1992). *Left Coast City: Progressive Politics in San Francisco*. Kansas: University of Kansas Press.

Della Porta, D. (1998). 'Immigrazione e Protesta'. *Quaderni di Sociologia*, 43/21: 14–44.

—— (1999). *La politica locale*. Bologna: Il Mulino.

—— and Diani. M. (1999). *Social Movements: An Introduction*. Oxford: Blackwell.

Dematteis, G. (1994). 'Global Networks, Local Cities'. *Flux*, 15: 17–24.

—— (1997). 'Il tessuto delle cento città', in P. Coppola (ed.), *Geografia politica delle regioni italiane*. Turin: Einaudi.

—— (2000). 'Spatial Representations of European Urbanism', in A. Bagansco and P. Le Galès (eds), *Villes en Europe*. Paris: La Découverte.

—— and Bonavero, P. (eds) (1997). *Il sistema urbano italiano nell spazio unificato europeo*. Bologna: Il Mulino.

Demazière, D. (2000). *Entreprise, développement économique et espace urbain*. Paris: Anthropos.

Demeestere, R. and Padioleau, J. G. (1990). *Politique de développement et démarches stratégiques des villes* (rapport pour le Plan Urbain). Paris: (Unpublished).

Dente, B. (1990). 'Metropolitan Governance Reconsidered or How to Avoid Errors of the Third Type'. *Governance*, 3: 55–74.

—— (1991). 'Italian Local Services: The Difficult Road towards Privatisation', in R. Batley and G. Stoker (eds), *Local Government in Europe*. Basingstoke: Macmillan.

—— and Kjellberg, F. (eds) (1988). *The Dynamics of Institutional Change: Local Government Reorganisation in Western Democracies*. London: Sage.

——, Bobbio, L., Fareri, P., and Morisi, M. (1990). *Metropoli per progetti: attori e processi di trasformazione ubrana a Firenze*. Turin, Milan, Bologna: Il Mulino.

Denters, S. (1999). 'Les démocraties urbaines aux Pays-Bas: changement socio-politique, continituité institutionnelle?', in O. Gabriel and V. Hoffmann-Martinot (eds), *Démocraties urbaines*. Paris: L'Harmattan.

De Rita, G. and Bonomi, A. (1998). *Manifesto per lo sviluppo locale: dall'azione di comunità al patti territoriali*. Turin: Bollati Bolinghieri.

de Roo, P. (1993). 'La métropolité', in A. Sallez (ed.), *Les villes, lieux d'Europe*. La Tour d'Aigues: Éditions de l'Aube/Datar.

De Rynck, S. (1997). 'Belgian Local Government, Far Away from Brussels', in M. Goldsmith and K. Klausen (eds), *European Integration and Local Government*. Cheltenham: Edward Elgar.

Descimon, R. (1988). 'L'échevinage parisien sous Henri IV', in N. Bulst and J.-Ph. Genet (eds), *La ville, la bourgeoisie et la genèse de l'État moderne*. Paris: Éditions du CNRS.

De Singly, F. (2000). *Libres ensemble: l'individualisme dans la vie commune*. Paris: Nathan.

de Swaan, A. (1995). *Sous l'aile protectrice de l'État*. Paris: PUF.

De Vries, J. (1984). *European Urbanization, 1500–1800*. Harvard: Harvard University Press.

Dezalay, Y. and Garth, B. (1998). *Dealing in Virtue*. Chicago: University of Chicago Press.

Diamanti, I. 'Nordest, si puo crescere senza politica?'. *Il Mulino*, 46: 1061–73.

Dieterich, H. and Drangsfeld, E. (1995). 'Düsseldorf', in J. Berry S. McGreal (eds), *European Cities, Planning Systems and Property Markets*. London: E&FN Spon.

DiGaetano, A. and Klemanski, J. (1993). 'Urban Regimes in Comparative Perspective'. *Urban Affairs Quarterly*, 29/1: 54–83.

—— and Lawless, P. (1999). 'Urban Governance and Industrial Decline: Governing Structure and Policy Agendas in Birmingham, Sheffield, England and Detroit, Michigan, 1980–1997'. *Urban Affairs Review*, 34: 546–77.

Dimaggio, P. and Powell, W. (eds) (1991). *The New Institutionalism in Organization Analysis*. Chicago: Chicago University Press.

Dollinger, P. (1970). *The German Hansa*. Basingstoke: Macmillan.

Donzel, A. (1998). *Marseille, l'expérience de la cité*. Paris: Economica/Anthropos.

Dowding, K. (2001). 'Explaining Urban Regime'. *International Journal of Urban and Regional Research*, 25: 7–19.

Dubet, F. (1987). *La Galère: jeunes en survie*. Paris: Fayard.

—— (1994). *Sociologie de l'expérience*. Paris: Seuil.

Dubet, F. and Lapeyronnie, D. (1992). *Les quartiers d'exil*. Paris: Seuil.
—— and Martucelli, D. (1998). *Dans quelle société vivons-nous?* Paris: Le Seuil.
Duby, G. (ed.) (1980). *La ville médiévale* (Histoire de la France urbaine, 2). Paris: Le Seuil.
Dumont, L. (1986). *Essays on Individualism: Modern Ideology in Anthropological Perspective*. Chicago: University of Chicago Press.
Duneier, M. (1999). *Sidewalk*. New York: Farrar, Strauss, Giroux.
Dunford, M. (1994). 'Winners and Losers: The New Map of Economic Inequality in the European Union'. *European Urban and Regional Studies*, 1: 95–114.
—— and Kafkalas, G. (eds) (1992), *Cities and Regions in the New Europe*. London: Pinter.
Dunleavy, P. (1981). *The Politics of Mass Housing in Britain*. Oxford: Clarendon.
—— and Hood, C. (1994). 'The globalization of public services: Can government be best in the world?'. *Public Policy and Administration*, 9/2: 9–16.
Dupuy, G. (1991). *L'urbanisme des réseaux*. Paris: Colin.
Dupuy, F. and Thoenig, J. C. (1986). *L'Administration en miettes*. Paris: Fayard.
Duran, P. (1999). *Penser l'action publique*. Paris:LGDJ.
—— and Thoenig, J. C. (1996). 'L'État et la gestion publique territoriale'. *Revue Française de Science Politique*, 46: 580–622.
Dyson, K. (1980). *State traditions in Western Europe*. Oxford: Martin Robertson.
—— and Featherstone, K. (2000). 'Italy and EMU as a "vincolo esterno": Empowering the Technocrats, Transforming the State'. *South European Society and Politics*, 1: 272–99.
Eade, J. (ed.) (1997). *Living in the Global City: Globalization as Local Process*. London: Routledge.
Economia Publicca, 30/3 (2000). Special issue: 'Milano e le aree metropolitane in Europa: un confronto'.
Edelman, M. (1964). *The Symbolic Use of Politics*. Chicago: University of Illinois Press.
Eisenschitz, A. and Gough, J. (1996). 'The Contradictions of Neo-Keynesian Local Economic Strategy'. *Review of International Political Economy*, 3: 434–58.
Eisenstadt, S. N. and Rokkan, S. (eds) (1973). *Building States and Nations*. London: Sage.
Ejersbo, N., Hansen, M. B., and Mouritzen, P. E. (1998). 'The Danish Local Government CEO: From Town Clerk to City Manager', in K. K. Klausen and A. Magnier (eds), *The Anonymous Leader: Appointed CEOs in Western Local Government*. Odense: Odense University Press.
Eldersveld, S., Strömberg, L., and Derksen, W. (eds) (1995). *Local Elites in Western Democracies: A Comparative Analysis of Urban Political Leaders in the US, Sweden and the Netherlands*. Boulder, CO: Westview Press.
Elias, N. (1962). *State Formation and Civilization* (The Civilizing Process, Part II). Oxford: Blackwell.
Elkin, S. (1987). *City and Regime in the American republic*. Chicago: University of Chicago Press.
Engbersen, G., Schuyt, K., Timmer, T., and Van Waarden, F. (1993). *Cultures of Unemployment*. Boulder, CO: Westview Press.
Engels, F. (1969). *The Conditions of the Working Class in England*. London: Panther.
Engelstoft, S. and Jorgensen, J. (1997). 'Copenhagen, the Redistributive City?', in C. Jensen-Butler *et al.* (eds), *European Cities in Competition*. Aldershot: Avebury.

Ercole, E. (1997). 'Yes in Theory. And Perhaps in the Future: European Integration and Local Government in Italy', in M. Goldsmith and K. Klausen (eds), *European Integration and Local Government*. Cheltenham: Edward Elgar.

Eskelinen, H. and Snickars, F. (eds) (1995). *Competitive European Peripheries*. Berlin: Springer.

Esping-Andersen, G. (1990). *The Three Worlds of Welfare Capitalism*. Cambridge: Polity Press.

—— (ed.) (1993). *Changing Classes: Stratification and Mobilities in Post-Industrial Societies*. London: Sage.

—— (ed.) (1996). *Welfare States in Transition*. London: Sage.

—— (1999a). *Social Foundations of Post-Industrial Economics*. Oxford: Oxford University Press.

—— (1999b). 'Politics without Class: Post-Industrial Cleavages in Europe and America', in H. Kitschelt *et al.* (eds), *Continuity and Change in Contemporary Capitalism*. Cambridge: Cambridge University Press.

Fainstein, S. (1994). *The City Builders: Property, Politics and Planning in London and New York*. Oxford: Blackwell.

——, Gordon, I., and Harloe, M. (eds) (1992). *Divided Cities: New York and London in the Contemporary World*. Oxford: Blackwell.

—— and Hirst, C. (1995). 'Urban Social Movements', in D. Judge, G. Stoker, and H. Wolman (eds), *Theories of Urban Politics*. London: Sage.

Faist, T. (1999). 'Transnational Social Spaces out of International Migration: Evolution, Significance and Future Prospects'. *European Archives of Sociology*, 39: 215–47.

—— (2000). *The Volume and Dynamics of International Migration and Transnational Socal Spaces*. Oxford: Clarendon Press.

—— (2001). 'Social Citizenship in the European Union: Nested Membership'. *Journal of Common Market Studies*, 39/1: 37–58.

—— and Haussermann, H. (1996). 'Immigration, Social Citizenship and Housing in Germany'. *International Journal of Urban and Regional Research*, 20/2: 83–98.

Farrar, M. (1999). 'Social Movement in as Multi-Ethnic Inner City: Explaining their Rise and Fall over 25 Years', in P. Bagguley and J. Hearn (eds), *Transforming Politics, Power and Resistance*. Basingstoke: Macmillan.

Faure, A. (1994). 'Les élus locaux à l'épreuve de la décentralisation'. *Revue Française de science politique*, 44/3: 462–79.

—— (1997a). 'Les apprentissages du métier d'élu local: la tribu, le système et les arènes'. *Pôle Sud*, 7: 72–9.

—— (ed.) (1997b). *Territoires et subsidiarité*. Paris: L'Harmattan.

Feagin, J. and Smith, M. (1987). *The Capitalist City*. Oxford: Blackwell.

Featherstone, M., Lash, S., and Robertson, R. (eds) (1995). *Global Modernities*. London: Sage.

Fevre, L. (1999). *L'Europe, Genèse d'une civilisation*. Paris: Perrin.

Fincher, R. and Jacobs, J. (eds) (1998). *Cities of Difference*. New York: Guildford Press.

Fisher, K. (forthcoming, 2002). 'Réseaux et coopérations régionales transfrontalières', in Commissariat au Plan, *L'Europe vue du bas: villes et régions en Europe*.

Fontaine, J. and Le Bart, C. (eds) (1994). *Le métier d'élu local*. Paris: L'Harmattan.

Forsé, M. and Mendras, H. (1983). *Le changement social*. Paris: Colin.

Fourcaut, A. (ed.) (1992). *La ville divisée: les ségrégations urbaines en question, France, XVIIIème–XXème siècle*. Grâne: Creaphis.

François, E. (1978). 'Des républiques marchandes aux capitales politiques: remarques sur la hiérarchie urbaine du Saint-Empire à l'époque moderne'. *Revue d'Histoire moderne et contemporaine*, 35: 587–603.

—— (1995). 'Négoce et culture dans l'Allemagne du 18ème siècle', in F. Angiolini and D. Roche, *Cultures et formations négociantes dans l'Europe moderne*. Paris: EHESS.

Frazer, E. (2000). *The Problems of Communitarian Politics, Unity and Conflict*. Oxford: Oxford University Press.

Friedberg, E. (1992). 'Organisation', in R. Boudon (ed.), *Traité de Sociologie*. Paris: PUF.

—— (1993). *Le Pouvoir et la règle*. Paris: Le Seuil.

Gabriel, O. (1999). 'Crise ou changement de la démocratie urbaine en Allemagne?', in O. Gabriel and V. Hoffmann-Martinot (eds), *Démocraties urbaines*. Paris: L'Harmattan.

—— and Hoffmann-Martinot, V. (eds) (1999). *Démocraties urbaines*. Paris: L'Harmattan.

Galland, O., Clémençon, M., Le Galès, P., and Oberti, M. (1995). *Le monde des étudiants*. Paris: PUF.

Gallie, D. and Paugam, S. (eds) (2000). *Welfare Regimes and the Experience of Unemployment in Europe*. Oxford: Oxford University Press.

Gamberucci, M. and Magnier, A. (1998). 'Italian Local Democracy in Search of a New Administrative Leadership', in K. K. Klausen and A. Magnier (eds), *The Anonymous Leader: Appointed CEOs in Western Local Government*. Odense: Odense University Press.

Garbaye, R. (forthcoming, 2002). 'A Comparison of the Management of Ethnic Conflicts in British and French Cities', in *International Journal of Urban and Regional Research*.

Garcia, S. (1991). 'Politique économique urbaine et autonomie locale: le cas de Barcelone'. *Sociologie du Travail*, 4: 485–502.

—— (1996). 'Cities and Citizenship: special issue'. *International Journal of Urban and Regional Research*, 20: 7–21.

Gasparini, A., Logan, J., and V. Mansurov (eds) (1994). *Riqualificazione et hinterland delle grandi città*. Milan: Franco Angeli.

Gaudin, J. P. (1999). *Gouverner par contrat*. Paris: Presses de Sciences Po.

Gaxie, D. (2000). *La démocratie représentative* (3rd edn). Paris: LGDJ.

Geddes, M. (2000). 'Tackling Social Exclusion in the European Union? The Limits of the New Orthodoxy of Local Partnership'. *International Journal of Urban and Regional Research*, 24: 782–800.

Gelli, F. (forthcoming, 2002). *Governments, Governance and Planning Systems in Italy*.

Gellner, E. (1983). *Nations and Nationalism*. Oxford: Blackwell.

Genet, J. P. (ed.) (1990). *L'État moderne: genèse*. Paris: Éditions du CNRS.

—— (1997). La genèse de l'État moderne. Les enjeux d'une programme de recherche'. *Actes de la Recherche en Sciences Sociales*, 118: 3–18.

Genieys, W., Smith, A., Faure, A., and Négrier, E. (2000). 'Le pouvoir local en débats, pour une sociologie du rapport entre leadership et territoire'. *Pôle Sud*, 13/November: 103–20.

Giddens, A. (1987). *The Nation-State and Violence*. Berkeley: University of California Press.

—— (1990). *The Consequences of Modernity*. Stanford: Stanford University Press.

—— (1994). 'Living in a Post-Traditional Society', in U. Beck, A. Giddens, and S. Lash, *Reflexive Modernization: Politics, Tradition and Aesthetics in the Modern Social Order*. Cambridge: Polity Press.

Gilbert, G. (1999). 'L'autonomie financière des collectivités locales est-elle en question?' *Les 2ème entretiens de la Caisse des Dépôts et Consignations*. La Tour d'Aigues: Éditions de l'Aube.

Gilroy, P. (1987). *There Ain't No Black in the Union Jack*. London: Hutchinson.

Goetz, E. and Clarke, S. (eds) (1993). *The New Localism: Comparative Urban Politics in a Global Era*. London: Sage.

Goldsmith, M. (ed.) (1986). *Essays on the Future of Local Government*. Salford: University of Salford.

—— (1992). 'Local Government'. *Urban Studies*, 29/3/4: 393–410.

—— (1993). 'The Europeanisation of Local Government'. *Urban Studies*, 30/4/5: 683–90.

—— (1995). 'Autonomy and City Limits', in D. Judge, G. Stoker, and H. Wolman (eds), *Theories of Urban Politics*. London: Sage.

—— and Klausen, K. (eds) (1997). *European Integration and Local Government*. Cheltenham: Edward Elgar.

Gomez, M. (1998). 'Reflective Images: The Case of Urban Regeneration in Glasgow and Bilbao'. *International Journal of Urban and Regional Research*, 22: 106–21.

Gourevitch, A. (1997). *La naissance de l'individu dans l'Europe médiévale*. Paris: Le Seuil.

Governa, F. (1997). *Il milieu urbano, l'identità territoriale nei processi di sviluppo*. Milan: Franco Angeli.

Graham, S. (2000). 'Constructing Premium Network Spaces: Reflection on Insfrastructure Networks and Contemporary Urban Development'. *International Journal of Urban and Regional Research*, 24/1: 183–200.

—— and Marvin, S. (1994). 'Cherry Picking and Social Dumping: Utilities in the 1990's'. *Utilities Policy*, 4/2: 113–19.

—— —— (1995a). 'More than Ducts and Wires: Post-Fordism, Cities and Utility Networks', in P. Healey *et al.* (eds), *The New Urban Context: Managing Cities*. London: J. Wiley.

—— —— (1995b). *Telecommunications and the City: Electronic Spaces, Urban Places*. London: Routledge.

—— —— (2001). *Splintering Urbanism: Networked Infrastructures, Technological Mobilities and the Urban Condition*. London: Routledge.

Green-Cowles, M., Caporaso, J., and Risse, T. (eds) (2001). *Transforming Europe*. Ithaca, NY: Cornell University Press.

Greenwood, J. (1997). *Representing Interests in the European Union*. Basingstoke: Macmillan.

Grossetti, M. (1995). *Science, Industrie, territoire*. Toulouse: Presses Universitaires du Mirail.

Gullesdat, M. and Segalen, M. (eds) (1995). *La famille en Europe, perpétuation et parenté*. Paris: La Découverte.

Gurr, T. and King, D. (1987). *The State and the City*. London: Macmillan.

Gyford, J. (1985). *The Politics of Local Socialism*. London: Allen and Unwin.

Habermas, J. (1996). 'The European Nation-State: Its Achievement and its Limits', in G. Balakhrisnan (ed), *Mapping the Nation*. London: Verso.

Hadjimichalis, C. and Sadler, D. (eds) (1995). *Europe at the Margins: New Mosaics of Inequality*. London: Wiley.

Haglund, R. (1998). 'Turbulence as a Way of Life: The Swedish Municipal CEO', in K. K. Klausen and A. Magnier (eds), *The Anonymous Leader: Appointed CEOs in Western Local Government*. Odense: Odense University Press.

Hall, J. and Ikenberry, G. J. (1989). *The State*. Minneapolis: University of Minnesota Press.

Hall, P. (1993). 'Policy Paradigms, Social Learning and the State: The Case of Economic Policy in Britain'. *Comparative Politics*, 25: 275–96.

Hall, T. and Hubbard, P. (eds) (1998). *The Entrepreneurial City: Geography of Politics, Regime and Representation*. Chichester: John Wiley.

Hamel, P., Lustiger-Thaler, H., and Mayer, M. (eds) (1998). *Urban Fields/Global Spaces, Urban Movements in a Global Environment*. London: Sage.

Hamnett, C. (1994). 'Social Polarisation in Global Cities'. *Urban Studies*, 31: 401–24.

—— (1995). 'Les changements économiques à London'. *Sociétés contemporaines*, 22/23: 15–32.

—— (1997). 'La polarisation sociale, déconstruction d'un concept chaotique', in A. Maertens and M. Vervaeke (eds), *La polarisation sociale des villes européennes*. Paris: Anthropos.

Hannerz, U. (ed.) (1996). *Transnational Connections, Culture, People, Places*. London: Routledge.

Hannigan, J. (1998). *Fantasy City, Pleasure and Profit in the Postmodern Metropolis*. London: Routledge.

Harding, A. (1992). 'Property Interests and Urban Growth Coalitions in the UK: A Brief Encounter', in P. Healey *et al.*, *Rebuilding the City: Property-Led Urban Regeneration*. London: E&FN Spon.

—— (1995). 'Elites Theory and Growth Machines', in D. Judge, G. Stoker, and H. Wolman (eds), *Theories of Urban Politics*. London: Sage.

—— (1997). 'Urban Regimes in a Europe of Cities?'. *European Urban and Regional Studies*, 4: 291–314.

—— (2000). 'Regime Formation in Edinburgh and Manchester', in G. Stoker (ed.), *The New Politics Of British Local Governance*. Basingstoke: Macmillan.

—— and Le Galès, P. (1998). 'Cities and States in Europe'. *West European Politics*, 21/3:120–45

——, Dawson, J., Evans, R., and Parkinson, M. (eds) (1994). *European Cities Towards 2000*. Manchester: Manchester University Press.

Harloe, M. (1995). *The People's Home*. Oxford: Blackwell.

—— (forthcoming, 2002). 'Social Justice and the City: The New Liberal Formulation'. *International Journal of Urban and Regional Research*.

——, Pickvance, C., and Urry, J. (eds), *Place, Policy and Politics: Do Localities Matter?* London: Unwin and Hyman.

Harvey, B. (1992). *Networking in Europe: Guide to Voluntary Sector Association*. London: NCVO.

Harvey, D. (1985*a*). *The Urbanisation of Capital*. Oxford: Blackwell.

—— (1985*b*). *Consciousness and the Urban Experience*. Oxford: Blackwell.

—— (1989). *The Condition of Postmodernity*. Oxford: Blackwell.

—— (1990). 'From Managerialism to Entrepreneurialism: The Transformation of Urban Governance'. *Geografiska Annaler*, 71B: 3–17.

Hassenteufel, P. (1997). 'Le Welfare state en entre construction nationale et crispation nationaliste', in P. Birnbaum (ed.), *Sociologie des nationalismes*. Paris: PUF.

—— and Surel, Y. (2000). 'Des politiques publiques comme les autres? Construction de l'objet et outils d'analyse des politiques européennes'. *Politique européenne*, 1/1: 8–24.

Haughton, G. and Williams, C. (eds) (1996). *Corporate City? Partnership, Participation in Urban Development in Leeds*. Aldershot: Avebury.

Healey, P. (1995). 'Infrastructure, Technology and Power', in P. Healey *et al.*, *Managing Cities: The New Urban Context*. London: J. Wiley.

—— (1997). *Collaborative Planning*. London: Macmillan.

——, Avoudi, S., O'Toole, M., Tavanoglu, S., and Usher, D. (1992). *Rebuilding the City: Property-Led Urban Regeneration*. London: E&FN Spon.

——, Cameron, S., Divoudi, S., Graham, S., and Madani-Pour, A. (eds) (1995). *Managing Cities: The New Urban Context*. London: J. Wiley.

——, Khakee, A., Motte, A., and Needham, B. (eds) (1997). *Making Strategic Spatial Plans: Innovations in Europe*. London: UCL Press.

Heers, J. (1990). *La ville au Moyen Âge*. Paris.

Heinelt, H. and Mayer, M. (eds) (1992). *Politik in Europäischen Städten*. Berlin: Birkhäuser.

—— and Smith, R. (eds) (1996). *Policy Networks and European Structural Funds*. Aldershot: Avebury.

Heinz, W. (ed.) (1994). *Partenariats public-privé dans l'aménagement urbain*. Paris: L'Harmattan.

Held, D. (2000). 'Regulating Globalization? The Reinvention of Politics'. *International Sociology*, 15: 394–408.

—— and McGrew, A. (1993). 'Globalization and the Liberal Democratic State'. *Government and Opposition*, 28: 261–85.

——, ——, Goldblatt, D., and Perraton, J. (1999). *Global Transformations: Politics, Economics and Culture*. Stanford: Stanford University Press.

Hendriks, F. and Toonen, T. (1995). 'The Rise and Fall of the Rinjmond Authority: An Experiment with Metro Government in the Netherlands', in L. J. Sharpe (ed.), *The Government of World Cities. The Future of the Metro Model*. Chichester: J. Wiley.

—— and Tops, P. (1998). 'Between Democracy and Efficiency: Trends in Local Government Reform in the Netherlands and Germany' (Communication au congrès de l'AIS). Montreal.

Héritier, A. (1996). 'The Accommodation of Diversity in European Policy-Making'. *Journal of European Public Policy*, 3/2: 149–67.

—— (1999). *Policymaking and Diversity in Europe*. Cambridge: Cambridge University Press.

—— (2001). 'Overt and Covert Institutionalization of Europe', in A. Stone Sweet, W. Sandholz, and N. Fligstein (eds), *The Institutionalisation of Europe*. Oxford: Oxford University Press.

——, Hill, C., and Mingers, S. (1996). *Ringing the Changes in Europe*. Berlin: De Gruyter.

Hermet, G., Braud, P., Badie, B., and Birnbaum, P. (1998). *Dictionnaire de science politique et des institutions publiques*, Paris: Colin.

Hervieu-Léger, D. (1997). 'Renouveaux religieux et nationalistes: la double dérégulation', in P. Birnbaum (ed.), *Sociologie des nationalismes*. Paris: PUF.

Hesse, J. and L. J. Sharpe (eds), *Local Government and Urban Affairs in International Perspective: Analyses of Twenty Western Industrialised Countries*. Baden-Baden: Nomos.

Hillmann, F. (1999). 'A Look at the "Hidden Side": Turkish Women in Berlin's Ethnic Labour Market', *International Journal of Urban and Regional Research*, 23: 267–81.

Hintze, O. (1991). *Féodalité, capitalisme et État moderne*. Paris: Éditions MSH.

Hirst, P. (2000). 'Democracy and Governance', in J. Pierre (ed.), *Debating Governance: Authority, Steering and Democracy*. Oxford: Oxford University Press.

—— and Thompson, G. (1999). *Globalization in Question*. Oxford: Polity Press.

Hitz, H., Schmid, C., and Wolff, R. (1996). 'Zurich Goes Global: Economic Restructuring, Social Conflicts and Polarization', in J. O'Loughlin and J. Friedrichs (eds), *Social Polarization in Post-Industrial Metropolises*. Berlin: De Gruyter.

Hix, S. (1998). 'The Study of the European Union II: The "New Governance and its Rival Agenda" '. *Journal of European Public Policy*, 5/1: 38–65.

—— and Goetz, K. (eds) (2000). 'Europeanised Politics?: European Integration and National Political Systems'. *West European Politics*, 23/4 (special issue).

Hobsbawm, E. (1987). *The Age of Empire: 1875–1914*. London: Weidefield and Nicolson.

Hoffman, J. (1995). *Beyond the State*. Oxford: Blackwell.

Hoffmann-Martinot, V. (1992). 'La participation aux élections municipales dans les villes françaises'. *Revue Française de Science Politique*, 42/1: 3–35.

—— (1995). 'La relance du gouvernement métropolitain en Europe: le prototype de Stuttgart'. *Revue Française d'administration publique*, 71: 499–514.

—— (1999). 'Les grandes villes françaises: une démocratie en souffrance', in O. Gabriel and V. Hoffmann-Martinot (eds), *Démocraties urbaines*. Paris: L'Harmattan.

Hohenberg, P. and Hollen Lees, L. (1985). *The Making of Urban Europe*. Cambridge, MA: Harvard University Press.

Hollingsworth, J. R. and R. Boyer (eds) (1997). *Contemporary Capitalism: The Embeddedness of Institutions*. Cambridge: Cambridge University Press.

Hood, C. (1995). 'Contemporary Public Management: A Global Paradigm?'. *Public Policy and Administration*, 10/2: 104–17.

—— (1999).*The Art of the State*. Oxford: Oxford University Press.

Hooghe, L. (ed.) (1996). *Cohesion Policy and European Integration: Building Multi-Level Governance*. Oxford: Oxford University Press.

—— (1999). 'EU Cohesion Policy and Competing Models of European Capitalism'. *Journal of Common Market Studies*, 36: 457–77.

—— and Keating, M. (1995). 'The Politics of European Union Regional Policy'. *Journal of European Public Policy*, 1: 367–93.

—— and Marks, G. (1999). 'The Making of a Polity: The Struggle over European Integration', in H. Kitschelt *et al.* (eds), *Continuity and Change in Contemporary Capitalism*. Cambridge: Cambridge University Press.

—— —— (2001). *Multilevel Governance and European Integration*. Lanham, MD: Rowman and Littlefield.

Houghton, C. and Williams, C. (1996). *Corporate City?* Aldershot : Avebury.

Isaacs, A. K. and Prak, M. (1996). 'Les villes, la bourgeoisie et l'État', in W. Reinhard (ed.), *Les élites du pouvoir et la construction de l'État en Europe*. Paris: PUF.

Isin, I. (ed.) (2000). *Democracy, Citizenship and the Global City*. London: Routledge.

Jacobs, B. (2000). *Strategy and Partnership in Cities and Regions*. Basingstoke: Macmillan.

Jaillet, M. C. (2001). 'Peut-on parler de sécession urbaine à propos des villes européennes ?', in J. Donzelot and M. C. Jaillet (eds), *La Nouvelle question urbaine*. Paris: PUCA/Ministère de l'Équipement, du transport et du logement.

Jauhianen, J. (1997). 'Social Movements and Local Politics in Turku', in *Milieu*, Helsinki conference, September.

Jayet, H. (1993). 'Territoires et concurrence territoriale'. *Revue d'économie régionale et urbaine*, 1: 62–75.

Jeffrey, C. (ed.) (1997). *The Regional Dimension of the European Union*. London: Frank Cass.

Jehel, G. and Racinet, P. (1996). *La ville médiévale*. Paris: Colin.

Jensen-Butler, C. (1997). 'Competition Between Cities, Urban Performance and the Role of Urban Policy: A Theoretical Framework', in C. Jensen-Butler, A. Sachar, and J. B. van Weesep (eds), *European Cities in Competition*. Aldershot: Avebury.

——, Sachar, A., and van Weesep, J. B. (eds) (1997). *European Cities in Competition*. Aldershot: Avebury.

Jessop, B. (1990). *State Theory: Putting the Capitalist State in its Place*. Cambridge: Polity.

—— (1994): 'Post-fordism and the State', in A. Amin, *Post-Fordism: A Reader*. Oxford: Blackwell.

—— (1995). 'The Regulation Approach, Governance and Post-Fordism: Alternative Perspectives on Economic and Political Change'. *Economy and Society*, 24: 307–33.

—— (1997*a*). 'Capitalism and its Future: Remarks on Regulation, Government, and Governance', *Review of International Political Economy*, 4/3: 435–55.

—— (1997*b*). 'The Entrepreneurial City: Re-Imagining Localities, Redesigning Economic Governance or Re-Structuring Capital?', in N. Jewson et S. MacGregor (eds), *Realising Cities: New Spatial Divisions and Social Transformation*. London: Routledge.

—— (1998). 'The Narrative of Enterprise and The Enterprise Of Narrative: Place Marketing and the Entrepreneurial City', in T. Hall and P. Hubbard (eds), *The Entrepreneurial City: Geographies of Politics, Regime and Representation*. Chichester: John Wiley.

—— (2000). 'The Crisis of the National Spatio-Temporal Fix and the Tendential Ecological Dominance of Globalizing Capitalism'. *International Journal of Urban and Regional Research*, 24: 321–60.

Jewson, N. and MacGregor, S. (eds) (1997). *Realising Cities: New Spatial Divisions and Social Transformation*. London: Routledge.

Jobert, B. (ed.) (1994). *Le tournant néo-libéral en Europe*. Paris: L'Harmattan.

—— (1999). 'L'État en interaction'. *L'Année de la Régulation*, 3: 77–98.

—— and Sellier, M. (1977). 'Les grandes villes: autonomie locale et innovation politique'. *Revue Française de Science Politique*, n.2: 205–27.

John, P. (1994). 'UK Subnational Offices in Brussels: Regionalisation or Diversification?'. *Regional Studies*, 28: 739–46.

—— (1996). 'The presence and influence of UK local authorities in Brussels'. *Public Administration*, 74: 292–313.

—— (1998). 'Urban Economic Policy Networks in Britain and France: A Sociometric Approach'. *Environment and Planning C: Government and Policy*, 16: 307–22.

—— (2001). *Local Governance in Europe*. London: Sage.

—— and Cole, A. (1998). 'Urban Regimes and Local Governance in Britain and France: Policy Adaptation and Coordination in Leeds and Lille'. *Urban Affairs Review*, 33: 382–404.

Jones, B. and Keating, M. (eds) (1995). *The European Union and the Regions*. Oxford: Clarendon Press.

Jopke, C. (ed.) (1998). *Challenges to the Nation-State*. Oxford: Oxford University Press.

Jouen, M. (2000). *Diversité européenne, mode d'emploi*. Paris: Descartes.

Jouve, B. (1998). 'D'une mobilisation à l'autre. Dynamique de l'échange politique territorialisé en Rhône-Alpes', in E. Négrier and B. Jouve (eds), *Que gouvernent les régions en Europe?* Paris: L'Harmattan.

—— and Lefèvre, C. (1996). 'Dynamique institutionnelle et culture politique territoriale: la cité métropolitaine de Bologna'. *Revue Française de Sociologie*, 36: 369–96.

—— —— (1997). 'When Territorial Political Culture Makes Urban Institution: The Case of Bologna'. *Government and Policy*, 15/1: 89–111.

—— —— (eds) (1999). *Villes, métropoles*. Paris: Economica.

Joye, D. and Leresche, J. P. (1999). 'Pouvoir local contre gouvernement métropolitain: l'exemple du bassin lemanique', in B. Jouve and C. Lefèvre (eds), *Villes, métropoles*. Paris: Economica.

Judd, D. and Fainstein, S. (eds) (1999). *The Tourist City*. New Haven: Yale University Press.

—— and Parkinson, M. (eds) (1990). *Leadership and Urban Regeneration*. London: Sage.

Judge, D., Stoker, G., and Wolman, H. (eds) (1995). *Theories of Urban Politics*. London: Sage.

Kaelble, H. (1988). *Vers une société européenne, 1880–1980*. Paris: Belin.

Kaika, M. and Swyngedouw, E. (2000). 'Fetishizing the Modern City: the Phantasmagoria of Modern Urban Network'. *International Journal of Urban and Regional Research*, 24/1: 120–38.

Kantor, P. (1995). *The Dependent City Revisited*. Boulder, CO: Westwiew Press.

Kastoryanno, R. (1996). *La France, L'Allemagne et leurs immigrés: négocier l'identité*. Paris: Colin.

—— (ed.) (1998). *Quelle identité pour l'Europe?: Le multiculturalisme à l'épreuve*. Paris: Presses de Sciences Po.

—— (2000). 'Des multiculturalismes en Europe au multiculturalisme européen'. *Politique Étrangère*, 65/1: 163–78.

Keating, M. (1991). *Comparative Urban Politics*. Aldershot: Edward Elgar.

—— (1997). 'The Invention of Regions: Political Restructuring and Territorial Government in Western Europe' , Environment and Planning C. *Government and Policy*, 15: 379–500.

—— (1998). *The New Regionalism in Western Europe*. Aldershot: Edward Elgar.

—— and Loughlin, J. J. (eds) (1997). *The Political Economy of Regions*. London: Frank Cass.

Keil, R. (1998a). 'Globalisation Makes Market: Perspectives on Local Governance in the Age of the World City'. *Review of International Political Economy*, 5: 616–46.

—— (1998b). *Los Angeles, Globalization, Urbanization and Social Struggles*. Chichester: John Wiley.

—— (2000). 'Governance Restructuring in Los Angeles and Toronto: Amalgamation or Secession'. *International Journal of Urban and Regional Research*, 24: 758–81.

—— and Ronneberger, K. (2000). 'Francfort-sur-le-main, capitale fatale dans une région métropolitanisée', in G. Benko and A. Lipietz (eds), *La richesse des régions*. Paris: PUF.

Kesteloot, C. (1995). 'The Creation of Socio-Spatial Marginalisation in Brussels: A Tale of Flexibility, Geographical Competition and Guestworker Neighborhoods', in C. Hadjimalis and D. Sadler (eds), *Europe at the Margins: New Mosaics of Inequality*. London: Wiley.

—— and Meert, H. (1999). 'The Geography of Informal Activities in Brussels'. *International Journal of Urban and Regional Research*, 23: 232–51.

Kickert, W., Lkijn, E. H., and Koopenjan, J. F. M. (eds) (1999). *Managing Complex Networks*. London: Sage.

Kilminster, R. (1997). 'Globalization as an Emergent Context', in A. Scott (ed.), *The Limits of Globalization*. London: Routledge.

King, D. (1987). *The New Right: Politics, Markets and Citizenship*. London: Macmillan.

—— and Pierre, J. (eds) (1990). *Challenges to Local Government*. London: Sage.

—— and Stoker, G. (eds) (1996). *Rethinking Local Democracy*. Basingstoke: Macmillan.

Kitschelt, H., Lange, P., Marks, G., and Stephens, J. D. (eds) (1999). *Continuity and change in Contemporary Capitalism*. Cambridge: Cambridge University Press.

Kjellberg, K. (1988). 'Local Government and the Welfare State: Reorganisation in Scandinavia', in B. Dente and F. Kjellberg (eds), *The Dynamics of Institutional Change: Local Government Reorganisation in Western Democracies*. London: Sage.

Klausen, K. K. and Magnier, A. (eds) (1998). *The Anonymous Leader: Appointed CEOs in Western Local Government*. Odense: Odense University Press.

Klingemann, H. D. and Fuchs, D. (eds) (1995). *Citizens and the State: Beliefs in Government*. Oxford: Oxford University Press.

Kloosterman, R. (1994). 'Amsterdamned: The Rise of Unemployment in Amsterdam in the 1980's'. *Urban Studies*, 31: 1325–44

—— (1997*a*). 'La polarisation du marché du travail à Amsterdam et Rotterdam', in A. Maertens and M. Vervaeke (eds), *La polarisation sociale des villes européennes*. Paris: Anthropos.

—— (1997*b*). 'Room to Manœuvre: Social Polarisation and Local Politics in Rotterdam', paper for the international seminar on 'Governing Cities: International Perspective', Brussels, EURA, 18–19 September.

—— , van der Leun, J., and Rath, J. (1999). 'Mixed Embeddedness: (In)formal Activities and Immigrant Businesses in the Netherlands', *International Journal of Urban and Regional Research*, 23: 252–66.

Knapp, A. and Le Galès, P. (1993). 'Top down to Bottom Up? Centre-periphery Relations and Power Structures in France's Gaullist Party'. *West European Politics*, 16: 271–94.

Knocke, D., Pappi, F. U., Broadbent, J., and Tsujinaka, Y. (1996). *Comparing Policy Networks*. Cambridge: Cambridge University Press.

Kocka, J. (1989). *Les Employés de l'Allemagne 1850–1980*. Paris: Éditions de l'EHESS.

Kohler-Koch, B. and Eising, R. (eds) (1999). *The Transformation of Governance in the European Union*. London: Routledge.

Kooiman, J. (ed.) (1993). *Modern Governance*. London: Sage.

—— (2000*a*). 'Societal Governance: Levels, Models and Orders of Social-Political Interaction', in J. Pierre (ed.), *Debating Governance: Authority, Steering and Democracy*. Oxford: Oxford University Press.

—— (2000*b*). 'Democratic theories of governance'. Paper presented at the conference 'Democratic and Participatory Governance: From Citizens to "Holders"', European Institute of Florence, 14 September.

Koolhaas, R., Boeri, S., Kwinter, S., Tazi, N., and Ubricht, H. O. (2001). *Mutations*. Bordeaux: Arc en rêve, centre d'architecture, ACTAR.

Korpi, W. (1983). *The Democratic Class Struggle*. London: Routledge and Kegan Paul.

Koter, P., Haider, D., and Penn, I. (1993). *Marketing Places: Attracting Investment, Industry and Tourism to Cities, States and Nations.* New York: Free Press.

Kotter, J. and Lawrence, P. (1974). *Mayors in Action: Five Approaches to Urban Governance.* New York: John Wiley.

Kriesi, H. P. (1998). 'Il cambiamento dei cleavages politici in Europa'. *Rivista Italiana di Scienza politica,* 28/1: 55–80.

——, Koopmans, R., Duyvendak, J. W., and Giugni, M. (1995). *New Social Movements in Western Europe.* London: UCL Press.

Krugman, P. (1995). *Development, Geography and Economic Theory.* Cambridge, MA: MIT Press.

Kübler, D. (2000). *Politique de la drogue dans les villes suisses: entre ordre et santé.* Paris: L'Harmattan.

—— and Wälti, S. (2000). 'Drug Policy-making in Metropolitan Areas: Urban Conflicts and Governance'. *International Journal of Urban and Regional Research,* 25: 35–44.

Kunzmann, K. (1998). 'World-city Regions in Europe: Structural Change and Future Challenges', in F.-C. Lo and Y.-M. Yeung (eds), *Globalization and the World of Large Cities.* Tokyo: United Nations University Press.

—— and M. Wegener (1993). *The Pattern of Urbanisation in Western Europe, 1960–1990.* Dortmund: Institut für Raumplanung Universität.

Kürpick, S. and Weck, S. (eds) (1998). 'Policies Against Social Exclusion at the Neighbourhood Level in Germany', in A. Madanipour, G. Cars, and J. Allen (eds), *Social Exclusion in European Cities.* London: Jessica Kingsley/Regional Science Association.

Lagroye, J. (1997). *Sociologie politique* (3rd edn). Paris: Presses de Science Po.

Laino, G. and Padovani, L. (2000). 'Le partenariat pour rénover l'action publique? L'expérience italienne'. *Pôle Sud,* 12: 47–56.

Lane, F. (1973). *Venise.* Paris: Flammarion.

Lane, J. E. and Magnusson, T. (1987). 'Sweden', in E. Page and M. Goldsmith (eds), *Central and Local Government Relations: A Comparative Analysis of West European Unitary State.* London: Sage.

Lange, P. and Regini, M. (eds) (1989). *State, Market and Social Regulation.* Cambridge: Cambridge University Press.

Lapeyronnie, D. (1993). *L'individu et les minorités.* Paris: PUF.

Lascoumes, P. and Le Bourhis, P. P. (1998). 'Le bien commun comme construit territorial, identités d'action et procédures'. *Politix,* no. 42: 37–67.

Lash, S. and Urry, J. (1987). *The End of Organised Capitalism.* Cambridge: Polity Press.

—— —— (1993). *Economies of Signs and Space.* London: Sage.

Lautman, J. (1981). 'Pour une théorie de la localité'. *Cahiers Internationaux de Sociologie,* 70: 323–8.

Leach, S., Stewart, J., and Walsh, K. (eds) (1994). *The Changing Organisation and Management of Local Government.* London: Macmillan.

Leboutte, R. (1997). *Vie et mort des bassins industriels en Europe, 1750–2000.* Paris: L'Harmattan.

Leca, J. (1973). 'Le repérage du politique'. *Projet,* 71: 11–24.

—— (1985). 'Sur la gouvernabilité', in J. Leca et R. Papini (eds), *Les démocraties, sont-elles gouvernables?.* Paris: Economica.

—— (1995). 'Gouvernance et institutions publiques. L'État entre sociétés nationales et globalisation'. Mimeo.

—— (1996). 'La gouvernance de la France sous la Vème République, une perspective de sociologie comparative', in F. d'Arcy and L. Rouban (eds), *De la Vème République à l'Europe: Hommage à Jean-Louis Quermonne*. Paris: Presses de Sciences Po.

Leemans, A. R. (1970). *Changing Pattern of Local Government*. The Hague: International Union of Local Authorities.

Lefèvre, C. (1995). 'Urban Governance in OECD Countries' (background paper). Paris: OECD.

—— (1998). 'Metropolitan Government and Governance in Western Democracies: A Critical Review'. *International Journal of Urban and Regional Research*, 22: 9–25.

—— and Offner, J. M. (1991). *Les transports urbains*. Paris: Celse.

Lefèvre, H. (1968). *Le droit à la ville*. Paris: Anthropos.

Le Galès, P. (1990). 'Crise urbaine et développement économique local en Grande-Bretagne, l'apport de la nouvelle gauche urbaine'. *Revue Française de Science Politique*, 40: 714–35.

—— (1993). *Politiques urbaines et développement local: une compaison franco-britannique*. Paris: L'Harmattan.

—— (1995). 'Du gouvernement local à la gouvernance urbaine'. *Revue Française de Science Politique*, 45: 57–95.

—— (1998). 'Regulation, Territory and Governance'. *International Journal of Urban and Regional Research*, 22: 462–505.

—— (2001*a*). 'Urban Governance and Policy Networks: On the Political Boundedness of Policy Networks'. *Public Administration*, 79: 167–84.

—— (2001*b*). ' "Est maître des lieux celui qui les organise": How Rules Change When National and European Policy Domains Collide', in A. Stone Sweet, W. Sandholz, and N. Fligstein (eds), *The Institutionalisation of Europe*. Oxford: Oxford University Press.

—— and Geddes, M. (2001). 'Conclusion: Local Partnership, Welfare Regimes and Modes of Governance in Europe', in J. Benington and M. Geddes (eds), *Local Partnership and Social Cohesion in Europe*. London: Routledge.

—— and Lequesne, C. (eds) (1998). *Regions in Europe: The Paradox of Power*. London: Routledge.

—— and Mawson, J. (1995). 'Contract versus Competitive Bidding: Rationalising Urban Policy in Britain and France'. *Journal of European Public Policy*, 2/2: 205–42.

—— and E. Négrier (eds) (2000). 'Partenariats et exclusion sociale dans les villes européennes du sud'. *Pôle Sud*, n.13 (special issue).

—— and Oberti, M. (1994). 'Lieux et pratiques sociales des étudiants dans la ville'. *Annales de la Recherche Urbaine*, 63–6: 252–64.

——, Oberti, M., and Rampal, J. C. (1993). 'Localité et Vote Front national à Mantes la Jolie'. *Hérodote*, 69–70: 31–52.

—— and Thatcher, M. (eds) (1995). *Les réseaux de l'action publique, débats autour des policy networks*. Paris: L'Harmattan.

—— and Voelzkow, H. (2001). 'The Governance of Local Economies in Europe', in C. Crouch *et al.* (eds), *Local Industrial Systems in Europe: Rise or Demise?* Oxford: Oxford University Press.

Lenschow, A. (1999). 'Variation in EC Environmental Policy Integration: Agency Push Within Complex Institutional Structures'. *Journal of European Public Policy*, 4: 109–27.

Lepetit, B. (1988). *Les villes dans la France moderne (1740–1840)*. Paris: Albin Michel.

Lequesne, C. (2001). *L'Europe Bleue*. Paris: Presses de Sciences Po.

Leresche, J. P. (ed.) (2001). *La gouvernance des villes suisses*. Paris: Pedone.

—— and Joye, D. (1995). 'The Emergence of the "Lemanique Metropole": A Process of Apprenticeship'. *Political Geography*, 14: 401–17.

——, ——, and Bassand, M. (eds) (1992). *Métropolisations: interdépendances mondiales et implications lémaniques*. Geneva: Georg.

Letho, J. (2000). 'Different Cities in Different Welfare States', in A. Bagnasco and P. Le Galès (eds), *Cities in Contemporary Europe*. Cambridge: Cambridge University Press.

Lever, W. (1997). 'Glasgow, the Post-Industrial City', in C. Jensen-Butler, A. Sachar, and J. B. van Weesep (eds), *European Cities in Competition*. Aldershot: Avebury.

Lévy, J. (1994). *L'Espace légitime: sur la dimension géographique de la fonction politique*. Paris: Presses de Sciences Po.

—— (1997). *Europe, une géographie*. Paris: Hachette.

Lewis, J. and Townsend, A. (1993). 'Universités et territoires en Grande-Bretagne, Essai de quantification'. *Annales de la Recherche Urbaine*, 61–2: 46–63.

Linklater, A. (1998). *The Transformation of Political Community: Ethical Foundations of the Post-Westphalian Era*. Chapel Hill: University of South Carolina Press.

Lipset, S. (1964). 'The Changing Class Structure and Contemporary European Politics'. *Daedalus*, 93/1: 271–303.

—— and Rokkan, S. (1967). Party System and Voter Alignments: Cross National Perspectives. New York: The Free Press.

Lloyd, C. (2000). 'Globalization: Beyond the Ultra-Modernist Narrative to a Critical Realist Perspective on Geopolitics in the Cyberage'. *International Journal of Urban and Regional Research*, 24: 258–73.

Lo, F-C. and Yeung, Y.-M. (eds) (1998). *Globalization and the World of Large Cities*. Tokyo: United Nations University Press.

Loftman, P. and Nevin, B. (1998). 'Pro-Growth Local Economic Development Strategies: Civic Promotion and Local Needs in Britain's Second city, 1981–1996', in T. Hall and P. Hubbard (eds), *The Entrepreneurial City: Geography of Politics, Regime and Representation*. Chichester: John Wiley.

Logan, J. and Molotch, H. (1987). *Urban Fortunes: The Political Economy of Place*. Berkeley: The University of California Press.

—— and Swanstrom, T. (eds) (1990). *Beyond City Limits. Economic Restructuring in Comparative Perspectives*. Philadelphia: Temple Press.

Loncle-Moriceau, P. (forthcoming, 2001). 'Les jeunes et L'État, un siècle d'action publique à la marge'.

Lorrain, D. (1989). 'La montée en puissance des villes'. *Économie et Humanisme*, 305: 6–21.

—— (1991*a*). 'Public Goods and Private Operators in France', in R. Batley and G. Stoker (eds), *Local Government in Europe*. Basingstoke: Macmillan.

—— (1991*b*). 'De l'administration républicaine ou gouvernement urbain'. *Sociologie du Travail*, 31: 461–83.

—— (1993). 'Après la décentralisation, l'action publique flexible'. *Sociologie du Travail*, no. 3, 285–307.

—— (1994). 'L'oligopole compétitif: la régulation en réseaux techniques urbains'. *Annales des Mines-Réalités Industrielles*, October: 85–90.

—— (ed.) (1995). *Gestions urbaines de l'eau*. Paris: Economica.

—— (1996a). 'The Extension of the Market', in D. Lorrain and G. Stoker (eds), *The Privatization of Urban Services*. London: Frances Pinter.

—— (1996b). 'Introduction', in D. Lorrain and G. Stoker (eds), *The Privatization of Urban Services*. London: Frances Pinter.

—— (2000a). 'The Construction of Urban Service Models', in A. Bagnasco and P. Le Galès (eds), *Cities in Contemporary Europe*. Cambridge: Cambridge University Press.

—— (2000b). 'Gouverner les villes. Questions pour un agenda de recherche'. *Pôle Sud*, 13: 27–40.

—— (2001). 'L'économie paradoxales des réseaux techniques urbains', in C. Henry and E. Quinet (eds), *Concurrence et services publics*, actes des conférences Jules Dupuit. Paris: L'Harmattan.

—— and Stoker, G. (eds) (1996). *The Privatization of Urban Services*. London: Frances Pinter.

Loughlin, J. (ed.) (2001). *Subnational Democracy in the European Union*. Oxford: Oxford University Press.

—— and Keating, M. (eds) (1997). *The Political Economy of Regionalism*. London: Frank Cass.

Lovering, J. (1995). 'Creating Discourses Rather Than Jobs: The Crisis in the Cities and the Transition Fantasies of Intellectuals and Policy Makers', in P. Healey *et al.* (eds), *Managing Cities: The New Urban Context*. London: J. Wiley.

—— (1999). 'Theory Led by Policy: The Inadequacies of the "New Regionalism"'. *International Journal of Urban and Regional Research*, 23: 379–95.

Lowe, P., Murdoch, J., and Cox, G. (1995). 'A Civilised Retreat? Anti-Urbanism, Rurality, and the Making of an Anglo-Centric Culture', in P. Healey *et al.* (eds), *Managing Cities: The New Urban Context*. London: J. Wiley.

Lowndes, V. (1995). 'Citizenship and Urban Politics', in D. Judge, G. Stoker, and H. Wolman (eds), *Theories of Urban Politics*. London: Sage.

—— (1999). 'Management Change in Local Governance', in G. Stoker (ed.), *The New Management of British Local Governance*. Basingstoke, Macmillan.

Mabileau, A. (ed.) (1993). *À la recherche du local*. Paris: L'Harmattan.

—— and Sorbets, C. (ed.) (1989). *Gouverner les villes moyennes*. Paris: Pedone.

McAleavey, P. and De Rynck, S. (1997). 'Regional or Local? The EU's Future Partners in Cohesion Policy' (Robert Schuman Centre working paper 97/55). Florence: European Institute of Florence.

McCarthy, R. (1997). 'The Committee of the Regions: An Advisory Body's Tortuous Path to Influence'. *Journal of European Public Policy*, 4: 439–54.

McDowell, L. (1997). *Capital Culture: Gender At Work in the City*. Oxford: Blackwell.

—— (1999). *Gender, Identity and Place*. Oxford: Polity Press.

McLaverty, P. (1998). 'The Public Sphere and Local Democracy'. *Democratization*, 5: 224–39.

MacLeod, G. (1999). 'Entrepreneurial Spaces, Hegemony, and State Strategy: The Political Shaping of Privatism in Lowland Scotland'. *Environment and Planning A*, 31: 345–75.

—— (2001). 'New Regionalism Reconsidered: Globalization, Regulation and the Recasting of Political Economic Space'. *International Journal of Urban and Regional Research*, 25: 804–29.

Madanipour, A., Cars, G., and Allen, J. (eds) (1998). *Social Exclusion in European Cities*. London: Jessica Kingsley/Regional Science Association.

Maertens, A. and Vervaeke, M. (eds) (1997). *La polarisation sociale des villes européennes*. Paris: Anthropos.

Magnier, A. (1996). *L'Europea delle grande città*. Padua: CEDAM.

—— (1999). 'La difficile renaissance des grandes villes italiennes', in O. Gabriel and V. Hoffmann-Martinot (eds), *Démocraties urbaines*. Paris: L'Harmattan.

—— (2001). 'Une nouvelle culture professionnelle européenne pour les administrateurs territoriaux'. Paper presented to the journée d'étude du Commissariat au Plan, 'L'Europe, vue du bas'. Paris: 27 June.

Mair, P. (1997). *Party System Changes*. Oxford: Oxford University Press.

Majone, G. (1996a). *La communauté européenne, un État régulateur*. Paris: Montchrestien.

—— (ed.) (1996b). *Regulating Europe*. London, Routledge.

Manin, B. (1995). *Principes du gouvernement représentatif*. Paris: Flammarion.

Mann, M. (1993). *The Sources of Social Power, vol. II. The Rise of Classes and Nation-states, 1760–1914*. Cambridge: Cambridge University Press.

—— (1997). 'Has Globalisation Ended the Rise and Rise of the Nation-State?' *International Review of Political Economy*, 4/3: 472–96.

—— (1998). 'Is there a Society Called Euro?', in R. Axtmann, R. (ed.), *Globalization and Europe*. London: Pinter.

March, J. and Olsen J. (1989). *Rediscovering Institutions*. London: Macmillan.

—— —— (1995). *Democratic Governance*. New York: The Free Press.

Marcou, G. (1993). 'New Tendencies of Local Government Development in Europe', in R. Bennett (ed.) (1993). *Local Government in the New Europe*. London: Pinter.

—— (1999). 'L'autonomie des collectivités locales en Europe', *Les 2ème entretiens de la caisse des Dépôts*. La Tour d'Aigue: Éditions de l'Aube.

——, Rangeon, F., and Thiébault, J. L. (eds) (1997). *La coopération contractuelle et le gouvernement des villes*. Paris: L'Harmattan.

Marcuse, P. (1993). 'What's so New About Divided Cities? *International Journal of Urban and Regional Research*, 17: 697–708.

—— and Van Kempen, R. (ed.) (2000). *Globalizing Cities: A New Spatial Order?*. Oxford: Blackwell.

Marks, G. and Hooghe (1996). 'Les accès des régions à Bruxelles', in V. Wright and S. Cassese (eds), *La recomposition de l'État en Europe*. Paris: La Découverte.

—— —— (2001). *Multi-level Governance and European Integration*. Lanham, MD: Rowman and Littlefields.

——, ——, and Blank, L. (1996). 'European Integration from the 1980's: State-centric versus Multi-level Governance'. *Journal of Common Market Studies*, 34: 341–78.

——, Sharpf, F, Schmitter, P., and Streeck, W. (eds) (1996). *Governance in the European Union*. London: Sage.

Marsh, D. and Rhodes, R. (eds) (1992). *Policy Networks in British Government*. Oxford: Clarendon Press.

Martin, R. and Sunley, P. (2000). 'L'économie géographique de Paul Krugman et ses conséquences pour la théorie du développement régional: une évaluation critique', in Benko, G. and Lipietz, A. (eds), *La richesse des régions. La nouvelle géographique socio-économique*. Paris: PUF.

Martinotti, G. (1992). *Metropoli, la nuova morfologia sociale della città*. Bologna: Il Mulino.

—— (1999a). 'A City for Whom? Transients and Public Life in the Second-Generation Metropolis', in R. Beauregard and S. Body-Gendrot (eds), *The Urban Moment*. London: Sage.

—— (ed.) (1999b). *La dimensione metropolitana, sviluppo e governo della nuova città*. Bologna: Il Mulino.

Massey, A. (ed.) (1997). *Globalisation and Marketisation of Government Services*. London: Macmillan.

Matejko, L. (2000). 'Du pouvoir éclaté au leadership urbain, patronat et classe politique dans l'aire lilloise'. Paper presented at a colloquium on 'leadership'. Bordeaux: CERVL, November.

Mattina, C. and Allum, F. (2000). 'La personnalisation du gouvernement municipal en Italie. L'expérience du maire de Naples'. *Pôle Sud*, 13: 57–70.

May, N., Veltz, P., Landrieu, J., and Spector, T. (eds) (1998). *La ville éclatée*. La Tour d'Aigues: Éditions de l'Aube.

Mayer, M. (1987). 'Restructuring and Popular Opposition in West German Cities', in M. P. Smith et J. Feagin (eds), *The Capitalist City*. Oxford: Blackwell.

—— (1995). 'Urban Governance in the Post-Fordist City', in P. Healey *et al.* (eds), *Managing Cities: The New Urban Context*. Chichester: John Wiley.

—— (2000a). 'Urban Movement and Urban Theory in the Late-Twentieth Century', in R. Beauregard and S. Body-Gendrot (eds), *The Urban Moment*. London: Sage.

—— (2000b). 'Social Movements in European Cities: Transition from the 1970's to the 1990's', in A. Bagnasco and P. Le Galès (eds), *Cities in Contemporary Europe*. Cambridge: Cambridge University Press.

—— and Ely, J. (1998). *The German Greens: Paradox between Movement and Party*. Philadelphia: Temple University Press.

Mayer, N. (2000c). *Ces français qui votent FN*. Paris: Flammarion.

Mayntz, R. (1993). 'Governing Failures and the Problem of Governability', in J. Kooiman (ed.) (1993). *Modern Governance*. London: Sage.

—— (1999). 'La teoria della governance: sfide e prospettive'. *Rivista Italiana di scienza politica*, 29/1: 3–21.

Mazey, S. and Richardson, J. (eds) (1993). *Lobbying in the European Community*. Oxford: Oxford University Press.

—— —— (2001). 'Institutionalizing Promiscuity: Commission-interest Groups in the EU', in A. Stone Sweet, W. Sandholz, and N. Fligstein (eds), *The Institutionalisation of Europe*. Oxford: Oxford University Press.

Mazza, L. (ed.) (1988). *World Cities and the Future of the Metropolis*. Milan: Electra.

Mendras, H. (1988). *La seconde révolution française: 1965–1984*. Paris: Gallimard.

—— (1995). *Sociétés paysannes, éléments pour une théorie de la paysannerie*. Paris: Gallimard.

—— (1997). *L'Europe des européens. Sociologie de l'Europe occidentale*. Paris: Gallimard.

Mény, Y. (1999). 'Démocratie locale, coopération, solidarité: défis et enjeux de la libre administration des collectivités locales'. *Les 2ème entretiens de la Caisse des Dépôts et Consignations*. La tour d'Aigues: Éditions de l'Aube.

——, Muller, P., and Quermonne, J. L. (eds) (1995). *Politiques publiques en Europe*. Paris: L'Harmattan.

Mény, Y. and Wright, V. (eds) (1985). *Centre-Periphery Relations in Western Europe*. London: Allen and Unwin.

Merton, R. (1965). *Éléments de théorie et de méthode sociologique*. Paris: Plon.
Meyer, D. and Tarrow, S. (eds) (1998). *The Social Movement Society: People, Passions and Power*. Lanham, MD: Rowman & Littlefield.
Meyer, J. (2000). 'Globalization: Sources and Effects on States and Societies'. *International Sociology*, 5: 233–48.
——, Boli, J., Thomas, G., and Ramirez, F. (1997). 'World Society and the Nation-State'. *American Journal of Sociology*, 103: 144–81.
Milanesi, E. (2000). 'Dal government alla governance nella regolazione locale: quale forma del piano? Riflessioni sul piano strategico del Nord Milan'. Contribution to a colloquium of DAEST, University of Venice, research programme 'Giovani ricercatori', MURST, September.
Mingione, E., (1991). *Fragmented Societies*. Oxford: Blackwell.
—— (ed.) (1996). *Urban Poverty and the Underclass*. Oxford: Blackwell.
—— (1997). *Sociologia della economia*. Rome: NIS.
—— (ed.) (1999*a*). *Le sfide dell'esclusione: metodi, lughi, soggetti*. Bologna: Il Mulino.
—— (1999*b*) 'Immigrants and the Informal Economy In European Cities' (Symposium). *International Journal of Urban and Regional Research*, 23/2.
—— and Morlicchio, E. (1993). 'New Forms of Urban Poverty in Italy: Risks Path Models in the North and South'. *International Journal of Urban and Regional Research*, 17: 413–27.
Ministère de l'Intérieur (1998, 2000). *Les collectivités locales en chiffres*. Paris: La Documentation Française.
Mollenkopf, J. and Castells, M. (ed.) (1992). *Dual City*. New York: Russell Sage Foundation.
Montagné, M. A. (2001). *Le leadership local*. Paris: L'Harmattan.
Montin, S. and Amna, E. (2000). 'The Local Government Act and Local Government Reform in Sweden', in E. Amna and S. Montin (eds), *Towards a New Conception of Local Self-government*. Bergen: Fagbokforlaget.
Moravscik, A. (1999). *The Choice of Europe*. London, Routledge.
Moriconi-Ebrard, F. (2000). *De Babylone à Tokyo. Les grandes agglomérations du Monde*. Paris: Ophrys.
Morris, L. (1993). 'Is There a British Underclass?' *International Journal of Urban and Regional Research*, 17: 404–22.
—— (1995). *Social Divisions: Economic Decline and Social Structural Changes*. Cambridge: Cambridge University Press.
Mouritzen, P. E. (ed.) (1993). *Defending City Welfare*. London: Sage.
Mumford, L. (1961). *The City in History*. New York: Harcourt, Brace and World.
Müsil, R. (1965). *L'homme dans qualité*. Paris: Le Seuil.
Musterd, S. and Ostendorf, W. (eds) (1998). *Urban Segregation and The Welfare State*. London: Routledge.
—— and de Winter, M. (1998). 'Conditions for Social Segregation: Some European Perspectives'. *International Journal of Urban and Regional Research*, 22: 665–73.
Nas, P. (1998). 'Congealed Time, Compressed Space: Roots and Branches of Urban Symbolic Ecology. Introduction to the Special Issue "Urban Rituals And Symbols" '. *International Journal of Urban and Regional Research*, 22: 545–9.
Nash, K. and Scott, A. (eds) (2001). *Blackwell Companion of Political Sociology*. Oxford: Blackwell.
Negri, N. and Sciolla, L. (eds) (1996). *Il paese dei paradossi. Le basi sociali della politica in Italia*. Rome: La Nuova Italia Scientifica.

Négrier, E. (1997). 'French Cultural Decentralization and International Expansion. Towards a Geometrically Variable Interculturalism?' *International Journal of Urban and Regional Research*, 21: 63–74.

—— and Jouve, B. (eds) (1998). *Que gouvernent les régions en Europe?*. Paris: L'Harmattan.

Neill, W., Fitzsimons, D., and Murtagh, B. (eds) (1995). *Reimaging the Pariah City: Urban Development in Belfast and Detroit*. Aldershot: Avebury.

Nevers, J. Y. (1985). 'Du clientélisme à la technocratie, cent ans de démocratie dans une grande ville, Toulouse'. *Revue Française de science politique*, 33: 428–54.

Neveu, C. (ed.) (1999). *Espace public et engagement politique*. Paris: L'Harmattan.

Neveu, E. (2000). *Sociologie des mouvements sociaux*. Paris: La Découverte.

Newman, P. and Thornley, A. (1996). *Urban Planning in Europe: International Competitions, National Systems*. London: Routledge.

Nordstat (1999). *Major Nordic Cities and Regions: Statistics on 16 Major Cities and their Regions*. Stockholm: Elander.

North, D. (1990). *Institutions, Institutional Change and Economic Performance*. Cambridge: Cambridge University Press.

North, P., Valler, D., and Wood, A. (2001). 'Talking Business: Towards an Actor-Centre Analysis of Business Agendas for Local Economic Development'. *International Journal of Urban and Regional Research*, 25/4: 830–46.

Oberti, M. (1995). 'Analyse localisée, quartiers et cités'. *Sociétés Contemporaines*, 22/23: 127–43.

—— (1996). 'La relégation urbaine en Europe', in S. Paugam (ed.), *L'exclusion, l'état des savoirs*. Paris: La Découverte.

—— (2000). 'Local Forms of Urban Anti-Poverty Strategies in Europe'. *International Journal of Urban and Regional Research*, 24: 536–53.

—— and Le Galès, P. (1995). 'Le rapport à la ville, les pratiques sociales et les lieux', in O. Galland *et al.*, *Le monde des étudiants*. Paris: PUF.

O'Brien, R. (1992). *Global Financial Integration: The End of Geography*. London: Pinter.

Observatoire du Changement Social (ed.) (1986). *L'esprit des Lieux*. Paris: Éditions du CNRS.

O'Connor, J. (1987). *The Meaning of the Crisis*. Oxford: Blackwell.

OECD (Organisation for Economic Cooperation and Development) (2001). *Economic Outlook*, 69. Paris: OECD.

Offe, C. (1985). *Disorganised Capitalism*. Cambridge: Polity Press.

—— and Wiesenthal, H. (1980). 'Two logics of collective action: theoretical note of social class and organizational form'. *Political Power and Social Theory*, 1. Greenwich, CT: Jai Press.

Offner, J. (2000). 'Territorial Deregulation: Local Authorities at Risk from Technical Networks'. *International Journal of Urban and Regional Research*, 24/1: 165–82.

—— and Pumain, D. (1996). *Réseaux et territoires*. La Tour d'Aigues: Éditions de l'Aube.

Ohmae, K. (1990). *The Borderless World: Power and Strategy in the Interlinked Economy*. New York: Harper Business.

—— (1995). *The End of the Nation-State*. New York: Free Press.

Osborne, D. and Gaebler, T. (1993). *Reinventing Government*. New York: Plume Books.

Pace, E. (1998). *La nation italienne en crise: perspectives européennes*. Paris: Bayard.

Paci, M. (1996). 'Ceti emergenti, aree territoriali e mobilizatione politica', in N. Negri and L. Sciolla (eds), *Il paese dei paradossi. Le basi sociali della politica in Italia*. Rome: La Nuova Italia Scientifica.

Padioleau, J. G. (1991). 'L'action publique urbaine moderniste'. *Politiques et Management public*, 9/3: 133–43.

Page, E. (1991). *Localism and Centralism in Europe: The Political and Legal Bases of Local Self-Government*. Oxford: Oxford University Press.

—— and M. Goldsmith (eds) (1987). *Central and Local Government Relations: A Comparative Analysis of West European Unitary State*. London: Sage.

Painter, J. (1998). 'Entrepreneurs are Made, Not Born: Learning and Urban Regimes in the Production of Entrepreneurial Cities', in T. Hall and P. Hubbard (eds), *The Entrepreneurial City: Geography of Politics, Regime and Representation*. Chichester: John Wiley.

Palier, B. and Bonoli, G. (2000). 'La montée en puissance des fonds de pension: une lecture comparative des réformes des systèmes de retraite entre modèle global et cheminements nationaux'. *Année de la Régulation*, 4: 209–50.

Papadopoulos, Y. (1998). *Démocratie directe*. Paris: Economica.

Pasquier, R. (2000). *La capacité politique des régions. Une comparaison France-Espagne*. Rennes: Doctorat IEP Rennes, Université de Rennes 1.

Paugam, S. (1993). *La société française et ses pauvres*. Paris: PUF.

—— (ed.) (1996). *L'exclusion, l'état des savoirs*. Paris: La Découverte.

Péchu, C. (1996). 'Quand les exclus pasent à l'action: la mobilisation des mal-logés'. *Politix*, 34: 115–34.

—— (1999). 'Black Immigrants in France and Claims for Housing'. *Journal of Ethnic and Migration Studies*, 25: 727–44.

Peck, J. (1996). *Work Place: The Social Regulation of Labor Markets*. New York: Guildford Press.

—— (1998). 'Geographies of governance: TECs and the Neo-liberalisation of "Local Interests"'. *Space and Polity*, 2/1: 5–31.

—— and Tickell, A. 'Searching for a New Institutional Fix: The After Fordist Crisis and the Global-Local Order', in A. Amin, *Post-fordism: A Reader*. Oxford: Blackwell.

—— —— (1995). 'Business Goes Local: Dissecting the "Business Agenda" in Manchester'. *International Journal of Urban and Regional Research*, 19/3: 55–78.

Perrineau, P. (ed.) (2001). *Les croisés de la société fermée: l'Europe des extrêmes droites*. La Tour d'Aigues: Éditions de l'Aube.

Perulli, P. (1992). *Atlante metropolitano. Il mutamente sociale nelle grandi citta*. Bologna: Il Mulino.

—— (1994). 'Lo stato delle città'. *Il Mulino*, 353: 479–89.

—— (1995). 'Stato, regioni, economie di rete'. *Stato e Mercato*, 2.

—— (ed.) (1998). *Neoregionalismo*. Turin: Bollati Bolinghieri.

—— (1999a). *La città delle reti*. Turin: Bollati Bolinghieri.

—— (1999b). 'Territorial Interests and the Governance of Local Economies in Italy', paper presented at the EURA colloquium. Paris, October.

Peterson, P. (1981). *City Limits*. Chicago: University of Chicago Press.

Petit-Dutaillis, Ch. (1971). *La monarchie féodale en France et en Angleterre*. Paris: Albin Michel.

Pichierri, A. (1995). 'Stato et identità economiche regionali'. *Stato e Mercato*, 45: 213–29.

—— (1997). *Citta Stato. Economia et political del modello anseatico*. Venice: Marsilio.
Pickvance, C. (1995*a*). 'Marxist Theories of Urban Politics', in D. Judge, G. Stoker, and H. Wolman (eds), *Theories of Urban Politics*. London: Sage.
—— (1995*b*). 'Where are Urban Movements Gone?', in C. Hadjimalis and D. Sadler (eds), *Europe at the Margins: New Mosaics of Inequality*. London: Wiley.
—— and Préteceille, E. (eds) (1991). *State Restructuring And Local Power: A Comparative Perspective*. London: Pinter.
Pierre, J. (1999). 'Models of Urban Governance: The Institutional Dimension of Urban Politics'. *Urban Affairs Review*, 34: 372–96.
—— (ed.) (2000). *Debating Governance: Authority, Steering and Democracy*. Oxford: Oxford University Press.
Pinçon, M. and Pinçon-Charlot, M. (1989). *Dans les beaux quartiers*. Paris: Seuil.
—— —— (2000). *Sociologie de la bourgeoisie*. Paris: La Découverte.
Pinçon-Charlot, M., Préteceille, E., and Rendu, P. (1986). *Ségrégation urbaine*. Paris: Anthropos.
Pinol, J. L. (1991). *Le monde des villes au XIXème siècle*. Paris: Hachette.
Pinson, G. (1999). 'Les échelles politiques du projet. Projets urbains et construction des gouvernements urbains'. *Les Annales de la recherche urbaine*, 82: 88–102.
—— (2000). 'Projet et projets urbains à Venise' (roneo). Rennes.
—— (forthcoming). 'Political government and governance. Strategic planning and political capacity in Turin'. FURS, *International Journal of Urban and Regional Research*. 26.2.
—— and Vion, A. (2000). 'L'internationalisation des villes comme objet d'expertise'. *Pôle Sud*, 13: 85–100.
Pirenne, H. (1969). *Histoire économique et sociale du Moyen Âge*. Paris: PUF.
—— (1971). *Les villes du Moyen Âge*. Paris: PUF.
Plaza, B. (1999). 'The Guggenheim-Bilbao Museum Effect'. *International Journal of Urban and Regional Research*, 23: 589–93.
Poggi, G. (1990). *The State: Its Nature, Development and Prospects*. Stanford, Stanford University Press.
—— (1996). 'La nature changeante de l'État: L'État et quelques aspects de son histoire', in V. Wright and S. Cassese (eds), *La recomposition de l'État en Europe*. Paris: La Découverte.
Polanyi, K. (1955). *The Great Transformation*. New York: Rinehart.
Pôle Sud (2000). 'Numéro spécial: Partenariats contre l'exclusion'. No. 12.
Pollitt, C., Birchall, J., and Putnam, K. (1999). 'Letting Managers Manage: Decentralisation and Opting Out', in G. Stoker (ed.), *The New Management of British Local Governance*. Basingstoke, Macmillan.
Poncela, Pierrette and Lascoumes, Pierre (1998). *Réformer le Code pénal. Où est passé l'architecte?*. Paris: PUF.
Porla, G. (1999). 'Perspectives de l'autonomie financière des collectivités locales en Europe'. *Les 2ème entretiens de la Caisse des Dépôts et Consignations*. La Tour d'Aigues: Éditions de l'Aube.
Poupeau, F. M. (2001). 'Libéralisation du service public et action publique locale'. *Sociologie du Travail*, 43/2: 179–95.
Poussou, J. P. (1992). *La croissance des villes au XIXème siècle*. Paris: SEDES.
Poussou, J. P. *et al.* (1983). *Études sur les villes en Europe Occidentale*. Paris: SEDES.
Powell, W. and Di Maggio, P. (1991). *New Institutionalism in Organizational Analysis*. Chicago: University of Chicago Press.

Pratchett, L. and Wilson, D. (eds) (1996). *Local Democracy and Local Government.* Basingstoke: Macmillan.

Préteceille, E. (1988). *Mutations urbaines et sociétés locales.* Paris: CSU.

—— (1995). 'Division sociale et globalisation'. *Sociétés Contemporaines,* 22/23: 33–68.

—— (1999). 'Inégalités urbaines, gouvernance, domination? Réflexions sur l'agglomération parisienne', in R. Balme, A. Faure, and A. Mabileau (eds), *Politiques locales et transformations de l'action publique locale en Europe.* Paris: Presses de Sciences Po.

—— (2000). 'Segregation, Class and Politics in Large Cities', in A. Bagnasco and P. Le Galès (eds), *Cities in Contemporary Europe.* Cambridge: Cambridge University Press.

Przeworski, A., Stokes, S., and Manin, B. (eds) (1999). *Democracy, Accountability and Representation.* Cambridge: Cambridge University Press.

Pugliese, E. (1995). 'New International Migrations and the European Fortress', in C. Hadjimalis and D. Sadler (eds), *Europe at the Margins: New Mosaics of Inequality.* London: Wiley.

Pumain, D. and Godard, F. (eds) (1996). *Données urbaines 1.* Paris: Anthropos.

—— and Mattei, M. F. (eds) (1998). *Données urbaines 2.* Paris: Anthropos.

Quassoli, F. (1999). 'Migrants in the Italian Underground Economy'. *International Journal of Urban and Regional Research,* 23: 212–31.

Quilley, S. (2000). 'Manchester First: From Municipal Socialism to an Entrepreneurial City'. *International Journal of Urban and Regional Research,* 24: 601–15.

Radaelli, C. (2000). 'Whether Europeanisation? Concept Stretching and Substantive Change', paper presented at the PSA conference. London, April.

Rallings, C., Temple, M., and Trasher, M. (1996). 'Participation in Local Elections', in L. Pratchett and D. Wilson (eds), *Local Democracy and Local Government.* Basingstoke: Macmillan.

Rao, A. M. and Supphellen, S. (1998). 'Les élites du pouvoir et les territoires "dépendants"', in W. Reinhard (ed.), *Les élites du pouvoir et la construction de l'État en Europe.* Paris: PUF.

Regini, M. (ed.) (1988). *The Future of the Labour Movement.* London: Sage.

—— (1995). *Uncertain Boundaries: The Social and Political Construction of European Economies.* Cambridge: Cambridge University Press.

Reidenbach, M. (1996). 'The Privatization of Urban Services in Germany', in D. Lorrain and G. Stoker (eds), *The Privatization of Urban Services.* London: Frances Pinter.

Reinhard, W. (ed.) (1996). *Les élites du pouvoir et la construction de l'État en Europe.* Paris: PUF.

Rex, J. (1996). *Ethnic Minorities in the Modern Nation-State.* Basingstoke: Macmillan.

—— (1997). 'Immigrants in Europe', in R. Axtmann (ed.), *Globalisation and Europe.* New York: Brookings.

Rhodes, M. (ed.) (1995). *Regions and the New Europe.* Manchester: Manchester University Press.

Rhodes, R. (1986). *The National World of Local Government.* London: Allen and Unwin.

—— (1997). *Modern Governance.* London: Macmillan.

—— (2000). 'Governance and Public Administration', in J. Pierre (ed.), *Debating Governance: Authority, Steering and Democracy.* Oxford: Oxford University Press.

Rigaudière, A. (1988). 'Réglementation urbaine et "législation d'État" dans les villes du midi français au XIIIème et XIVème siècles', in N. Bulst and J.-Ph. Genet (eds), *La ville, la bourgeoisie et la genèse de l'État moderne*. Paris: Éditions du CNRS.

—— (1993). *Gouverner la ville au Moyen Âge*. Paris: Anthropos. Paris.

Robertson, R. (1992). *Globalization: Social Theory and Global Culture*. London: Sage.

Rodriguez Posé, A. (1998). *Dynamics of Regional Growth in Europe*. Oxford: Oxford University Press.

Rogowski, R. (1999). 'The Zipf Law and the Future of European Cities' (memo.). Los Angeles: UCLA.

Rokkan, S. (1973). 'Cities, States and Nations: A Dimensional Model for the Study of Contrasts in Development', in S. N. Eisenstadt and S. Rokkan (eds), *Building States and Nations*. London: Sage.

—— (1975). 'Dimensions of State-Formation and Nation-Building: A Possible Paradigm for Research on Variations Within Europe', in C. Tilly (ed.), *The Formation of National States in Western Europe*. Princeton: Princeton University Press.

Rose, L. (1990). 'Nordic Free-Commune Experiments: Increased Local Autonomy or Continued Central Control?', in D. King and J. Pierre (eds), *Challenges to Local Government*. London: Sage.

Rose, N. (2000). 'Governing Cities, Governing Citizen', in Isin, I. (ed.), *Democracy, Citizenship and the Global City*. London: Routledge.

Rösener, W. (1994). *Les paysans dans l'histoire de l'Europe*. Paris: Seuil.

Roth, R. (1991). 'Local Green Politics in West German Cities'. *International Journal of Urban and Regional Research*, 15: 75–89.

Rouban, L. (1998). 'L'Europe comme dépassement de l'État'. *Revue suisse de science politique*, 4/4: 56–79.

Rousseau, M. P. (1998). *La productivité des grandes villes*. Paris: Economica.

Rucht, D. (1998). 'The Structure and Culture of Collective Protest', in D. Meyer and S. Tarrow (eds), *The Social Movement Society: People, Passions and Power*. Lanham, MD: Rowman & Littlefield.

Rucquoi, A. (1990). 'Genèse médiévale de l'Espagne moderne: du pouvoir et de la nation, 1250–1516', in J. P. Genet (ed.), *L'État moderne: genèse*. Paris: éditions du CNRS.

Ruggie, J. (1993). 'Territoriality and Beyond: Problematizing Modernity in International Relations'. *International Organisation*, 47/1: 139–74.

Ruggiero, V. (2000). *Movimenti nella città: Gruppi in conflitto nella metropoli europea*. Milan: Bollati, Boringhieri.

Ruggiu, F. J. (1997). *Les élites et les villes moyennes en France et en Angleterre (XVIIème et XVIIIème siècles)*. Paris: L'Harmattan.

Sadler, D. (1995). 'Old industrial Regions: Limits to Reindustrialisation', in C. Hadjimalis and D. Sadler (eds), *Europe at the Margins: New Mosaics of Inequality*. London: Wiley.

Sallez, A. (ed.) (1993). *Les villes, lieux d'Europe*. La Tour d'Aigues: Éditions de l'Aube/Datar.

Salone, C. (1997). 'Le politiche urbane et territoriali nell'europa comunitaria', in G. Dematteis and P. Bonavero (eds), *Il sistema urbano italiano nell spazio unificato europeo*. Bologna: Il Mulino.

Sandberg, S. (1998). 'The Strong CEOs of Finland', in K. K. Klausen and A. Magnier (eds), *The Anonymous Leader: Appointed CEOs in Western Local Government*. Odense: Odense University Press.

Sandholtz, W. and Stone Sweet, A. (eds) (1998). *European Integration and Supranational Governance*. Oxford: Oxford University Press.

Saraceno, C., Bonny, Y., Garcia, M., Gustafson, B., Mingione, E., Oberti, M., Pereirinha, J., and Voges, W. (eds) (1998). *Evaluation of Social Policies at the Local Urban Level: Income Support for the Able Bodied* (Research report for DX XII). Brussels: European Union.

Sassen, S. (1991). *The Global City*. Princeton: Princeton University Press.

—— (1994). *Cities in a World Economy*. London: Pine Forge Press.

—— (1998a). 'The Impact of the New Technologies and Globalization on Cities', in F.-C. Lo and Y.-M. Yeung (eds), *Globalization and the World of Large Cities*. Tokyo: United Nations University Press.

—— (1998b). *Globalization and its Discontents*. New York: The New Press.

—— (2000). 'Territory and Territoriality in the Global Economy'. *International Sociology*, 15: 372–93.

Saunders, P. (1979). *Urban Politics: A Sociological Interpretation*. London: Hutchinson.

—— (1986). *Social Theory and the Urban Question* (2nd edn). London: Hutchinson.

Saunier, P. Y. (2000). 'Sketches from the Urban Internationale, 1910–1950: Voluntary Associations, International Institutions and US Philanthropic Foundations'. *International Journal of Urban and Regional Research*, 25: 380–403.

Sauvage, A. (1996). 'Villes estudiantines'. *Espaces et sociétés*, 80/81: 35–48.

Savage, M., Barlow, J., Dickens, P., and Fielding, T. (1992). *Property, Bureaucracy and Culture: Middle Class Formation in Contemporary Britain*. London: Routledge.

Savino, A. (1998). 'Università, città, studenti: aspetti complessi di interdepenze non sempre note', *Archivio di studi urbani e regionali*, 60–61: 13–84.

Sbragia, A. (1996). *Debt Wish, Entrepreneurial Cities, US Federalism and Economic Development*. Pittsburgh: University of Pittsburgh Press.

Scharpf, F. (2000). *Governing Europe*. Oxford: Oxford University Press.

Schmitter, P. (1997). 'The Emerging Europolity and its Impact upon National Systems of Production', in J. R. Hollingsworth and R. Boyer (eds), *Contemporary Capitalism: The Embeddedness of Institutions*. Cambridge: Cambridge University Press.

—— (forthcoming, 2002). 'Governance', in H. Heinelt, J. Grote *Participatory governance: political and societal implications*. Berlin: Leske and Budrich.

Schnapper, D. and Lewis, B. (eds) (1994). *Muslims in Europe*. London: Frances Pinter.

Schulze, H. (1996). *État et Nation dans l'Histoire de l'Europe*. Paris: Seuil.

Schumpeter, J. (1972). *Capitalisme, socialisme et démocratie*. Paris: Payot. (First edition in English, 1942.)

Schweisguth, E. (1995). 'La montée des valeurs individualistes'. *Futuribles*, 200: 131–60.

Scott, A. (ed.) (1997). *The Limits of Globalization*. London: Routledge.

Scott, A. J. (1988). *Metropolis: From the Division of Labour to Urban Form*. Berkeley: University of California Press.

—— (1998). *Regions and the World Economy*. Oxford: Oxford University Press.

—— (ed.) (2001). *Global City-Regions, Trends, Theory, Policy*. Oxford: Oxford University Press.

Sebastiani, C. (1998). 'Citizen's Committees, Social Protest and Urban Democracy' (paper presented to IPSA conference). Charlottesville, September 1998.

—— (1999). 'Spazio e sfera pubblica: la politica nella città'. *Rassegna Italiana di Sociologia*, 38: 223–43.

Sellers, J. (1995). 'Post Industrial Expansion and the Local Left: Growth Politics and Green Milieux in French and German University Towns' (paper delivered to the APSA conference). Chicago, September.

—— (2001). *Governing from Below: Urban Politics and Post-Industrial Economy*. Cambridge, Cambridge University Press.

Selznick, P. (1957). *Leadership in Administration*. New York: Harper and Row.

Sennett, R. (1990). *The Conscience of the Eye: The Design and Social Life of Cities*. New York: Alfred Knopf.

Seyd, P. (1987). *The Rise And Fall of the Labour Left*. Basingstoke: Macmillan.

—— (1990). 'Radical Sheffield: From Socialism to Entrepreneurialism'. *Political Studies*, 38: 335–44.

Sharpe, L. J. (1970). 'Theories and Values of Local Government'. *Political Studies*, 18: 153–74.

—— (ed.) (1993). *The Rise of Meso Government in Europe*. London: Sage.

—— (ed.) (1995). *The Government of World Cities: The Future of the Metro Model*. Chichester: John Wiley.

Shaw, K. (1993). 'The Development of a New Urban Corporatism: The Politics of Urban Regeneration in the North East of England'. *Regional Studies*, 27: 251–86.

Shaw, M. (1997). 'The State of Globalization: Towards a Theory of State Transformation'. *Review of International Political Economy*, 4: 497–513.

Shields, R. (1999). 'Culture and the Economy of Cities'. *European Urban and Regional Studies*, 6: 303–11.

Shonfield, A. (1965). *Modern Capitalism*. Oxford: Oxford University Press.

Shore, C. and Black, A. (1996). 'Citizens' Europe and the Construction of European Identity', in V. Goddard *et al.* (eds), *The Anthropology of Europe*. London: Berg.

Silver, H. (1993). 'National Conceptions of the New Urban Poverty'. *International Journal of Urban and Regional Research*, 17: 336–54.

Simmel, G. (1965). *Les grandes villes et la vie de l'Esprit*, French translation in F. Choay, *L'urbanisme, utopies et réalités*. Paris: Seuil.

Sklair, L. (1995). *The Sociology of Globalisation*. London: Harvester and Wheatsheaf.

—— (1997). 'The Nature and Significance of Economic Sociology' (review essay). *Review of International Political Economy*, 4: 239–44.

—— (2001). *The Transnational Capitalist Class*. Oxford: Blackwell.

Smith, A. (1995). *L'Europe au miroir du local: La réforme des fonds structurels*. Paris: L'Harmattan.

—— and Genyes, W. (eds) (forthcoming, 2002). *Leadership et territoire*.

Smith, M. P. and Guardino, L. E. (eds) (1998). *Transnationalism from Below*. New Brunswick: Transaction Publishers.

Smith, N. (1995). 'Remaking Scale: Competition and Cooperation in Prenational and Postnational Europe', in H. Eskelinen and F. Snickars (eds), *Competitive European Peripheries*. Berlin: Springer.

—— (1996). *The New Urban Frontier: Gentrification and the Revanchist City*. London: Routledge.

Smouts, M. C. (ed.) (1998a). *Les nouvelles relations internationales*. Paris: Presses de Sciences Po.

—— (1998b). 'Region as a New Imagined Community?', in P. Le Galès and C. Lequesne (eds), *Regions in Europe: The Paradox of Power*. London: Routledge.

Soysal, Y. (1994). *Limits of Citizenship: Migrants and Post-National Membership in Europe*. Chicago: Chicago University Press.

Spybey, T. (1996). *Globalization and World Society*. Cambridge: Polity Press.
Stacey, M. (1969). 'The Myth of Community Studies'. *British Journal of Sociology*, 20: 134–47.
Stoker, G. (1995*a*). 'Grande-Bretagne, Le volontarisme politique', in D. Lorrain and G. Stoker (eds), *La Privatisation des Services Urbains en Europe*. Paris: La Découverte.
—— (1995*b*). 'Regime Theory and Urban Politics', in D. Judge, G. Stoker, and H. Wolman (eds), *Theories of Urban Politics*. London: Sage.
—— (ed.) (1999). *The New Management of British Local Governance*. Basingstoke, Macmillan.
—— (ed.) (2000). *The New Politics Of British Local Governance*. Basingstoke, Macmillan.
—— and Mossberger, K. (1994). 'Urban Regime in Comparative Perspective'. *Government and Policy*, 12/2: 195–212.
Stone, C. (1989). *Regime Politics: Governing Atlanta, 1946–1988*. Lawrence: University Press of Kansas.
—— (2001). 'The Atlanta Experience Reexamined'. *International Journal of Urban and Regional Research*, 25: 20–34.
Stone Sweet, A. (2000). *Governing with Judges: Constitutional Politics in Europe*. Oxford: Oxford University Press.
——, Sandholz, W., and Fligstein, N. (eds) (2001). *The Institutionalization of Europe*. Oxford: Oxford University Press.
Storper, M. (1997). *The Regional World*. New York: Guildford Press.
Strange, S. (1996). *The Retreat of the State, The Diffusion of Power in the World Economy*. Cambridge: Cambridge University Press.
Streeck, W. (1992). *Social Institutions and Economic Performance*. London: Sage.
Strom, E. (1996). 'The Political Context of Real Estate Development: Central City Rebuilding in Berlin'. *European Urban and Regional Studies*, 3/1: 3–17.
Surel, Y. (2000). 'The Role of Normative and Normative Frames in Policy-Making'. *Journal of European Public Policy*, 7: 495–512.
Swedberg, R. (1987). *Current Sociology*. London: Sage.
Swyngedouw, E. (1989). 'The Heart of the Place: The Resurrection of Locality in the Age of the Hyperspace'. *Geografisca Annaler*, 71(B): 31–42.
Tabard, N. (1993). 'Des quartiers pauvres aux banlieues aisées'. *Économie et Statistique*, 270: 5–22.
Tajbakhsh, K. (2001). *The Promise of the City*. Berkeley: University of California Press.
Tarr, J. A. and Dupuy, G. (eds) (1988). *Technology and the Rise of Networked City in Europe and America*. Philadelphia: Temple University Press.
Tarrius, A. (1992). *Les fourmis d'Europe*. Paris: L'Harmattan.
—— (2000). *Les nouveaux cosmopolitismes*. La Tour d'Aigues: Éditions de l'Aube.
Tarrow, S. (1977). *Between Center and Periphery: Grassroots Politicians in Italy and France*. New Haven: Yale University Press.
—— (1994). *Power in Movement*. Cambridge: Cambridge University Press.
Terhorst, P. and Van de Ven, J. (forthcoming, 2001). 'Territorialisation of the State and Urban Trajectories: Amsterdam and Brussels Compared'.
Therborn, G. (1985). *European Modernity and Beyond*. London, Sage.
—— (2000). 'Globalizations: Dimensions, Historical Waves, Regional Effects, Normative Governance'. *International Sociology*, 15/3: 151–79.

Thompson, E. P. (1963). *The Making of the English Working Class*. London: Penguin.

Thureau-Dangin, P. (1995). *La concurrence ou la mort*. Paris: Syros.

Thoenig, J. C. (1995). 'De l'incertitude en gestion territoriale'. *Politiques et Management Public*, 13/3: 1–27.

Thoonen, T. (1991). 'Change and Continuity: Local Government and Urban Affairs in the Netherlands', in J. Hesse and J. Sharpe (eds), *Local Government and Urban Affairs in International Perspective: Analyses of Twenty Western Industrialised Countries*. Baden-Baden: Nomos.

—— (1998). 'Provinces versus Urban Centres in the Netherlands', in P. Le Galès and C. Lequesne (eds), *Regions in Europe: The Paradox of Power*. London: Routledge.

Tilly, C. (ed.) (1975). *The Formation of National States in Western Europe*. Princeton: Princeton University Press.

—— (1990). *Coercion, Capital and European States, AD 990–1990*. Oxford, Blackwell.

—— (1992). *Contrainte et capital dans la formation de l'Europe, 1990–1990*. Paris: Aubier.

—— and Blockmans, W. (eds) (1994). *Cities and the Rise of States in Europe*. Boulder, CO: Westview Press.

Todd, E. (1990). *L'invention de l'Europe*. Paris: Le Seuil.

—— (1994). *Le destin des immigrés*. Paris: Le Seuil.

Tomlinson, J. (1998). 'Locating Culture'. *European Urban and Regional Studies*, 6: 316–19.

Topalov, C. (1987). *Le logement en France, Histoire d'une marchandise*. Paris: Presses de Sciences Po.

—— (1990). 'From the "Social Question" to "Urban Problems": Reformers and the Working Classes at the Turn of the Twentieth Century'. *International Social Science Journal*, 135: 319–36.

Touraine, A. (1990). 'Existe-t-il encore une société française'. *Tocqueville Review*, 11: 143–71.

—— (1994). 'La crise de l'État-nation'. *Revue Internationale de Politique Comparée*, 1: 341–9.

—— (1997): 'Le nationalisme contre la nation', in P. Birnbaum (ed.), *Sociologie des nationalismes*. Paris: PUF.

Trigilia, C. (1986). *Grandi partiti e piccole imprese. Comunisti e democrastiani nelle regioni a economia diffusa*. Bologna: Il Mulino.

—— (1996). 'Dinamismo privato e disordine pubblico', in N. Negri and L. Sciolla (eds), *Il paese dei paradossi. Le basi sociali della politica in Italia*. Rome: La Nuova Italia Scientifica.

Unnia, M. and Bertaccini, P. (eds) (1996). *Milano Città-stato, Equidistante da Roma e da Bruxelles*. Milan: Libro bianco, Forum Federalista.

Unwin, D. and Rokkan, S. (1982). *The Politics of Territorial Identity*. London: Sage.

Urban Studies, 35/10 (1998). Special issue on Ethnic minorities in European cities.

Urry, J. (1990). *The Tourist Gaze*. London: Sage.

—— (2000). *Mobility beyond Society*. London: Routledge.

Vallat, C., Marin, B., and Biondi, G. (1998). *Naples, Démythifier la ville*. Paris: L'Harmattan.

Vandelli, L. (1991). *Pouvoirs locaux*. Paris: Economica.

—— (1997). *Sindaci e miti*. Bologna: Il Mulino.

—— (2000). *Il governo locale*. Bologna: Il Mulino.

Van den Berg, L., Braun, E., and Van der Meer, J. (1997a). 'The Organising Capacity of Metropolitan Regions'. *Government and Policy*, 15: 253–72.
—— —— —— (eds) (1997b). *Metropolitan Organising Capacity*. Aldershot: Ashgate.
Van der Veer, J. (1997). 'Metropolitan Government in Amsterdam and Eindhoven: A Tale of Two Cities'. *Government and Policy*, 16: 25–30.
Veltz, P. (1996). *Mondialisation, villes et territoires*. Paris: PUF.
—— (2000). *Le nouveau monde industriel*. Paris: Gallimard.
—— (forthcoming, 2002). *Métropolitisation et formes économiques émergentes*.
Vergès, V. (1999). 'Le grand Rotterdam, entre territorialité locale et uniformité nationale', in B. Jouve and C. Lefèvre (eds), *Villes, métropoles*. Paris: Economica.
Verpraet, G. (1991). 'Le dispositif partenarial, pour une typologie des rapports publics/privés'. *Annales de la Recherche Urbaine*, 51: 102–12.
—— (1999). 'Coordinations urbaines et lieux du politique'. Miméo.
Vervaeke, M. and Lefebvre, B. (1997). 'La mobilité résidentielle et la réorganisation sociale de l'agglomération lilloise', in A. Maertens and M. Vervaeke (eds), *La polarisation sociale des villes européennes*. Paris: Anthropos.
Viard, J. (2000). *Court traité sur les vacances, les voyages et l'hospitalité des lieux*. La Tour d'Aigues: Éditions de l'Aube.
Vigar, G., Healey, P., Hull, A., and Davoudi, S. (2000). *Planning, Governance and Spatial Strategy in Britain*. Basingstoke: Palgrave.
Villechaise-Dupont, A. (2000). *Amère banlieue. Les gens des grands ensembles*. Paris: Grasset/Le Monde.
Vion, A. (2001). 'La constitution des enjeux internationaux dans le gouvernement des villes françaises (1947–1995)' (Ph.D. thesis). Rennes: University of Rennes I.
Voelzkow, H. (forthcoming, 2002). *Urban Redevelopment in Duisburg*.
Wachter, S. (1995). *La ville contre l'État*. Montpellier: GIP Reclus.
Wacquant, L. (1993). 'Urban Outcasts: Stigmata and Division in Black American Ghetto and the French Urban Periphery'. *International Journal Of Urban And Regional Research*, 17: 366–80.
Walby, S. (1997). *Gender Transformation*. London: Routledge.
Waldinger, R. and Bozorgmehr, M. (eds) (1996). *Ethnic Los Angeles*. New York: Russell Sage Foundation.
Wallace, H. and Wallace, W. (eds) (2000). *Policy-making in the European Union*. Oxford: Oxford University Press.
Waller, P. J. (1991). *Town, City and Nation: England, 1850–1914*. Oxford: Clarendon.
Wallerstein, I. (2000). 'Globalization or the Age of Transition?'. *International Sociology*, 15: 249–65.
Walsh, K. (1995). *Public Services and Market Mechanisms*. London: Macmillan.
Walton, J. (1990). 'Theoretical Methods in Comparative Urban Politics', in J. Logan and T. Swanstrom (eds), *Beyond City Limits. Economic Restructuring in Comparative Perspectives*. Philadelphia: Temple Press.
—— (1998). 'Urban Conflict and Social Movements in Poor Countries: Theory and Evidence of Collective Action'. *International Journal Of Urban And Regional Research*, 22: 460–81.
Ward, S. (1998). 'Place Marketing: A Historical Comparison of Britain and North America', in T. Hall and P. Hubbard (eds), *The Entrepreneurial City: Geography of Politics, Regime and Representation*. Chichester: John Wiley.
Weber, Max (1951). *General Economic History*. Glencoe, Il: Free Press.
—— (1978). *Economy and Society*. Berkeley: University of California Press.

Weiler, J. (1994). 'A Quiet Revolution: The European Court of Justice and its Interlocutors'. *Comparative Political Studies*, 26: 510–34.

Weiss, L. (1998). *The Myth of the Powerless State*. Cambridge: Polity Press.

Whitley, R. (1993). *European Business Systems: Firms and Markets in their National Context*. London: Sage.

—— and Kristensen, P. H. (eds) (1997). *The Changing European Firm*. London: Routledge.

Wieviorka, M. (ed.) (1997). *Une société fragmentée*. Paris: La Découverte.

Wijmark, B. (1997). 'Stockholm: Welfare and Well-being', in C. Jensen-Butler *et al.* (eds), *European Cities in Competition*. Aldershot: Avebury.

Williamson, O. (1995). *The Mechanisms of Governance*. Oxford: Oxford University Press.

Wilson D. (1999). 'From Local Government to Local Governance: Recasting British Local Democracy'. *Democratization*, 5/1: 90–115.

Wolmann, H. (2000). 'Local Government Systems: From Historic Divergence Towards Convergence? Great Britain, France and Germany as Comparative Cases in Point'. *Environment and Planning C: Government and Policy*, 18/1: 33–55.

—— and Goldsmith, M. (1992). *Urban Politics and Policy: A Comparative Approach*. Oxford: Blackwell.

World Bank (1996). *The Growth of Government and the Reform of the State in Industrial Countries*. Washington, DC: World Bank.

Wright, V. (ed.) (1993). *Les privatisations en Europe*. Arles: Actes Sud.

—— and Cassese, S. (eds) (1996). *La recomposition de l'État en Europe*. Paris: La Découverte.

Yates, D. (1977). *The Ungovernable City: The Politics of Urban Problems and Policy Making*. Cambridge: MIT Press.

Zanfrini, L. (1998). 'Economic Sociology and the Study Of Local Societies', *Italian Sociology*, 20: 167–208.

Zidjerveld, A. C. (1998). *A Theory of Urbanity*. New Brunswick, NJ. Transaction Publishers.

Zukin, S. (1988). *Loft Living, Culture and Capital In Urban Change*. New York: Radius.

—— (1995). *The Cultures of Cities*. Oxford: Blackwell.

NAME INDEX

SUBJECT INDEX

poverty
   anti-poverty strategies 103, 107,
      214–16, 261–2, 267
   in European cities 124
   in the European Union 123
   and social segregation 120–30
privatization 92, 162, 256–8
   and regulation 95
problem-solving, and governance 18
property market regulation 218–21
proto-industries 53
public investment, and the state 90–1,
   92
public policies
   and collective actors 11
   and entrepreneurial cities 206
   and governance 17
   and the state 79–80, 94–5

RECITE Programme 107
Redcliffe-Maud Commission 232
regional capitals 52, 67, 69, 70, 94, 176
regional identity 142–3
regions
   and the European Union 96, 98–9,
      99–103
   national spaces fragmented into
      156–9
regulation
   and competition 202–3
   diverse forms of 213–25
   economic 79–80, 91–3
   and governance 14–15, 17–18
   market 15, 18, 202, 228
   and privatization 95
regulations, and actors 183–226
religion, and immigrant populations
   137
restructured city councils 227–59
Rhineland League 46
road networks 69
robustness of European cities 115–20,
   260
Roman Empire 33, 34
Rome 27

Saxon League 46
Scandinavia
   cities 27, 47, 50, 128, 217–18
   local government 230–1, 231–2, 238,
      242–3
   mayors 240
   states 81, 117, 118
segregation, poverty and social
   segregation 120–30, 261
self-regulation, and governance 17
SMEs (small and medium-sized
   companies) 158

social change 22
social cohesion 8
social democracy 270
social exclusion *see* exclusion
social mobility 130, 144
social movements 140–1, 186–93, 223
social structure 6, 8, 31, 112–45,
   213–14
   the bourgeoisie 127–30, 133, 145,
      196–7
   and globalization 131–4, 154
   and identity 140–3
   immigrants and trans-national
      networks 134–5
   in industrial cities 57, 115–20
   and local government 83
   in medieval cities 34, 37–8, 41, 51
   and urbanization 68
society, and territories 4–5
space of flows 24
Spanish cities 6, 27, 49
   local government 82, 245–6, 252
   medieval 35, 37
states 75–111
   capital cities of 47, 58–9, 69, 157
   and European integration 6, 76, 84–7,
      95–6, 97–111
   and local government 80–4
   loosening grip of the state 87–96,
      108
   relations between cities and 40–52,
      70–1
   reshaping of the state in Europe
      77–96
   state expenditure 79, 80, 117, 207
   state regulation 15, 17–18
Stockholm 32, 35, 68, 217–18, 243
Strasbourg 40, 193
suburbs 28, 178
surveillance-style communications 24
Sweden 81, 135
Switzerland 45, 49
   Zurich 223

taxation, and the state 90–1, 94
technological change and innovation
   23–4, 141
   and globalization 147–8
   and industrial cities 56
   and medieval cities 66
territories, and society 4–5
time-space compression 147, 174
Toulouse 218
tourism 139–40
town planning
   and local government 83
   medieval cities 31, 37, 40, 67
trade, globalization of 152